Looking Past the Screen

LOOKING PAST THE SCREEN

Case Studies in American Film History and Method

Edited by Jon Lewis and Eric Smoodin

DUKE UNIVERSITY PRESS
Durham & London 2007

Designed by Jennifer Hill
Typeset in Adobe Jenson Pro by
Tseng Information Systems, Inc.

Library of Congress Cataloging-
in-Publication Data appear on
the last printed page of this book.

For Richard deCordova, 1956–1996

CONTENTS

ACKNOWLEDGMENTS

This collection began as a panel about developments in the practices of film history at the Society for Cinema Studies meeting in 1998. For several months after the meeting we solicited essays from some terrific film scholars. These contributors have stayed with the project for the long period of manuscript formation and revision, and they have been rigorous and creative in their writing and rewriting. We thank them for their hard work, friendship, and, most of all, patience.

At Duke University Press, Ken Wissoker has been supportive and encouraging from the beginning. Indeed, everyone we have worked with at Duke has been wonderful—in particular Courtney Berger.

On the home front, our spouses and kids have given us all kinds of support as this project has taken its slow journey from SCS in 1998 to its present form. For all of their encouragement along the way, we give very special thanks to Martha, Adam, and Guy Lewis and to Caren Kaplan and Sofia Smoodin-Kaplan.

Portions of this collection have appeared in earlier publications. A version of "Going Hollywood Sooner or Later" appeared in *Regarding Frank Capra: Audience, Celebrity, and American Film Studies* (Duke, 2004). A version of "Murnau in America" was published in

Film History 14, no. 1 (2002). A version of "The Perfect Money Machine(s)" appeared in *Film International* 1, no. 1 (2003). A version of "Lois Weber and the Celebrity of Matronly Respectability" was published as "Presenting the Smalleys: 'Collaborators in Authorship and Direction'" in *Film History* 18, no. 2 (2006). Richard deCordova's "Ethnography and Exhibition" was published in *Camera Obscura* 23 (May 1990).

Richard was our colleague in graduate school and a close friend for many years. He died all too young in 1996. His scholarship was very much the inspiration for this collection, and we are pleased to include this example of his work here. We dedicate this book to his memory.

INTRODUCTION
The History of Film History
Eric Smoodin

There are other people who make the movies besides the artists and technicians in Hollywood. Eighty-five million Americans go to see a picture every week . . . [and] it is undoubtedly true that no art has ever been so shaped and influenced by its audience as the art of cinema.

So began Margaret Farrand Thorp in her 1939 sociological study *America at the Movies*.[1] We can learn a great deal about Thorp's methodology from the title of her book as well as the chapters in it—for example, "Eighty-Five Million a Week," "What Movie Tonight?" "Glamour," "Cinema Fashions," "The Industry," and "Reforming the Movies." For Thorp, the proper study of cinema was the audience, the relationships between films and consumers, and the practices of the film industry. With her frontispiece photograph of a theater full of viewers watching a movie she turned the audience into the stars of her book.

At about the same time as Thorp's study, Robert Gessner at New York University began teaching a class titled "History and Appreciation of the Cinema" (the syllabus I found dates from 1938). Gessner examined a different facet of cinema each week, with such headings as "The Early American Spectacle," "Legend and Fantasy in Germany," "The Moving Camera in Germany," "The Psychological Film," "Contemporary Soviet Naturalism," "The American Film of Protest," and "An American Classic" (*It Happened One Night*). The title of the class and the topic headings give a strong indication of Gessner's approach, which clearly appears to be centered on the history of texts, on the films themselves, and on ways of making meaning from them by clustering them around national and generic concerns, differentiating one film from the other, and ranking them.[2]

Thus film scholars might speak of the possibility of alternative film historiographies, that is, the prospect that in 1910 or 1925 or 1940 the study of cinema, at least in the United States, might have gone one way instead of another. Robert Gessner's approach, which owes much to art history and literary history, has become the dominant mode for the practice of film scholarship in the United States. Thorp's methodology had ample scholarly precedents, but the social science model of *America at the Movies*, which deemphasized the film text and stressed issues of industry and consumption, did not become the primary model for organizing the study of the cinema or for understanding its history.

This is not to say that an analytical method owing more to the social sciences than to the humanities has simply vanished from film studies. Instead, we can find a number of examples, many of them from the last twenty years or so. Neither is it to romanticize a lost historiographic option, one that would have provided unimaginable possibilities for film scholars. Instead, we want to point out that film scholarship most broadly, and the analysis of film history more narrowly, has at least since the mid-1950s been dominated by the study of the film itself, often organized around genre, nation, or authorship in much the same manner as Gessner's class. The essays in this collection together demonstrate the possibility for film scholarship without films; for using primary materials other than films themselves for examining the history of the cinema in the United States.

This volume addresses shifts in film studies, specifically with the writing of film history—a project that connects the essays here to the efforts of those made fifty, sixty, and seventy years ago. It is important to point out that at the time of Thorp, Gessner, and others, scholars clearly understood that film did possess a history, and one well worth studying. Indeed, Gessner's overtly historical approach, moving from early short films to silent

feature films to sound films, and charting narrative and aesthetic developments, would have struck no one interested in film as at all odd. In the case
of Thorp, while her concerns were sociological—that is, with the effects of
cinema on Depression-era consumers—her methodology was largely historical given that most of her chapters have some sense of chronology and
development. In "The Industry," for example, Thorp compares the number
of directors working in Hollywood in 1926 with the number in 1937 (246
vs. 234) and then measures this finding against the number of feature films
(743 vs. 484).[3] But in addition to such historical anecdotes Thorp insists
on fully understanding the long view. Her chapter "Reforming the Movies,"
for instance, begins in 1897 with the famous fire at the Bazaar de la Charitè
screening outside Paris, and then moves carefully through various projects
aimed at making movie screenings safe in terms of protecting patrons from
physical harm and also emotional damage.[4]

The period of these scholarly concerns was also an era for the creation
of institutions that would both safeguard and produce film history. The
Academy of Motion Picture Arts and Sciences founded its research library
in 1928, and the Museum of Modern Art in New York formed its film
library in 1935. As Iris Barry, the museum's film curator for many years,
wrote in 1946, the film library's founding was based on the notion that
the cinema has a history worth preserving, analyzing, and viewing. With
this in mind, such Hollywood dignitaries as Will Hays, Walt Disney, Sam
Goldwyn, and Mary Pickford promised "to contribute to the collection
of outstanding films of the past which the Museum planned to amass,"
so that "films may be studied and enjoyed as any one of the other arts is
studied and enjoyed."[5] In fact, the first films to be deposited at the library
were Harold Lloyd's silent comedies *Grandma's Boy* and *The Freshman*.[6]
A few years later, in 1942, the Library of Congress, in "recognizing the importance of motion pictures and the need to preserve them as a historical
record," began collecting films rather than just requiring descriptive material relating to individual motion pictures.[7] The birth of the film archive,
then, along with the scholarly developments from the same period, show
the consolidation of the idea of film history and of film history itself being
a significant aspect of film studies.

Very broadly speaking, we can identify four general categories for practicing and teaching this history. The first is that of industrial systems. This
category includes modes of making films—for example, the producer sys-

tems introduced into Hollywood during the 1920s or the more artisanal models from the era just before the 1920s. Such studies also concentrate on studios or on the manner in which star systems organized production, or they focus on labor issues or on the divisions of labor particular to various forms, from feature films to animation. Another consideration is technological development, for instance in color or in sound, and the ways in which that development affected filmmaking. Such a category, then, takes in all manner of film production, but it also includes studying modes of distribution and exhibition. Examples here include Douglas Gomery's monograph on the studios, Richard deCordova's examination of the development of the star system, Kristin Thompson's analysis of the distribution of American films abroad, and John Belton's history of the widescreen film.[8]

The second category involves the regulatory systems that have so much control over content, industry structure, audience, and so on. Typically, a study of regulation has meant a study of censorship, but it can also include an analysis of the tax laws that facilitated certain production styles and practices (the American emphasis on overseas epics in the 1950s, for instance). The *Mutual Film Corporation v. Ohio's* first amendment case of 1915 could also be studied here, or the various stages of the Paramount case, or foreign quota systems. Lea Jacobs's *The Wages of Sin* stands out in this category, as does Ruth Vasey's *The World According to Hollywood*, and Jon Lewis's *Hollywood v. Hard Core*.[9] Numerous shorter studies also come to mind, for example William Boddy's examination of congressional concern over television violence in the 1960s and the governmental discussion about controlling television content.[10]

The third category is reception—that is, the audiences who watched films, where they saw them, and how they made sense of them. This option helps to give us an idea of how audiences differ (and, in some cases, stay the same) in relation to location, gender, race, class, age, and other categories, and in relation to different kinds of film. The exemplary work here has been done by Janet Staiger and, probably most significantly, by Jackie Stacey in her study of the relationships between female fans and stars.[11]

The final category is that of representation—the images and narratives that make up the text. This is precisely the interest of most textual analysis, which charts strategies of representation in different genres, directors, studios, and so on. This is also the mode of film study that has dominated the discipline since the 1950s.

Industry, regulation, reception, and representation: none of these categories necessarily excludes the others, and each concerns itself with distinct but sometimes overlapping primary materials. Censorship reports, for instance, some of the basic materials for the study of regulation, might provide excellent information about reception. While studying representation, we might also use the evidence of lighting and mise-en-scène to help us understand issues related to industrial practice. In the most brute terms, however, the primary materials for studying industry, regulation, and reception cannot be the films themselves. Instead, they will most typically be on paper (and on microfilm and the Internet) as the material evidence left, for instance, by fans, censors, critics, and government officials; in other words, the very materials most often studied by historians working in other disciplines.

THE HISTORY OF FILM STUDIES

Evidence exists that shows that as soon as intellectuals began taking the cinema seriously they focused on broad institutional issues. As early as 1909 Jane Addams, in *The Spirit of Youth and City Streets*, paid far more attention to theaters than to the films themselves. This interest was very much in keeping with the era's reformist concern over the sites of children's leisure; not only movie theaters but also schools and playgrounds come to mind here.[12] About twenty years later, film fully entered the academy, not only as a humanities discipline related to literature and art but also as a practice in the social sciences. During the late 1920s the Harvard Business School began its lecture series on the economics of film, and the sociologists Robert Lynd and Helen Lynd produced their study of Muncie, Indiana—the famous *Middletown*—in which filmgoing habits and other modern consumer activities received significant attention.

Shortly after the Lynds, issues of reception came to dominate film studies with the publication of the research sponsored by the Payne Fund, which concentrated on the effects of the cinema on children and adolescents. Then, in 1939, Thorp published her volume, which analyzed industrial structures, advertising, exhibition, reception, and other related areas. During World War II, film studies largely became the domain of psychiatrists, psychologists, and sociologists. Working primarily for the government, these social scientists, influenced as they were by progressive New Deal ideology, believed in the cinema, especially the documentary, as the best means to a liberal postwar modernism. These were the men who conducted research on the recruits watching Frank Capra's *Why We Fight* films. Hoping to determine the films' pedagogical powers—their ability to convince soldiers of the rightness of the war effort—these experts sought to use their findings about Capra's films to establish the possibility for a postwar documentary practice that might help viewers unlearn racism, class biases, and hypernationalism.[13]

In 1950, in something of an apotheosis of these various projects, Leo Handel published *Hollywood Looks at Its Audience*, a work that still stands out as the most thorough analysis of reception in the United States. Just two years later, David Riesman and Evelyn T. Riesman's "Movies and Audiences" appeared in *American Quarterly*, the journal of the American Studies Association.[14] Although the Riesmans called for a thorough examination of how various audiences interact with the movies they see, the moment for this kind of research had already begun to pass.

Around this time the intellectual discourse on film shifted toward more literary concerns, and film studies came to occupy a place in the academy alongside disciplines in the humanities rather than those in the social sciences. The reasons for this development remain unclear, but they may have had something to do with the diversification of English departments in universities during the period, with film classes becoming something of a staple and popular offering. In just one example of this disciplinary shift, the postwar period witnessed an extraordinary movement in American studies. The professoriate finally started to include scholars whose connection to elite culture was somewhat tenuous—Jews, for instance, or those who had attended state universities rather than private institutions—and whose main interests were more regional, vernacular, and popular. The emergence of vast state systems of university education in Wisconsin, California, and elsewhere also led to a determination to study the regional and to examine the ideological connection between artistic production and the project of building the nation. Most of this movement was a literary one largely focused on finding distinctive American voices in Whitman, Stowe, Twain, and others. The movies, along with other such apparently "American" aesthetic practices as jazz, seemed the perfect match for these interests. Hence, the movies themselves, rather than their modes of production, their audiences, or other institutional practices, seemed to merit the most serious study.

The history of the most enduring film journal in the United States exemplifies these shifts. In 1945 a group of Southern California leftist intellectuals and Hollywood studio workers founded the *Hollywood Quarterly*, which until 1957 was published in cooperation with the University of California Press. The journal's editors hoped that the *Quarterly* might become a forum for advancing a politicized, socially responsible cinema, one that was freed from what they called in an opening editorial statement the "'pure entertainment' myth which had served to camouflage the social irresponsibility and creative impotence of much of the material presented on the screen and over the air" both before and during the war.[15]

Film needed to teach, to enlighten, to persuade. The *Hollywood Quarterly*'s editors, in their opening statement of principles, stressed not only their desire to understand the "aesthetic" principles of film and other media but also the "social" and "educational" possibilities of these forms. In so saying, the editors aligned themselves with the war era's social science approach to film studies as well as to Gessner's auteurist, textual analysis model. The formation of the editorial board itself also demonstrated this methodological mixture; Franklin Fearing, for instance, who specialized in the effects of mass communication, as well as the literary historian Franklin Rolfe, the Paramount producer and UCLA film school founder Kenneth Macgowan, and the hard-line communist (and soon to be blacklisted) screenwriter John Howard Lawson.

Subscriptions languished for many years, with the editorial board and the University of California Press seeing the problem largely in terms of content. Ellen Seacoat, the periodicals manager at the press, in a 1954 memo to press director August Frugé, worried precisely about a kind of disciplinary unpredictability built into the journal. "I feel frustrated," she wrote, adding, "Who is sufficiently interested in all or most of these subjects [covered by the journal] to pay for a subscription?" Seacoat wondered whether "the person primarily interested in social science articles [would] be willing to pay for the other types of articles in which he is not particularly interested?" She then commended the direction of recent issues, with "their heavy emphasis on Shakespeare and literature as brought to the public through mass media," which apparently convinced many readers teaching in universities and other schools to think of the journal "as an exciting adjunct to the teaching of English and related subjects."[16]

Frugé himself worried about the continued influence of the social sciences in the journal, lamenting that, throughout the 1950s, the journal "continued . . . running gradually down . . . as the emphasis became more sociological and less cinematic."[17] Indeed, in 1958 the press reconfigured the journal into *Film Quarterly*, which is still published today. The new journal was modeled on the British *Sight and Sound* and the French *Cahiers du cinéma*—that is, according to Frugé, it was "devoted to film as an art and not as communication."[18] In American film studies this development as much as anything marked the disciplinary shift, placing cinema scholarship firmly within the realm of the humanities.

Over the next two decades film studies doctoral programs were founded at several American universities, and scholarly publishing on film proliferated in both the United States and the United Kingdom. These programs and this scholarship generally reflected the literary nature of film studies, with textual analysis serving as the primary methodological practice. Certainly the *Cahiers du cinéma* analysis of *Young Mr. Lincoln* published in 1970 marked the maturation of this mode of film study, with the journal's editorial collective demonstrating the manner in which the film rendered visible or suppressed the popular front politics of the 1930s.[19] We can trace the importance of the *Cahiers* work through many of the most significant contributions to the field published in the subsequent ten-year period; for example, in the essays by Raymond Bellour, Thierry Kuntzell, Stephen Heath, and Nick Browne and in the analyses of directors such as Douglas Sirk, Alfred Hitchcock, and Fritz Lang who became particularly important to the era's scholars.[20]

This scholarship served the absolutely central purpose of demonstrating the workings of the textual systems of American and European classical-era cinema. This is not to say, however, that scholars with different priorities were not doing other kinds of work. At the risk of dramatically reducing the history of the discipline from the period, one issue of one journal pointed out both the options available to film scholars and the choices that they made. During the 1970s, in large part because of how it adapted the French film studies tradition of the 1960s and also combined European and American models, the British publication *Screen* emerged as the most significant film journal, at least in the United States and the United Kingdom. In volume 16, number 3, from autumn 1975, *Screen* published the essay that has become almost certainly the most cited and most influential contribution to film studies over the last thirty years, Laura Mulvey's "Visual Pleasure and Narrative Cinema."[21]

Mulvey's essay has been celebrated and critiqued for the manner in which it details identificatory relationships between spectator and image. In the same issue, though, *Screen* also published Edward Buscombe's *Notes on Columbia Pictures Corporation, 1926–1941*.[22] Using Frank Capra's films and the studio for which Capra worked as his objects of study, Buscombe sought to interrogate the relationships between the structure of the Hollywood film industry and the films that Hollywood produced. In so doing, he discussed the reductionist impulse of even the most sophisticated, progressive textual analysis (*Cahiers du cinéma* on *Young Mr. Lincoln*, among others), which assumed, for example, that films unproblematically reflected the corporate interests of the studios that made them. Buscombe also warned that even the most ingenious reading of a film often did more to demonstrate the virtuosity of the scholar rather than the "meaning" of a movie. "Surely," he wrote, "it would have to be demonstrated that such a reading was available to an audience at the time."[23]

Thus Buscombe called for a type of film study and historiography that has inspired the contributors to the present collection. But he also served notice as to why, at least in the mid-1970s, this kind of scholarship proved so difficult. Buscombe noted that a general neglect of industry history among scholars was "not only a consequence of critical attitudes and priorities," but was "also the result of very real practical problems." He further explained that "many of the basic materials that would be needed" to produce this sort of scholarship "are simply not available."[24] Studios typically provided very little assistance, even if they maintained records, and there were few archival sources available with pertinent primary materials.

Nevertheless, Buscombe's call for a different emphasis in film studies was part of a movement in a number of scholarly fields—a movement against the literariness of so many humanities disciplines that began at least in the early to mid 1970s. Although we think of that period as being marked in film studies and other fields by semiotic, Marxist, and psychoanalytic approaches to texts, as well as by other, perhaps less rigorously applied, versions of textual analysis, some significant theorists already seemed wary of such methodologies. In 1973, Michel Foucault and a team of editors produced *I, Pierre Rivière, Having Slaughtered My Mother, My Sister, and My Brother*, a virtuoso compilation of primary materials documenting, as the rest of the title indicates, "a case of parricide in the nineteenth century." In explaining their approaches to the material, the editors insisted that "the outdated academic methods of textual analysis and all the concepts which are the appanage of the dreary and scholastic prestige of writing on writing can very well be eschewed in studying" the evidence around Rivière's case.[25] Thus the editors placed the emphasis on collection and presentation; on providing as complete a dossier as possible of the materials of the case, from newspapers, court records, medical reports, and other sources. Of course, the editors did not believe that these sources simply presented themselves—indeed, they provide commentaries at the end of their project. But to the extent that these practices can be kept separate, the commentaries produce a historiography of crime, judgment, and punishment through the materials rather than analyzing the materials themselves. Foucault's project takes on particular interest because it is precisely an interdisciplinary one, examining as it does standard literary and historical texts (memoir, court proceedings, etc.) in order to determine relations of power between such institutions as legal systems, journalism, science, and the family.

During this time there were, of course, film scholars who made extremely sophisticated historiographic interventions in the field through the use of primary materials. Garth Jowett's *Film: The Democratic Art*, from 1976, still stands out as an important social history of the cinema, one in which American cinematic institutions—regulatory, educational, governmental, etc.—come to be examined through an intensive analysis of the documents produced by those institutions. The book also presents a modest effort to make some of those documents available to the reader, with the publication, in appendices, of a variety of censorship materials, including the Production Code of the Motion Picture Producers and Distributors Association (better known as the Hays Code), which starting in 1930 governed Hollywood representational and narrative practices.[26]

Almost ten years later, in 1985, Robert Allen and Douglas Gomery's co-written *Film History: Theory and Practice* appeared.[27] To my knowledge, this was one of the first books published in the United States to take motion picture historiography as its subject, rather than the history of a particular aspect of cinema. Thus while Jowett's book was a history of the social impact of the cinema in the United States, Allen and Gomery's project asked questions and developed ideas about historical methodologies that might be applied to a number of film-related topics.

Allen and Gomery provided chapters on different kinds of film history—aesthetic, technological, and economic, for example—as well as on the problems of researching that history. Here they discussed, quite under-standably, "film evidence," that is, the films themselves. But they also pro-posed the study of what they called "nonfilmic evidence," by which they meant primary materials such as trade papers and secondary materials such as the various film encyclopedias.[28] As they noted, "For certain inves-tigations, film viewing is really an inappropriate research method," and in so doing they helped to coalesce a historical movement around documen-tary evidence rather than the movies themselves.[29]

Many of the film histories of the next decade emphasized such nonfilmic evidence, and in fact brought film studies closer to the kind of project en-dorsed by Foucault in *I, Pierre Rivière*. Jowett and those he influenced used documentary evidence to produce broad narrative histories. In the case of *Film: The Democratic Art*, that narrative was of the industrial growth of the cinema and its perceived effects on audiences. Gomery and Allen outlined the broad contours of a theory of film history that would include primary materials, but the film historians who followed looked at specific historical cases and the documents they produced in order to theorize histories of power relations and discursive practices.

Two of the significant histories following Gomery and Allen's project—Jacobs's *The Wages of Sin: Censorship and the Fallen Woman Film, 1928–1942*, which was published in 1991, and Danae Clark's 1995 volume *Negoti-ating Hollywood: The Cultural Politics of Actors' Labor*—provide interesting examples and also, finally, attest to the entrenched power of textual analysis in film studies during the 1980s and early 1990s.[30] Jacobs took the case of a cycle of films and the mechanisms of Hollywood censorship in her ex-amination of the files on individual movies from the Hays Office. Jacobs's project was "to reconstruct the grounds on which . . . [certain films] had been defined and experienced as offensive."[31] Additionally, she analyzed the manner in which censorship, as practiced by the Hays Office, was itself productive by creating, in debate and discussion with filmmakers, accept-able representational practices. It is difficult to overestimate the impor-tance of Jacobs's work, both in practical and historiographic terms. First, *The Wages of Sin* presented primary materials, those from the Hays Office, that scholars had not yet examined. Second, Jacobs's book provided us with a methodology for studying the discourses of censorship in order to determine the relationships between industrial practice, representational systems, and beliefs about the effects of movies on the film audience.

With its interdisciplinarity and analysis of intersecting discourses, Jacobs's book helped introduce contemporary cultural studies to film studies and film history. Of course, part of this project might well have been that of showing the relationships between this kind of analysis and traditional textual analysis. And Jacobs does indeed provide sections of just such analysis—for example, her extended examination of a few shots in the 1935 Greta Garbo film *Anna Karenina*, which demonstrates the connections between visual style and Hays Office edicts. But it is also true that a film studies monograph from this period would be almost unthinkable without this kind of analysis. That is, textual analysis was a methodological requirement, even in a book focusing on primary materials from the Production Code Administration.

This requirement becomes even clearer in Clark's *Negotiating Hollywood*, which examines actors' labor under the studio system and pays special attention to the formation of the Screen Actors Guild. In so doing, Clark theorizes and historicizes the role of the actor "outside" of the cinema, that is, as an employee, as an organizer, and as a commodity. In conducting this analysis, her evidence comes from *Variety*, various newspapers, the *Screen Guilds Magazine*, and other primary materials. But Clark also includes a chapter called "Labor and the Film Narrative," which is largely an examination of acting as a profession in such films as *42nd Street* and *Morning Glory*. Of the six chapters in the book, only "Labor and the Film Narrative" employs typical textual and narrative analysis; as such it seems to stand out from the other chapters, which take as their evidence the primary materials of actors' labor. But as with *The Wages of Sin*, Clark's book was both conceived and published during an era in film studies when at least some acknowledgment of textual analysis was a virtual requirement of any monograph taking seriously theory and history. Thus, although these are vitally important books because of how they advance the possibilities of the field, they also tell us about the structure of knowledge in the field at a specific time. At least through the early 1990s, sophisticated historiographic work usually needed to include at least some gesture toward traditional textual analysis.

Other scholars have noted these tensions. In a 1990 essay (reprinted in this collection) about the history of the construction of children as film audiences, Richard deCordova wrote that in 1970s film theory, "an abstract, psychoanalytically-inflected notion of the textual subject . . . permitted a way of theorizing spectatorship without straying from what was largely a theory of textual determinism." He then added that "textual processes placed a pliant spectator in a position from which sense could emerge." DeCordova goes on to argue that contemporary ethnographic research might provide a way of "challenging this abstract and deterministic view" by giving us access to "the concrete evidence of the ways audiences make sense of texts."[32]

The approaches taken by Jacobs, Clark, deCordova, and others have still only been fully accepted by film studies in fits and starts. Judith Mayne, in her 1993 work *Cinema and Spectatorship*, laments the "excessive emphasis on cinematic textuality in film studies," by which she means the emphasis on the analysis of individual films. Annette Kuhn, writing more recently in her 2002 project on the relationships between memory and film viewing, writes that "a humanities-based study of cinema ... will take films as the starting point for exploring the cinema-consumer relationship," and she adds that "as a discipline, film studies models itself largely on literary studies, and to this extent is predominantly text-centred: films as texts are its primary objects of inquiry, and textual analysis its method of preference." Then, echoing deCordova more than a decade earlier, Kuhn writes that "even debates within film studies concerning the nature of spectatorship in the cinema are predominantly about a spectator addressed or constructed by the film text."[33]

A recent debate in *Screen* underscores the centrality of the method that Kuhn describes and also addresses some of the tensions between text-centered projects and those that take a broader view of evidence. In two issues, published in 2001 and 2003, *Screen* devoted its "Reports and Debates" section to a discussion titled "Trauma and Screen Studies: Opening the Debate."[34] Trauma studies, of course, had by this time become significant to literary theory, intellectual history, philosophy, and historiography, through the work of Cathy Caruth, Dominick LaCapra, Shoshana Felman, and others. In *Screen*, scholars from film studies and other fields responded to the questions of why, as noted by Susannah Radstone, "so many of us are sharing this fascination [with memory and trauma] and what this might mean ... intellectually, historically and culturally."[35]

In the essay that opened the debate, Radstone provided some of the ground rules for considering the relations between film studies and the analysis of trauma, and she did so in ways that centered squarely on the film text: "Should such analysis take its impetus from texts, and if so, should the focus fall primarily on narration, or on mise-en-scène or on editing and so on? Or does trauma make itself felt in . . . these media in the relation between their texts and their spectators—and if so, then how?"[36] For Radstone, then, the proper study of trauma and cinema relies either on films themselves—their stories, editing, and staging—or, in the manner of much 1970s-style film theory, on a describable, precise interaction between those films and the undifferentiated viewers who watch them.

Most of the work that followed tacitly accepted these precepts and asked questions about representation or about the audience-text relationship. E. Ann Kaplan examined the ways in which melodrama introduces the spectator to trauma—namely how "the spectator" is vicariously traumatized" by melodrama or "positioned as a voyeur" or "addressed as a 'witness.'"[37] Maureen Turim looked at the representation and narrativization of trauma in *The Pawnbroker* (1965) and other films. Janet Walker wrote about the links between traumatic memory and a series of women's experimental autobiographical documentaries; Peter Thomas provided an extended analysis of *Memento* (2000); and Daniel Humphrey examined Derek Jarman's *The Last of England* (1987).[38]

Here I am hardly doing justice to the complexity of these and other contributions, and certainly film scholars must theorize both representation and spectatorship. Only one of the scholars participating in the debate, however, chose to explore the relationships between cinema and trauma through an examination of primary materials. Michael Hammond, in "Laughter during Wartime: Comedy and the Language of Trauma in British Cinema Regulation, 1917," directly tied the terms of trauma to British World War I–era debates about film regulation and reception, two of the categories that have motivated so much of the significant historical work of the last twenty years.[39] Hammond sought to explore "the etiology of trauma and the stresses of everyday life in the discursive practices that underpinned debates on the social function of entertainment and, specifically, cinema."[40] In so doing, he examined reports from the National Council of Public Morals' Cinema Commission in order to determine an official British understanding of the merits of showing both war films and escapist comedies to the public. This is not necessarily a superior approach to that of Radstone, Jarman, Walker, or any of the other contributors. But it does demonstrate a different kind of historiographic practice, one that

is based on a broader sense of film culture and not just on the films themselves. Trauma might be read in films, but it can also be examined in the
documentary evidence surrounding those films and the attempts to regulate them and judge their effects on audiences.

This is, of course, more of an imbalance than balance, where Hammond is the only scholar looking at nonfilmic evidence. But we can see
these methodological tensions played out more evenly in perhaps the most
significant historical project of the last two decades in film studies—the
History of American Cinema multivolume series copublished by Macmillan
and the University of California Press. Each volume in the series to date
examines both films and the documentary evidence that they produced,
although to varying degrees. Eileen Bowser's volume on the cinema from
1907 to 1915 largely addresses the films themselves.[41] Donald Crafton, however, in the 1999 volume *The Talkies*, explains early on that his emphasis is
"more on end-use than on production," that is, on the manner in which the
new technology of synchronized sound came to be understood, appreciated, or dismissed by a variety of audiences.[42] As a result, Crafton decided
to study primarily "one form of documentation, the exhibitors' trade news,
which provides a roundabout clue to how audiences in general received
the talkies."[43] I would suggest that this marks a significant moment in the
practice of film history; a volume written by a major film historian and
designed to provide a broad range of readers, from undergraduates to film
scholars, with an introduction to one of the more significant periods in
cinema history, places its emphasis on documentary evidence rather than
on a selection of films.

HISTORICAL PEDAGOGIES AND PRACTICES

In the broadest terms, however, and in a return to that 1975 issue of *Screen*,
film studies and the practice of film history have followed in a Mulveyan
mode focused on the film text rather than in the style advocated by Buscombe. To justify this, one might argue that the cinema as a medium is
relentlessly textual, providing us with fairly easy access to films. Movies
are available for classroom use and for extended study in 16mm format, in
video, in laser disc, in DVD, and also on the Internet. And frequently these
movies come directly to us, without the viewer having to leave the house.
We can watch movies on broadcast television. We can, with increasingly

greater ease, download them from the Internet. We can also have DVDs sent directly to us by mail order rental companies. Of course, other film-related texts are more and more readily available, often on the Internet; many FBI files can be found there, for instance, as well as some clippings files (from the Pacific Film Archive in Berkeley, for example).[44] But the relative ease with which we can see films certainly influences the kind of scholarship we produce. In addition, many film scholars, at least in the United States, work at institutions with extensive video and DVD holdings, while other forms of text might be harder to come by. Many of these same institutions, however, have newspapers on microfilm or have access to university databases, and they also have other kinds of records that often relate directly to cinema—for instance, records from the Department of State either in published volumes or on microfilm. We assume and expect the availability of film texts, but we also might be surprised to learn about the accessibility of so many other records that teach us the history of cinema.

Primary materials of all kinds have been available at some sites for decades, but particularly over the last twenty-five years more archives have been developed and more collections opened to the public.[45] The Library of Congress, for instance, opened its researcher-friendly Motion Picture Reading Room in 1983, and USC became a significant archival resource with its Warner Bros. Collection, which was deposited at the university in 1977. The Academy of Motion Pictures Arts and Sciences Library acquired the Hays Office records in 1983, allowing for a much more nuanced understanding of American regulatory practices, and even some individual studios, such as Disney, have begun to realize the potential importance of their holdings. To the extent, then, that institutional attitudes toward paper collections can influence intellectual work, these improvements have lead to important shifts in film studies scholarship and in the writing of film history. These institutional shifts themselves have led to more sophisticated practices among film historians, who now, with a greater emphasis on a variety of primary materials, have moved the discipline far closer to traditional historical practices and away from literary criticism.

But even while film scholars during this period have shown the possibilities for film history and other historical practices to merge, historians from more traditional fields seem determined to show their bona fides as film critics. Such, then, is the influence of the humanities-based film study of the last forty or fifty years. All too commonly, when these historians try to talk about a film's relationship to "history," for instance, they do so through the rather useless binary of text versus context; that is, history is "out there," all around a film, and the film in some manner or other "reflects" it. So, to understand "history" we need only to interpret the film.

When the American Historical Association makes an institutional foray into film studies, as just one example, the results are often depressingly stodgy. In the organization's professional newsletter, *Perspectives*, scholars periodically weigh in on the manner in which history has been represented in cinema. The AHA's rightly respected journal, the *American Historical Review*, usually discusses the cinema only in order to review individual films, and then only when they deal specifically with a historical subject, so that a movie's "accuracy" may be judged (*The Tuskegee Airmen*, for instance). Or, in special sections, the *Review* will give historians space to engage in the requisite scholarly handwringing over how well or how poorly a film like *JFK* depicts the past.[46] These scholars seem most interested in the relationship of a film to history, rather than in advancing the practices of film historiography.

Attempts to shift methodologies and practices for any scholar interested in doing so run into the problem of the formation of film studies within the academy. University film studies classes, in history, literature, or other fields, tend to be taught in theater-type spaces and are given time slots— three to four hours—that are appropriate for showing movies. My own experiences at three institutions seem representative; four-hour classes meeting twice a week, seventy-five-minute classes that meet two times a week with an evening screening time, and two-to-three-hour classes that meet once or twice a week. Thus film studies classes in which films are not shown or that form a secondary part of the curriculum seem unthinkable, primarily because of the architecture of the classroom and the time devoted to each class. Similarly, most of the standard textbooks teach students how to read films, to understand genres, to appreciate issues of authorship, and to consider film movements. Film history thus largely becomes the history of styles, aesthetic practices, and narrative structures.

Even in the ideal setting, what would a revised pedagogical and intellectual project look like? In part because of the documentary evidence that has been made available about the cinema, a number of film historians have adapted the recent work of such intellectual and cultural historians as Hayden White, Dominick LaCapra, and Natalie Zemon Davis, who have been instrumental in developing the possibility of treating all discursive practices—and for film studies this means fan magazines, theater manager reports, studio memos, and of course films—as worthy of being "read" as texts, thereby creating meaning through interrelationship rather than in isolation. This method of reading has, in fact, become part of a broad cultural studies project that includes film as well as other disciplines. I point here to the work of Jackie Stacey in sociology, John Bodnar and Mary Ryan in urban history, and Jane Gaines in such hybrid fields as critical legal theory and film studies.

Such practices are not opposed to textual interpretation, the primary goal of so many methodologies associated with film studies. The very status of interpretation has become a vexing one in film studies, often in terms of whether different methodologies view films through rigid grids or more flexible ones. The contributors to this collection, however, and scholars concerned with similar issues, view interpretation as possible only with the help of a variety of different kinds of evidence, in addition to or often excluding films themselves. The goal, of course, is not for "truth" or for absolute certainty through exhaustive research. Instead, these scholars seek to expand the number of interpretable texts and to begin to chart the relationships between, and make meaning from, various discursive practices. Pedagogically, this means, of course, getting film students into libraries and other archives; intellectually, it means getting them to understand that films do not "reflect" culture, or history, or attitudes, as well as teaching them to treat movies as aspects of a complex system of cultural production.

This collection proceeds through a series of case studies. For the last forty years or so, the case study—based on materials from archival collections, case files, dossiers, and so on—has become the dominant genre among social historians. As Franca Iacovetta and Wendy Mitchinson have stated, such scholars typically seek "the recovery of the lives of those individuals and groups . . . traditionally dismissed or ignored as marginal, inarticulate, and powerless."[47] Film scholars, and the contributors to this book are no exception, have taken part in the same project. But another kind of recovery has been going on as well—namely, the recovery of often neglected materials, at least in relation to film, including censorship reports, government documents, trade journals, fan mail, and the like. Thus the multiple project of this collection is to show how our understanding of what constitutes film history has expanded over the last twenty-five years, to increase our sense of the participants in that history, and to provide methodologies for the uses of a variety of primary materials that, in some cases, may have seemed only tangentially connected to the cinema.

A look at these primary materials as used by the contributors to this volume provides a sense of the possibilities for historical research. These materials fall broadly into eight categories:

1 Collections of personal papers. The contributors to this volume examined the collections of Mark Hellinger, Cecil B. DeMille, Robert Flaherty, F. W. Murnau, and others. These collections include personal correspondence, drafts of scripts, contracts, etc.

2 Newspapers and magazines. Popular journalism serves as wonderful primary material about movies. Sources range from the obvious (the *Los Angeles Times*) to the less so (the *Tulsa Daily World*) and also include such staples as *Life* magazine.

3 Trade materials. Such journalism, including *Film Daily*, *Moving Picture World*, and *Variety*, is specifically about the film industry and thus directed to an industry audience.

4 Fan magazines. *Photoplay* and similar publications offer valuable information about the ways that fans learned about movies and movie stars.

5 Studio publications. These materials, such as *Paramount News*, *Fox Folks*, and *Universal Weekly*, designed for internal use or to alert exhibitors about future movies, tell us how the movie companies described themselves and their products.

6 Industry records. The Production Code Administration files, for instance, explain classical-era censorship practices.

7 Educational materials and research publications. Textbooks about film have been published at least since the 1920s, while publications in related fields, such as the *Research Memorandum on Recreation in the Depression*, explore a number of film-related topics.

8 Government records. Large government organizations such as the Department of State, along with the small ones such as the short-lived pornography commissions, often deal with the cinema or with issues directly connected to film production, distribution, and consumption.

To examine these and other materials, the contributors to this volume went to a variety of institutional sites, including, among others, the National Archives, the National Museum of American History, the Margaret Herrick

Library, the Lyndon Baines Johnson Library, the Oklahoma Historical Society in Oklahoma City, the New York State Appellate Court Law Library in Rochester, the New York Public Library, and the Bibliothèque du Film in Paris.

Let us now consider the methodological practices that these primary materials facilitate. As a term, methodology can be understood, in the sense that Bill Nichols has explained it, as "a conceptual model or framework that helps organize individual impressions," and that helps us make "assumptions about how we should . . . punctuate an undifferentiated universe of experience in order to make better sense of it." These methodologies "offer explanatory or descriptive concepts," so that Andrew Sarris, writing in the late 1960s, might propose an auteurist analysis for understanding not only individual films but the process of film history, or that Garth Jowett, just a few years later, will suggest ways of studying interactions between films and audiences that created, between about 1895 and 1950, fundamentally new forms of social interaction.[48]

For understanding American film and American film history, the contributors to this volume take the usual question, posed most famously by Bazin, of "What is cinema?" and rework it into "What is cinema culture?" That is, they propose a conceptual model of history and of understanding films that lessens the priority of the film text itself. These scholars, of course, understand that cinema culture includes individual movies and groups of them, and also the thematic and aesthetic considerations that would be familiar to Sarris and others. But they also consider that which took place in theaters before and after screenings, such as theater architecture, the business decisions of movie companies, or movie ballyhoo. In addition, moving somewhat further afield from the experience of seeing movies, they examine the interaction of other institutions with the cinema, including the government, the library, the school, the museum, and so on. An understanding of film culture acknowledges that fan magazines, censorship reports, State Department documents about overseas film markets, and other such materials are as deserving of analysis as the movies themselves.

The questions emphasized by the contributors include: What other modes of consumption took place in theaters? How did government action, or inaction, develop audiences for movies? In what ways did journalism and other forms of writing create awareness about films and filmmakers? How has the film industry imagined the child and adolescent audiences? These and other similar questions require a conceptual framework both varied and specific, and the essays in this volume provide a multidisciplinary approach to evidence and history. For example, Richard deCordova's work about the development of children as consumers might most properly be considered anthropological; David Lugowski's analysis of the understanding of gay subtexts in films owes much to recent queer cultural theory; and Shelley Stamp's consideration of Lois Weber's stardom owes a debt to feminist historiography. However, all of the contributors assume that the questions they raise and the frameworks they pose for answering these questions require an analysis of a broad textual field of various primary materials.

The contributors to this volume view movies as multiple sites of interpretation. Interpretation can, of course, be produced by the films themselves, but it can also occur through other means—publicity, fan magazines, and so on. The scholars here understand that film audiences occupy competing and contradictory positions; positions that are themselves influenced by different forms of exposure to film culture. Moreover, possible interpretations can be made through texts such as government documents, newspapers, trade journals, and other sources.

Most of the essays here in some way or other deal with the classical Hollywood cinema—that mode of studio production developed and perfected from about 1915 to 1960. But these essays also acknowledge that there may be alternative practices and ideologies at work within that system; practices that might become apparent only through an analysis of a variety of primary materials. Such an analysis tends to break down the absolute hegemony of the classical system, so that, for example, in the case of Mark Anderson's essay, independent production during the silent era falls well outside Hollywood's ability to control it, or, in the case of Lugowski's work, queer interpretations of major studio sound films seem accessible to many audiences.

The major concern of this collection, of course, is the practice of film history, and so the volume begins with essays on "institutional histories," which still is an area of general neglect in the field. One essay deals broadly with the formation of film studies as a discipline, while another proposes a case study of the manner in which film history came to be written during a fairly brief period. From this analysis of practices, the contributors turn to practicing film history itself and in relation to three broad but central areas of interest.

The analysis of stars has been something of a subfield of film history. In particular over the last decade, however, "star studies," which forms the second section of this volume, has depended upon an examination of an array of materials beyond films in order to understand the connections of stardom to journalism, publicity, and advertising, as well as to fans. Thus this subfield of film studies stands out as one of the primary means for carrying out a different kind of film history, one that is interested in the cinema as a network of practices.

The next sections move toward a consideration of those areas discussed above that can be deemed central to historiographic examinations of primary material relating to cinema in the United States: regulation, reception, and production. Regulation, the first such section, has most often been examined in terms of the practices of the Production Code and also of local governmental censorship organizations. The essays here follow in this mode but also show the global reach of negotiations over censorship as well as the more loosely organized grassroots efforts at domestic control. Regulatory activity emerges here as a significant practice among a number of institutions working cooperatively at times and also, just as often, in conflict. The next section of the collection deals with reception, which was perhaps the principal area of concern in the social science based film studies of the 1930s and 1940s. This interest, however, centered on influence; the capacity for gangster films to turn young boys into criminals or for wartime training films to explain as convincingly as possible the reasons for combat. More recent work on audiences has understood that viewers are not quite so passive and that movies are not nearly so powerful, at least in terms of influence. This work does not attempt to reconstruct the "real" audience, as if that might ever be possible. Instead, the current work on reception, and the work in this volume, seeks to understand the variety of relationships between spectators and the cinema as an institution. Finally, the contributors examine the primary evidence of production. The case studies here provide a focused look at one director's films over a short period and also an extended analysis of the development of a genre. In so doing, these studies show how the evidence of production can serve as the primary material of artistic inspiration as well as of narrative and representational histories.

INSTITUTIONAL HISTORIES

One of the embarrassments of film studies, and something that separates it from many other humanities and social science disciplines, is the lack of attention paid by scholars to the history of the discipline itself. Many in the field assume that film studies began in the 1950s and 1960s, and to my knowledge there are few if any regular classes on the subject taught in film studies doctoral programs. To help us understand the history of the discipline, Dana Polan, in "The Beginnings of American Film Study," examines the entrance of film study into the academy. This is, of course, a complicated history, and much of it is impossible to know because so much of the evidence, ranging from syllabi to course schedules to lecture notes to records of discussions within departments and between institutions, has disappeared. What Polan's essay makes clear, however, is that even before 1930 there existed a significant movement to teach film studies at all educational levels and to the general public. In addition, there were ideological and institutional relationships between such sites as Stanford, Harvard, and USC, the Museum of Modern Art in New York as well as other museums, the newly formed Academy of Motion Picture Arts and Sciences, the Hays Office, and the studios, which led to the formation of specific forms of film study. Polan's essay corresponds to, expands upon, and differs from the history of the discipline that I relate here. In each instance, though, we understand that the discipline cannot be practiced effectively if we make little effort to understand its history and the connections between the discipline and other scholarly fields, research organizations, and professional pursuits. A historiographic method that diminishes the significance of the films themselves makes little sense if we fail to understand how and why certain emphases in film studies developed.

Much of the historiographic work on American cinema from the last twenty years has concentrated on the classical period, particularly the eras before 1940. Thus we have a much more complex understanding of the beginnings of cinema in the United States, or of the workings of censorship during the Depression. Far fewer historians have paid attention to the last thirty years, which is precisely the period that Jon Lewis covers in his essay "The Perfect Money Machine(s): George Lucas, Steven Spielberg, and Auteurism in the New Hollywood." Lewis uses film journalism as his primary source material in exploring how at least some "expert" observers understood the arrival and acceptance of auteurist cinema to Hollywood

in the early 1970s, and then the arrival of the blockbuster ethos just ten or
fifteen years later. Most critics, Lewis observes, wax nostalgic for the personal cinema of Scorsese and Coppola from the 1970s and hold up Steven
Spielberg and George Lucas as a combined "public enemy number one" responsible for the demise of sophisticated motion pictures. In other words,
in order to understand the prevalent narrative of the development of the
American cinema from the last few decades, Lewis writes the history of the
people constructing film history. This becomes, as well, the story of institutional relationships, with the contemporary motion picture studios often
controlled by the same corporations that run the print sources that most
frequently report on films and filmmakers.

STAR STUDIES

In "Lois Weber and the Celebrity of Matronly Respectability," Shelley
Stamp uses press materials, primarily from fan magazines and trade journals, to understand the construction of the director Lois Weber's public persona and the manner in which that persona may have influenced
readings of Weber's films and worked through World War I–era concerns about femininity, feminism, and marriage. Of course, the fan magazine industry has always been viewed as one of the least respectable aspects of the American film industry, where it is deemed the domain of
fictional publicity that attends mostly to the desires of young, underedu-
cated women. As a result, such publications tend not to be collected and
archived by libraries and other institutions. Stamp, then, has helped to accomplish a major task of scholarly retrieval, as she shows how *Photoplay*,
Movie Pictorial, and other fan magazines worked as partners with movies
themselves in the development of what Richard deCordova called "picture
personalities." Although Weber was not a movie star in the sense of Mary
Pickford or Lillian Gish, Stamp shows that as a director from the period
Weber entered into the industry's star machinery. Indeed, directors such as
Weber, perhaps to a greater extent than the performers themselves, might
have been viewed in relation to significant political discourses—including
companionate marriage, gender equality, and the movies' responsibility to
engage with serious ideas.

Mark Anderson examines a different kind of female star construction
in his essay on the career of Clara Smith Hamon. Scholars interested in

celebrity have routinely looked at how film companies developed stars—to produce publicity, regularize production, standardize reception practices, and so on. But Anderson analyzes a kind of star production that is at odds with the film industry's perception of its own best interests, and he further argues that movie companies sought to regulate stardom in the same manner that they sought to regulate film content. If Clara Smith Hamon, who murdered her lover, could become a star based solely on her criminal notoriety—a notoriety enhanced in an unsanctioned, "runaway" film production—then the established film companies would almost certainly lose their battle to establish the cinema as the approved leisure preoccupation for children and other audiences. Through his reading of newspapers, trade journals, and community political activity, Anderson demonstrates the fluidity of stardom during the period, from the courthouse to the movie theater. He also shows how different kinds of institutional activity—journalism and cinema as just two examples—create stars but also come into conflict with each other over the development of celebrity. Finally, the case of Clara Smith Hamon amply underscores that, even before the Fatty Arbuckle case, Hollywood sought to claim movie stardom as the sole province of the studios and aimed to regulate as carefully as possible the development of film celebrity in America.

Andrea Slane's "The Crafting of a Political Icon: Lola Lola on Paper" demonstrates how nonfilmic materials make both a film and its star "readable" to audiences, and it shows the ways that industrial activity influenced representational strategies. Paramount capitalized on Marlene Dietrich's most famous starring role, as Lola Lola in *The Blue Angel* (1930), in its publicity for the star's 1948 film *A Foreign Affair*. Thus Dietrich's last and greatest German film became the means, almost twenty years later, to influence the reception of her postwar return to Berlin. Just as the studio worked to produce Dietrich's star image, so too did the Hays Office, the overseer of the motion picture production code. But while studio publicity attempted to bridge an almost two-decade divide, the regulatory activity around *A Foreign Affair* typified the breaks in the Hollywood censorship system. Following upon Lea Jacobs's findings in *The Wages of Sin*, Slane shows that while the production code was preoccupied with representations of sexuality in the prewar era, after the war the issue of politics became just as important, and the Hays Office's concerns over Dietrich's film were almost exclusively directed at the depiction of fascism.

REGULATION

Hollywood films served as significant international commodities, and as such they entered into trade negotiations between governments in the United States and those in other countries. My essay on Frank Capra's *The Bitter Tea of General Yen* (1932) analyzes the balance between Hollywood autonomy, the studios' relationships with the federal government, and the influence of foreign governments on American films. Through an examination of the State Department records from the period, the essay shows that censorship occurred at international levels, and that as a result a Hollywood film might be a very different product from country to country. Indeed, the Hollywood studios hardly cared. Their concern with content was always overshadowed by their interest in access. Other countries—in this case, China—typically threatened to bar a studio's entire product if changes were not made to a particular film. After routine minor protests, from filmmakers and from the State Department, Hollywood almost always complied.

Eric Schaefer examines a more localized and less organized form of regulatory activity in "Plain Brown Wrapper: Adult Films for the Home Market, 1930–1969." In his reading of trade journals, men's magazines, Supreme Court cases, and other materials, Schaefer studies an alternative mode of production—soft-core pornography—and the grassroots as well as more formal legal efforts to control it. The films that Schaeffer discusses tended to be shown in clubs, smokers, bars, and, of course, in private homes. He finds that regulatory efforts seemed to be in inverse proportion to these films' visibility and public acceptance. The more underground the film, the more diligent was the work on the part of arbiters of propriety and moral well-being.

RECEPTION

In "Ethnography and Exhibition: The Child Audience, the Hays Office, and Saturday Matinees," Richard deCordova examines a single, very large audience and a specific industry practice. DeCordova himself, of course, was one of the scholars who helped to develop the new interest in film history through his work on early stardom, and this essay first appeared in the second of two extraordinary volumes of *Camera Obscura* focusing on film history and leisure activity that helped establish the terms of current historiographic practice.[49] DeCordova's essay demonstrates the range of relations between institutions, audiences, and an era's social and political discussions. In this case the links between the motion picture industry, developments in child psychology during the period after World War I, and the concerns of parents, teachers, and reformers over children's leisure activities worked to make the movie matinee of the 1920s the site of attempts at both control and uplift in relation to the child audience, and thus a primary location for working out the very definitions of childhood and adolescence.

We understand that Hollywood films mobilized audience desires and fantasies, and that filmmakers endeavored to keep viewers coming back for more. But Kathryn Fuller-Seeley, in her "Dish Night at the Movies: Exhibitor Promotions and Female Audiences during the Great Depression," explains that the institution of the cinema produced desires and created audiences in ways unrelated to the content of the movies themselves. During the Depression, these audiences showed up for dinnerware—for the plates and saucers and gravy boats distributed by theaters. The site of exhibition thus came to construct a gendered narrative of consumption, with female patrons completing their collections from week to week. Despite an apparent orderliness, dish nights and other giveaways from the period also created a potentially angry audience, or at least the perception of one. Fuller-Seeley's reading of trade reports and advertising materials shows the period's concern, on the part of exhibitors and some authorities, with audiences motivated to mob action not by the films that they saw but by their disappointment over not being awarded any money on bank night or by a theater running out of china. From Fuller-Seeley's account, we can come to a more complete understanding of what it meant to "go to the movies" during the 1930s, including the full range of activities available to audience members and the relationships and tensions between the cinema and other institutions and consumption practices.

A significant contribution of queer theory to film studies has been to show that the representational strategies of numerous mainstream, classical-era Hollywood films might be queered, that is, understood as engaging either openly or covertly with images ostensibly condemned by the Production Code. David Lugowski, in "'A Treatise on Decay': Liberal and Leftist Critics and Their Queer Readings of Depression-Era U.S. Film," has retrieved and analyzed the "voices" of a select group of viewers to show that such interpretations are not simply the inventions of contemporary scholars but rather were readily available to classical period audiences. Lugowski's primary materials are film reviews from identifiably right-wing and leftist sources, as well as memos from the Production Code Administration. These reviews and memos are astonishingly sensitive to the sexual politics of films like *Stage Door* and to characterizations like those of Mae West and Franklin Pangborn. But film reception is never monolithic, and Lugowski's essay demonstrates the range of interpretation available even after audiences may have accepted the queer possibilities of Hollywood films. Those interpretations varied from assertions of immorality and ethnic and political depravity by the Right to connections of "deviant" sexuality with decaying capitalism by the Left.

PRODUCTION

Janet Bergstrom, in "Murnau in America: Chronicle of Lost Films (*4 Devils* and *City Girl*)," examines the intense negotiations between the famous emigré director F. W. Murnau and those with whom he worked at Fox Studio (including William Fox himself). In her essay Bergstrom's aim is not to add to the history and mythology of the European artist betrayed by an American assembly-line system of production, but rather to examine the place of the director—as a celebrity, commodity, and acknowledged artist—in the economy of the film studio. Murnau's movies for Fox figured prominently in the studio's expansionist practices of the late silent period and in its determination to produce films that could be considered art as well as be perfectly suitable to a global mass audience. From Murnau's career at Fox we can understand the period's frequent conflation of art film and popular cinema. Over the last eighty years, Murnau has earned a reputation as a sort of cinematic visionary; at the end of the 1920s, however, Fox saw no contradiction between such aesthetic practice and the idea of the super-production designed to establish the studio's reputation and guarantee its financial stability.

Sumiko Higashi, in her essay "The American Origins of Film Noir: Realism in Urban Art and *The Naked City*," investigates one of the givens of film history—that the film noir emerged more or less directly from German expressionism, with more marginal influences from French poetic

realism and American hard-boiled fiction. In its determination to emphasize the text/context binary, this history would also have it that film noir
somehow reflected a pervasive late-1940s psychological malaise as a result
of a weariness from war coupled with anxieties about modernity. Higashi,
however, uses the Ashcan school paintings and the work of photographers
from Jacob Riis to Weegee as evidence that demonstrates new and compelling antecedents to this cycle of movies. She also uses the studio correspondence about *The Naked City* (1948) to examine the very deliberate efforts
of the production team to make a film that incorporated this American
brand of realism. But Higashi's point is not simply to use these materials
to make a nationalist claim for a popular grouping of films—there were,
of course, multiple influences on these movies. The usual explanation of
film noir tends to psychologize it, from Freud to Caligari to a victorious
but uncertain postwar America. Higashi uses her materials to politicize
the genre by showing that the American realist tradition, dating at least to
the middle of the nineteenth century, sought to represent the urban scene
in order to control it, particularly in order to control the racial and ethnic
diversity that so marked the American city.

This volume is designed largely for use by undergraduates in film history classes and also by film scholars. It is our goal that the essays collected
here will be instructive in terms of how to do historical research and how
to examine and make sense of historical materials. In addition, we see the
essays as contributing to an ongoing historiographic project in film studies,
one that asks questions about methods in history and theories of historical
understanding. In doing so, we do not propose either a return to a golden
age in film studies or a rejection of the methods that have dominated the
field since the 1950s. We do hope, however, that the essays here encourage film scholars and students to ask questions about methodologies and
about film studies as a scholarly discipline, and to consider new subjects
and modes of historical inquiry. We are not advocating removing the text
from film studies, but instead we aim to develop the notion of the textuality of the historical field. Such a field includes a broad variety of primary
materials, with movies holding a significant position but not always the
central one.

This approach does not, then, insist on a final perfection of historical
research. In fact, such a teleology works against everything that motivates
these essays. All of us included in this project hope that our work con-

tributes to a continuing history of the history of film scholarship itself, so that we can properly understand the contributions of Thorp, Gessner, Buscombe, Jacobs, and others. These writers have taught us that films need not be the main object of study for film scholars, but in doing so they perhaps provide a link to, rather than a rejection of, more text-based studies.

One of the historical clichés of film studies is that the field only emerged in the academy in the 1960s and 1970s. This is certainly not true, as this introduction and several of the essays demonstrate. But it may well be true, as Jennifer Bean has written, that there was a crisis of legitimation of film studies during that period, with scholars meeting the crisis by attempting "to secure, outline, and theorize *the* unique object of . . . inquiry," the film itself, in order to justify the serious study of cinema.[50] As the current secure place of film studies in the academy attests, these attempts were successful. So now, more than three decades later, our very ability to critique the idea of the centrality of the film text is possible largely because of that notion itself as well as through the efforts of the scholars who proposed it.

NOTES

1 Margaret Farrand Thorp, *America at the Movies* (New Haven, Conn.: Yale University Press, 1939), 1.

2 Gessner sent his syllabus to Frank Capra, because of his ranking of *It Happened One Night*, and Capra deposited it with his papers at the Cinema Archive at Wesleyan University. The fee for the class itself was fifteen dollars for all of the sessions or a one dollar fee for individual sessions, and because of this it seems to have been an adult education course or perhaps an extension course and not part of the regular university curriculum.

3 Thorp, *America at the Movies*, 144.

4 Ibid., 173–215.

5 Iris Barry, "Why Wait for Posterity?" in *Hollywood Quarterly: Film Culture in Postwar America, 1945–1957*, ed. Eric Smoodin and Ann Martin (Berkeley: University of California Press, 2002), 244. The article originally appeared in *Hollywood Quarterly* 1, no. 2 (January 1946): 131–37.

6 Ibid.

7 See the Web site for the Library of Congress Motion Picture and Television Reading Room at http://www.loc.gov/rr/mopic/.

8 Douglas Gomery, *The Hollywood Studio System* (New York: St. Martin's Press, 1986); Richard deCordova, *Picture Personalities: The Emergence of the Star System in America* (Urbana: University of Illinois Press, 1990); John Belton, *Widescreen Cinema* (Cambridge, Mass.: Harvard University Press, 1992).

9 Lea Jacobs, *The Wages of Sin: Censorship and the Fallen Woman Film, 1928–1942* (Madison: University of Wisconsin Press, 1991); Ruth Vasey, *The World According to Hollywood, 1918–1939* (Madison: University of Wisconsin Press, 1997); Jon Lewis, *Hollywood v. Hard Core: How the Struggle over Censorship Saved the Modern Film Industry* (New York: New York University Press, 2000).

10 William Boddy, "Approaching *The Untouchables*: Social Science and Moral Panics in Early Sixties Television," *Cinema Journal* 35, no. 4 (summer 1996): 70–87.

11 Janet Staiger, *Interpreting Films: Studies in the Historical Reception of American Cinema* (Princeton, N.J.: Princeton University Press, 1992); Jackie Stacey, *Star Gazing: Hollywood Cinema and Female Spectatorship* (London: Routledge, 1994).

12 Jane Addams, *The Spirit of Youth and City Streets* (New York: Macmillan, 1909).

13 For an examination of these uses of Capra's wartime documentary, see my *Regarding Frank Capra: Audience, Celebrity, and American Film Studies, 1930–1960* (Durham, N.C.: Duke University Press, 2004).

14 Leo A. Handel, *Hollywood Looks at Its Audience* (Urbana: University of Illinois Press, 1950); David Riesman and Evelyn T. Riesman, "Movies and Audiences," *American Quarterly* 4, no. 3 (fall 1952): 195–202.

15 See the editorial statement at the beginning of *Hollywood Quarterly* 1, no. 1 (1945). For a history of *Hollywood Quarterly* (*The Quarterly Review of Film, Radio, and Television*), see Eric Smoodin and Ann Martin, eds., *Hollywood Quarterly: Film Culture in Postwar America, 1945–1957* (Berkeley: University of California Press, 2002).

16 Ellen Seacoat, memo to August Frugé, "*Quarterly* Statement of Purposes and Principles," November 3, 1954. The memo is housed at the University of California Press.

17 August Frugé, *A Skeptic among Scholars: August Frugé on University Publishing* (Berkeley: University of California Press), 161.

18 Ibid.

19 The essay appeared originally in *Cahiers du cinéma*, no. 223 (1970): 29–47. An English translation first appeared in *Screen* 13, no. 3 (autumn 1972): 5–44, and was reprinted in *Movies and Methods*, ed. Bill Nichols (Berkeley: University of California Press, 1976), 493–529.

20 Raymond Bellour, "Alterner/raconter," in *Le cinéma americain: Analyses de films*, vol. 1, ed. Raymond Bellour (Paris: Flammarion, 1980), 69–88; Thierry Kuntzell, "Savoir, pouvoir, voir," in *Le cinéma americain: Analyses de films*, vol. 1, 161–72; Stephen Heath, "Narrative Space," *Screen* 17, no. 3, (autumn 1976): 68–112; Nick Browne, "The Spectator-in-the-Text: The Rhetoric of *Stagecoach*," *Film Quarterly* 29 (winter 1975–76): 26–38. For representative works on the directors, see Jon Halliday, ed., *Sirk on Sirk* (London: Secker and Warburg,

1971); for Hitchcock, see Heath, "Narrative Space"; for Lang, see Bellour, "On Fritz Lang," *Sub-Stance*, no. 9 (1974): 25–34.

21 Mulvey's essay appears on pp. 6–18 of the journal.

22 Buscombe's essay appears on pp. 65–82 of the journal. In my discussion of the essay, the numbers refer to the anthologized version in *The Studio System*, ed. Janet Staiger (New Brunswick, N.J.: Rutgers University Press, 1995), 17–36.

23 Ibid., 24.

24 Ibid., 20.

25 *I, Pierre Rivière, Having Slaughtered My Mother, My Sister, and My Brother . . . A Case of Parracide in the 19ᵗʰ Century*, ed. Michel Foucault (Lincoln: University of Nebraska Press, 1982). The project first appeared in France, from Éditions Gallimard, in 1973.

26 Garth Jowett, *Film: The Democratic Art* (Boston: Little, Brown, 1976). For the Production Code, see appendix 4, 468–72.

27 Robert C. Allen and Douglas Gomery, *Film History: Theory and Practice* (New York: Knopf, 1985).

28 Allen and Gomery cite Roger Manwell, *The International Encyclopedia of Film* (New York: Crown, 1972); and Ephraim Katz, *The Film Encyclopedia* (New York: Lippincott and Crowell, 1979).

29 Allen and Gomery, *Film History*, 38.

30 Lea Jacobs, *The Wages of Sin: Censorship and the Fallen Woman Film, 1928–1942* (Madison: University of Wisconsin Press, 1991); Danae Clark, *Negotiation Hollywood: The Cultural Politics of Actors' Labor* (Minneapolis: University of Minnesota Press, 1995).

31 Jacobs, *The Wages of Sin*, ix.

32 Richard deCordova, "Ethnography and Exhibition: The Child Audience, the Hays Office and Saturday Matinees," *Camera Obscura*, no. 23 (May 1990): 91–106. The discussion of 1970s film theory and ethnography can be found on p. 92.

33 Judith Mayne, *Cinema and Spectatorship* (London: Routledge, 1993), 157; Annette Kuhn, *Dreaming of Fred and Ginger: Cinema and Cultural Memory* (New York: New York University Press, 2002), 3–4.

34 "Special Debate: Trauma and Screen Studies," *Screen* 42, no. 2 (summer 2001): 188–216; "The Trauma Debate II," *Screen* 44, no. 2 (summer 2003): 200–28.

35 Susanna Radstone, "Trauma and Screen Studies: Opening the Debate," *Screen* 42, no. 2 (summer 2001): 188.

36 Ibid., 189.

37 E. Ann Kaplan, "Melodrama, Cinema and Trauma," *Screen* 42, no. 2 (summer 2001): 204.

38 Maureen Turim, "The Trauma of History: Flashbacks upon Flashbacks," *Screen* 42, no. 2 (summer 2001): 205–10; Janet Walker, "Trauma Cinema: False Memories and True Experience," *Screen* 42, no. 2 (summer 2001): 211–16; Peter Thomas, "Victimage and Violence: *Memento* and Trauma Theory," *Screen* 44,

no. 2 (summer 2003): 200–207; Daniel Humphrey, "Authorship, History and the Dialectic of Trauma: Derek Jarman's *The Last of England*," *Screen* 44, no. 2 (summer 2003): 208–15.

39 Michael Hammond, "Laughter during Wartime: Comedy and the Language of Trauma in British Cinema Regulation, 1917," *Screen* 44, no. 2 (summer 2003): 222–28.

40 Ibid., 223.

41 Eileen Bowser, *The Transformation of Cinema, 1907–1915* (Berkeley: University of California Press, 1994).

42 Donald Crafton, *The Talkies: American Cinema's Transition to Sound, 1926–1931* (Berkeley: University of California Press, 1999).

43 Ibid., 6.

44 The FBI/Freedom of Information Act Web site (http://foia.fbi.gov/) provides files for a number of film personalities, ranging from Bud Abbott to John Wayne. Many of the files of the Pacific Film Archive can be accessed at http://www.bampfa.berkeley.edu.

45 Examples of longstanding collections include those at UCLA (papers from Paramount and Twentieth Century-Fox, for instance, as well as such personal collections as that of Walter Lantz); the New York Public Library (documents from the National Board of Review); and the Library of Congress (invaluable motion picture copyright records).

46 For example, see Robert Brent Toplin, "Film and History: The State of the Union," in *Perspectives: American Historical Association Newsletter* 37, no. 4 (April 1999): 1, 8–9. The AHA tends to review films in the *American Historical Review* in the fourth edition of each year's volume.

47 Franca Iacovetta and Wendy Mitchinson, "Social History and Case File Research," in *On the Case: Explorations in Social History*, ed. Iacovetta and Mitchinson (Toronto: University of Toronto Press, 1998), 7.

48 Bill Nichols, "Introduction," in *Movies and Methods*, vol. 1 (Berkeley: University of California Press, 1976), 1; Andrew Sarris, *The American Cinema: Directors and Directions, 1929–1968* (New York: Dutton, 1968); Jowett, *Film*, 11.

49 These volumes of *Camera Obscura* were published by the Johns Hopkins University Press. The special issue editors for number 22, "Feminism and Film History," were Lea Jacobs and Patrice Petro. For number 23, "Popular Culture and Reception Studies," the special issue editor was Lynn Spigel (deCordova's essay appears on pp. 91–106 of this issue).

50 Jennifer Bean, "Introduction: Toward a Feminist Historiography of Early Cinema," in *A Feminist Reader in Early Cinema*, ed., Jennifer M. Bean and Diane Negra (Durham, N.C.: Duke University Press, 2002), 9.

I   INSTITUTIONAL HISTORIES

THE BEGINNINGS OF AMERICAN FILM STUDY

Dana Polan

In a version of this study that I was preparing to present at Stanford University (one of the historical sites of importance for the story I propose to tell), I had originally intended to use the word "origins" instead of "beginnings" in my title. But then it struck me that the idea of "origins" might be misleading, for it could suggest lineages, developments, traditions, and legacies—that is, successful continuities across time. In fact, the story of the earliest days of American film study is instead one of breaks and gaps—of projects begun but not followed through, of initiatives that concretized into nothing enduring. For all the effort of a new historiography to break away from singular events and deal with gradual movement (as in the Annales school's emphasis on *longue durée*, or the long duration of history), the history of early film study in particular reveals itself to be highly punctual and highly fragmentary.

To be sure, as the following pages will bear out, in the early days there were precise institutional linkages between the various attempts at bringing film into the academy. Indeed, much of the early history has to do with the ways in which, with the support of established institutions, various initiatives could seem to gain solidity. But to the extent that any initiative depended on larger institutional support and promotion, its existence and endurance could be fragile when the support dried up. To anticipate just one example, it is clear that soon after its founding the Academy of Motion Picture Arts and Sciences (hereafter, AMPAS or "the Academy") became a central player in the push to introduce film education into universities. The Academy sponsored several such educational projects and was key to their start-up. But it seems that when the Academy came to feel it no longer needed special university instruction and could rely on the studios to train their own personnel, it lowered its support to academic ventures, and the diverse university initiatives under its aegis had to fight on their own or flounder.

In fact, if the early history of cinema study is one of punctual events that do not add up to an enduring lineage, we can in particular pinpoint an ultimate punctuation to these beginning moments, one that cuts early film study off from later developments that more clearly form part of a legacy for the current state of the discipline. This terminal event, which takes place in the mid-1930s, is the founding of the Museum of Modern Art's Department of Film and its creation of a circulating library of film titles. As disconnected as are the beginnings of film study, the formation and dissemination of the MOMA canon brings together the fragments and gives a sense of direction to a new field of film study in the university. Almost as if overnight, we see the creation of courses all mentioning the MOMA collection and all resembling each other in terms of their sense of just what the history of film has been canonically. To take just one example, in the late 1920s Stanford University hesitantly tried to introduce a film course (under the aegis of AMPAS). But this hesitancy disappeared in the second half of the 1930s when the university began a new, more enduring course based on the MOMA collection. Significantly, where the earlier course had been housed in the Department of Psychology (a sign in this case of an uncertainty of just how film should be imagined as an object of study), the new course was in the Department of Fine Arts and reflected a newfound respectability for film as an aesthetic object.[1]

In the following study my goals are both modest and complex. On the one hand, I want simply to tell the story of early film study as I see it. The primary goal here is to present things as I think they were, as captured in all their concrete facticity. But here even the modesty becomes complex. I have already used language—"the story . . . as I see it," for example—that implies that this history is very much one filtered through a narrative consciousness (in this case, mine). Perhaps this is inevitable in all historiography but it is especially necessary in the case at hand, for there is much that went on in the early days of film study that is unknown to us—so many parts of the narrative at which the historian can only guess. In some cases, a document that might fill out the narrative is simply unavailable and the researcher has to imagine what it might say; historians live perhaps in the hope of the last piece of paper that will bring everything together. To take just one example, in the early 1930s, the USC film professor Boris Morkovin tried to set up a series of regular visits by classes to Hollywood studios to aid in a professionalization of film-inclined students. Something went wrong, however, and studios' relations with the budding USC film program soured a bit. Wondering what happened is intriguing, but all I have for the moment is a letter of apology to the Academy (which evidently facilitated the visits) by a friend of Morkovin asking that what happened during one particular studio visit be forgotten. What happened, what the affront or impropriety might have been, is never explained. Perhaps somewhere in some studio file there is the other side of this correspondence, the bit that would put it all together. But how do we know that it is even there, and how do we begin to imagine the research effort it would take to track it down? Instead, it is better to guess simply that some lapse of protocol occurred and then leave it at that. We can at least posit that the triangular relations between the academic world, the Academy, and the studio system were no doubt fraught with tensions and mutual suspicions. Individual facts can sometimes be less important than the intuition of general attitudes and tensions.

There is much about the details of the history of early film study that is simply not available to us—the facts are not available, the records are not to be found, the documents are missing. To take another example (which I also will return to later), there is next to nothing known about one of the very first film instructors in the university, Frances Taylor Patterson, who taught at Columbia. When a few years ago one of the Columbia professor John Belton's students, Vassilios Koronakis, set out to learn about Patterson, his study became as much a commentary on the difficulty of finding information as it was a study of Patterson herself. Virtually nothing could be found out about Patterson except the basic evidence, such as her syllabi, that she did in fact teach courses.[2]

But if simple tales turn out to be difficult to develop because of empirical gaps in the historical record, there is another, deeper difficulty in the easy modes of the simple retelling of the historical past of film study. As I see it, to make full sense of the history of film study we need to go beyond the immediate chronicle to engage with larger issues of social and cultural history. To be sure, presented in and of itself the story of the beginnings of film study is a fascinating one that is filled with great anecdotes and amusingly eccentric characters. It is salutary, no doubt, for disciplines to look back on their founding moment, and the story of film study can be both pleasurable and educational. But this story, as I want to tell it, is about more than just a discipline—more than a fun tale of curious characters in intriguing narratives. Among other things, the story of film study as I will tell it is part of a bigger tale, that of American higher education as it emerged into the modern age and had to deal with new, nontraditional media technologies such as the emergent culture of cinema.

In fact, the tale I tell has contemporary relevance and is not just an amusing oddity from the past. Take, for instance, the way film is configured in some of today's debates about value and the humanities—debates that have been summed up under the rubric of "the culture wars." Notorious is an early issue of the *New Criterion* with Hilton Kramer's strident diatribe against the teaching of film in the university. For Kramer, the supposed breakdown of morals and civic confidence beginning in the 1970s comes less from the Vietnam experience and a loss of American mission than from the demoralizing, relativizing effect that film instruction has in a university world ostensibly geared to higher knowledge. Neoconservatives like Kramer need for their arguments the nostalgic positing of a golden age of intellection before the imputed fall into the morass of mass culture. They posit, for instance, an integrity of the great books tradition and of pedagogy in that tradition, and they see the popular arts as a potential threat to its sanctity. But a look at the history of higher education with attention both to great books instruction *and* to academia's engagement with mass culture reveals a much more complicated picture—one of interference and influence between the high and the low. For all the resistance by neoconservatives to mass culture, the earlier days of intellectual interaction reveal a frequent openness to the educational and even aesthetic possibilities of mass cultural forms such as film. Many of the central proponents of great books education turn out to be central advocates also of an open and even laudatory approach to popular arts such as cinema.

One example involves Scott Buchanan, the first president of Saint John's College, which was famous for fully basing its curriculum on great books education and serving as a symbol of a supreme education concerned with the "best that has been thought and said." In his draft plan for the college, Buchanan ended his discussion of the proposed curriculum with the strong recommendation that the planned four years of great books education be followed by a fifth year of instruction within an Institute of Cinematics (to be run, he suggests, by Lewis Mumford, whose 1934 *Technics and Civilization* had also argued for the need to engage in positive fashion with the arts and crafts of everyday life).[3] Following in the lineage of so many commentators in the period from around 1910 to the 1930s, Buchanan argues that cinema is not merely one among many arts (whether popular or fine), but rather it is the ultimate art, a veritable Hegelian synthesizer that realizes the potential of all other arts and brings them to their greatest import and intensity. Significantly, Buchanan's discussion of just what would be learned in this institute is somewhat vague: it is not clear to what extent the emphasis would be on the craft of filmmaking or on critical reflection, the elaboration of an aesthetic appreciation of the lively art. But in his welcoming of film, Buchanan is in fact typical of many of the great books intellectuals of his day. For example, the philosopher Mortimer Adler (also a key figure in great books education to the point of later becoming a veritable salesperson for the Encyclopedia Britannica's postwar popularization of the canon) was one of Buchanan's closest friends (and an obvious partner in dialogue on the positive virtues of cinema). In 1934, Adler wrote one of the most extended defenses of film as a humanist endeavor, the Aristotelian *Art and Prudence* (a book that became a bible for the Hays Office in its attempts to stave off the condemnation of film as more sociological—an influence on behavior—than aesthetic). And the willingness in Buchanan and Adler to engage with the popular can be traced back to their graduate school work at Columbia, where both participated in John Erskine's great books program and became committed to adult education as a way of making higher education responsive to the popular, public realm.

In the first decades of the century, education found itself forced to come to grips with the new demographic conditions in the United States: in particular, the shift to city living; the influx of immigrant cultures; and, with industrialization, the growing need for a trained labor force and, some might say, for a working class that was disciplined and trained to be subservient. Progressivism is the term commonly employed to describe the various initiatives in government, religious organizations, reform institutions, Chautauqua institutes, and so on to deal with these new factors in American life by trying to find points of integration for such new forces within the dominant mode of production and its corresponding cultural and social realms. It is my contention that the efforts of progressivism to argue the potentially beneficent aspects of everyday culture help explain the increasingly positive acceptance of film as object of academic study.

It is important to understand that progressivism was not so much a single movement as a series of initiatives and debates engaged in by individuals, organizations, and institutions that did not necessarily have a direct relation to each other and that could, indeed, have conflicting notions of purposes and methods of social-cultural reform. In its first guise, a moralistic discourse dominated progressive reform with a notion that the new conditions of everyday life in America offered both advantages and risks, and therefore that there should be moral instruction in proper behavior. But where many of the moralists came as amateurs and applied their efforts as such in the civic realm, the rising professionalization of the American university meant that it increasingly was able to take on the mission of progressivism without enclosing amelioration within moralistic and religious frames. Film, regarded as both an embodiment of potentially moral contents and as the result of an applied professional activity (the craft of filmmaking), found a place within this transition from moral guardians to academics as the ostensible arbiters of everyday ethics.

The moral guardians in the first decade of the twentieth century tended to regard film with suspicion as one of the seductions into the salacious that faced ordinary people in the public sphere. The closing of New York's moving picture exhibition venues at the end of 1908 is the most famous example of the moral disciplining of cinema in this first moment. But this moralistic disapprobation received a quick riposte: first, in the form of a secular and practical-oriented reformism manifested in the influential efforts of reform groups such as the People's Institute (a key player behind the foundation of the National Board of Censorship) and, second, through the efforts of academia to make film into the object of a positive analysis and approbation where it is imagined that exposure to film and its workings could have an uplifting and ameliorative effect. In fact, the People's Institute had a major academic component, as its teaching staff included a number of professors and graduate students from Columbia University. Implicit in the idea of the People's Institute was a concern for a positive education that would respect much of the mass culture that ordinary citizens possessed. In their rejection of practices of moral condemnation, reform organizations like the People's Institute promoted instead an affirmative emphasis on training as the means to integrate populations into the American way of life.

Subsequently, this concern with ameliorative forms of instruction was continued by universities such as Columbia that increasingly understood the need to target new constituencies for educational benefits. As Thorstein Veblen in *The Higher Learning in America* (1918) attests (albeit in critical fashion) the American university was undergoing a transition from gentlemanly refinement to a much more pragmatic concern with the industrial applicability of academic lesson. Indeed, the concern of the nineteenth-century elite universities had been as much to improve and confirm the character of a hereditary elite as it had been to give that elite any socially useful knowledge—members of such elites famously set out to get no more than a C grade in their courses (known as the "gentleman's C's") as anything higher would have indicated that too much time was being devoted to learning and not enough to the sort of social life that builds character and forges ties of honor among a future business class. By Veblen's time, there was a shift toward a notion of education that would be practical and popular, reaching out to many nonelite members of the culture.

Progressivism offered at least three different approaches to an affirmative understanding of film as force of uplift and positive pedagogy. (As I will show, a fourth option emerges later in the history I relate here.) First, the very terms of a philosophy of high culture—as evident, for instance, in the concurrent promotion of great books courses—could simply be transferred over to film. In other words, film would be seen to take up its rightful place among the fine arts and, significantly, this place could be one either of equivalence (that cinema is as worthy as the other arts) or of superiority (that there are ways in which cinema brings to a supreme point the aesthetic tendencies of the other arts). The breakthrough volumes on film in 1915–1916 by Vachel Lindsay and Hugo Munsterberg offer key articulations of this philosophy (and it is worth noting how many subsequent volumes reference these two establishing texts): for Lindsay, for instance, each fine art has its refinement in a cinematic equivalent; and for both Lindsay and Munsterberg, film establishes itself as an art by its systematic, imaginative deformation of reality.

Intriguingly, then, a second option for progressivism has, quite the contrary, to do with an appreciation of film for its representational qualities rather than for any aesthetic propensity to deform reality: that is, film is to be valued for its ability to provide a record of the world—a veritable archive of human history's great moments. Throughout the first decade of the twentieth century, and especially in the second decade, there is a recurrent reference in studies of film to its potential to serve as a universal language, a "visual esperanto" as Edward Van Zile refers to it in his 1923 volume *That Marvel, the Movie*.[4] If the aesthetic appreciation of film relied on a notion of the autonomy of art, this second approach imagines film in a virtual documentary mode, a transparent registration of events. Intriguingly, this emphasis on cinema as itself a pedagogy that derives from contents transmitted through the transparency of realism could, and often did, lead logically to the conclusion that there did not need to be education *about* film. Since film carried its educational lessons on its sleeve, in its explicit presentation of worldly knowledge, it could substitute for other forms of learning. Cinema supposedly transmitted the world with greater immediacy and greater impact than the more mediated, distanced efforts of the traditional verbal discourse of pedagogy. Vachel Lindsay's *Art of the Moving Picture* (1915), even within its aesthetic framework, also buys into a notion of film as direct universal language: as many commentators have noted, Lindsay's notion of film as a hieroglyphic form assumes a directness and intensity of film effect far superior to that of the word (including Lindsay's own words as a popular bard coming increasingly to realize that film could have a much greater extensive and intensive impact than his poems ever could). Even more extreme, in Van Zile's *That Marvel, the Movie* we find the author proposing an end to universities and their replacement by a universal archive of film images that could recount all of human knowledge. (It is worth noting that this assumes the necessity of re-creating past events through staged performances; even as it intends to valorize film as documentary, the philosophy of film as a universal language has a necessary place for fiction and imaginative reconstruction.) But in this very notion of a universal image archive, we can find another way in which the seemingly opposed goals of aesthetic appreciation and documentary instruction come together: from the sorts of images that Van Zile cites as worthy of inclusion in the archive (for example, great moments from history), it becomes clear that not every human accomplishment merits archiving but rather only those that are valuable and that are in themselves uplifting and capable of serving as moral models for their viewers. In other words, the documentary impulse is limited by the sentiment that not everything should be archived and offered to citizens; indeed, what should be included are just those human practices that, to extend Matthew Arnold, picture the best that has been thought, said, and visually enacted.

In contrast, the third move by which progressivism enables a receptiveness to cinema has little to do with the specific content—whether aesthetic or documentary—of individual films. Here instead the emphasis is on the production process per se, rather than on the specific films produced, and cinema comes to be celebrated for its applied procedures for making images come to life. Film historians such as Richard deCordova have noted how one of the most prominent and earliest discourses on film has to do with marveling at the technology that produces the cinema;[5] to this initial awe at the science of moving images, progressivism adds a more balanced, less bewildered appreciation of the concrete work that goes into movie making. Here, the progressivist attitude to film in particular derives from a larger impulse in the historical moment to celebrate human effort, activity, industry. Throughout the first and second decades of the twentieth century, two words recur constantly in progressivist texts: workmanship and craftsmanship. The idea of human skill and dexterity—which no doubt also is the fuel for the growing American interest in hobbies, science fairs, basement tinkering, gadgetry and invention, and everyday arts and crafts—becomes a celebration of the American dream less as the pioneer adventure it had been in the nineteenth century than as an adventure in place, the discovery of the ingenuity by which one copes industriously with the objects in one's immediate purview. Before a professional industry of movie making geared to the creation of aesthetically or pedagogically rich objects could be appreciated, there is the act of making per se, and this industrious activity is itself to be admired and imagined to be one of the means for self-amelioration. There is an interesting lineage to be drawn from this valorization of workmanship in the progressivist moment to the more recent Bordwellian appreciation of film as directly a poesis, not just cultural creation but a fundamental crafting of something valuable from raw material; a codified set of procedures for concrete and quite practical problem solving.[6] A significant step in this lineage, then, would be the craft, and reflection on craft, in the work of the former engineer Sergei Eisenstein; thus it is logical that David Bordwell treats Eisenstein as a key early figure in the understanding of filmmaking as scientifically modeled craft.

We should note, though, that in the first moments of practical instruction in film, the emphasis on industriousness is seen in highly personal terms rather than business ones. In other words, the goal is to offer individuals self-improvement by means of a training in personal workmanship that is to be valorized in and of itself, independent of any usefulness of the objects created from that workmanship and even independent of any supposed gain other than that of personal accomplishment. Thus, while the training manuals from the period on the various elements of filmmaking may mention the eventual possibility of financial reward, the overriding emphasis is on the moral benefit that skilled effort brings to the self. In fact, an emphasis on pecuniary rather than moral benefit emerges only as an explicit goal of film education in the 1920s, especially toward the end of the decade, through the work of correspondence schools and professional university curricula. The notion of training for purposes of financial gain is the fourth of the impulses that drive progressivism toward cinema and, as I indicated earlier, it is a topic that I will return to as I draw this history to a close. For the moment, I would like to note that the initial interest in film as an activity of craftsmanship was presented as being independent of monetary concerns (even if, in fact, the very notion of amelioration had obvious ties to the needs of a new industrialism both to train and to discipline its citizens).

The progressivist valorization of craftsmanship as a moral virtue in its own right accounts for an enduring central duality in film education from its very beginnings: film instruction was sometimes imagined to concentrate best on practical training in the work of actually making films; sometimes, in contrast, such instruction was deemed to be best applied in the service of film appreciation. From the start, film courses were concerned with issues both of production and of aesthetic reception. Indeed, it is important to note how this confusion of two pedagogies—a confusion that is often deliberate in the progressivist ideology in which all forms of self-improvement from the moral-aesthetic to the practical are promoted—is the force behind the first courses in film. Victor Freeburg and Frances Taylor Patterson's photoplay courses that began around 1915 at Columbia University were targeted both at providing practical training in hands-on practice to aspiring photoplay writers and at giving the ordinary citizen a critical framework to aid in the effective reception and consumption of films. Significantly, as Freeburg makes clear in his *Art of Photoplay Making*, the two goals blur: Freeburg posits a feedback loop between filmmakers and film consumers in which better discernment on the part of viewers will lead to a demand for better quality films that will then spur better photoplays.[7] Both the activities of photoplay making and of photoplay appreciation are integral components of an overall process of film's function as moral, aesthetic, and practical self-amelioration, and film education thus began out of the impulse to touch upon all of these elements together. The duality of concerns in film education remains in today's film study in the complicated relationship between production courses and those in the history and aesthetics of the art of cinema.

Central to the new mission of the universities was an emphasis on outreach forms of pedagogy—for example, correspondence classes, evening colleges, extension programs, adult education programs, and off-campus instruction (for example, in meeting halls). To be sure, we should not overemphasize the democratic impulse or effect of such outreach. On the one hand, as I have already hinted, the desire by the universities to address a new constituency was not disconnected from the need of industrial capital to refine a workforce and to hone working-class submissiveness (both through uplift and through an ostensible disabusing of criminal or other antisocial inclinations). On the other hand, the universities still kept as much of their mission to maintain the powers of a refined elite and to police boundaries between classes and the sort of education provided to them (thus film remained marginalized in extension programs). In fact, in falling himself for a myth of a golden age of higher learning for its own sake Thorstein Veblen laments that a new elite is being created by the modern university: namely, a professionalized elite concerned crassly with business practice that thereby substitutes economic benefit for moral or aesthetic self-improvement. Veblen tries to stave off a professionalization of academia by promoting craftsmanship and disinterested learning as salutary alternatives. But increasingly the modern university both called out to new populations and carefully regulated the sites in which their instruction could occur. In particular, many of the outreach programs offered noncredit courses targeted for nonmatriculating students (who were often told emphatically in promotional and course registration materials that they could not aspire to a real, elite university education but would instead be engaging in discrete learning experiences that would not add up to a whole higher learning).

Film study rose within this context. Around 1915, as noted above, Columbia University began to offer courses in the photoplay through its extension program (created, in large part, to compete with New York University, which had been making great efforts to reach out to a larger population in metropolitan New York). It seems not coincidental that the course developed at virtually the same moment as the publication of works on the aesthetics of film by such luminaries as Munsterberg and Lindsay. For film to become constituted as a positive object for university education, it had to achieve a certain level of respectability and aesthetic ambition, and this happened concurrently with the shift at the time to the feature film. Certainly, it would be possible to imagine educators attending to the social role of film in earlier moments. There is obviously writing on film from the moment of its invention, although rarely within academia: for example, as deCordova notes in his *Picture Personalities*, the emergent fan discourse on stars around 1910 was in fact preceded by a more scientific discourse on the technology of cinema and its ability to bring reproduced pictures to life. There even was some sense of a positive pedagogy through film at science centers, museums, Chautauqua activities, and public lectures (for example, the early travelogues shown by itinerant exhibitors at opera houses). But these earliest forms of educated attention to film were limited and could not lead to a full-fledged curriculum for the study of film: on the one hand, film was considered too much of a form of carnival culture to merit anything more than attention to its technology; on the other hand, positive pedagogy through film tended to see cinema as a neutral and transparent medium for the conveyance of knowledge (for instance, the travelogue as a direct representation of exotic places) and thereby it excluded the possibility of understanding the specific aesthetics of film.

With the transition to the feature film, the potential of film to appear as an ambitious cultural form and even a mode of art became harder to avoid. At the same time, the sense of what film can achieve is counterbalanced by a fear of what will happen if films refuse to realize their potential. In Victor Freeburg's books from the period, for instance, the notion that one can be trained to write morally and aesthetically qualified photoplays coincides with an admission of the dangers of bad films. In the best cases, the increased length of the feature film brings with it a greater attention to nar-

rative coherence—revealingly, so much of the education on film in this moment centered on visual composition and on an Aristotelian elaboration of
rules for the unified construction of long plots. The constant and consistent
reference in Munsterberg, Lindsay, Freeburg, and others in this moment to
the films of D. W. Griffith is revealing since we find there a manifestation
of the three primary impetuses seen earlier in the progressivist attention to
film. First, Griffith's intensive use of editing confirmed the ways in which
cinema as an art form could use medium-specific techniques in service of
an aesthetic transformation of reality. And this aesthetic refinement could
perhaps be tied to a valorization of art as not only artistic but moral uplift:
the Griffith films had a clear message about the proprieties of Victorian
life and the threats posed to it by ostensibly dangerous outsiders and mis-
creants. Second, the feature films of Griffith are seen to embody a documentary or archival ideal: Griffith's "history told with lightning" shows the
ability of film to range across time and offer a record of great human events
(thus, the intertitles in *The Birth of a Nation* insist on a photographic accuracy, albeit reconstructed, in the images). Third, the strikingly visible use of
editing in Griffith's works—an editing that called attention to itself rather
than participated in a transparent artifice of continuity—reiterated the appreciation of film as a craft, a skilled accomplishment of workmanship.

The courses at Columbia were shared by Victor Freeburg and Frances
Taylor Patterson, although Freeburg shifted directions after World War I
and increasingly moved away from film education. Their courses hesitated,
as we have seen, between practical training and instruction in aesthetic
discernment at the point of consumption. But the photoplay courses at
Columbia hovered as well between a professional, rigorous emphasis on
codified pedagogic procedures befitting a course from an Ivy League institution (today's students and scholars may be amused to note that the syllabus for one of Patterson's courses is twenty-six pages long) *and* a lighter
concern for adult education as a sort of hobbylike dabbling in which the
demands on the "students" cannot be too great. In this respect, the very
location of the photoplay courses in the extension program offered both
benefits and disadvantages to this beginning effort in film pedagogy. On
the one hand, that the extension courses were designed for nonmatriculating students and were assumed not to be a central part of the university's
primary mission in higher education meant that the photoplay course enjoyed an autonomy that allowed it to merge the practical and the aesthetic

more than mainstream curricula might have. The photoplay courses flourished, and even as late as the 1940s there are still listings of such courses
offered by Frances Taylor Patterson. On the other hand, that the courses
are located in a special program outside the regular curriculum allowed the
administration to treat the courses as less serious, less integral. It is clear
that there was an intellectual marginalization of film courses even as these
helped the financial mission of the university (something that is often all
too true today, where film is considered a "sexy" offering that brings in en-
rollment fees).

As mentioned earlier, research has turned up little about Patterson
(there is a little more on Freeburg but probably because he had important
career developments before and after his brief foray into film). Speaking
to the marginalization of female instructors, especially when they taught
in areas such as film that were not deemed to be serious components of
a bona fide higher education, the best available details on Frances Taylor
Patterson can be found in her husband's obituary.

The Columbia courses may also have borne the limitations of their emphasis on practicality. Insofar as a strong aspect of what they offered was
the promise of direct, usable gains (whether moral, aesthetic, or financial),
they paralleled—and were rivaled by—offerings in the private sector. The
period between 1910 and the late 1920s was a moment in which myriad businesses arose whose primary commodity was instruction: self-help manuals,
correspondence courses, trade schools, and the like. Indeed, the early 1920s
appear to present no other academic initiatives in film instruction than
the Columbia program, while the private sector witnessed a flourishing of
modes of training in film. For example, the New York School of Photography offered a range of correspondence courses (one of the school's students from the early 1930s told me that he took the cinematography class
for $100, a fee that provided weekly installments of at-home lessons as well
as a 35mm camera and film). Likewise, as a number of film historians have
shown, there was a strong presence of the correspondence school program
known as the Palmer Plan, which offered courses that used an impressive
range of textbooks and supporting materials (including, for example, the
fascinating *Photoplay Plot Encyclopedia* which presented an enormous list
of basic plot premises for prospective photoplay writers to build upon).[8]

It is clear from the paucity of real pedagogy in many of the manuals
that many of the home instruction courses offered in the period came

from companies that were more concerned with their own financial benefit than with any truly useful instruction they could provide to customers. Certainly, some of the courses from these companies seem to have been veritable acts of con artistry. But even the best-intentioned firms admitted limits to the quality and usefulness of their instruction. The material often reveals a modesty in the claims to success that the courses advertise; perhaps because of fears of legal action, company publicity often backs away from promising the customer too much. For instance, the photoplay writing manual of the New York Institute of Photography offers instruction on how to become a photoplay writer, but then reiterates to the reader just how tight the market is for new writers. To demonstrate this issue, a photo in the volume shows Norma Talmadge along with a revealing caption that states, "Norma Talmadge pays high for her stories favoring successful stage productions and published stories. Small chance here for the amateur writer to sell anything!"[9] On the other hand, given the fact that many of the correspondence schools were actually not located in Hollywood and were not actually staffed by Hollywood personnel (like the LSAT courses taught today by graduate students in other fields), the instruction in filmmaking and in industrial practice could only go so far. Many of the textbooks from the 1920s evidence a relative ignorance of just what goes on inside studios by reverting to broad homilies. For example, the New York Institute of Photography's motion picture directing manual states that the key to becoming a director is to gain experience—not experience in the industry but in life itself: "The greatest directors of today are the men who have run the greatest gamut of emotional experience. To converse with D. W. Griffith is to instantly realize that here is a man who has suffered, sacrificed, lost, loved, triumphed."[10] As one screenwriter, Frederica Maas, recounts in her memoirs, there was often a quite evident gap between what the commercial firms offered and the direct, hands-on experience of actually learning to work in the industry: "The Palmer School promised to read and correct your film scenarios. When the alleged textbook of 'The Palmer Method' arrived in the mail, it was an obvious moneymaking scheme from start to finish, a fraud, a false come-on for novices like myself."[11]

As film historians such as Richard Koszarski have shown, the period of the 1920s was one in which the film industry was engaged in intense consolidation, the rationalization of means and modes of production, the establishment of industry standards, and the professionalization of the labor force. This is the period, as Bordwell, Kristin Thompson, and Janet Staiger famously note, of the rise of trade organizations and professional societies in the film industry. If one reads books from around 1926 and 1927 on American film, it is clear that the coming of sound would add a new complexity to the industry's attempt to refine itself into a big business with advanced production methods. Clearly, those in the industry felt that this highly rationalized industry would need a professionally trained work force, and in the texts around 1926–1927 there are several overlapping initiatives to develop a nonamateurish, rigorous training in aspects of the business of film. Additionally, as the founding purposes of AMPAS make clear, we need to note how the need for professional training had direct political impetus behind it. The rationalization of the means and modes of production brought with it a corresponding worker activism—one that would culminate in the labor struggles of the 1930s and 1940s—and training was one of the means by which management could attempt to construct a docile, disciplined labor pool. We might note also that the first decades of the century saw a shift in the overall mission of higher education from moral or aesthetic character building to greater pragmatic concern with training in business success. Veblen, in his *Higher Learning in America*, laments the rise of professional schools within the university (his example is the burgeoning programs in business education and the very establishment of schools of business), and he takes this emphasis on training toward financial success to represent a loss of the university's true vocation of cultivating disinterested workmanship. What Veblen is responding to is a transition from the view of craft as an activity that is practical only to the extent that it helps develop the fiber of the individual, to the view of industry as an activity that is practical because it brings financial reward.

Interestingly, one of these 1926–1927 initiatives to professionalize film training centered on Columbia University, and yet the initiative seems to have bypassed Frances Patterson and the extension program. In the university's archives there is correspondence between Will Hays at the MPPDA and the university's president, Nicholas Murray Butler, about the possibility for the establishment of an accredited and accrediting degree program in film. The initiative appears to have originated with the MPPDA side of things, and it may well parallel other efforts by Hays in the 1920s, such as the establishment of Central Casting, to present as professional an image of mainstream American filmmaking as possible. For a subsequent

stage of the story I'm telling, it is important here to note that Hays's suggestion is for a curriculum divided into three tracks—one on photoplay
construction, one on cinematography, and one on set design and related
aspects of mise-en-scène. Butler promises Hays that he will set up a committee to investigate the possibility of a film curriculum, but the initiative
seems to have died out because there is no follow-up correspondence. My
guess is that while the main offices of the MPPDA were in New York—as,
obviously, is Columbia University—it became apparent that an effective
training in aspects of film production had to take place in the burgeoning
center of the industry: in other words, in Los Angeles.

Indeed, it is this geographic distance that may be one of the factors
in the termination of another endeavor in 1927. In that year, the Harvard
alumnus Joseph P. Kennedy organized a course in the Graduate School of
Business on the business aspects of the film industry. Kennedy used his
film industry connections to bring major luminaries from the film world
to speak to students. The Harvard Graduate School of Business had a required course each spring in which students engaged in intensive study
of a major industry. The very fact that Kennedy was able to convince the
administration that the film business was a worthy object of attention is
itself a mark of the extent to which film had grown up and was no longer
seen as the hobby art of a few isolated inventors or as an unrationalized
pseudo business (like that of other entrepreneurs of the fairgrounds). The
course had people from the industry speak on all of the stages of film's
circulation as a commodity, from production to distribution to exhibition,
and the transcripts were even published as a major book, *The Story of the
Film*.[12] Will Hays was a major presence in the course (issues of the campus
newspaper *Harvard Crimson* from the time report that he gave additional
lectures—such as a luncheon for four hundred students—and held extra
meetings with participants), and it may well be that, as with the Columbia
University initiative, Hays was in part responsible for the push to have
Harvard address the industry of film. Whatever its origin, the course was
not to be repeated. On the one hand, the course rubric implied that the
subject matter (i.e., the industry to be studied) would change from time to
time. But there were also problems specific to the film course. It was apparent that Cambridge, Massachusetts, was positioned a considerable distance from the film industry—both its centers of production in Los Angeles and its centers of finance and distribution on the East Coast—and this

factor made it hard to orchestrate. Indeed, one speaker, Marcus Loew, was advised by his doctor not to travel to Harvard; he disregarded the advice, however, and a few months later passed away, an event commented on in the published volume of *The Story of the Film*. Again, the initiative of an Ivy League university to find a place for film within a solid university curriculum was a beginning without follow-up.

Evidently it was apparent to people in the film industry that any regularized and professionalized training in film would have to take place in Los Angeles. The Academy of Motion Picture Arts and Sciences, founded in 1926, had an education division run by Lester Cowan (a Stanford graduate who would later go on to become an important film producer). Douglas Fairbanks, the first president of the Academy, had as one of his fencing partners Rufus von Kleinsmid, president of the University of Southern California, and the two began a discussion about developing a program at the university. As Manuel P. Servin and Iris Higbie Wilson recount in their history of the university, von Kleinsmid and the Trustees were involved in a major campaign to make the university seem more professional (indeed, a number of professional schools begin their life at usc in this period), and the proximity of the film industry may well have suggested that here too there was the possibility of evolving a program that would provide practical professional training.[13] There are two initiatives toward film education undertaken in the collaboration between usc and ampas, but despite the professionalizing hopes for these intiatives, it is necessary to emphasize the fragility of these first undertakings.

Take, for instance, the first plan by which usc and ampas decided to create a regular program in film study. Starting in 1929, a course called "Introduction to Photoplay" was convened by the dean of Arts and Sciences, a psychology professor named Karl Waugh. The course centered on lectures by visiting luminaries from the film business (the first year advertised presentations by Will Hays, Frank Wood, Irving Thalberg, Ernst Lubitsch, and J. Stuart Blackton, among others).[14] Undoubtedly ampas was instrumental in setting up these visits and convincing representatives from the film business to give up valuable time to come lecture to students. The contribution by ampas seems to have been quite organized; here, clearly, an industry organization saw that the professional training of its future workforce would increasingly be necessary and would involve assertive action to make sure programs developed and did so in ways that the industry leaders desired. Perhaps nothing indicates more the diligent effort of AMPAS around the photoplay course than its attempt soon after the USC version to push for a second course at Stanford (where, we will recall, Lester Cowan of the AMPAS education division had gone to school). Despite its relative distance from Los Angeles, Stanford had the advantage of reputation; already it was considered a site for the production of a professional elite, and no doubt AMPAS wanted to cultivate connections there. Indeed, at the same time as the planning of a Stanford version of the USC course, AMPAS was instrumental in getting the university to hold a centennial tribute for the famous horse-locomotion experiments of Muybridge at Leland Stanford's ranch in Palo Alto. For the Muybridge ceremony, Louis B. Mayer was the primary guest speaker (Mayer had been one of the key figures in the founding of AMPAS), and in his speech he specifically indicated that Stanford would be creating a program in film study. Karl Waugh was put in touch with a colleague of his in the Psychology Department at Stanford, and a young professor, Paul R. Farnsworth, who dealt with experimental aesthetics (and had written on music) was put in charge of the course. Significantly, Farnsworth appears to have had little special interest in film (and little professional background—predictably since he would be teaching one of the first courses on the subject), but in any case, he did not have to worry about preparedness, since AMPAS offered to make transcripts, and even perhaps films of the USC course, available to Stanford. It seems that AMPAS viewed the Stanford course as a veritable replay of the one at USC. But Farnsworth's lack of commitment, augmented by AMPAS's own increasing disinvestment in its education division in the 1930s, meant that the Stanford course never really developed into anything central to the university curriculum (significantly, in some years, it is not even identified in departmental catalogues as a course on film but instead is promoted as a general course on aesthetic issues). The course lumbered on until the mid 1930s when it was replaced, quite predictably, by one based on the new MOMA circulating library of films; significantly, this new course was offered in fine arts, not psychology.

At the beginning, at least, AMPAS clearly had coherent ambitions for the photoplay course that enabled it to imagine it could play an instrumental role in the curriculum at USC and elsewhere. On the USC side of the initiative, the situation was a bit more complicated and was symptomatic both of the still somewhat frivolous relationship of the academic world to the new art and business of film and of the larger hesitation in academia regarding the issue of a university devoting itself to professional training (in this respect, USC replays the broader debates about higher education at the time). Thus, while the administrative prestige held by Karl Waugh as dean no doubt explains some of the logic of why he was chosen, the deeper reason is purely anecdotal and suggests the potentially eccentric relationship of academia to subjects deemed popular, such as cinema. In the 1920s, as part of his experimental work in psychology, Waugh had developed a sort of galvanometer that he claimed could be used as a "truth" machine. To gain publicity for his "invention," he visited various Los Angeles film studios to hawk his machine as an instrument that film companies could use to test the believability of their actors. Indeed, there is a marvelous photo—obviously a sort of publicity still—in the USC archives of Waugh hooking up his gadget to Buster Keaton with a caption explaining that the scientist could get no meter reading at all from the great "stone face." Waugh's contacts with administrators in the film business no doubt accounts for some of the university's success in getting luminaries to come to the class, but it also shows how early professional education in the university world was still a curious blend of science and hokum, of training and hucksterism.

At the same time—and again, with strong supervision by AMPAS—the university began to develop a second project around film education. It was quickly decided that the "Introduction to Photoplay" course would become the first offering in a larger film-related curriculum—namely, a fully professional degree in hands-on film work. Intriguingly, the idea revolved around three tracks that are virtually identical to those that the Hays Office had tried to get Columbia University to develop: photoplay writing; cinematography; and directing and mise-en-scène. Each track would develop out of courses in already established departments: photoplay writing would use courses from English, cinematography would use courses from physics (insofar as camera work involved the science of optics), and directing and mise-en-scène would develop out of theater arts. The strong resemblance between this proposal and Hays's proposition to Columbia University at virtually the same time is intriguing. I have found no documentation to establish any direct connection, but my intuition is that all three initiatives in 1927—the Columbia project, the Harvard course, and the USC curriculum—all developed in response to educational plans promoted by Hays and AMPAS together, concerned as both were with perfecting a professionalized labor force.

In choosing a head of the new film program, USC was limited by a perceived need to have a full professor in charge. Waugh himself appears to have had no special interest in film except for his pecuniary efforts to market his truth meter. In any case, he was readying himself for a move into the presidency of a midwestern college. Thus USC turned instead to one of its few full professors in the humanities—a White Russian named Boris Morkovin from the Comparative Literature Department. In addition to his rank, perhaps it was felt that Morkovin's literary interests made him an appropriate organizer for courses on a new narrative art.

Interestingly, when I interviewed industry old-timers about Morkovin's supervision of the budding film program, most of them were dismissive because they felt he had little practical knowledge of filmmaking and little commitment to the program. Already, then, we can see a split in the goals of film education between a very hands-on practical training in the nuts-and-bolts of production and a more general education that aims to study film aesthetically as one of the narrative forms of art in our culture. Morkovin, indeed, stood primarily for the latter view (although he did teach a production course that, by all accounts, was not very good). In the early 1920s, Morkovin had come to the United States for a series of lectures (designed clearly to gain the attention of American universities as prospective employers) in which he used magic lantern projection for illustrative materials. He thus possessed that progressivist faith, as noted above, in the documentary educational power of images. And by the 1930s he added to this a more specific attention to film as an aesthetic and moral force as well as an educational one. Throughout the 1930s, for instance, he worked as a consultant to Walt Disney's company, for which he conducted a course for the animators on the comedic structures of narrative as inspired by Aristotelian poetics. At the same time, like the more classic progressives, he founded a league for the promotion of film as a form of moral uplift, and he edited a journal, *Cinema Progress*, that reviewed films and offered a general reflection on film's place in culture. As important a scholarly figure as Rudolf Arnheim was listed as a member of the journal's editorial board.

But the humanistic interest in film as an object for critical study would have only a fragile presence in USC's developing program. The preference—among students and administration—was for a professional program of hands-on training. Morkovin himself was increasingly marginalized, and by the end of the 1930s he clearly was looking for another field to devote his attentions to. Ironically and amusingly, his chance to leave film study, which he felt was being overrun by business-oriented professional training, came by means of the film industry itself. The presence of two hearing-impaired students in his introductory film course got him thinking about the pedagogical needs of face-to-face communication among the hard of hearing, and this new interest got a boost when the wife of Spencer Tracy contacted him about her hearing-impaired son. With financial support from Mrs. Tracy, the John Tracy Clinic for the Hearing Impaired was founded at USC. To conduct research in that area of concern, Morkovin left the film department to join psychology, where he remained for the rest of his career. In a further ironic twist, his greatest accomplishment was the production in the 1950s of what came to be called the "life-situation" films—namely, short narratives of everyday life produced by USC film production students and presented to the hearing-impaired.

Morkovin's departure from the film program led to its increasing professionalization as a training ground for documentary and industry-oriented filmmakers. This professionalizing tendency would intensify during World War II where the needs of documentary film production in such venues as the Signal Corps created a great demand for practically trained and hands-on experienced film workers. And a very different constitution of film as an object of professional academic study occurred through the attention that social scientists and political theorists began to pay to film as a form of mass media or mass communication. There is, for instance, another story of film education to be told around initiatives that gain momentum in the 1920s and 1930s, such as the Payne Fund studies, and that take on a new impetus during World War II (for example, the Rockefeller Foundation's aid to Siegfried Kracauer for research on representations of Nazism).

At the same time, as I suggested earlier, a less practical and more aesthetically oriented approach to film was gaining a new impetus through the success of the MOMA Film Library and its construction of a historical canon of film. In the postwar moment, the critical study of film within the terms of the humanities would also begin to be developed in such programs as UCLA where the program director Kenneth MacGowan combined up-close knowledge of the film business, a left-liberal concern for film as a form of moral instruction, and an interest in the aesthetic history of film (culminating in his book *Behind the Screen* from 1965).[15] By the end of the 1950s, with the push to create a Society for Cinematologists (eventually to mutate into the Society for Cinema Studies and then into the Society for Cinema and Media Studies), there would be a new interest in the academic study of film as an aesthetic and moral form; significantly, some of the key figures in this new push for critical study came from outside of film production programs (for example, Erwin Panofsky from art history) and thus signal a shift in film study from professional schools to humanities departments. With this humanistic turn, a new moment in the history of American film studies begins.

NOTES

This essay represents a work in progress on the early days of film study. I offer thanks to the archive staff members at the University of Southern California, Harvard University, Stanford University, and the Academy of Motion Picture Arts and Sciences. I also extend deep thanks to my graduate student researcher John Frankfurt, who aided me in the initial stages of this research. Finally, I thank Haidee Wasson and Jon Lewis for their extremely helpful comments on earlier drafts of this paper.

1 Haidee Wasson's book on the MOMA Film Library gives a wonderful and detailed account of this early history. See Wasson, *Museum Movies: The Museum of Modern Art and the Birth of Art Cinema* (Berkeley: University of California Press, 2005).

2 My thanks to John Belton for making Koronakis's seminar paper available to me.

3 Buchanan, "In Search of a Liberal College Program for the Recovery of the Classics and the Liberal Arts," unpublished text in the Special Collections archives of Saint John's College.

4 Edward S. Van Zile, *That Marvel, the Movie* (New York: Putnam, 1923).

5 See Richard deCordova, *Picture Personalities: The Emergence of the Star System in America* (Urbana: University of Illinois Press, 1990).

6 See, for instance, David Bordwell, *On the History of Film Style* (Cambridge, Mass.: Harvard University Press, 1997).

7 See Victor Freeburg, *The Art of Photoplay Making* (New York: Macmillan, 1918).

8 William Lord Wright, *Photoplay Plot Encyclopedia* (Los Angeles: Palmer Photoplay Corporation, 1920).

9 William Lord Wright, *Photoplay Writing* (New York: Falk Publishing, 1922); the photograph appears between pp. 20 and 21.

10 See Peter Milne, *Motion Picture Directing* (New York: Falk Publishing, 1922), 17.

11 See Frederica Sagor Maas, *The Shocking Miss Pilgrim: A Writer in Early Hollywood* (Lexington: University Press of Kentucky, 1999), 17.

12 See Joseph P. Kennedy, ed., *The Story of the Film* (Chicago: A. S. Shaw, 1927).

13 See Manuel P. Servin and Iris Higbie Wilson, *Southern California and Its University* (Los Angeles: Ward Ritchie Press, 1969), 97–121.

14 Transcripts of the first year's course have been published in John Tibbets, ed., *Introduction to the Photoplay* (Shawnee Mission, Kan.: National Film Society, 1977).

15 See MacGowan, *Behind the Screen: The History and Technique of the Motion Picture* (New York: Delacorte, 1965).

THE PERFECT MONEY MACHINE(S)

George Lucas, Steven Spielberg, and
Auteurism in the New Hollywood

Jon Lewis

After seeing Steven Spielberg's 1975 film *Jaws* at a press screening, the *Saturday Review* critic Hollis Alpert glibly described the picture as "a perfect money machine."[1] He was right of course; the film went on to become the highest-grossing motion picture in Hollywood history—a title it lost two years later to George Lucas's *Star Wars*.

Lucas's and Spielberg's success accompanied, perhaps even fueled, a dramatic economic recovery in Hollywood, and their role in this recovery has complicated both the critical and the historical accounts of their work. Between 1975 and 2000, no two American filmmakers had reached a wider international audience. Further, no two filmmakers have been more fundamentally regarded as emblematic of America, where their work represents valued American ideals and their success is a victory for an American style and form of film production and promotion. But the price of this success may well be steep. Exactly what historians will make of these two auteurs will have less to do with films per se—that is, with films as texts somehow removed from their place and time—and more to do with the ways in which their films so influenced a blockbuster-oriented new Hollywood that for over a generation dominated box offices worldwide.

THE BOX OFFICE

A survey of the historical record on American film from the mid-1970s to the end of the century—a record comprised of articles in the popular entertainment magazines and trade press—reveals an increased public interest in and media attention to the box office. A film is reported to be successful because it makes money; it is a simple matter of mathematics and not aesthetics.

The studios have always measured success in terms of dollars and cents, and Hollywood players have long looked to the two primary industry trades, *Variety* and the *Hollywood Reporter*, to keep track of weekly box office numbers. But as the industry has changed over the last twenty years or so, so has the popular reportage. Today, mass media venues like *Entertainment Weekly, Premiere, Vanity Fair, USA Today*, and *Entertainment Tonight*, with their readership largely outside of the industry, highlight the performance of films at the box office; it's the stuff that feature story lines are now made of. This tells us a lot about the interconnectedness of today's mass media and about the ways in which popular magazines participate in the marketing of motion pictures in the United States.

This public record of the new Hollywood is produced by companies with a vested interest not only in the medium's continued success but in the success of specific, astoundingly expensive products: motion pictures. *Entertainment Weekly*, for example, which covers the box office the way sports editors track baseball box scores, is owned by the media conglomerate Time Warner. Time Warner owns a number of film distribution companies (Warner Bros., New Line, Fine Line) with a significant profit interest in many of the films covered in the magazine. The premium cable channel HBO, also owned by Time Warner, picks up exclusive screening rights to selected Warner Bros. films. Like Time Warner, the media venues of Fox, Viacom-Paramount, Sony, and Disney all sport vast vertical and horizontal monopolies that include newspaper and magazine publishing, cable TV software and hardware, video and music production, and distribution and sales.

The notion that a movie's success could ever be mathematically determined is at once intellectually lazy and, given the ways in which information gets "cooked" in the industry, spurious. In *The Gross: The Hits, the Flops—The Summer that Ate Hollywood*, Peter Bart (*Variety* editor and former Paramount executive) notes that the box office figures that have become so interesting to contemporary moviegoers are almost always inaccurate. As with the vast majority of studio press releases and statistical information compiled by studio marketers, truth takes a back seat to spin. Studio distribution executives understand that filmgoers and film information consumers are apt to believe and remember only what they read first. If the numbers that get published first are later revised and reduced, few readers seem to notice or care. As Bart writes: "By Sunday morning the distribution chiefs, having filled in their colleagues, start calling key members of the press [like Bart himself] to spread the word. Often the process of achieving the number one position becomes a test of gamesmanship. A distribution chief, for example, may call *Variety's* box office reporter, Andrew Hindes, and inquire what his rivals at other studios have reported. If his film is running neck-and-neck with a competitor, he will offer a higher number. Not until Tuesday morning [are] the official numbers announced . . . By that time the ads would already be in newspapers claiming that the film in question is 'the number one movie in America.' Given the herd instincts of the moviegoing public, this information helps build momentum, even if the basic data itself may be exaggerated. The machinery of hitmaking had been set in motion."[2]

Bart is particularly well situated to appreciate how Hollywood data can be purposefully misleading, especially if the release of the data is timed just right. Not only are the facts, the specific numbers, at issue here but so is the larger question of box office significance. Domestic theatrical revenues—that is, box office numbers in the United States and Canada—account for only 16 percent of the total revenue of a studio film in release that year. The remaining 84 percent, comprised of domestic home video (26 percent), international theatrical box office (16 percent), international home video (19.9 percent), domestic television (11 percent), and licensing and merchandising (11.1 percent), goes largely unreported.[3] Box office is only the first and fastest money that is counted. The media attention to a film's first weekend reflects a familiar postmodern impatience (and shortsightedness). It enables the filmgoer, like the film executive, to assess the value of a film in the least amount of time using as little data as possible. Though accuracy is at issue here, the media attention paid to the box office has fundamentally changed how the filmgoing public has come to think about success, importance, significance, and value. If the studios are driven at all by audience demand, filmgoers now clamor for the supply of success-ful films. The studios are, of course, inclined to comply.

In the late 1960s and early 1970s, as the auteur theory dominated the popular literature, how a film performed at the box office was hardly the most pressing story at hand. For example, at the end of each year film-goers anxiously awaited their favorite reviewer's annual ten best list. These lists of the ten best films of the year were topics of discussion and dispute. Films mattered. An avid film culture concerned itself with the aesthetic and political rationale in assessments of success, importance, significance and value. Such lists persist of course. But these days they are of less inter-est to the filmgoing, information-devouring public than are the so-called power lists of those with the most influence and clout in the movie business and the celebrity rankings based on complex financial formulas regarding salaries, profit points, and endorsement revenues. These lists are published in magazines as distinct as *Entertainment Weekly* and *Forbes* . . . magazines that today only superficially appear interested in film for different reasons.

GEORGE LUCAS AND STEVEN SPIELBERG

The increased media coverage of box office numbers and features attending the movement of money within the industry have inextricably linked the films directed and produced by George Lucas and Steven Spielberg to a larger Hollywood story regarding recovery, conglomeration, multination-alization, and vertical and horizontal integration. Such a history—such a story line—raises a key question. Did the astonishing box office and an-cillary industry success achieved by these two filmmakers usher in a major shift in Hollywood policy and practice, or were these policies and practices already taking form at the very moment that their particular new Ameri-can cinema was poised to cash in?

Lucas's and Spielberg's initial impact at the box office was unprece-dented and remain unmatched. Lucas's breakthrough film, *American Graf-fiti* (1973), was until 1999 the highest-grossing low-budget film in motion picture history.[4] In what was a sign of things to come, the film, picked up reluctantly by Universal only after Francis Coppola signed on as executive producer in 1973, was brilliantly cross-marketed with an LP of its nostal-gic pop music score.[5] Spielberg's *Jaws* broke the box office record set by Coppola's *The Godfather* (1972). Its success *created* the summer season and

Steve (Ron Howard) and Laurie (Cindy Williams) embrace after the crash on Paradise Road at the end of George Lucas's *American Graffiti* (Universal, 1973).

Elliot (Henry Thomas) introduces "his alien" to his sister (Drew Barrymore) in Steven Spielberg's *ET: The Extraterrestrial* (Universal, 1982).

in doing so presented a model of filmmaking for a generation of "summer films." In 1977, Lucas's *Star Wars* broke in dramatic fashion the record held by *Jaws*. Like *American Graffiti*, *Star Wars* was a model new Hollywood product. It was easily cross-promoted and it exploited markets in several parallel entertainment and consumer industries.

Lucas and Spielberg completely dominated film in the 1980s. *Raiders of the Lost Ark* (1981) and its sequels *Indiana Jones and the Temple of Doom* (1984) and *Indiana Jones and the Last Crusade* (1989) along with *ET: The Extraterrestrial* (1982), all directed by Spielberg, were monumental box office hits. The Spielberg-produced films *Poltergeist* (1982), *Gremlins* (1984), *Back to the Future* (1985) and its sequel, *Back to the Future Part II* (1989), *Who Framed Roger Rabbit* (1988), and the feature animation pictures *An American Tail* (1986) and *The Land before Time* (1988) are all evidence of Spielberg's range of popular moviemaking and ability to tap a variety of entertainment markets.

The three Indiana Jones films were produced by Lucas, as were the two blockbuster *Star Wars* sequels, *The Empire Strikes Back* (1980) and *Return of the Jedi* (1983). Although Lucas did not a direct a single film in the 1980s, he is one of the decade's two most successful, important, significant, and valued auteurs. His reputation was sustained through his production work (mostly with Spielberg) at Lucasfilm and through the many successful films that passed through his postproduction house, Industrial Light and Magic (ILM). In the 1980s, *Star Trek II: The Wrath of Khan* (1982), *Poltergeist*, *Starman* (1984), *The Witches of Eastwick* (1987), *The Last Temptation of Christ* (1988), *Field of Dreams* (1988), and *The Abyss* (1989) showcased ILM's expertise.

To fully appreciate Lucas's and Spielberg's fiscal impact on the movie business it is worth looking back at the industry and the entertainment market before the release of *American Graffiti* in 1973 and *Jaws* in 1975. The Hollywood studios struggled throughout the 1960s and early 1970s. The number of theater screens showing Hollywood fare reached a postwar low in 1966 and, adjusting for the changing value of the dollar, annual ticket sales dipped from $8 billion in 1956 to a low of less than $5 billion in 1970 and 1971.[6] In 1970, as yet another wave of bloated epics and dated musicals reached American screens, studio revenues hit an all-time low and industry unemployment an all-time high.

Just as several studios contemplated scaling back or shutting down altogether,[7] the first wave of auteur films scored at the box office. Films like *Bonnie and Clyde* (1969), *MASH* (1970), *The Godfather* (1972), and *The Exorcist* (1973) began to pull the studios out of their slump. But the studio indulgence of projects produced by such an elite group of auteur directors was from the start a short-term strategy; after all, the auteur theory required executives to abdicate authority and control. By mid-decade, Spielberg's *Jaws* and Lucas's *Star Wars* took things to another level (financially at least) while at the same time hinting at another sort of moviemaking that did not require such big concessions to talent.

Jaws was the first film to break the $100 million mark. *Star Wars* nearly doubled the domestic revenues earned by *Jaws* and it exploited ancillary/ merchandising tie-ins in ways that no film—even the animated films made at the Disney Studios—had done before it. The near fiscal disaster of *Apocalypse Now* (1979) and the very real losses netted by the big-budget auteur projects like *Heaven's Gate* (1981) and *One from the Heart* (1982) gave the studios the opportunity they had been waiting for. The studios' short-lived embrace of the auteur theory ended just as Lucas and Spielberg presented them with a new formula for making movies and money.

The transition from the auteur renaissance to the blockbuster era—

a transition set in motion by *Jaws* and *Star Wars*—is of keen interest to contemporary film historians. Many of these historians first fell in love with the movies in the 1970s. Their work justifiably values the past over the present and it targets Lucas and Spielberg as the first of a bad lot of blockbuster "auteurs." A quick survey of what was screened in American theaters between 1972 and 1974 reveals just how lucky this generation was, at least at first, at the movies: *A Clockwork Orange, The French Connection, Klute, Dirty Harry, The Last Picture Show, Deliverance, The Godfather, Cabaret, 2001: A Space Odyssey* (in reissue), *American Graffiti, Mean Streets, High Plains Drifter, Pat Garrett and Billy the Kid, Badlands, Chinatown, The Conversation, The Godfather Part II, Blazing Saddles, The Exorcist,* and *Serpico.* Then add to this list of studio-distributed films the following foreign-made pictures: *The Garden of the Finzi Continis, The Go-Between, Dodes-ka-den, WR: Mysteries of the Organism, Murmur of the Heart, The Sorrow and the Pity, The Merchant of Four Seasons, Chloe in the Afternoon, The Goalie's Anxiety at the Penalty Kick, The Discreet Charm of the Bourgeoisie, Celine and Julie Go Boating, Day for Night, Last Tango in Paris, Ali—Fear Eats the Soul, Amarcord,* and *Lacombe, Lucien.*

Today, the 1970s seem an ever-distant memory. Blockbuster Hollywood persists, now for over twice as long as the golden age it replaced. The question of relative importance—quality versus duration—drives new Hollywood history. "Blockbuster hits," Thomas Schatz writes in putting this dilemma into context, "are, for better or worse, what the new Hollywood is all about, and thus are the necessary starting point for an analysis of contemporary cinema."[8] The notion that film history might be comprised of important films and important filmmakers, Schatz implies, is an old-fashioned notion based on media less clearly industrial than the cinema. The auteur theory has become as outdated as the very "auteur films" that many of us still so deeply admire.

A REVISED AUTEUR THEORY

The first wave of new Hollywood auteurs began in the early 1970s and was led by Coppola, Martin Scorsese, and Robert Altman. Their importance in the industry declined just as the second wave, headed by Lucas and Spielberg, emerged a few years later. The similarities and differences between these two "new waves" are noteworthy. Lucas and Spielberg, like the first-wave auteurs, were, as the biographer and critic David Thomson notes, "young, industrious, hopeful, smart, well intentioned, and, in their way, brilliant."[9] But, as Thomson concludes, their instincts were far more akin to producers, to "presenters," to showmen. Like Coppola and Scorsese, for example, Lucas and Spielberg exhibit in their work an extensive awareness if not understanding of film history. But unlike Coppola and Scorsese, who used both a formal and informal film education as a starting point in the development of a self-conscious signature style, Lucas and Spielberg are throwbacks to a bygone era before the term *auteur* meant anything in the film business.

As Hollywood evolved into a blockbuster industry in the late 1970s, Lucas and Spielberg provided the formula for high-concept entertainment. "If a person can tell me the idea in 25 words or less," Spielberg boasted to J. Hoberman in 1985, "it's going to make a good movie. I like ideas, especially movie ideas, you can hold in your hand."[10] With such an embrace of simple, striking narratives—narratives that support mass marketability— Spielberg displayed a penchant for deliberating upon marketing schemes in advance of principal photography.

Lucas also adopted the high-concept formula and took it one step further. When Fox balked at fully financing *Star Wars*, Lucas brokered a deal that secured for him a significant percentage of the film's merchandising revenues. The deal revealed a canny understanding on his part of the importance of pre-selling films as multi-industry products. As the Fox executive Mark Pepvers reflected in a 1983 *Business Week* article, "George Lucas created *Star Wars* with the toy byproducts in mind. He was making much more than a movie."[11] Indeed, he was. Within its first year, *Star Wars* merchandise accounted for $300 million in revenue.

In the new Hollywood, auteurism and celebrity intersect in interesting ways. Auteurs gain notoriety less for a signature style than for a signature product. Lucas's and Spielberg's films are easy to package and multiply in form and format. Their oeuvre presents a model of contemporary filmmaking in an industry that is no longer (just) about making movies.[12] But success is never so simple. Auteurism in the present tense is about celebrity and reputation and how a particular director or producer might use his or her celebrity and reputation to make deals and thus films and money. On that score, Lucas and Spielberg are unrivalled.

Studio executives have for purely practical reasons always regarded auteurism as a marketing tool. But film historians take a larger, more long-term view. When the dust finally settles on a career, one's work is routinely assessed in a new and different context that is not empirical or objective. For historians, auteurism regards the relative quality of an artistic signature. The evaluation of a given oeuvre becomes a matter of posterity and legacy. On that score—in some future account of late-twentieth-century American filmmaking—Lucas and Spielberg may well have plenty to worry about.

A preview of this final accounting can be found in a number of new Hollywood commentaries penned by independent-minded reviewers, critics, and academic film historians. This work views the two filmmakers as turncoats, as industry players who have achieved success by all too willingly accepting and all too deftly accommodating the studios' formula for successful filmmaking. The films that have so captured the public interest are in these accounts blithely dismissed as juvenile, simplistic, and politically retrograde—as empty divertissements in an era in which entertainment has become an end in itself. At the heart of this new critique is a suspicion about pop culture in general.

Consider the following comments from Pauline Kael, writing for the *New Yorker* in 1977 on the release of *Star Wars*. "The loudness, the smash-and-grab editing, and the relentless pacing drive every idea from your head, and even if you've been entertained, you may feel cheated of some dimension—a sense of wonder, perhaps. It's an epic without a dream. Maybe the only real inspiration involved was to set the sci-fi galaxy in the pop culture-past, and to turn old movie ineptness into conscious Pop art. The writer and director, George Lucas, has got the tone of bad movies down pat: you never catch the actors deliberately acting badly; they just seem to be bad actors, on contract to Monogram or Republic, their clunky enthusiasm polished at the Ricky Nelson school of acting." [13]

Kael is now hardly alone in her critique. In a 1996 essay titled "Who Killed the Movies?" David Thomson looks back and laments the end of the auteur renaissance and the emergence in its place of a "medium [that has] sunk beyond anything we dreamed of, leaving us stranded, a race of dreamers. This is more and worse than a bad cycle . . . and I blame Spielberg and Lucas." Thomson's essay is nostalgic and rueful. "Twenty-five years ago," he writes, "the best directors were identifiable. They had their own language, the deepest sense of personal style." Spielberg and Lucas, Thomson adds, were and still are far less pretentious: they're "recyclers, geniuses of pastiche." [14] Thomson finally dismisses Spielberg as an efficient but anonymous filmmaker, a master of presentation, a showman, not unlike his character Oscar Schindler, "who stumbles onto a side entrance to the kingdom of heaven." Lucas, Thomson adds, is an even less intriguing figure: "a functionary, an enabler, a man content to head a very large operation that still has many secrets in the burgeoning area of special effects." [15]

For Thomson and for a number of other contemporary film reviewers, critics, and historians, the root of the problem with this new American cinema lies in its embrace of big special effects. This embrace has at its core an attempt to reproduce the thrill ride that *Jaws* and *Star Wars* provided when they first hit the screens in the mid-1970s. Special effects have gained prominence at the expense of mise-en-scène, performance (of the human kind), and narrative/thematic depth. The primacy of special effects is never more apparent than it is in two Spielberg-produced films. The first, *Who Framed Roger Rabbit*, directed by Spielberg's protégé Robert Zemekis features animated characters with which live-action actors occasionally interfere. The film is at its most interesting in Toon Town where the effects bedevil and overwhelm the flesh and blood on screen. In the Zemekis follow-up hit *Forrest Gump* (1995), Spielberg (who produced the film) reveals what he and Lucas (who postproduced it) have been up to all along: what they're really interested in is the possibility of making movies without human actors—that is, in simulating the production phase entirely in a postproduction studio.

While the first-wave auteurs focused primarily on mise-en-scène and took pride and care in directing actors during the production phase, Lucas and Spielberg are almost exclusively postproduction directors. When Lucas quit directing in 1977 and let Irwin Kershner and then Richard Marquand, two directors with modest track records, handle the *Star Wars* sequels, little in terms of visual style seemed changed from the first picture. Indeed, there is the sense that anyone in the Directors Guild could have shot these films so long as Lucas got to tinker with the footage at Lucasfilm and ILM. As recent interviews have revealed, while making *American Graffiti* Lucas frustrated his talented ensemble by offering no performance-related direction at all. From the start of principal photography, Lucas told his actors that the film (which was shot "wild" and "live" with three mostly handheld cameras running simultaneously) would come together, that it would match his vision, only after they went home and he got to work in the editing room.[16]

Postproduction can be painstakingly slow and lonely. But historically it has been the phase of filmmaking during which the battle to control a movie has been keenest. In an editing suite there are no temperamental actors to contend with, no bad weather to botch a shot. Instead, there is a movie executive looming over your shoulder, or worse, tinkering, after you've moved on to another project. After weeks, maybe months, of trimming and tweaking the film without you, the studio releases "your" movie. It is fundamentally changed in accordance with test market surveys conducted at some mall in some suburban backwater and the peculiar preferences of a single studio executive (who may not still be at the studio when the film finally comes out). Lucas and Spielberg understood that films are made and sometimes unmade once the talent and crew go home. In order to protect the final cut of their films, they technically complicated the postproduction process. Their films thus were shot (and still are) in such a way that no one else could ever hope to make sense of the footage except them. Footage functions primarily to set up complex postproduction effects—effects that depended on their particular expertise.

If a director or producer's claim to auteur status regards the degree to which he or she has controlled a project, Lucas and Spielberg are auteurs of the highest, strictest order. Such a degree of control was from the start dependent on a similarly high degree of box office success. Thomson and others are right to downplay Lucas's and Spielberg's commitment to a directoral, auteur cinema. Lucas and Spielberg used their postproduction expertise to establish another sort of auteur project. As much as the old studios—MGM, Warner, etc.—cultivated a signature look in the so-called classical era, Lucasfilm, ILM, and Spielberg's production unit, Amblin, have produced a recognizable, signature product.[17] Like no other directors before or since, Lucas and Spielberg successfully challenged studio control over postproduction, and they did so in order, as auteurs, to control their products completely. Lucas has gone so far as to exert control over the exhibition of his films through his THX-line of theater sound systems and videocassette and DVD sound reproduction.

Lucas and Spielberg have exploited their auteur celebrity more deftly than did any of their predecessors. Most film historians damn them for this particular skill, or at least insist that we need to put their oeuvres in the context of certain significant changes in the film industry. As the film historian Henry Jenkins writes: "By treating filmmakers as independent contractors, the new production system places particular emphasis on the development of market value of an individual director."[18] This market value is tied to the consistent supply of a familiar, visual, and narrative formula. Directors are wont to develop and consistently adhere to such a recognizable style and form because familiarity breeds success. And success insures control.

BLISSING OUT

Lucas's and Spielberg's filmmaking focuses decidedly outward. Both men insist that they are interested primarily, even solely, in entertaining their audience. Such a priority has served them well within the industry, but at the same time it has left them open to a scathing critique from Left-leaning film historians anxious to call attention to the inherent political function of (such a) popular entertainment. For example, in his essay "Blissing Out: The Politics of Reaganite Entertainment," Andrew Britton, leaning heavily on Adorno and the rest of the Frankfurt school, contends that divertissement in and of itself has a significant political function. "Entertainment," Britton writes, "refers to itself in order to persuade us that it doesn't refer outwards at all. It is purely and simply entertainment—and we all know what *that* is."[19] He then continues by stating, "Entertainment tells us to forget our troubles and to get happy, but also tells us that in order to do so we must agree deliberately to switch life off . . . we are not told not to think, but we are told, over and over again, that there is nothing to think about." The prevailing effect of these films, Britton concludes, is one of "conservative reassurance," a *feeling* consistent with the prevailing political climate of the times. He laments the "delirious, self reference—the interminable solipsism" of such quintessentially "Reaganite entertainment." *Raiders of the Lost Ark* is, according to Britton, "the key Reaganite nuclear film"; and *ET* is "the ultimate Reaganite movie about patriarchy."[20]

Britton further points out that the other significant 1980s film franchises—the *Rocky* and *Star Trek* films, for example—are highly derivative of the Spielberg-Lucas formula. They are films driven by personality (as opposed to character), like TV. Their narratives are compact and redundant in order to facilitate serialization—again, like TV. For Britton, the popularity and influence of Lucas's and Spielberg's films reveals a problematic media politics in which escapist entertainment distracts from the real conditions in America. Despite, in the 1980s, for example, a decade of recession, mounting national debt, and the failure of trickle-down economics—in other words, despite hard times—Lucas's and Spielberg's films affirm an America locked into some false nostalgic past. The past depicted in these films is one that never existed or at least never existed anyplace except in the populist and escapist cinema that Lucas and Spielberg so love and emulate.

Out of arrogance or naiveté, especially early in his career, Spielberg paid little attention to establishing a reputation as a serious creative artist. Through the first half of the 1980s, Spielberg seemed content and even anxious to discuss his work as at once nostalgic, accessible, and, ultimately, ideologically reductive and manipulative. "*Raiders of the Lost Ark* is like popcorn," Spielberg told Todd McCarthy in 1982, "it doesn't fill you up and it's easy to digest and it melts in your mouth and it's the kind of thing you can just go back and chow down over and over again. It's a rather superficial story of heroics and deeds and great last minute saves; but it puts people in the same place that made me want to make movies as a child, which is wanting to enthrall, entertain, take people out of their seats to get them involved—through showmanship—in a kind of dialogue with the picture you've made. I love making movies like that. I mean, I'd still like to do my *Annie Hall*, but I love making films that are stimulus-response, stimulus-response. Anyway, I haven't met my Annie Hall."[21] With regard to the 1970s auteur renaissance, Spielberg remarked to Michael Sragow in *Rolling Stone*, also in 1982: "You see, George and I have fun with our films. We don't take them as seriously (as Scorsese, for example, does his). And I think that our movies are about things that we think will appeal to other people, not just to ourselves. We think of ourselves first, but in the next breath we're talking about the audience and what works and what doesn't."[22]

In virtually all of the early interviews, Spielberg espouses a pure joy in filmmaking. But at the same time he discounts the very pretensions that supported 1970s auteurism: personal signature, marginal and/or antagonistic relations with studio Hollywood, a priority on artistic integrity, and a seeming disinterest, though it need not be altogether honest or true, in a film's stake in the marketplace. By embracing high-concept filmmaking, Spielberg expressed (according to his critics at least) undue interest in what works and what doesn't work with audiences. By seeming to prioritize public relations over personal artistic principals, he effectively snubbed the very filmmaking practice that reviewers, critics, and historians had come to idealize. Reviewers and critics and film teachers routinely maintain that certain American filmmakers, those deserving of the title auteur, *transcend* the system and make great art. In idealizing films made for audiences, Spielberg at once celebrated pure entertainment as an end in itself and critiqued a filmmaking practice that dared to take itself more seriously. The history of his own oeuvre—a history that begins here in his own words—suggests an opportunism and anti-intellectualism that will hardly play well when the matter of his historical legacy is considered.

Compare, by way of example, Spielberg's self-promotion with that of Coppola. Coppola, like Spielberg, is a master showman, the producer/director of a number of very popular movies. But unlike Spielberg, from the moment Coppola finished film school he created a serious context for his work. In doing so he introduced a story, a film history, in which he played the part of an artist at odds with the industry. Such a reputation is profoundly misleading, of course. But it is a reputation that promises to preserve the impression that Coppola, unlike Spielberg, was once upon a time a serious filmmaker. As to his own role within 1980s American cinema, Spielberg concluded, again off the cuff: "Francis [Coppola] lives in a world of his own, George [Lucas] lives in a galaxy far, far away but close to human audiences, and I'm an independent moviemaker working within the Hollywood establishment."[23] Spielberg's deceptively simple remarks here are revelatory. Independence is and always has been an ideal in Hollywood. But while Spielberg's success at the box office has enabled him to maintain control over his movies, the notion that he was ever making films somehow independent of the studios is patently ridiculous.

THE LUCAS/SPIELBERG CYCLE

Lucas and Spielberg worked together on all of the Indiana Jones films and routinely share credit for the films' success. The inside story is that Lucas first developed *Raiders* with Philip Kaufman, later the director of *The Right Stuff*. When the two parted company, Spielberg stepped in to supervise the production of the films himself, and then he pretty much let Lucas run things in the editing room. Spielberg's *ET* (which included effects produced at ILM) and the Lucas-produced *The Empire Strikes Back* and *Return of the Jedi*—which, along with the Indiana Jones films, comprise six of the top ten titles of the 1980s—are cut from the same mold. If both men are auteurs—and it seems silly to argue that they are not—their peculiar artistic signatures intersect so often and in so many ways that it just isn't possible to distinguish them.

In *Hollywood from Vietnam to Reagan*, the contemporary film historian Robin Wood elaborates six "ingredients" that coordinate and comprise what he terms "the Spielberg-Lucas syndrome." The first symptom of this cinematic malady is "childishness"—that is, narrative predictability, a thematic emphasis on childhood, and a calculated attempt to construct the audience as unsophisticated and uncomplicated children. The second ingredient involves the emphasis on special effects that works to provide viewers with a visual and aural spectacle. Such a spectacle distracts from and at the same time enhances the simplistic plot and calculated appeal to the inner child. The third element is a narrative dependence on unoriginal, superficial comic book fantasy. The films are nostalgic, allusive, and derivative. They hearken back to early film serials, comic books, and 1950s sci-fi and horror. Several of these films regard some apocalyptic event—the Nazis gaining access to the Ark and winning the war, the Empire seizing control of the galaxy—all in service of Wood's fourth ingredient, a peculiar end-of-the-century "nuclear anxiety": "There's nothing you can do, so don't worry."

The fifth element regards the depiction of evil in the films, which is often based on the Nazi or Soviet fascism of the 1940 and 1950s. The films pit rule by force against rule by democracy or at least rule by popular consent. The sixth distinguishing characteristic involves the narrative trope of "the restoration of the father." Wood argues that this narrative concern exposes a crisis in masculinity in the 1980s and 1990s, one in which fathers—in films as in *real life*—are either absent or, as in the case of Luke Skywalker's dad, temporarily gone evil.[24]

The signature symptom of the Spielberg-Lucas syndrome is, according to Wood, "the curious and disturbing phenomenon of children's films conceived and marketed for adults."[25] Life for most everyone in these films is characterized by constant locomotion. The films depict a child's world constructed entirely of brief forays of activity that never last long enough to be either boring or meaningful. Heroes and villains alike leave behind a mess they have no intention of ever cleaning up. The hero in these films has adventures because in the childlike and childish vision perpetuated by these auteurs, that is what men do, or would do if they could. Luke Skywalker and Indiana Jones take us by the hand and lead us into and then out of wonderland. The rest is detail, cool gadgets, and backstory . . . stuff to be explained in ancillary materials purchased between viewings of the movies (e.g., books, comics, theme park rides, and computer, board, and card games). The films are so dependent on a rhythm created in the editing room that they fall flat during virtually all of the expository sequences. As a result, why stuff happens is never interesting enough; it is never rendered interesting enough. The audience comes to view exposition as a kind of intermission—as time wasted, time better spent at the candy counter or staring into the fridge—during which the filmmaker sets up the next gag or chase sequence.

LUCAS, SPIELBERG, REAGAN

Wood's unflattering auteurist study does well to reduce the films to a simple formula. But, and Wood seems to recognize this, the significance of the films has less to do with their form and style than with the larger and more complex interaction between the films and the filmgoing, video- and merchandise-buying public. What historians have to account for now and in the future is not the content of the films taken on their own or as serials but the various larger contexts of their use. Here again there are signs of trouble for Lucas and Spielberg vis-à-vis an auteur legacy. In *Visions of Empire*, the film historian Stephen Prince puts the culture-commerce dichotomy in Lucas's and Spielberg's oeuvre into a specifically Reaganite context—a context at once reflected in and refracted out from the world of movies and moviemaking. "Relationships between culture and commerce, film characters, and commodities," writes Prince, "are being reorganized in the era of the blockbuster as an economy of advertising comes to regulate film production and its representations of our cultural life in new ways. Some films become ads, and characters like ET become products." Such a "merging of the real and the symbolic," Prince concludes, "was a hallmark of the Reagan presidency" and of cinema during the Reagan-Bush regime.[26]

Many of Lucas's and Spielberg's most popular films were released during Ronald Reagan's presidency. For a number of film historians, like

Prince, this is no mere temporal coincidence. It is hard to miss the inter-sections between the politics of nostalgia that lies at the heart of, for ex-ample, the *Star Wars* and the Indiana Jones films and the public relations mythology attending Reagan's run for presidency and tenure at the White House. The films, like Reagan, are conservative and populist. In ways that the producer-directors never intended, the *Star Wars* and Indiana Jones films anticipated and then helped to define Reaganism, and they did so in a particularly accessible and attractive package. Six of Lucas's and Spielberg's most popular films star Harrison Ford. In these films, Ford is the embodi-ment of the very rugged, straight, white masculinity that Reagan courted in the political ads showing him riding into view on horseback: Reagan the cowboy, the strong, certain, populist movie hero. Genius is as much about timing as it is about talent. Lucas's and Spielberg's films were popular for the very same reason that Reagan was popular. And this legacy is one that both directors will have to both live with and live down.

There is plenty of evidence that Spielberg is a good Hollywood liberal: he is rich, white, and something of a humanist. Leftist historians and crit-ics grudgingly acknowledge a superficial liberal politics in his oeuvre, but they refocus attention from intent and content to how the films are rou-tinely read and used in the popular culture at large. In *Camera Politica*, for example, Michael Ryan and Douglas Kellner affirm Spielberg's apparent humanism. "In Spielberg's cozy home world of cuddly beasts and warm-hearted social relations," they write, "liberal ideals thrive of a sort that else-where in American society and Hollywood cinematic culture were being shunted aside in favor of a brutish, quasi-fascist cinematic and economic realism." But while such a cinematic world was on its surface progressive, Ryan and Kellner conclude that Spielberg's "white liberal sentimentality" failed to make any sort of impact on the society at large. In terms at once dramatic and typical of this line of critique, Ryan and Kellner argue that Spielberg's penchant for populist nostalgia seems "criminal when it is mea-sured against the rise in the black infant mortality rate provoked by the Reagan domestic budget cuts or the increase in deaths among workers af-fected by reductions in federal safety standards or the numerous killings perpetrated by bombs and death squads in Latin America as a result of the foreign policy of white conservatives in power in the eighties." For Ryan and Kellner, Spielberg's "family fantasies" should be viewed as "strained at-tempts to close ears to the sound of suffering elsewhere."[27]

Ryan and Kellner are even harder on Lucas. They refer to *Star Wars* as "the paradigmatic conservative movie series of the period." The *Star Wars* films, they argue, make conservatism appear revolutionary by presenting "a conservative past (both temporally as a prior, postmodern era and morally as a set of simpler, more 'natural' values and institutions) as something to be fought for in the present and future."[28] Lucas disconnects revolutionary action from progressive politics.

WHO KILLED THE MOVIES?

The questions that contemporary film critics have asked—"Who killed the movies?" (David Thomson); "Why don't people love the right movies anymore?" (the *New Yorker* reviewer David Denby); "Why are movies so bad?" (Denby's predecessor at the *New Yorker*, Pauline Kael)—presume a decline in film culture after 1980 that is at once tragic, significant, and specific. Whether Lucas and Spielberg are symptoms of this decline, avatars of this decline, unlucky bystanders to this decline, or just savvy players profiteering on this decline will be a matter of real concern to those who write the history of late-twentieth-century American cinema.

To that end, one last scholarly history is worth a close look here, namely, Robert Kolker's *A Cinema of Loneliness*—now in its much transformed third edition. In the first edition, published in 1980, Kolker presented a history of Hollywood's golden age by focusing on the work of five key auteurs: Arthur Penn, Stanley Kubrick, Coppola, Scorsese, and Altman.[29] The book's continued popularity—its endurance now through two revisions and twenty more years of new Hollywood history—testifies to the auteur renaissance's importance to a generation that came of age at the movies at this wonderful and, alas, brief moment in American film history. For this generation of filmgoers and film scholars, movies still matter.

Kolker's third edition, published in 2000, retreats from the first edition's auteur orthodoxy—the notion that movies and the directors who made them have a historical value completely divorced from market concerns. The third edition's changes reveal less about Kolker as a historian—he's still an auteurist after all these years—than they do about an industry that has in many ways complicated his historical argument. Kolker's response to these complications reveals his growing discomfort with the new Hollywood and what it has done to American filmmaking. Kolker's book reveals the difficulty of doing auteurist history in the blockbuster era—an era that marks the industrial demise of the auteur. For example, in the third edition he adds a section on Spielberg, a director that he tries to like but in the final analysis regards as merely the best director in a particularly bad era "of minimal experimentation and large scale repetition." For Kolker, Spielberg is the avatar of a pervasive "cinema of retrenchment."[30]

As for Lucas, Kolker quips that *Star Wars* is less a movie or movie franchise than a "reference point for a kind of cinema" that Spielberg comes to make better than Lucas or anyone else in the business. What makes Spielberg's films *better* than those made by other blockbuster auteurs is that they are "obviously well-crafted." This is a distinction Kolker makes not only because he believes it's true, but because it's necessary if he is going to discuss Spielberg alongside auteur-directors like Scorsese, Kubrick, and the other significant addition to the third edition, Oliver Stone. The term "well crafted" is carefully chosen and I think it aptly reveals Kolker's reservations about Spielberg and, by extension, Lucas. Kolker argues that Spielberg's films are "technologically overdetermined, [too] dependent in special effects, and at the same time determinedly realistic and manipulative." Kolker allows Spielberg to share a stage otherwise set for Scorsese, Kubrick, and Stone. But despite all efforts to support an auteur argument and evaluation to accommodate Spielberg's obvious "importance," Kolker gets discouraged whenever he has to talk about the films themselves. Spielberg's embrace of a cinema of spectacle, Kolker observes, "divert(s) the viewer into the mise-en-scène, providing aural and visual wonder and fear to make up for the moral uncertainty that very mise-en-scène creates."[31] The more serious-minded Spielberg films that tackle serious subject matter (the holocaust, combat, race relations), are all, finally, too politically flexible; for Kolker, they are all too user friendly.

Kolker uses Spielberg to track key changes in filmmaking between the publication of the first edition and the third—a period of twenty years that has seen fundamental changes in industry policies and procedures. But he is an auteurist at heart. And try as he might, he can't help but evaluate Spielberg's work harshly. He ends his account of Spielberg in much the same place that Kael, Thomson, Denby, Wood, Britton, Prince, Ryan, and Kellner begin theirs. Spielberg's cinema, Kolker concludes finally, "provides narrative closure without having to reach any definite conclusions: it totally evades politics and history; it gives men an excuse for their behavior; and most obviously, it hails the redeemed character . . . without the audience having to act on anything but their ability to look at the screen."[32]

INDEPENDENCE: CAN WE SAVE LUCAS
AND SPIELBERG FOR POSTERITY?

In the film business, independence is a relative term. One is always independent of or to something.[33] And while Lucas and Spielberg have had the power and prestige to secure studio-backed financing and distribution for pretty much anything they have made, they have never released so much as a single film fully independent of the major studio production/distribution apparatus.

Both auteurs have sought relative autonomy and independence, but they have expressed or outlined their endeavors differently. Though Lucas's work has been no less mainstream or commercial than that of Spielberg, Lucas has historically been far less willing than Spielberg to publicly embrace the Hollywood system. Lucas's account of his decision to seek a modicum of autonomy from Hollywood reveals a film student's notion of independence based in large part on the European model championed by the auteur critics and French New Wave filmmakers whose work dominated the film school curriculum in the 1960s and 1970s.

When Lucas received a special Academy Award in 1992, he thanked his parents, his teachers, and his mentor, Francis Coppola. For those who know both men, the tribute was hardly a surprise. Despite a power shift in Hollywood—Lucas was a major player in the 1980s; Coppola was just as big an auteur celebrity in the 1970s—the two men have remained friends and have, on the record, voiced similar concerns about doing business with studio Hollywood. Coppola's Zoetrope Studios project was founded in 1980 and financed against moneys earned by the first two *Godfather* films and *Apocalypse Now*. It was at once more ambitious and a whole lot less sensible than Lucasfilm and ILM. As a result, Coppola's studio project went up like a rocket and came down like a stick. Coppola took on the big studios but after one expensive film, the notorious box office flop *One from the Heart*, his studio went into foreclosure and was ultimately auctioned off by one of its several lien holders.[34]

Lucasfilm's and ILM's success, on the other hand, offer an object lesson on how to establish a position on the near margins of Hollywood. In retrospect, it seems clear that, quite unlike Coppola, Lucas understood the emerging new Hollywood, or at least that his continued interest in the postproduction of mostly high-concept films was shared by the studios with whom he still routinely did business. Lucas has over the years made a lot of money for the studios, especially Twentieth Century-Fox, and as a result he has maintained a reputation for being a studio player. But he is a pragmatist, not a true believer.

Dating back to the end of the 1960s at American Zoetrope, Lucas has consistently expressed an antipathy for studio Hollywood.[35] For example, when executives at Warner Bros. failed to appreciate the shooting script for *American Graffiti*, Lucas bristled: "The studios don't understand . . . that scripts should be more like blueprints than novels. They don't even know who McLuhan is over there."[36] In 1981, as Lucasfilm and ILM were beginning to take shape, Lucas explained his desire to circumvent the studio system in terms not unlike those more predictably pronounced by his mentor: "LA is the place where they make deals, do business in the classic corporate way, which is screw everybody and do whatever you can to turn the biggest profit. They don't care about people. It's incredible the way they treat filmmakers . . . I don't want anything to do with them."[37]

While historians tend to value a sort of obstinate independence that routinely leads to ruin—Orson Welles is, of course, the prototype here—Lucas's independence reveals an understanding of the business of making movies that is at once cynical and accurate. For example, in 1981, before Coppola had released a single film at Zoetrope, Lucas doubted his mentor's ability to succeed: "I disagreed with Francis when he said he was going to Los Angeles. We both have the same goals, we both have the same ideas and we both have the same ambitions . . . [but we have] a disagreement in the way it should be done . . . Being down there in Hollywood, you're just asking for trouble, because you're trying to change a system that will never change." As to the "electronic cinema" system—Coppola's Industrial Light and Magic–like computer/video postproduction system researched and developed at Zoetrope—Lucas quipped prophetically: "The studios will never come to understand it at all."[38]

Comparing Lucasfilm (then in its infancy) to Coppola's (off and running) Zoetrope in 1981, Lucas aptly characterized the fundamental difference in temperament and managerial style that would spell disaster for Coppola and, as it turned out, success for him. "It's going to take six years for me to get my facility functioning the way his is right now," Lucas mused, "He just went 'Boop' and it was done . . . I'll have mine, and it will take a lot longer to get it built, but I don't think it will ever collapse."[39] Even before

The young protagonist Jim Graham (Christian Bale) in Steven Spielberg's sentimental adaptation of J. G. Ballard's World War II novel *Empire of the Sun* (Warner Bros., 1987).

the release of *One from the Heart,* Coppola seemed inclined to agree."If I'm like America," Coppola mused, "George was my Japan—he saw what I did wrong and perfected what I did right." As the gap widened between them in the wake of the success of *Raiders* and the *Star Wars* sequels, Coppola put into eerie perspective their relative stock in the industry: "George is so wealthy now, he doesn't need a partner anymore. And he's a practical person who doesn't want to be saddled with a diseased organ."[40]

Spielberg's independence *within* the system is worth acknowledging if only to highlight the ways in which the larger production and distribution system in Hollywood accommodates and controls any and all "independent" work with a stake in the marketplace. Spielberg has moved freely within the studio industry. Between 1975 and 1994 he made films for Paramount (all three Indiana Jones films), MCA/Universal (which distributed *Jaws, ET,* the two *Jurassic Park* films, and *Schindler's List* and provided his production company, Amblin, with posh executive office space), Columbia/Tri-Star (*Hook*) and Warner Bros. (which released two of his most ambitious films: *The Color Purple* [1985]; and *Empire of the Sun* [1987]).

In 1994 Spielberg joined the recording industry billionaire David Geffen and the recently dismissed Disney second-in-command Jeffrey Katzenberg to found DreamWorks SKG. It seemed from the start yet another effort on Spielberg's part to find independence within the system. By all accounts Spielberg proved to be a canny studio executive. A quick look at the studio's releases between 1997 and 2005 (when the studio was sold to Viacom, the parent company of Paramount) testifies to his continued knack for popular moviemaking: *Mousehunt* (1997), *Antz* (1998), *Saving Private Ryan* (1998), *American Beauty* (1999), *Almost Famous* (2000), *Cast Away* (2000), *Gladiator* (2000), *Small Time Crooks* (2000), *A Beautiful Mind* (2001), *AI: Artificial Intelligence* (2001), *Shrek* (2001), *Catch Us If You Can* (2002), *Seabiscuit* (2003), *Anchorman: The Legend of Ron Burgandy* (2003), *Shark Tale* (2004), and *Shrek 2* (2004). DreamWorks' release slates sport a near-perfect balance of pure entertainment and serious filmmaking ranging from a string of family-audience hits to Academy Award best picture winners three years in a row (*Saving Private Ryan*, *American Beauty*, and *Gladiator*).

But throughout its brief independence DreamWorks never emerged as the producer of anything like alternative films—instead it did what the other studios did (only with a slightly better success rate at the box office). The difference between DreamWorks and Coppola's Zoetrope is fundamental and revealing: the former aspired to be a better studio within the studio system; the latter aimed to be an independent alternative. Neither proved viable in the end: the movie business is just too expensive these days. After years of seeking partnerships in order to release big films (five films with Fox, ten with Paramount, eight with Universal, six with Warner Bros., and five with Columbia), the DreamWorks partners sold out to the media conglomerate Viacom and their studio became in pretty much every way a subsidiary brand for a company that already owned a number of other recognizable media brands (e.g., Paramount, MTV, Showtime).

This discussion of relative autonomy and independence begs two key questions. Do directors or their big films, however influential, ever actually propel the movie history? Is the history of film really about films and filmmakers, or is it a lot more complicated? Blaming Lucas and Spielberg for what far more powerful players in the media industries have done with their films—the ways in which Lucas's and Spielberg's auteur legacy has been mediated in the industry—ignores the key issue of volition. Neither Lucas nor Spielberg has ever claimed a desire to put an end to anything (good or bad) in American filmmaking. And neither has ever publicly supported political causes or candidates who embraced or represented conservative, populist causes. Reviewers, critics, and historians tend to blame Lucas and Spielberg for what their films are not and what they failed to do with the media access they acquired.

It is important to remember that the freedom to make movies "independently" in Hollywood comes at a cost. Lucas and Spielberg found a formula for success with the film-going public. But more significantly, they found a formula for success in their dealings with the studios. In the mid-1970s, when Lucas and Spielberg first hit the scene, auteurs were under significant pressure to turn things around at the box office. And that's exactly what these two auteurs did.

The 1970s studios' conglomerate owners, the likes of Transamerica, Coca-Cola, and Gulf and Western, dealt with their studios like any of their subsidiaries—as units held accountable to consistent business practices, marketing policies, and bottom-line performance. As the entertainment market expanded in the 1980s, these corporations began to insist that films be distributed in a variety of forms and formats to better exploit the vertically and horizontally integrated marketplace. Lucas and Spielberg were the first and the best at the very sort of filmmaking designed to succeed under such an economic policy. In light of this we might ask here, at the end, had Lucas and Spielberg not arrived on the scene just when they did, would studio executives in 1980s Hollywood have had to invent them?

NOTES

1 Alpert as cited by Douglas Brode, *The Films of Steven Spielberg* (New York: Citadel, 1995), 61.

2 Peter Bart, *The Gross: The Hits, the Flops—The Summer that Ate Hollywood* (New York: St. Martin's Press, 1999), 177–78.

3 Leo Rice-Barker, "Industry Banks on new Technology, Expanded Slates," *Playback*, May 6, 1996, 19.

4 *American Graffiti* was bested in summer 1999 by *The Blair Witch Project*. But once again box office figures can be misleading. Ticket prices are far higher now than they were in 1973, and there have also been significant improvements in film marketing.

5 Lucas first wrote *American Graffiti* for American Zoetrope, Coppola's production company, in the late 1960s. When American Zoetrope folded, Warner Bros., which had financed Coppola's company and had first crack at the film, decided not to finance its production even though Lucas had set the budget at a mere $750,000. For a few years Lucas shopped the project around, but there were no takers until Coppola, fresh off his box office success with *The Godfather*, put his name in the opening titles. Though he is credited as executive producer, Coppola did virtually nothing in the production and postproduction of the film.

6 Constance L. Hays, "The Vast Picture Show," *New York Times*, December 29, 1997, c8.

7 In 1970, Paramount ranked ninth in the industry, behind the other six majors and two independents, National General and Cinerama. Gulf and Western, which owned Paramount at the time, attempted to unload the legendary Melrose Avenue production facility for real estate development. However, the sale fell through at the last minute when the conglomerate was unable to get an adjacent property, a cemetery, rezoned.

8 Thomas Schatz, "The New Hollywood," in *Film Theory Goes to the Movies*, ed. Jim Collins, Hilary Radner, and Ava Preacher Collins (New York: Routledge, 1993), 10–11.

9 David Thomson, "Who Killed the Movies?" *Esquire*, December 1996, 57.

10 Justin Wyatt, *High Concept: Movies and Marketing in Hollywood* (Austin: University of Texas Press, 1994), 13.

11 "ET and Friends Are Flying High," *Business Week*, January 10, 1983, 77.

12 Here again it is worth noting that domestic box office revenues account for less than 20 percent of a blockbuster's total value to the studio.

13 Pauline Kael, *Star Wars* (review), *New Yorker*, February 3, 1997, 27.

14 Thomson, "Who Killed the Movies?" 56, 62. Spielberg hardly disputes his tendency to recycle and allude. "I essentially pulled from the same air, the same sense of popcorn pleasure that Ford, Curtiz, Hawks, King Vidor, and even C. B. DeMille had available to them," Spielberg remarked to Michael Sragow. "We drank from the same well. It's always been there for anybody who wants to dip a ladle" (Michael Sragow, "A Conversation with Steven Spielberg," *Rolling Stone*, July 22, 1982, 28).

15 Thomson, "Who Killed the Movies?" 62.

16 An hour-long tribute to Lucas was produced by PBS in their *American Masters* series. Several of the actors (including Ron Howard and Harrison Ford) who had performed in Lucas's films agreed that the director expressed little interest in helping them develop their onscreen performances.

17 I am purposefully leaving DreamWorks off this list. To date, the slate of films produced and codistributed by DreamWorks seem of a kind with any of the other major studios.

18 Henry Jenkins, "Historical Poetics," in *Approaches to Popular Film*, ed. Joanne Hollows and Mark Jancovich (Manchester: Manchester University Press, 1995), 111.

19 The title of Britton's essay alludes to Pauline Kael's glib *New Yorker* review (June 14, 1982, 119) of Spielberg's *ET: The Extraterrestrial*. "*ET*," writes Kael, "is a bliss out."

20 Andrew Britton, "Blissing Out: The Politics of Reagnite Entertainment," *Movie*, no. 30/31 (1982): 4–5, 2, 21, 27.

21 Todd McCarthy, "Sand Castles," *Film Comment* (May/June 1982): 58.

22 Sragow, "A Conversation with Steven Spielberg," 28.

23 Chris Auty, "The Complete Spielberg," *Sight and Sound* (autumn 1982): 279.

24 Robin Wood, *Hollywood from Vietnam to Reagan* (New York: Columbia University Press, 1986), 162–88.

25 Ibid., 163.

26 Stephen Prince, *Visions of Empire: Political Imagery in Contemporary American Film* (New York: Praeger, 1992), 22.

27 Michael Ryan and Douglas Kellner, *Camera Politica: The Politics and Ideology of Contemporary Hollywood Film* (Bloomington: Indiana University Press, 1990), 258–59.

28 Ibid., 234.

29 Robert Kolker, *A Cinema of Loneliness: Penn, Kubrick, Coppola, Scorsese, Altman* (New York: Oxford University Press, 1980).

30 Robert Kolker, *A Cinema of Loneliness: Penn, Stone, Kubrick, Scorsese, Spielberg, Altman*, 3rd ed. (New York: Oxford University Press, 2000), 247, 248.

31 Ibid., 306.

32 Ibid., 324.

33 Chuck Kleinhans, "Independent Features: Hopes and Dreams," in *The New American Cinema*, ed. Jon Lewis (Durham, N.C.: Duke University Press, 1998).

34 This is discussed at greater length in my *Whom God Wishes to Destroy: Francis Coppola and the New Hollywood* (Durham, N.C.: Duke University Press, 1995).

35 American Zoetrope, for which Lucas was vice-president and principal filmmaker, was a short-lived alternative studio project set up by Coppola at the end of the 1960s. *THX-1138* and a shooting script for a Lucas-helmed *Apocalypse Now* were two of the four projects developed at the "studio" before Warner Bros., which had financed the production company, got cold feet and American Zoetrope folded.

36 Louise Sweeney, "The Movie Business Is Alive and Well and Living in San Francsico," *Show*, April 1970, 82.

37 Lucas quoted in David Thomson, *Overexposures* (New York: Morrow, 1981), 40.

38 Mitch Tuchman and Anne Thompson, "I'm the Boss," *Film Comment* 17, no. 4 (1981): 50–51.

39 Ibid.

40 Audie Bock, "George Lucas: An Interview," *Take One*, August 1976, 6.

II   STAR STUDIES

LOIS WEBER AND THE CELEBRITY OF MATRONLY RESPECTABILITY
Shelley Stamp

L ois Weber was a filmmaker unquestionably associated with cinema's rising cultural cachet in the
mid-1910s. Renowned for her early literary and
dramatic screen adaptations, Weber wrote and directed ambitious multi-reel films at a time when features were almost universally associated with elevated
cinematic fare designed to appeal to highbrow tastes.
In her belief, moreover, that films of social conscience
were equal ingredients in cinema's uplift, Weber also
made controversial films on drug addiction, capital
punishment, anti-Semitism, contraception, and wage
equity for women—topics less readily associated
with upscale taste, perhaps, but fully consistent with
Weber's view of the medium's serious social mandate.
Known as "one of the forward looking directors," she
was said to be "a large shareholder in holding up the
standards of the moving picture industry."[1] Significant though these films were, Weber's elevated reputation had as much to do with the kinds of pictures
she made as it did with the type of woman she presented herself to be—married, matronly, and decidedly middle class. Indeed, it is unlikely that she would
have enjoyed such success in repeatedly tackling contentious social issues were it not for her persona cultivated behind the scenes.

Within the relatively new culture of Hollywood celebrity in the late 1910s and early 1920s, Weber offers a unique case study. As a woman more noted for her creative control behind the camera than for her charming onscreen personality, Weber stood out, akin neither to contemporary actresses like Mary Pickford and Pearl White, nor to male directors like D. W. Griffith and Cecil B. DeMille, figures to whom she was often compared. No other female star was associated with such unqualified professional accomplishment, and no director could claim equal personal fame. At a time when rapidly changing gender norms were mapped through celebrity discourse, and when women still vied for creative and financial control of the fledgling film industry, Weber's image was instrumental in defining both her particular place in filmmaking practices and women's roles within early Hollywood more generally. Her wifely, bourgeois persona, relatively conservative and staid, mirrored the film industry's idealized conception of its new customers: white, married, middle-class women perceived to be arbiters of taste in their communities. At the same time, Weber's frequent creative collaborations with her husband Phillips Smalley offered a more forward-looking portrait of gender equality in the workplace modeled on new ideas of companionate marriage. Ultimately, though marriage helped to anchor Weber's upright persona and also helped to define a professional role for her within the industry, portraits of Weber's marriage to Phillips Smalley also complicated her image by blurring the boundaries between home and workplace and, ultimately, by destabilizing the very gender norms they appeared to uphold.

"A PERPETUAL LEADING LADY"

As a noted picture personality early on, Weber appeared frequently in the trade press beginning in the early 1910s. In one of her earliest publicity notices, from *Photoplay*'s 1912 "Players' Personalities" column, her association with upper-crust material and utmost respectability was already evident: Weber, *Photoplay* told its readers, "is grace personified as she moves through the society plays."[2] By 1916 she was included in the *New York Dramatic Mirror*'s list of "prominent directors," and in 1921 she was described by the movie trade *Wid's Daily* as "one of our foremost directors."[3] In fact, *Wid's* consistently encouraged exhibitors to mention Weber when promoting her films, claiming, "I needn't tell you the value of Miss Weber's name."[4] Beyond the trades, Weber's notoriety was cultivated in early fan magazines, where she was trumpeted as "Lois the Wizard," "The Muse of the Reel," and "Photo-Genius, in Front or Back of the Camera."[5] Even general-interest publications took notice: *Sunset* magazine, promoter of "western living," introduced readers to Weber in its "Interesting Western-ers" column in 1914, and *Overland Monthly*'s 1916 essay cast her as "one of the big personalities in the photo-play world."[6] Newspaper articles pub-lished throughout the country described the director in various hyperbolic alliterative configurations as the "wonder woman of the films," the "super-woman of the silent drama," and "the director deluxe of filmdom"—all sug-gesting a celebrity status reaching far beyond the confines of movie buffs, and certainly eclipsing that of any other director or screenwriter at the time.[7]

In many profiles Weber came to stand for the very image of twentieth-century womanhood: "Among the modern women who are accomplishing big things," Weber provided a "splendid example of what may be accom-plished by a woman both in a creative and an executive capacity," an ex-ample that "opens up vistas for other women."[8] Indeed, one writer cast the filmmaker as an idealized embodiment of modernity: "The twentieth cen-tury woman, with her ingenious charm, has reached the pinnacle of success in every calling. It is said that out of the many trades and professions, there are very few which do not number women as adept. And now comes the confirmation that [this is so] even in the pictures. Lois Weber, a young and talented woman, is without a doubt the best known woman-producer of films in the world."[9]

Within such general celebrations of her stature, three overlapping nar-ratives fueled Weber's particular association with respectability and refine-ment. First were her oft-repeated comments about future directions in filmmaking. Beginning in 1912 and continuing for the next five years of her most concentrated fame, Weber was frequently quoted in trade columns and interviews advocating the changes she hoped to see in motion picture entertainment: more-nuanced screenplays, longer film lengths, educated film fare, and specifically cinematic modes of performance that would im-prove motion picture quality.[10] "If pictures are to make and maintain a position alongside the novel and the spoken drama," Weber told the *New York Dramatic Mirror*, "they must be concerned with ideas that get under the skin and affect the living and the thinking of the people who view them."[11] In this view she was aligned not only with many in the industry pushing for similar changes, most notably trade journals like *Moving Picture World*, which quoted her thoughts at length; she was also aligned with women's clubs that were very active in the "better films" movement during these years. As a frequent speaker at club gatherings, Weber addressed the Woman's City Club of Los Angeles in 1913 on the topic of "the making of picture plays that will have an influence for good on the public mind," and early in 1917 she hosted a luncheon at Universal City for women concerned about the fate of young women descending on Hollywood eager for movie work.[12] Both moviegoing and work behind the scenes in Hollywood, she seemed to insist, were wholesome and decent.

Equally central to Weber's star persona was the oft-repeated story of her "origins," a narrative that stressed her background as a pianist, an evangelical Church Army Worker, and a stage performer. Lois Weber was a "distinguished woman," one profile insisted, a person whose interests in classical music and theater had brought her to motion pictures.[13] Weber herself was particularly apt to bring up the association between her earlier efforts as an urban missionary and her later interests in topical screenplays, claiming she enjoyed working in a "voiceless language" like the cinema that allowed her to "preach to my heart's content."[14] Together these details of her background worked to dissociate her from commercial entertainment, that sphere of less reputable leisure establishments, and instead anchor her film work within a fine arts and social services tradition. In doing so she became aligned with forces in the industry promoting a conception of cinema that was itself strongly aligned with bourgeois femininity. Exhibitors cultivated bourgeois women as patrons, hoping their presence might lend legitimacy to filmgoing, at the same time that Weber's celebrity image trafficked in a similar ladylike decorum.[15] In embodying this idealized model of patronage, Weber's persona demonstrated that a similar degree of cultivation existed on the side of production as well as reception.

Even more important than the professional resume rehearsed in so many promotional pieces were depictions of Weber's home life—"personal" profiles that situated her as a married woman and as the denizen of well-appointed, but not too lavish, middle-class surroundings. As movie star culture took off after 1910, celebrity writing increasingly focused on performers' personal lives and living spaces. Fame in early Hollywood was built as much through audience knowledge of a star's onscreen roles as it was through familiarity with her or his off-screen, "private" life, as Richard deCordova has shown.[16] Romances, marriages, divorces, childhoods, and children all became targets of increased curiosity, as did dwellings, kitchens, closets, and dressing tables. This was a fan culture that, Kathryn Fuller argues, increasingly tailored its appeal to women by catering to "feminine" interests in romance, beauty, decorating, and family life, rather than the technical and scientific details that had colored much of the earliest film publicity.[17] If the circulation of biographical tidbits shifted the fan's gaze toward an invisible, extratextual realm hidden from the screen, as Gaylyn Studlar stresses, we should not lose sight of the degree to which this other scene assumed its own visuality.[18] Amelie Hastie, in her reading of Alice Guy Blaché's memoirs, suggests that celebrity portraits often take on a cinematic quality where visual symbolism and narrative juxtaposition play key signifying roles.[19] Thus even as "visits" to celebrity homes gave early motion picture fans vicarious, voyeuristic access to the private lives of the stars by furnishing imaginary entry into an unseen, off-screen world, such imagery also blurred the boundaries between this realm and the screen by fictionalizing domestic spaces and staging events and conversations for their readers.

Weber's marriage to Phillips Smalley, with whom she collaborated on most of her early films, stood at the heart of both her professional persona and depictions of her private life. Initially billed as "The Smalleys, collaborators in authorship and direction," the couple's working partnership was from the very beginning of their fame intertwined with their marital status.[20] One oft-repeated story of their courtship suggested that they tried motion picture work only after realizing that life in touring stage companies would keep them apart for too much of the year. This anecdote implied that film work saved their marriage (rather than undermining it). Many pieces celebrated Weber and Smalley's "marital resolve," their "bride and groom determination" not to work in separate fields, forging instead an artistic alliance that represented "one of the most illuminating examples of marital happiness."[21] Their equanimity and companionability were usually played up in such profiles: the two were seen as "congenial co-workers" with Smalley described as Weber's "co-director, husband—and *chum*," while the director herself trumpeted their habit of working "brain to brain, shoulder to shoulder in all our endeavors."[22]

As a particularly striking example of how these different threads were

Weber and Smalley's marriage
is central to Bosworth's promotion of the couple's filmmaking
work in 1914.

woven together in Weber's persona, consider the publicity that Bosworth
issued for the couple when they joined the company in 1914 to produce
upscale feature films. Images of Weber and Smalley in profile face one another on the page as if the two were gazing fondly into one another's eyes;
surrounding these images are little cartoon figurations highlighting (sometimes apocryphal) details about their past lives and career achievements.
In a pictorial, even cinematic, narrative showing their professional rise
alongside their emergence as a couple, romantic union serves as an explicit
metaphor for the logical melding of their interests. In fact, their wedding is
presented as a significant event in Weber's *professional* evolution, poised between her triumphant stage performance and her by-then most celebrated
feature-length release, *Hypocrites*. Promoting nothing in particular, save its
own highbrow reputation, Bosworth trafficked in the couple's status—not
simply the exaggerated pedigree claimed in the cartoon captions but their
standing as a solid, bourgeois couple.[23] Weber and Smalley's marriage and
their creative partnership did as much to promote the company's highbrow
reputation, it seems, as the films they were to produce there.

Weber and Smalley, "conferring on a manuscript." (Courtesy of the Academy of Motion Picture Arts and Sciences)

Although Bosworth's figuration of the couple's coexistence was spectacularly cinematic it certainly was not unique, for publicity photos often pictured the pair side by side in analogous poses, where the visual parallelism seems to echo their broader artistic synchronicity. A portrait of Weber and Smalley "conferring on a manuscript" depicted the two posed intimately together with their bodies literally intertwined as they worked.[24] With domestic furnishings visible in the soft-focus background, Weber rests her elbow on Smalley's thigh as she holds a script in her lap. Such allusions offered marriage as an appropriate template for working partnerships between men and women, and egalitarian collaboration as a new blueprint for modern romance. Indeed, these images seem to suggest that films produced by such a partnership, however controversial they might appear to be, could surely only be grounded in the finest bourgeois virtues.

The degree to which Weber's marriage underscored her reputation for respectability is most notable in celebrity profiles structured around visits to her Los Angeles bungalow. Interviews staged in stars' homes became familiar conceits in celebrity writing of the mid-1910s, focused as it was on private lives and living spaces. Beginning with a reporter's approach to the dwelling—"she met me on the deep veranda of her pearl-gray bungalow"[25]—such pieces offered fans a virtual tour of stars' off-screen lives. One might suspect in the case of such a professionally accomplished woman that portraits of Weber's home life might be used to "domesticate" her, to sketch her within the lines of a more conventionalized femininity designed to temper her groundbreaking power within the industry. Certainly some profiles served this function, anxiously assuring readers that the filmmaker "loves her work as she loves her home" and that she had "not sacrificed her home life for her public career."[26] Yet the interplay between Weber's creative endeavors and her personal affairs was not always so clearly defined, especially given her professional collaboration with Smalley.

Weber's name and her marital status, for instance, were belabored in virtually every publicity item, each of which offered some version of the statement "in private life Miss Weber is Mrs. Phillips Smalley."[27] Domestic architecture, in one case, was even employed to delineate boundaries between these facets of Weber's persona: "In her home," readers learned, "this writer-actress-director lays aside the sternness of the 'firing line,' drops her professional name and becomes Mrs. Phillips Smalley, wife of one of the best-known actor-directors in California."[28] But in another iteration of this same arrangement—"in private life Miss Weber is Mrs. Phillips Smalley, and her talented husband is associated with her in all her productions"—the boundaries failed to hold, for the couple's marriage appears to sustain their working partnership.[29] Certainly the most interesting twist on this recital described Weber's performance as wife and homemaker as masterful. In *Sunset* magazine's portrait of the director, titled "A Perpetual Leading Lady," Weber's "lead" slipped between starring roles onscreen to positions of creative control behind the camera to her convincing performance as devoted wife. "The part of Mrs. Phillips Smalley," author Bertha Smith noted, "is not the least picturesque role of Lois Weber."[30] Trivial though they may seem, deliberations over a woman's name were not without significance in the early years of Hollywood when so many women juggled their own fame in relation to their status within a celebrity couple. Mark Lynn Anderson has demonstrated, for instance, that the actress and director Dorothy Davenport played a vital role in domesticating her husband, the matinee idol Wallace Reid, after his accidents and overdoses. By changing her professional name first to Dorothy Davenport Reid, then to Mrs. Wallace Reid, the star posthumously recovered her husband's wayward image in the guise of a man beloved by a wife who remained devoted even after his death.[31]

Weber and Smalley were, of course, only one of many celebrity couples in early Hollywood; indeed, they took a decided backseat to the likes of Davenport and Reid or Mary Pickford and Douglas Fairbanks.[32] What distinguished Weber and Smalley's "collaboration" from these other partnerships, however, was how closely their filmmaking accomplishments were overlaid with their marriage and how solidly the couple was associated with bourgeois values rather than Hollywood glamour. Unlike Pickford and Fairbanks, whose marriage was presented as a fairy-tale romance played out in the imaginarily unified realm of "Pickfair," Weber and Smalley were cast as a married couple of long standing (not starry-eyed lovers) and solid citizens of the middle class (rather than denizens of that new fantasyland called Hollywood). Whereas these other more glamorous couples had met in Hollywood after already having achieved some fame, Weber and Smalley were married outside of the industry and entered motion picture work together, a fact nearly always stressed in their profiles. Moreover, Weber and Smalley frequently appeared together onscreen playing husband and wife, thus encouraging connections between their creative endeavors and their marriage. By comparison, Pickford and Fairbanks starred together in only one film, a historical drama that muted the connections between the diegetic couple and their off-screen counterparts. Pickford formalized a professional collaboration with Fairbanks through United Artists in 1919, but there was little evidence of this working relationship in their screen life. Indeed, Pickford continued to hide her growing industry stature beneath a celluloid persona that seemed to remain eternally prepubescent.[33]

In perhaps the most striking contrast, fan magazines dwelt on the "majesty" of Pickfair and the "royalty" of its inhabitants, as Christina Lane has shown, while items on Weber and Smalley emphasized the well-ordered hominess of their quintessential California bungalow. Unlike so many other early star profiles that played up lavish Hollywood lifestyles, portraits of Weber's life at home did not celebrate the glamour of her surroundings. Rather, it was precisely the ordinariness of the couple's "beautiful little vine-covered flower garden bungalow," their "charming house in Hollywood," and their "modest little bungalow" that was cherished.[34] Associated almost exclusively with a romanticized view of California living, bungalows were by far the most prevalent housing innovation of the second decade of the twentieth century. Targeted toward middle-class homeowners, bungalow designs broke down the rigid formality of nineteenth-century dwellings by permitting easier flow within the space and greater integration with its adjoining landscape.[35] Pictured in such a home, Weber and Smalley were quite pointedly identified with middle-brow taste and quite explicitly set apart from more upscale Hollywood residences then being erected by the industry's new stars.

Emphasis on the couple's quotidian existence often served to accentuate their views on cinema, particularly their investment in the medium's refinement. Exemplary in this regard is a 1915 *Movie Pictorial* feature on Weber and Smalley that is structured around a visit to their bungalow.[36] The reporter, Richard Willis, narrated his visit with the pair from the moment he "duly pressed the little button by the door of the bungalow and was accorded the welcome," to the point when he left them standing "in the doorway of their cheery home with the subdued lights behind them." Between these moments the couple, mainly Weber, discussed the progress of motion pictures—including the ill effects of recent melodramatic serials, ideal film lengths, literary adaptations, and stage performers—surrounded by the couple's modest, tastefully decorated interiors. Here we see that in Weber's case, highbrow filmmaking was associated above all with bourgeois domesticity, in striking contrast to her contemporary Cecil B. DeMille who, as Sumiko Higashi demonstrates, was linked to improved motion picture standards and "famous players" chiefly through his professional background and his family's pedigree in the theater, not through details of his personal lifestyle.[37] Speaking with Willis in her living room, Weber once again played the idealized film industry patron of these years—the temperate, educated, married, middle-class woman looking for refined entertainment for her family. The interview's setting also implicitly tied motion picture entertainment to older forms of leisure and socializing based in the family parlor. In fact, fans learned in another profile that Weber "shuns press agents" and "the cafe life of 'The City of Angels,'" preferring instead to spend "every leisure moment in the bungalow which the Smalley's call home."[38] Although Weber worked within the industry, she remained associated with more traditional forms of leisure centered around the home. Weber's sister Ethel, who appeared in several of the director's films, underscored the point further when she insisted that "the most extraordinary thing about my sister is that she is so ordinary."[39]

Cozy living room conversations about the future of motion picture drama also suggest that while glimpses of Weber's private life anchored her in a domestic setting, they also provided an opportunity to showcase her labor. Boundaries between the home and the workplace were complicated still further when interviews conducted in her residence invariably led Weber to discussions of her working methods, given that she spent so much of her time writing screenplays at home. Considering the invisibility of much of her labor as a screenwriter and director, this was all the more significant. The books that lay within easy reach on her desk, the light streaming in her windows, her preference for writing in pencil on yellow pads propped on her knee—all of these details became crucial to the film-maker's persona. One such profile focused on her "exceptional" mahogany desk: "A gift from my husband," Weber noted, an explanation that simultaneously inscribed her writing within domesticity and marriage, even as it hinted at something altogether different—a husband's value and support of his wife's chosen profession.[40]

Photos of the couple also stressed this integration of domesticity and motion picture work, often overlaid with the couple's working partnership. In a photo essay on "The Smalleys" published in *Photoplay* magazine, Weber was posed sitting at her desk with pencil in hand and a writing pad on her knee, deep in concentration. Smalley, seated in a comfortable chair on the other side of a dividing screen, reads a book or perhaps a film script. It is a portrait of the couple comfortably and companionably working at home, their familial bond underscoring their creative partnership. Though they are not physically intertwined, as they are in the portrait showing them "conferring on a manuscript," the balanced composition reinforces a sense that the two are engaged in corresponding, complementary activities that together support their combined creative endeavor as "The Smalleys." And here again household space is framed as work space, not as a sanctified domestic realm set apart from studio labor.[41]

Weber's domestic and professional interests were further integrated when she purchased an estate on Santa Monica Boulevard in 1917 to set up her independent company, Lois Weber Productions—thus emerging quite prominently from under the banner of "The Smalleys." Preserving much of its landscaping for use in exterior shots, Weber converted the main house into administrative offices and erected a studio on the property. The company's first publicity bulletin told the story of how a potato patch on the original property had been preserved amid the renovations, acknowledging that a healthy potato crop was likely to bring in more revenue than movie making—a jest that only served to underscore the residential origins of the premises.[42] Profiles of the filmmaker at the time were invariably structured around a tour of this home/studio, as if to foreground the very problem of situating Weber as a professional woman. Visiting the "cottage studio" in 1921, the *Motion Picture Magazine* writer

Weber and Smalley, shown
at home in *Photoplay*, 1916.

Aline Carter's eyes roamed around the director's "cozy study," catching "the dancing flames in the fireplace . . . the great bowls of gorgeous dahlias, the wide couch, heaped with pillows, drawn invitingly near the fire, and the stunning carved teakwood desk," declaring "I felt the definite touch of a woman's hands."[43] "You would never guess this is a studio," another fan magazine "tour" announced. "Nothing suggests business . . . You walk right into a huge, cheery room with comfortable divans and rockers and a great log-fire burning and blinking cheerfully at you, while its long fiery arms invite you to draw up a chair and be comfy."[44] Noting Weber's penchant for calling the studio "My Old Homestead," *Photoplay*'s Elizabeth Peltret described how the estate's "broad grounds, with rose bushes and shade trees, the swing in the backyard, the wide, hospitable doors, and the long, handsomely furnished reception room are all reminiscent of some Southern manor house."[45] Weber herself, apologizing for sounding "sentimental and feminine," assured *Moving Picture World*'s interviewer Arthur Denison, "that we will make better pictures all the way around from having an in-spiring and delightful environment in which to work."[46] If these glimpses inside Weber's studio seemed to stress its tranquillity and hominess (and her talents for interior decorating over film directing) while ignoring the facility's technical sophistication, Weber was also quick to point out how significantly her working methods would be improved by the new studio setup.[47] Eager to experiment with new filmmaking strategies, Weber spoke of her desire to assemble all of the sets and props ahead of time so that entire pictures could be shot in sequence, a costly and time-consuming method of shooting that was discouraged within conventional studio set-tings.[48] Building on the strengths of her new quarters, Weber developed a significant production innovation of the teens, one that decisively refused the increasing standardization of studio production methods.

Portraits of Weber at home, then, refused much of the accustomed func-tion of celebrity profiles: rather than domesticating a notable professional woman, they blurred the boundaries between work and leisure; rather than reinserting Lois Weber under the banner of "Mrs. Phillips Smalley," they furnished an alternate model of a nonhierarchical marriage based upon common creative interests and mutual support; and rather than spinning a portrait of otherworldly glamour, akin to that found on the screen, the visits insisted, rather forcefully, on the couple's commonplace tastes and habits. Such portraits marshaled Weber's matronly persona in the service of the more general project of uplifting the cinema, while at the same time creating not only a legitimate place for women in the industry, but a privi-leged one.

"DOMESTIC DIRECTRESS"

When Weber's domestic talents *were* mentioned in the press, they did not always serve the purpose of relegating her to the more traditionally feminine roles of wife and homemaker. More often than not, celebrity pro-files drew connections between the skills necessary for efficient household management and those associated with filmmaking. "Hers is the leading role in her Hollywood home," one piece quipped, adding that Weber "di-rects her household."[49] Another magazine, hailing Weber as "The Do-mestic Directress," celebrated her ability to combine a creative career with household science: "Domestic hours are well interspersed in the life of Directress Weber and her efficiency behind the megaphone in the studio fails to interfere with her efficiency in her well-ordered home."[50] As one might expect with a female artist, culinary and handicraft metaphors abounded in descriptions of her work: as one piece suggested, "She is to the modern propaganda film what yeast is to dough."[51]

Weber herself participated in the construction of her "domesticated" persona, comparing screenwriting in one instance to "making a dress," adding that one must have a complete mental conception of the finished project from the beginning, otherwise "when you begin fixing this, altering that, and inserting something else, the pattern is spoiled."[52] In another instance Weber outlined her ambition to give the public the filmmaking equivalent of "little afternoon teas ... light, artistic production[s]" that "charm the eye" and "leave a pleasant fragrance behind."[53] Here we find more traditional avenues of female creativity—dressmaking, handiwork, decorating, cooking, entertaining—quite legitimately compared to the artistic demands of filmmaking, not, I must stress, to downplay Weber's cinematic endeavors, but precisely to assert her rightful place behind the megaphone. Indeed, Weber often played up these associations, claiming that feminine virtues were precisely those that enabled her to be a gifted filmmaker: "I like to direct, because I believe a woman, more or less intuitively, brings out many of the emotions that are rarely expressed on the screen. I may miss what some of the men get, but I will get other effects that they never thought of," she maintained.[54] She offered in her persona exactly the kind of femininity that many in the industry hoped would uplift the social standing of the country's new entertainment pastime.

Indeed, many of the talents for which Weber was praised in both the trade press and the popular press drew upon this image of her uniquely feminine skills. Weber was, for instance, often celebrated for her realism, particularly her attention to detail in shooting interior settings.[55] Universal drew attention to the fact that while making *Shoes* in 1916, the director had the entire contents of a five-and-dime store transported to the studio in order to film the shop sequences, and in the domestic scenes "real corned beef and cabbage were cooked on a real stove, with real fire in it, and the furniture which was used in the interior of the Meyer home was specially bought from just such people as the Meyers were."[56] Noting her penchant for filming interior locations in private homes rather than on studio sets, *Moving Picture World* gave Weber considerable credit for the skill involved in such realizations. "This ability, which requires an exceptionally keen sense of light values and technical knowledge of the proper placing of artificial lights, has enabled her ... to secure life-like detail ... which helps give her productions an atmosphere of reality." [57]

Weber's femininized aesthetic virtues, like attention to detail in interiors, costumes, and locations, was thus linked in these profiles to a particularly well-developed mastery of filmmaking technique that was itself uniquely feminine. Portraits of the director at work on film sets stressed her efficient control of all aspects of shooting. "As a director she attends not only to the details of productions, but personally goes over every inch of films, scrutinizing each tiny detail closely, keen to detect ... any false trick of the camera or error of the actor," one newspaper profile reported. [58] In filming *The Dumb Girl of Portici* on location in Chicago in 1916 Weber remained at the center of all activity, "wanted here, there and everywhere," according to the *Chicago Herald*, as "Phillips Smalley came to her for advice upon every question that presented itself." [59] When a distressed actor appeared at her side worried that there was no hat to match his suit, Weber accompanied him to the wardrobe room to find a suitable cap. [60] In these depictions Weber seemed simultaneously to be overseeing her busy home, serving as a loving wife, and shepherding her children to their closets, none of which appeared out of place in this era of filmmaking.

Alongside these filmmaking talents, Weber was also often celebrated for her ability to nurture acting talent, as *Moving Picture World* acknowledged in 1921 when it noted that she "has been a star maker for years." [61] Still again, this expertise was given a specifically feminine cast, for her relationships with others in the field, particularly younger women, were often couched in maternal imagery. Weber's discovery of the actress Mary McLaren on the Universal lot and her subsequent mentoring of the young star was a story often repeated in press accounts of both women's careers. [62] "She's only sixteen and beautiful," Weber said of McLaren, "but, more than that, she is the most sensitive and intelligent girl I ever directed." [63] Two years later Weber described Mildred Harris, another young actress with whom she worked, in similar terms: according to the director, Harris was "the dearest little thing" going about the "grounds and studio home" busily improving things. [64] Directorial and mothering skills were also conflated in an article on a school that Weber operated for "young actor folks" at her studio. In an accompanying photo, the director was shown leaning over one boy's shoulder to correct his homework, her other arm encircling his shoulders in a nurturing posture. As Universal's trade paper proudly proclaimed: "Miss Weber is noted for the interest she takes in the younger members of the acting faces at Universal City."[65]

Though Weber had no children of her own—or perhaps *because* she had none—maternal tropes were often used to define her support of younger women working in the field. Placing herself in an explicitly motherly relation to other screenwriters, Weber recounted how she "had under [her] care many of the girls who are now famous in the writing field, notably Frances Marion . . . one of the very brightest girls writing today, and my close friend."[66] Although Marion was only five years younger than Weber, the tenor of Weber's commentary simultaneously stressed her relative seniority within the profession and her mothering role. Even at home, Weber's sister Ethel posed as surrogate child during the *Movie Pictorial* feature, spending the entire interview sitting on the floor at Weber's feet gazing adoringly upward at her elder sister in a pose more reminiscent of a daughter than a sibling.[67]

By aligning Weber's filmmaking talents with more traditionally feminine skills like decorating, entertaining, handiwork, and childcare, celebrity portraits insisted on the uniquely female perspective that she brought to the cinema. Rather than detracting from her professional stature, however, accounts of her domestic acumen actually served to affirm Weber's rightful place in motion picture production precisely because of her ability to straddle these realms, not in spite of it. Rather than downplaying Weber's filmmaking accomplishments then, such profiles anchored her directorial voice within the home, the family, and marriage—and, through the intersection of these fields, within a particularly feminine worldview welcome within the industry at the time.[68]

"A BRIDE AND GROOM DETERMINATION"

Weber's marriage to Phillips Smalley, and the couple's frequent creative collaborations, stood at the heart of the filmmaker's persona: a matronly stature enhanced her claims to cinematic respectability, as I have shown, and her marriage, far from competing with her creative interests, was cast as the couple's emotional and creative center. In a mutually reinforcing scenario Weber and Smalley's unusual male-female business partnership was tempered through less-threatening matrimonial imagery, while at the same time the couple's personal relationship, modeled on the workplace, offered a fresh portrait of gender equality in marriage. However forward looking, these overlaid metaphors could not always mask the fundamental reorientation of gender roles that Weber and Smalley's partnership implied. Indeed, a closer look at portraits of the couple's relationship reveals a less celebratory tenor, an undercurrent of tension indicating something of the stress placed on their "bride and groom determination."

Fan magazines and newspaper profiles, eager to provide readers with an inside peek into the couple's relationship, were very fond of staging conversations between Weber and Smalley in which each modestly deferred to the other about who should be given credit for their success. Witness the following dialogue:

> "Give Mrs. Smalley all the publicity," said her husband, "for hers is the hand that is instrumental in creating the most important scenes."
>
> "He always does that," said his wife. "He would obliterate himself entirely if he felt it would give me more honor."[69]

The tensions over creative control that surface in this playful debate came to the fore in another behind-the-scenes episode sketched for *Photoplay* readers. In this vignette Smalley was depicted approaching Weber on the set with a proposed script change to which she readily agreed:

> "You're right," said the wife.
>
> "Say, 'as usual,'" ordered the husband.
>
> "I won't," she answered, and added in the manner of a side-show lecturer: "Here you see the only theatrical couple in captivity married thirteen years and still in love with each other."[70]

What is so remarkable about this exchange is not only the way that Weber and Smalley cloak their creative rivalry within an apparently healthy matrimonial tussle, but also the degree of self-consciousness that each brought to the enterprise: Weber, narrating the episode, appeared fully cognizant of their performance "onscreen" as husband and wife. Employing zoo imagery to characterize the lens of media scrutiny, she knowingly played up the exoticism of the working couple on display, all but acknowledging the presence of curious fan magazine "onlookers." Perhaps more significantly, in serving as sideshow lecturer Weber took decisive directorial control away from her husband who had presumed to give her direction in the first place. Even while ceding creative decisions to Smalley, then, Weber appeared to retain an illusion of control. Asked, in another piece, how she and Smalley worked together, Weber replied, "We boss each other," once again underscoring their equality while also pointing out the tensions underlying it.[71]

Similarly self-conscious jockeying for power surfaced in the *Los Angeles Times* writer Samuel M. Greene's account of his trip to Universal City in 1916, where Smalley was presented to be even less certain about the exact nature of his and Weber's partnership and his status within it. When Weber and her husband were introduced as "Mr. and Mrs. Smalley," Smalley jokingly offered a correction, insisting that the two be referred to as "Mrs. Smalley and husband," a change that reordered the implied hierarchy of their partnership, asserting Weber's dominance in the professional sphere while still holding her under the rubric of his name and their marriage.[72]

These humorous little episodes, however staged or manufactured they might have been, performed two functions simultaneously. By offering behind-the-scenes glimpses of the pair together in seemingly typical spousal moments, they intertwined all the more decisively the couple's off-screen bond with their working partnership, thereby normalizing the uncommon sight of men and women functioning together as equals not only in marriage but, even more profoundly, in the workplace. At the same time, however, each episode pointed to the remarkable destabilization of gender roles that this egalitarian arrangement posed, which was evident especially in the ongoing power struggle enacted in each incident. Obviously these scenes yield no access to the couple's "true" coexistence. However, such attempts to imagine their interactions, to evoke their simultaneous status as coworkers and spouses, necessarily revealed cracks in the fiction of their harmonious union and the mutually reinforcing metaphors of marriage and collaboration. Ideas of romantic companionability could not erase professional rivalry any more than ideas about egalitarian working conditions could stand for the significant changes that equality might have introduced into their marriage.

It is no coincidence that Smalley's stature stood at the core of these jokes. In fact, the scope of his involvement in the couple's creative projects has always been a source of uncertainty for film historians. Reviews from the time do not shed much light on the matter; indeed, many seem concerned to distinguish each partner's contribution or to resurrect individual identities blurred under the joint signature of "The Smalleys." One writer, adopting a conservatively gendered assessment of the pair's division of labor, suggested that "to Mrs. Smalley is given the credit for the delicacy of the picture, the pictorial artistry, but her husband is said to be responsible for the big mob scenes and bolder masculine workmanship."[73] More often than not, however, Weber's contribution was elevated above her husband's, sometimes in spite of their equal billing. In reviewing *Sunshine Molly* in 1916, another commentator openly questioned the film's attribution: "It is attributed to Mr. Smalley," he noted, "but since he and his wife, Lois Weber, worked on the film, and knowing her handiwork so well, somehow I say it is the work of 'The Smalleys.'"[74]

Publicity materials also offer contradictory evidence, for they identify many titles as Weber's work and Weber's vision while also noting Smalley's contributions and invariably stressing how the couple's marriage sustained their collective endeavors. A brief item in *Moving Picture World* announcing the completion of *Where Are My Children?* in 1916, for instance, began with the headline "Lois Weber Molds Artistic Surprises," stressing the work as her sole creation. Information that "Phillips Smalley co-directed with his talented wife" remains buried halfway into the item. Thus, in the same moment that the democratic nature of their filmmaking was noted, it was simultaneously erased.[75] When Weber left Universal to form Lois Weber Productions, her outfit's first publicity bulletin was, as always, careful to delineate the nature of the couple's creative interaction: Smalley, it noted, "will be associated with Miss Weber as he has been in all of her productions in the past."[76] Since nothing in particular was said about the nature of Smalley's "association" with the company, we must assume that it was at once immediately apparent, and therefore not worth belaboring, and simultaneously embarrassing because of its inadequacy in relation to Weber's own accomplishments, so celebrated in the main body of the piece.

That same summer *Photoplay* ran a spread on celebrity marriages in Hollywood, including Weber and Smalley among its featured couples. A caption beneath separate photos of the two described them, rather baldly, as "Phillips Smalley and his talented wife, Lois Weber, whose directorial fame has eclipsed his."[77] Smalley is shown in profile, his eyes are downcast,

Weber dominates the goings on at Universal City in 1916.

his mood somber, as he appears to focus on something unseen beyond the frame. Weber, by contrast, looks directly into the camera, smiling. Cut out from the original background, her portrait is re-pasted slightly on top of Smalley's, accentuating an inequity already stated so unequivocally in the photo caption. Smalley's marginalization was also acutely figured in a *Los Angeles Times* cartoon depicting the goings-on at Universal City that year.[78] Under the heading "The Center of the Stage," Weber dominates the image in a way that identifies her as the studio's chief asset. Beneath her the caption reads, "Lois Weber: Wonderful Lois, her note book always filled with clever ideas." Smalley, drawn much smaller, stands noticeably in her shadow. As his eyes remain fixed upon Weber, she looks outward meeting the reader's gaze, reinforcing the notion that she is the central object of attention, not her husband.

Indeed, a closer look at visual representations of the couple reveals other instances where the metaphor of "bride and groom determination" became strained. The mirrored compositions in which Weber and Smalley were so frequently pictured not only emphasized their modern and egalitarian bond, as I have stressed, but also they were inflected with a competing tenor, one that subtracted substantially from the theme of harmo-

nious union and indeed suggested its very manufacture. Turning again to
the rhyming layout of Bosworth's 1914 advertisement shown above, we see
that while it trumpets the couple's synchronous achievements on stage and
screen, it also literally creates their partnership by pasting their two separate images together. In lieu of portraying the pair in the same frame, the
ad juxtaposes solo portraits of Weber and Smalley in a mirrored composition that seeks to create an effect of the couple gazing into one another's
eyes. And it would be an engaging effect but for the fact that their sightlines do not match. The egalitarian image of their partnership has been
literally pasted together, we are forced to realize, much as we are forced to
recognize how much the fiction of bourgeois marital happiness has been
marshaled to prop up their image of cultural sophistication.

Similarly misaligned sightlines fracture the intimacy of several other
portraits as well. The photo of the couple "conferring on a manuscript,"
for instance, would seem to be the quintessential encapsulation of their
mutual interaction, however staged. Yet, once again, the composition
might be considered in another light. While Weber faces forward, her
eyes cast downwards reading the script, Smalley appears in three-quarters
view, his back very nearly to the camera. His unfocused gaze lingers somewhere just beyond the frame, engaged neither with Weber nor the material
upon which they are supposedly "conferring." In a half-controlling, half-
protective stance he appears to hover over her, yet he remains isolated from
the project she is undertaking. Although the composition emphasizes a
mirrored and therefore egalitarian placement within the frame, as well as
the intertwining of the couple's bodies on one single project and the intimacy of the domestic interior visible in the background, it also emphasizes
to an equal degree how composed this portrait is and how disengaged they
are from one another.

Smalley's marginalization in their endeavors is also readily suggested
by the *Photoplay* portrait of the couple at work in their Hollywood home.
Although the composition again seems to stress their complementary activities, Smalley is confined to the far right of the frame, contained within
a much smaller portion of the image and in a much darker corner of the
room. Weber, by contrast, is nearly centered within the frame, bathed by
light from the window behind her and surrounded by empty, unrestrict-
ing space. As another clearly staged portrait of their supposed companionability, it unwittingly points to the fissures in the image itself.

Photos of Weber and Smalley with the famed Russian dancer Anna

Pavlova on the set of *The Dumb Girl of Portici* in 1916 also betray contradictions in the discourse surrounding the couple's working relationship,
even as they accompany a *Motion Picture Magazine* story on the project.[79]
In one image Smalley stands to the right of the frame beside a camera
embossed with "The Smalleys" on its side, while Weber stands to the left
holding a script. At first glance the composition might seem to reinforce
traditional ideas about the gendered division of labor on the couple's productions, with Weber handling script details while Smalley assumes the
task of directing and shooting the action. But other facets of the composition belie this interpretation: Weber confers with Pavlova in an animated
manner, meeting the other woman's gaze. Smalley, isolated on the other
side of the frame, appears removed from the directing process and, once
again, his unfocused gaze does not rest on anyone or anything in the frame.
A second photo accompanying the article shows a closer view of the happy
interaction between Weber and her star overlaid on top of the first. The
juxtaposition only underscores how Smalley is displaced by the dialogue
between the women, how theirs remains the true collaboration, outpac-
ing any interaction between "The Smalleys." As I stressed earlier, Weber
herself frequently mentioned her friendships with actresses and writers
working on her productions. Here we see more clearly how those directorial alliances might vie with her partnership with Smalley. Perhaps most
significantly, Weber's association with Pavlova, a woman of considerable
fame and artistic stature, refused the maternal and matrimonial tropes that
had been used to soften her working relationships in other celebrity portraits. Collaborating with the dancer on a high-profile project, Weber could
neither be cast as an adoring "mother" nurturing a young actress's career,
nor as a faithful "wife" toiling alongside her husband in the family business.
Instead, she risked a much more politicized interpretation of the relationship, one echoed in the text accompanying the photos. Because Weber so
often favored screen stories with central female roles adapted from properties written by women, *Motion Picture* described her work as "suffraget [*sic*]
propaganda."[80]

These illustrations, staged in some collaboration between fan magazines, studio publicity machines, and the savvy stars themselves, offer us
no greater access into the couple's "real" interactions than do the dialogue
scenes examined earlier. On the contrary, they allow us to see just how
fabricated the couple's image was. Once we read this artifice back into

LOIS, THE WIZARD   43

THE SMALLEYS AND PAVLŌWA CAUGHT IN INFORMAL SNAPSHOTS IN AND AROUND THE STUDIO

actors who seem to be peculiarly adapted for her particular work. Most of her pictures have been based on morality —in fact, I think she was one of the very first to produce this type of picture. In every picture of hers there is a hidden and appealing sermon. Her pictures not only interest and amuse, but also genuinely help her audiences. Her company includes such sterling actors as Edna Maison, Rupert Julian, Wadsworth Harris, Douglas Gerrard, Betty Schade, John Holt, Hart Hoxie, William Wolbert, Laura Oakley, and many others, all of whom have won

Weber's collaboration with Anna Pavlova on *The Dumb Girl of Portici* (1916) is pictured in *Motion Picture Magazine*.

written narratives of the couple's "bride and groom determination," we see the labor involved not only in filmmaking but in creating a portrait of the congenial couple, a process so often disrupted by jokes (usually put in Smalley's mouth) that called attention to the fundamental destabilization of gendered professional and familial roles that the couple's partnership represented.

If Weber's private life structured her star persona then, it did so in a contradictory fashion. Without a doubt, her reputation for high-minded feature filmmaking traded upon her celebrity image as married, middle-class matron at a time when the industry was eager to present someone so upstanding, so righteous, so ladylike as its public face—someone whose behind-the-scenes persona mirrored that of the industry's idealized female clientele. Similarly, depictions of Weber's creative endeavors with husband Phillips Smalley provided mutually reinforcing metaphors that furnished new means of framing gendered roles at home and in the workplace. Yet the weight placed upon these combined analogies strained the marital imagery, revealing gaps in what had first been presented as the consummate model of professional and personal collaboration between equals. Ironically, rather than displacing her creative accomplishments, the emphasis placed on Weber's marital status ended up foregrounding her *husband's* marginalization. What ultimately suffered was not the ideal of female professional accomplishment but the ideal of marital equality. Thus, the fiction of "The Smalleys" did not serve to erase Weber's filmmaking accomplishments under her husband's signature, as one might expect; rather, it served to preserve a fiction of egalitarian relations between men and women that her success ultimately challenged.

In the end, Weber's fame seems wedded to a particular moment in early Hollywood, for her reputation began to suffer in the early 1920s as her films were increasingly perceived to be too stuffy, too preachy, and too lacking in fun. Reviewers began to complain about having to sit through her "simplified sermons," suggesting that her matronly persona quickly lost its currency.[81] How could Weber compete, in the long run, with Hollywood's embrace of youth culture in the Jazz Age, with younger stars like Clara Bow, Colleen Moore, and Louise Brooks—flappers who embodied a new feminine ideal? Casting off propriety, marital fidelity, even common sense, they rejected precisely those values in which Weber had trafficked. Ironically, Weber's persona, which had stressed her independence within marriage, paved the way for newer forms of female independence outside of marriage that came into vogue with the youthful flapper stars. Ultimately, Weber's persona did not serve modern Hollywood, where femininity, no longer the signifier of dignity and gentility, now signaled playfulness, rebellion, and above all, sexuality, an issue that is deftly sidestepped in Weber's matronly persona. For a time, however, what Weber offered her fans was a model of female professional accomplishment that would for decades not be seen again in the film industry. Her persona was perfectly suited to a time when films of serious social import were Hollywood's desired product, not entertainment and glamour, and when married, middle-class women, not young dating singles, were the desired clientele.

NOTES

My thanks to Sirida Srisombati for her expert research assistance, to Madeline Matz, Barbara Hall, and Jan Lorentz for their help with the illustrations, and to Amelie Hastie for her generous, astute reading of the manuscript.

1 Ernestine Black, "Lois Weber Smalley," Overland Monthly 68 (September 1916): 198.

2 *Photoplay*, October 1912, 86.

3 *New York Dramatic Mirror*, July 15, 1916, n.p.; "Biographies of Important Directors," *Wid's Daily*, April 24, 1921, 112. Weber was one of only four women on a *Wid's* survey list of close to 250 "important directors" in Hollywood (Alice Guy Blaché, Frances Marion, and Mrs. Sidney Drew were the others).

4 *Wid's Daily*, November 22, 1917, 744. See also *Wid's Daily*, March 16, 1919, 3; and *Wid's Daily*, May 22, 1921, 7.

5 H. H. Van Loan, "Lois the Wizard," *Motion Picture Magazine*, July 1916, 41–44; Aline Carter, "The Muse of the Reel," *Motion Picture Magazine*, March 1921, 59–61, 126; and Fritzi Remont, "The Lady behind the Lens: Lois Weber, Photo-Genius, in Front of, or Back of, the Camera," *Motion Picture Magazine*, May 1918, 62–63, 105.

6 Bertha H. Smith, "A Perpetual Leading Lady," *Sunset* 32, no. 3 (March 1914): 636; Black, "Lois Weber Smalley," 198.

7 "Lois Weber, Film Genius, Has Spectacular Rise to Fame," unidentified newspaper clipping, n.d., n.p. Envelope 2518, Robinson Locke Collection, Billy Rose Theater Archive, New York Public Library for the Performing Arts (hereafter RLC); "'Scandal' Terrific Denunciation of the Gossiping Evil, Seen at Orpheum Today," *Fort Wayne Journal Gazette*, n.d. (c.1915), RLC; and Florence Lawrence, "Lois Weber in Studio De Luxe," *Los Angeles Examiner*, 6 June 1917, n.p., RLC.

8 Unidentified newspaper clipping, *Ohio State Journal*, September 2, 1915[?], n.p., RLC; *Moving Picture World*, August 21, 1915, 1322; and Black, "Lois Weber Smalley," 200.

9 Unidentified newspaper clipping, c.1915. Photo Collection, Billy Rose Theater Archive, New York Public Library for the Performing Arts.

10 See "Lois Weber on Scripts," *Moving Picture World*, October 19, 1912, 241; "Lois Weber Talks Shop," *Moving Picture World*, May 27, 1916, 1493; and "Lois Weber Talks of Film Future: Producer Discusses Possibilities and Professes Faith in Picture with Ideas," *New York Dramatic Mirror*, June 23, 1917, 30.

11 "Lois Weber Talks of Film Future," 30.

12 "Lois Weber—Mrs. Phillips Smalley," *Universal Weekly*, October 4, 1913, 8; *Photoplay*, September 1913, 73; and "Lois Weber Club Women's Hostess," *Moving Picture Weekly*, January 7, 1917, n.p., RLC.

13 Carolyn Lowrey, *The First One Hundred Noted Men and Women of the Screen* (New York: Moffat, Yard and Co., 1920), 190.

14 Smith, "A Perpetual Leading Lady," 634. For more on this aspect of Weber's persona, see my "Lois Weber, Progressive Cinema and the Fate of 'The Work-A-Day Girl' in *Shoes*," *Camera Obscura* 56 (2004): 140–69.

15 On the industry's desire around 1915 for upscale female patronage, see Russell Merritt, "Nickelodeon Theatres, 1905–1914: Building an Audience for the Movies," in *The American Film Industry*, ed. Tino Balio, 2nd ed. (Madison: University of Wisconsin Press, 1985), 83–102; Eileen Bowser, *The Transformation of Cinema, 1907–1915* (Berkeley: University of California Press, 1990), 37–47; Miriam Hansen, *Babel and Babylon: Spectatorship in American Silent Film* (Cambridge, Mass.: Harvard University Press, 1991), 114–20; and Shelley Stamp *Movie-Struck Girls: Women and Motion Picture Culture after the Nickelodeon* (Princeton, N.J.: Princeton University Press, 2000), 10–40.

16 Richard deCordova, *Picture Personalities: The Emergence of the Star System in America* (Urbana: University of Illinois Press, 1990), 98–107.

17 Kathryn Fuller, *At the Picture Show: Small-Town Audiences and the Creation of Movie Fan Culture* (Washington, D.C.: Smithsonian Institution Press, 1996), 115–32.

18 Gaylyn Studlar, "The Perils of Pleasure? Fan Magazine Discourse as Women's Commodified Culture in the 1920s," *Wide Angle* 13, no. 1 (1991): 28.

19 Amelie Hastie, "Circuits of Memory and History: The Memoirs of Alice Guy Blaché," in *The Feminist Reader in Early Cinema*, ed. Jennifer Bean and Diane Negra (Durham, N.C.: Duke University Press, 2002), 29–59.

20 "The Smalleys, Collaborators in Authorship and Direction," slogan used in ads, including *New York Dramatic Mirror*, November 11, 1914.

21 Black, "Lois Weber Smalley," 198; unidentified newspaper clipping, *Columbus Dispatch*, March 12, 1916, n.p., RLC.

22 Smith, "A Perpetual Leading Lady," 636; Remont, "The Lady behind the Lens," 126; Carter, "The Muse of the Reel," 105.

23 Advertisement, *Moving Picture World*, November 21, 1914, 1028.

24 Remont, "The Lady behind the Lens," 60.

25 L. H. Johnson, "A Lady General of the Picture Army," *Photoplay*, June 1915, 42.

26 Carter, "The Muse of the Reel," 105; Remont, "The Lady behind the Lens," 126.

27 "Lois Weber, Film Genius," n.d.

28 Van Loan, "Lois the Wizard," 42.

29 "Lois Weber, Film Genius," n.d.

30 Smith, "A Perpetual Leading Lady," 636.

31 Mark Lynn Anderson, "Shooting Star: Understanding Wallace Reid and His Public," *Headline Hollywood: A Century of Film Scandal*, ed. Adrienne L. McLean and David A. Cook (New Brunswick, N.J.: Rutgers University Press, 2001), 86.

32 For analyses of the fan discourse surrounding the Pickford/Fairbanks marriage, see deCordova, *Picture Personalities*, 121–24; and Christina Lane, "Pick-

ford and Fairbanks: Winning and Losing at the Game of Marriage," in *Holly-wood Star Couples: Classical-Era Romance and Marriage* (Ph.D. dissertation, University of Texas at Austin, 1999).

33 Coincidentally, Weber was featured in Pickford's (likely ghostwritten) syn-dicated newspaper column, "Personalities I Have Met," in which the actress describes the director as "one of the most interesting women in the history of motion pictures" ("Daily Talks by Mary Pickford. Personalities I Have Met: Lois Weber," unidentified newspaper clipping from the McClure Newspaper Syndicate, 1916, n.p., RLC.

34 Unidentified newspaper fragment, n.p., n.d., RLC; Black, "Lois Weber Smalley," 198; Van Loan, "Lois the Wizard," 42.

35 Clifford Edward Clark Jr., *The American Family Home, 1800–1960* (Chapel Hill: University of North Carolina Press, 1986), 163–67, 171–73, 181–82; Gwendolyn Wright, *Building the Dream: A Social History of Housing in America* (Cam-bridge, Mass.: MIT Press, 1981), 164–68.

36 Richard Willis, "Lois Weber and Phillips Smalley—A Practical and Gifted Pair with High Ideals," *Movie Pictorial*, May 1915, n.p. (reprinted in *Taylorology* 59, http://silent-movies.com/Taylorology/Taylor59.txt).

37 Sumiko Higashi, *Cecil B. DeMille and American Culture: The Silent Era* (Berke-ley: University of California Press, 1994), 7–58.

38 Remont, "The Lady behind the Lens," 126.

39 Elizabeth Peltret, "On the Lot with Lois Weber," *Photoplay*, October 1917, 91.

40 Johnson, "A Lady General of the Picture Army," 42.

41 "The Smalleys," *Photoplay*, January 1916, 152.

42 "News of Lois Weber Productions," *Lois Weber Bulletin*, no. 1, June 1917, RLC. See also Lawrence, "Lois Weber in Studio De Luxe,"; and "Lois Weber Starts Production," *Moving Picture World*, June 30, 1917, 2106.

43 Carter, "The Muse of the Reel," 62.

44 Remont, "The Lady behind the Lens," 59.

45 Peltret, "On the Lot with Lois Weber," 89.

46 "A Dream in Realization: Interview with Lois Weber by Arthur Denison," *Motion Picture World*, no. 21, July 1917, 417.

47 *Moving Picture World* provides the following description of the facilities at Lois Weber Productions: "A stage of 80 by 150 feet is now under construction. There will be sixteen dressing rooms, administrative offices, scenic and prop-erty rooms; in fact, everything pertaining to an up-to-date and well-equipped modern picture plant" ("Lois Weber Starts Production," *Moving Picture World*, June 30, 1917, 2106).

48 "A Dream in Realization," 417–18.

49 Smith, "A Perpetual Leading Lady," 636.

50 "Domestic Directress." *Motion Picture*, July 1920, 67.

51 Black, "Lois Weber Smalley," 199.

52 Carter, "The Muse of the Reel," 63.

53 Remont, "The Lady behind the Lens," 60.

54 Johnson, "A Lady General of the Picture Army," 42. Alice Guy Blaché made very similar claims in her article "Woman's Place in Photoplay Production," *Moving Picture World*, July 11, 1914, 195.

55 *Moving Picture World*, December 18, 1920, 913.

56 "Shoes," *Moving Picture Weekly*, June 24, 1916, 34.

57 "Lois Weber Sails for Europe; Plans Production of Big Films," *Moving Picture World*, October 8, 1921, 676.

58 Unidentified newspaper clipping, *Ohio State Journal*, n.d., n.p., RLC.

59 Unidentified newspaper clipping, *Chicago Herald*, 1916, n.p., RLC.

60 Unidentified newspaper clipping, 1915, n.p., RLC.

61 "Lois Weber Sails for Europe," 676.

62 "The Strange Case of Mary McLaren," *Moving Picture Weekly*, June 24, 1916, 34.

63 "Lois Weber Talks Shop," 493.

64 Remont, "The Lady behind the Lens," 61.

65 "Lois Weber Club Women's Hostess," n.p.

66 Remont, "The Lady behind the Lens," 60.

67 Willis, "Lois Weber and Phillips Smalley."

68 A related argument can be made about celebrity profiles of serial stars during these same years. If at first the portraits of adventure queens baking pies, tending gardens, and rearing children seem to detract from their spectacular adventures onscreen, in fact this is not the case. "Real life" portraits of these women's attempts to combine work and motherhood, marriage and professional life belie the strict separation of these realms enforced in onscreen serial narratives where marriage invariably marked the end of the heroine's exploits in the final episode. I develop these ideas further in *Movie-Struck Girls*, 141–53.

69 See unidentified newspaper clipping, *Columbus Dispatch*, March 12, 1916, n.p., RLC.

70 Peltret, "On the Lot with Lois Weber," 90.

71 Unidentified newspaper clipping, 1915, n.p., RLC.

72 Samuel M. Greene, "The Hay-Day of Universal," *Los Angeles Times*, April 9, 1916, part 2, 14.

73 Unidentified newpaper clipping, *Columbus Dispatch*, March 12, 1916, n.p., RLC.

74 Unidentified newspaper clipping, March 6, 1915, n.p., RLC.

75 *Moving Picture World*, March 11, 1916, 1668.

76 "News of Lois Weber Productions." The same phrase is repeated in *Moving Picture World*'s article, "Lois Weber Starts Production," on the new company.

77 *Photoplay*, July 1917, 81.

78 *Los Angeles Times*, April 9, 1916, part 2, 14.

79 Van Loan, "Lois the Wizard," 43.

80 Ibid., 44.

81 *New York Times*, November 14, 1921, 18.

TEMPTING FATE

Clara Smith Hamon, or,
The Secretary as Producer
Mark Lynn Anderson

Thus science and belles-lettres, criticism and production, education and politics, fall apart in disorder. The theater of this literary confusion is the newspaper, its content "subject matter," which denies itself any other form than that imposed on it by the readers' impatience. —Walter Benjamin, "The Author as Producer"

During Clara Smith Hamon's ten-day trial for murder in March 1921, reports surfaced that she had received several offers to appear in motion pictures. She declined these offers because she feared that signing a film contract before a verdict was reached might influence the jury against her. Immediately following her acquittal, however, the twenty-eight-year-old secretary informed reporters that she planned to enter the movies so that she could tell her life story to the world.[1] A week later, the *New York Times* reported that Smith Hamon had "signed a two-year contract with the Oklahoma Moving Picture Company of Oklahoma City under the terms of which she [was to] receive $25,000 as an advance payment and fifty percent of the profits of the company." *Moving Picture World* reported her motion picture contract as $50,000 a year. Other sources claimed that she was to receive a salary of $1,000 a week and that all

This photo of Clara Smith Hamon
shows a young woman whose attrac-
tiveness is defined more by the smart-
ness of her professional presentation
than by the reigning codes of Hollywood elegance as emphasized by the
prosecution. (Courtesy of the Library
of Congress)

motion pictures in which she was featured would bear the trademark
"Clara Smith Hamon Pictures, Inc."[2] Whatever the actual terms of her
post-trial employment, Clara Smith Hamon entered into the film business
at a significant level of bankable popularity.

In order to appreciate Clara Smith Hamon's celebrity and to understand
the effects of her film work on the development of the Hollywood star system, it is first necessary to recount the publicized facts of her life, since it
was during the immediate postwar period that the identity of the film star
relied on a notion of "personality" that was almost thoroughly biographical.
Smith Hamon's sudden star potential in early 1921 is itself indicative of this
particular cultural moment. Her celebrity status was the direct result of
the extensive newspaper coverage after she became the principal suspect in
the shooting death of Jake Hamon, a national Republican committeeman
from Oklahoma. When Clara Smith Hamon shot Jake Hamon in a hotel
room in Ardmore, Oklahoma, on November 21, 1920, he, too, was on the
verge of becoming a recognizable public figure. He was thought by many
political insiders to have been Warren Harding's choice for secretary of the
interior, having helped the newly elected president into the White House
by successfully leading the traditionally Democratic state of Oklahoma to

vote Republican in the 1920 election. Like so many others with close financial and political ties to the Harding administration, Jake Hamon was a multimillionaire with significant holdings in oil and railroads. And like Albert Fall who eventually became secretary of the interior, Hamon was primarily interested in holding the cabinet post in order to secure the lease of federal lands for private oil developers.[3]

In 1898 Jake Hamon married Georgie Perkins, with whom he had two children. Originally from Kansas, the Hamons moved to Lawton, Oklahoma, shortly after the federal government opened the Comanche-Kiowa territory to white settlement. While in Lawton, Hamon involved himself deeply in the economic development and regional politics of the territory, becoming the first chairman of the Oklahoma Republican Party when statehood was achieved in 1907. An aggressive lobbyist and a resourceful businessman, Hamon was charged in 1910 with attempting to bribe U.S. Senator Thomas P. Gore of Oklahoma for favors relating to the private allocation of native lands.[4] Soon afterward, Georgie Hamon moved to Chicago with the two children, as she later claimed, to "send them to better schools."[5] With his family hundreds of miles away, Jake Hamon devoted even more time to developing his investments and landholdings in southern Oklahoma, eventually entering into a business partnership with John Ringling (of Ringling Brothers Circus fame) to build a railroad line connecting the oil fields of southern Oklahoma.[6]

When Hamon's personal secretary and purported mistress shot him in 1920, the event immediately became front-page news in Oklahoma. Guests at the Randol Hotel in Ardmore, Oklahoma, claimed to have overheard a violent argument between the millionaire and his "alleged consort" on the night of the shooting. As Hamon lingered in an Ardmore hospital during the week of Thanksgiving, his personal secretary vanished and was rumored to be fleeing toward California or the Mexican border. Associates of Hamon claimed that he had accidentally shot himself with his own .25 caliber pistol, but the attorney general for Carter County immediately issued a warrant for the arrest of Clara Smith Hamon on a charge of assault with intent to kill, and he charged both her and Jake Hamon with adulterous relations. Throughout the first week of news coverage, Smith Hamon was almost always referred to as "Miss Clara Smith," and she was variously identified as Jake Hamon's "stenographer," "secretary," "protégé," "sweetheart," and "financial advisor." The papers also indulged in comparisons of Jake Hamon's gunshot wound to the "wound which resulted in the death of President McKinley."[7] When the Oklahoma entrepreneur died after languishing five days in the hospital, the story became national news and Smith Hamon became a fugitive wanted for murder.[8]

While the case was clearly exploitable for its sensationalistic aspects, the newspapers quickly began telling a more compelling story about the abuses of male privilege and the hypocrisies of political power. During the four weeks that Smith Hamon was a fugitive from justice, reporters were often more successful in following her trail than were the law-enforcement officials responsible for carrying out the warrants for her arrest. Early in December, a Texas newspaperman claimed to have obtained an interview with Smith Hamon after sighting her shopping in a San Antonio department store. He refused to disclose any further information to investigators or to other reporters, though, until the attorney general of Carter County promised to honor Smith Hamon's request for a trial by an all-woman jury.[9] This news was fairly unremarkable since the understanding of the homicide as principally a women's issue had been established several days earlier when the contents of scrapbooks and a diary found among Smith Hamon's belongings were serially published by the *Chicago Herald and Examiner* and made available to newspapers around the world through the International News Service. Authorities had seized these autobiographical materials from trunks belonging to Smith Hamon that had been shipped from Oklahoma to Kansas City in an effort, it was surmised, to divert law-enforcement officials from following her.[10]

Smith Hamon had collected numerous press clippings and articles documenting Hamon's career, but she had also kept a personal record of recent events in a diary that narrated a story that cast her as a patient and loving companion suffering at the hands of a manipulative alcoholic who was increasingly given over to romantic indifference, emotional neglect, and fits of sadistic violence. Usually written during the many long train journeys she had made attending to Jake Hamon's business affairs, Smith Hamon's diary chronicled a life of despair and boredom that sought relief in the glamour of Hollywood. In the entry dated May 30, 1920, Smith Hamon compares a desert landscape to a William S. Hart picture and mentions spotting Charles Chaplin in the dining room of a Los Angeles hotel, only to conclude: "Movies are a godsend for the unhappy."[11] Sandwiched between accounts of reading movie magazines, sharing train cars with film stars such as Sessue Hayakawa, and visiting beauty parlors to stave off despondency, entries referring to physical assaults, presumably by Jake Hamon, sometimes ended with words of warning to other young women. For example, an entry made after an especially terrible attack on May 12, 1920 reads:

> Know your man before you give him your soul, and when I say "know him" I mean not only know the good and funny side—the sugar-coated side, the pretentious, flattering, false side, but know the side that is not its best. Know the side the world fails to see. Know the side that only comes to life in the presence of "four walls." . . . Know him at his worst, not at his best, before you sell your soul and become ever afterward his slave. For once you give it to him you can NEVER GET IT BACK AGAIN, no matter how hard you try.
>
> A woman has power—real power—once with a man and that is when he is madly in love and wants all she's got to give.
>
> Once given the charm is broken—for him the battle is won.
>
> This is not justice, but it is a tradition as old as civilization and in spite of the light that is coming ([but] not yet come) remains a cold-blooded fact at this time.
>
> Women fit their lives to men; men never fit their lives to women.[12]

Other entries show a similar concern with social justice and express similar longings for political change. Smith Hamon's diary appeared in the newspapers just four weeks after American women voted in their first presidential election. While some readers might have connected Smith Hamon's longing for "the light that is coming" with women's recent political enfranchisement, the diary's most subversive effect was to make the murder legible as an act of retributive justice.

Clara Smith met Jake Hamon in Lawton, Oklahoma, around 1910 when she was a seventeen-year-old clerk in a hardware store.[13] He was a prosperous and ambitious businessman, approximately twenty years her senior and married with two young children. He courted the young sales clerk, eventually paying her way to business schools in Missouri and Oregon so that she could enter his employ with a rudimentary knowledge of business and law. Ending her studies before receiving a degree, Clara Smith returned to Oklahoma to become Hamon's stenographer and personal secretary. Immediately after the shooting in 1920, information about her early relationship with Jake Hamon was used by newspapers to portray

Clara Smith as an upwardly mobile teenage vamp who had manipulated Hamon into a long-term commitment by threatening him with prosecution under the Mann Act and other federal laws regulating sexual relations between adults and minors.[14] But after her diary was discovered and published a week later, Smith Hamon was represented as an intelligent but naive young woman who had slowly arrived at a feminist understanding of society because of the hardships and disappointments she had endured in her romantic and professional experiences. Reporters described how Jake Hamon had rented adjoining rooms for himself and his young secretary in the Randol Hotel in Ardmore soon after she had gone to work for him. Furthermore, it was revealed that in 1917 he arranged for Clara Smith to marry his nephew, Frank Hamon, so that he and his secretary could share the same last name, thus making travel and hotel bookings easier under the pretense of being husband and wife. Clara Smith and Frank Hamon divorced within three months, but she kept the Hamon name.[15]

These events in Smith Hamon's life were familar to the public when she surrendered to authorities at Christmas. By that time, as the *New York Times* noted, "a pronounced sentiment [had grown] against her arrest and prosecution," and several individuals had sent hostile letters to the Carter County attorney general for attempting to apprehend the "fugitive woman."[16]

At the trial in March, most of the published details about Smith Hamon's life were repeated and corroborated by the testimony she and others gave at the trial.[17] And some new information surfaced about Smith Hamon's own investments in oil leases and other properties, some of which were part of the Jake Hamon estate.[18] Hamon's former business manager, Frank Ketch, testified that he and Smith Hamon were currently financial partners in several business projects and that she also held shares in a motion picture concern.[19] Even though the murder case was prosecuted by the Oklahoma state attorney general at the special request of Oklahoma Governor J. B. A. Robertson,[20] the lawyers for the defense successfully argued that Jake Hamon had entrapped Clara Smith Hamon in a sexually exploitive and physically abusive relationship and that she had shot her employer in self-defense during an exceptionally brutal episode in which he had threatened her with a knife and attacked her with a chair. After the defense attorneys waived their right to final argument, the jury of twelve men took less than forty minutes to return their decision: "not guilty."[21]

Clara Smith Hamon placed herself in the custody of Ardmore Sheriff Buck Garrett, who met her at the Mexican border near El Paso, Texas. This photograph was taken shortly after her surrender and shows her with Garrett (left), her uncle, Benjamin F. Harrison (center), and Fort Worth Sheriff Carl Smith (right). (Courtesy of the Library of Congress)

The nation's newspapers reported that the courtroom burst into wild applause when the verdict was pronounced declaring Smith Hamon's action a case of "justifiable homicide."[22] It was at this moment that Smith Hamon announced to the world her intention to perform in motion pictures.

The first and probably only film that Clara Smith Hamon made was *Fate* (W. E. Weathers, 1921). She played herself in the film, while John Ince took the part of Jake Hamon.[23] *Fate* was produced by at least one of Hamon's business associates and was probably funded by Smith Hamon herself and by others in the Oklahoma oil business.[24] No prints of *Fate* appear to have survived. The film was in production at the Warner Bros. studio on Sunset Boulevard in Los Angeles during summer 1921 and was ready for release just prior to Roscoe "Fatty" Arbuckle's arrest on charges of rape and murder.[25] Kevin Brownlow maintains that *Fate* might have enjoyed greater popular success and acceptance had it not been for the unfortunate timing of the film's release and the decision to open the film in San Francisco (where Arbuckle had been arrested). That city was, he notes, "the wrong town in which to open. The Arbuckle case had aroused deep feeling against the entire motion picture profession."[26] Ultimately, however, it was not so much the Arbuckle scandal that decided *Fate*'s reception and censorship; in fact, the production of *Fate* was potentially a far more disruptive event for the film industry than the famous comedian's troubles. Indeed, instead of the Arbuckle scandal determining the reception of *Fate*, the film provided the grounding context for the many star scandals that immediately followed. This is why the Hamon murder trial is an important event in the development of the star system. The Hamon case significantly exacerbated the damage to Arbuckle's career by dramatically posing the real possibility that film celebrity could be based solely upon the notoriety of the featured performer and that audiences were primarily interested in scandalous stars not in spite of their transgressions but precisely because of them.

Fate's fate had already been determined as early as March 1921 when exhibitors in California announced their opposition to any film appearance by Smith Hamon, declaring "that an exhibition of this sort would unduly and improperly put a premium on violence."[27] Exhibitor organizations in other states quickly followed suit, calling for self-imposed bans on any and all films in which Smith Hamon might appear. The Motion Pictures Theatre Owners of New York, for example, went on record as "emphatically opposed to the exploitation of criminal sensationalism as illustrated in a proposal to film Clara Smith Hamon."[28] Exhibitors were not alone in their calls for voluntary censorship. Apparently, many film producers and distributors also supported a nationwide ban on any and all pictures featuring Hamon. William Brady, president of the National Association of the Motion Picture Industry (NAMPI), the principal regulatory agency in the film industry before the formation of the Hays office, reported that the members of his organization were "unilaterally opposed" to Hamon's appearance on the screen and that they were actively seeking means to stop the production and distribution of any such films.[29]

Why was there all this fuss about a small independent production company's plans to feature this young woman in films, even before the production of any such pictures had begun? Indeed, the newspapers had treated Smith Hamon quite sympathetically before and during her trial, and afterward many concluded that the "Oklahoma melodrama" had provided the nation with an entertaining moral lesson "end[ing] in an acquittal, as all canons of dramatic construction required."[30] From the very beginning, news coverage of the case had sought to clear Smith Hamon of all charges of moral turpitude, while Jake Hamon was thoroughly demonized. Moreover, in the immediate post-trial publicity, Smith Hamon was simultaneously represented as a potential film actress *and* as an evangelist who might help other young women avoid the costly mistakes she had made.[31] While the film industry's concerns about a film featuring Clara Smith Hamon were real,[32] these concerns are explained less by a commitment to social propriety and an adherence to professional standards of decency than by the sheer disruption that Smith Hamon's film celebrity would have caused for the regular functioning of the Hollywood star system. Since the film industry had continually represented itself as the ultimate source of film stardom and as the supplier of stars to the public, the popular appeal and success of a film performer such as Clara Smith Hamon would mean that Hollywood was no longer capable of authorizing film celebrities in the same way it had in the past. At stake was not just the idea that movie stars were stars because they had proven themselves through long apprenticeships as picture personalities in the industry, but also the increasingly real possibility that star identities could actually be defined and sustained by a public interest that had little or nothing to do with the ostensible products of the industry: motion pictures. While it might be argued that the nation's newspapers had usurped Hollywood's prerogative to create compelling mass celebrities, the threat posed to the star system by Smith Hamon (a threat so dramatically reenacted months later by Arbuckle) was a result of the internal logic of the star system itself.

As Richard deCordova has shown, by the late 1910s, as more information about the private lives and the personal experiences of Hollywood's most successful actors and actresses was revealed to the public, the star system functioned as a fairly coherent and codified system of knowledge.[33] For film audiences, screen appearances by stars were not just pleasurable displays of the faces, the bodies, and the wardrobes of their favorite players but also a unique way of knowing each of them and the industry in which they worked. The American cinema was presenting itself to the public as a new and particularly powerful way of understanding personality, and there was absolutely no substitute for the knowledge to be gained by the appearance of a particular player in a featured role. As the private life of the star became increasingly more a part of the information that constituted the star's identity, the "epistemological gap" between a star's screen appearances and his or her private life became increasingly less; in other words, the star performer brought to the screen an elaborate biography that was available for further inspection by the film audience. Any information revealed about the stars in magazines or newspapers could quickly become an integral part of their identities on the screen.

Since the motion picture screen had become such an important instrument for producing knowledge about the stars, it was only a matter of time before the screen was proposed as a way of knowing other interesting individuals, ones who lived quite apart from the film industry but who shared with Hollywood stars a lifestyle that was in some way exceptional and indicative of the most current social trends. Clara Smith Hamon had proposed to perform in pictures immediately after her acquittal because she believed that a large portion of the American public had a particular interest in her life experiences and might welcome the opportunity to learn more about her at the cinema. Such an interest on the part of the public was, however, a rather radical appropriation of the star system, one that went far beyond the film industry's own deployment of personalities in order to build and sustain a mass market for its products. The film industry's initial responses to these developments were entirely defensive. Besides rather disingenuously claiming that Hamon and her associates were "attempting to commercialize [her] life history,"[34] industry leaders also felt it necessary to portray any audience interest in any such personalities as deviant. However, the activity of this pathological audience had to be carefully distinguished from the will to knowledge that characterized the Hollywood star system proper.

One way to make this distinction was to claim that the reception of scandalous celebrities was essentially static and defined only by a morbid fixation on a particular individual's transgressive behavior or immoral condition, whereas the reception of genuine Hollywood stars was a dynamic process that continually revealed new aspects of a performer's identity. In the latter case, fame was well deserved since the star was talented enough and, by implication, healthy enough to support an ever-changing popular interest in his or her identity. On the other hand, audience fascination with notorious individuals was portrayed as perversely arrested by a single quality.

Consider the example of Fred Beauvais. Beauvais, a professional wilderness guide from Quebec, had been named as a corespondent in the highly publicized Stillman divorce case, another of the major news stories of 1921. His name had featured quite prominently in the extensive coverage given to the legal proceedings in the nation's newspapers. When James Stillman filed for divorce from his wife, Anne Urquhart Stillman, he claimed that Beauvais was the father of Mrs. Stillman's youngest child. At the time, Mr. Stillman was a prominent figure in financial circles and the president of the National City Bank of New York in which he, along with the Rocke-fellers, held the controlling shares. In her repeatedly appended answers to her husband's suit, Mrs. Stillman named a former showgirl of musical revues along with several other young women, all of whom had been al-legedly "kept" by Mr. Stillman at one time or another during his marriage to Mrs. Stillman. The intense and protracted publicity given to this case forced Mr. Stillman to resign his post as bank president, and several love letters purported to have been sent to Anne Stillman by Beauvais were published as part of the press coverage.[35] In summer 1921, Florence "Flo" Leeds, a former Ziegfeld chorine who was named by Mrs. Stillman in the divorce proceedings as one of her husband's many dalliances and who was said by the *New York Times* to possess "beauty and personality," was ru-mored to have been planning to star in a Hollywood production about the Stillman affair. Around the same time there was also some talk in the industry that Mrs. Stillman herself might attempt to perform in motion pictures.[36] Finally, when some exhibitors in New York State began adver-tising the appearance of Fred Beauvais in *The Lonely Trail* (Credit-Canada Productions, 1921), NAMPI president William Brady once again spoke out strongly against the screen appearances of immoral individuals.

Brady contended that if Clara Hamon and Roscoe Arbuckle were barred by popular sentiment from appearing on the screen, the same held in the case of Fred Beauvais. He was an attraction only because of his con-nection with a notorious divorce case, the details of which might best be kept from the public in the papers, on the screen, or in the courts. If one can become famous through murder, divorce, or scandal, then such encour-agement only goes to spread the present wave of crime.[37]

Brady's condemnation of exhibitor sensationalism suggests that the only possible interest in pictures featuring Arbuckle, Beauvais, or Hamon was that of a prurient fascination with their immorality or their crimes; in other words, there was nothing to be gained or to be learned by patroniz-ing the motion pictures in which they appear. Furthermore, by permitting movie audiences to publicly indulge a continued interest in such people by displaying their images and screening their films, exhibitors were inadvertently allowing a misguided sector of the public to make these individuals into celebrities to be envied and emulated, and that is why, Brady claims, such films ultimately "encourage" crime.

What is interesting in Brady's account of the problem is how far his representation of the scandalous celebrity in motion pictures departs from the industry's previous discursive construction of film stardom. Unlike traditional film stars, the appearance of immoral or criminal individuals in motion pictures is nonproductive in terms of any new or useful experience. More importantly, their very status as celebrities is now represented as entirely derived from and supported by the *public's interest in them*; the industry no longer bears primary responsibility for authorizing the identity of the film performer in such cases. These individuals remain prominent public figures in spite of the efforts of most of the film industry to ban their film appearances. Furthermore, the possibility that film audiences could have a more dynamic interest in the personalities of notorious individuals, a reception that sought to further understand the different situations and experiences of these people, is completely discounted in the industry's condemnation of showing the films of Arbuckle, Hamon, or Beauvais. Yet, since *Fate* was more or less a recounting of Smith Hamon's exploitation at the hands of the Oklahoma oilman, and since in *The Lonely Trail* Fred Beauvais played a character resembling himself, it is clear that there was a potential public interest in their individual stories. Though some film exhibitors denounced any attempt to tell the Hamon story, regardless of who performed it, the film industry as a whole was far less concerned with the suitability of the Hamon murder or the Stillman divorce for the motion picture screen than it was with controlling the screen appearances of the individuals involved in these public scandals.[38] The industry's bottom line was that these individuals did not deserve attention and did not properly belong in feature films. As *Variety* stated, "There is a movement on the part of the industry to blacklist stars recruited through the medium of sensationalism and with no other known talents to recommend them than the notoriety accruing through court proceedings."[39] However, the industry's attempt to regulate the identity of the performer faced a serious contradiction since Arbuckle, a major Hollywood star who had performed in hundreds of films before his arrest, was now on a list with the likes of Hamon and Beauvais.

Clara Smith Hamon was not, of course, the first person to achieve celebrity status through notoriety based principally upon public scandal. Evelyn Nesbit, who had been a central personality in the Thaw-White sex and murder scandal of 1906, sustained a career on the vaudeville stage and eventually performed in motion pictures. Undoubtedly, many of the people who went to see Nesbit on the stage or on the screen were interested in her precisely because of her notorious past. Yet there are important differences between Nesbit and Smith Hamon that entail different audience receptions. First of all, Nesbit had a career on the stage before the scandal broke in 1906. She was performing in a revue when she first met the wealthy architect Stanford White, who allegedly drugged and raped her when she was only sixteen years old. By the time Nesbit's husband, the millionaire Henry Thaw, shot and killed White five years later, Nesbit was easily identifiable as belonging to a metropolitan world of entertainment and popular amusements. While both Nesbit and Smith Hamon shared similar class positions, and while both were romantically involved with wealthier men, their class identities were necessarily represented and perceived quite differently. Nesbit's life as an artist's model and chorus girl was closely associated with questions of urban leisure and an emerging consumerist culture, thereby making Nesbit's identity readable within a context of the pursuits of a leisured class. Nesbit belonged, however troublesomely, to "sophisticated" society. Smith Hamon's world was different. As a business secretary for a midwestern oil developer and Republican politician, Smith Hamon's identity related far more coherently to the context of women's productive labor and the conditions women experienced in the modern corporate workplace than it did to the extravagant metropolitan milieu of glamour and mass entertainment. Indeed, H. H. Brown, one of the prosecuting attorneys at Smith Hamon's trial, discovered how inappropriate a comparison between the two women could be when he referred to Smith Hamon as "another Evelyn Nesbit Thaw, who has made more prostitutes than any other person."[40] According to the press, Brown's attacks were received in the courtroom as vitriolic and unwarranted. His asking jurors if they were "going to write another Evelyn Thaw case" produced in the silent courtroom only scowls from the relatives of Smith Hamon, a sharp contrast to the applause that would erupt the next day when the verdict was read. The defense lawyers waived their right to argument and sent the case to the jury immediately following Brown's comparison of Clara Smith Hamon to Evelyn Nesbit, presumably on the belief that Brown's attacks were far more destructive of the prosecution's credibility than damaging to their client.[41] Whether people objected to the comparison itself, or whether some of them also objected to the ease with which Brown was able to connect Nesbit's name to prostitution, the comparison of these two women was seen by many in March 1921 as saying more about a particular type of outmoded moral conservatism than about the true identity of Clara Smith Hamon.

Another important difference in the two scandals is their respective historical moments. As Lee Grieveson has shown, the Thaw-White scandal occurred at the beginning of the nickelodeon era and became a key historical event in the regulation of the cinema as a social space.[42] One concern at that time was the suitability of particular stories and representations for a mass audience, especially as those stories and representations may have related to "real" events reported in the newspapers. In 1906 there was no star system yet in place, but by the time Smith Hamon proposed to enter the movies in 1921, that system had been firmly established as a particularly powerful means of addressing and sustaining a mass audience, offering a unique and dynamic means for understanding celebrity personalities. It was only after World War I that the regulation of motion picture personalities became a significant concern for reformers, politicians, scientists, and educators, all of whom were interested in the social effects of the cinema. Similarly, while Smith Hamon's murder trial was the immediate occasion for her film stardom, Nesbit entered motion pictures almost ten years after her husband was tried for shooting Stanford White. While it is true that each woman's appearance could call to mind the story of the scandal with which she was associated, Nesbit's status as a "fallen woman" was first negotiated on the stage where noticeably less regulatory scrutiny of this particular genre occurred than in motion pictures.[43] Though Nesbit's scandalous past continued to inform her identity and to cause her problems, her status as a controversial and provocative personality gradually diminished. Nesbit was already history when she made her first film in 1914, whereas Smith Hamon was still news when she starred in *Fate* in 1921.

In pointing out these differences, I am not claiming a privileged or unique role for Smith Hamon in the history of the cinema. Rather, I am attempting to demonstrate how she represents the problems and institutional contradictions of the Hollywood star system at a particular moment; a moment that has often been obscured by an overemphasis on and preoccupation with the Arbuckle scandal as a sort of violent rupture in Hollywood's ability to unproblematically represent itself through its stars. By the end of March 1921, more than five months before Arbuckle's Labor Day party, all branches of the industry were negotiating the threat posed by Smith Hamon's film stardom. Furthermore, Smith Hamon's success in producing *Fate* was often explicitly connected to stories about other film contracts offered in summer 1921 to similar individuals involved in high-profile divorce and murder cases. Not only were Fred Beauvais, Flo Leeds, and Mrs. Stillman mentioned in the papers as possibly embarking on film careers, but Peggy Hopkins-Joyce was also rumored to be considering offers to star in motion pictures. Like Leeds, Hopkins-Joyce had been a Ziegfeld Follies performer, and like Mrs. Stillman, she was involved at that time in a protracted divorce settlement with a millionaire. The lives of Hopkins-Joyce and her estranged husband were revealed daily through the lurid details of their contentious legal proceedings that for weeks occupied the front pages of the nation's newspapers.[44]

In short, during summer 1921 and continuing through the following year, a moral panic ensued about the possible film appearances of scandalous individuals. In June 1921, an editorial in the *Daily News* of New York attacked movie producers in a piece titled "Capitalizing Indecency." The author charged that the film industry's demand for self-regulation appeared preposterous since numerous women involved in recent scandals had "been offered a big salary to act for the screen."[45] Brady took the editorial seriously enough to publicly demand an apology from the anonymous writer, and—in a direct reference to the production of *Fate*—he made clear that the members of NAMPI, an organization representing all the major studios, had actually "repulsed the efforts of unscrupulous outsiders to foist such a picture upon the public."[46] In a satirical piece in *Variety* on the production of *Fate*, the famous director/producer Marshall Neilan blasted Actor's Equity for failing to restrain its members from performing in the film, as well as NAMPI for failing to halt the production of the picture altogether. Neilan reserved his highest praise for the American Society of Cinematographers (ASC) since they immediately expelled the cameraman André Barlatier when he agreed to shoot *Fate* for $500 a week, after the ASC had passed a formal resolution forbidding its members from working on the Smith Hamon project.[47] Despite Brady's earlier pronouncements in March against Smith Hamon's film ambitions, and his subsequent guarantees that *Fate* would never make it to the screen, he was widely perceived both inside and outside of the industry as too indecisive and too ineffectual in his handling of regulatory issues. With the passage of film censorship legislation in New York State in May 1921, and with the ongoing production of the Smith Hamon film in Hollywood, Brady and the trade organization that he headed were in a precarious position. The Arbuckle scandal would be only another event in a series of crises concerning the industrial regulation of film personalities during summer and fall 1921. That a long-standing film star such as Arbuckle could be so easily scandalized, despite the lack of credible evidence for the debauchery and crimes of which he was accused,[48] is partially explained by the previous conflation of film stardom with immorality, crime, and scandalous notoriety, a conflation in which the industry itself had inadvertently participated and in which Smith Hamon played a determining role.

The fact that Clara Smith Hamon posed such a threat to the corporate integrity of the film industry came not only because she was able to successfully produce a film version of her life story, but also because she was different in one respect from the other notorious individuals rumored to be considering film careers in 1921—she had shot and killed her employer. Her specific claim to violence made her especially vulnerable to those reactionary and conservative discourses that sought to preserve a state monopoly on the legitimate use of violence. Even though she had been found "not guilty" of murder, the rationale of Smith Hamon's defense was that the shooting had been entirely justified. The specific statute that allowed for Smith Hamon's acquittal defined "justifiable homicide" as an act of self-defense committed when "resisting an attempt to murder a person or commit any felony upon such person."[49] Yet the larger ideological justification for killing Jake Hamon was the widely shared belief that he had finally got what was coming to him. For many in the courtroom and, undoubtedly, for many newspaper journalists and readers around the country, Clara Smith Hamon was warranted in killing Jake Hamon not only because of the immediate threat he had to posed to her in their adjoining rooms at the Randol Hotel on the night of the shooting but also because of the abuse and exploitation to which he had subjected her to for nearly a decade.

The New Republic felt obliged to refigure and reduce this popular reception of the Smith Hamon case to a quaint and amusing regional moralism. Under the heading, "How God Works in Oklahoma," one of the lawyers for Smith Hamon's defense was quoted as saying, "There was never a bible in Jake Hamon's room, because he died as he lived, cursing, swearing, and in debauchery. . . . My contention is that God Almighty took a hand in the affair. When a man deserts his wife, a boy and girl, as that man did, he ought to be killed."[50] By switching the popular justification for the murder from Jake Hamon's abuse of his personal secretary to his moral transgressions against God and family, *The New Republic* was attempting to stall and to contain a public's interest in a compelling female heroine who had successfully used deadly force (whether liberatory, vengeful, or defensive) against her imminent oppressor. Smith Hamon's popular appeal, and therefore the threat that she posed to corporate authority, is more adequately understood in terms of the possibilities that her celebrity posed for mass cultural representations of justifiable violence outside state control. As Walter Benjamin observes: "Violence, when not in the hands of the law, threatens it not by the ends that it may pursue but by its mere existence outside the law. The same may be more drastically suggested if one reflects how often the figure of the 'great' criminal, however repellent his ends may have been, has aroused the secret admiration of the public. This cannot result from the deed, but only from the violence to which it bears witness. In this case, therefore, the violence of which present-day law is seeking in all areas to deprive the individual appears really threatening, and arouses even in defeat the sympathy of the mass against the law. By what function violence can with reason seem so threatening to law, and be so feared by it, must especially be evident where its application, even in the present legal system, is still permissible."[51]

Benjamin turns to the labor strike as an example of still-permissible violence outside the law. Yet, the popular understanding of Smith Hamon's acquittal as it was articulated in the newspapers provides us with a more spontaneous but no less effective instance of law-threatening violence, since her acquittal was generally seen as a moral and political vindication of a violent act taken against a man whose power resided in the patriarchal underpinnings of corporate state power. Allowing Smith Hamon to tell her own story on the screen would presumably only further indulge a popular interest in versions of social justice that were *popularly defined*.

By looking only at the trade journals, one would think that *Fate* was the unlikely realization of a few misguided individuals who sought quick riches by infiltrating the industry with a sensationalized story of adultery and murder. Industry representatives continually characterized the film and its potential audiences as entirely aberrant. But how did media representations of Smith Hamon change so quickly? Before her acquittal she was depicted as a tragically brave heroine who resisted the excesses and abuses of male privilege by standing up to a tyrant. When she announced her intention to make a film about her life, she immediately became a vulgar opportunist scandalously turning herself and her past into a spectacle for a prurient crowd of gossipers and degenerates whose spectatorship could only be defined as morbid. The day before the Smith Hamon case went to the jury, the judge revealed to reporters that he had received letters daily from individuals throughout the country asking to "substitute for Clara" in serving out her sentence. One woman reportedly requested: "If she is sentenced to be electrocuted let me take her place in the chair."[52] Such pleas were not yet offered as evidence of a pathological fandom for Clara Smith Hamon, but served only as the visible evidence for a popular sympathy extended to a young woman's suffering. Yet the film industry almost immediately mobilized the language of popular consent—"unilaterally opposed," "clearly voiced opinion of the country," "justified reception"—to support its campaign against the motion picture that promised to bring Smith Hamon and her life story to the masses.[53] This transformation of Smith Hamon and her public was not as easy as it appears, despite the near obliteration of *Fate* from film historical memory. Smith Hamon remained a contested figure throughout and after the production of *Fate*. In order to get a glimpse of the sustained political struggles that surrounded her and the making of the film, we need to look to the more fragmentary evidence of the local and regional debates on the *Fate*'s censorship.

During the trial of Clara Smith Hamon, people stood in line for hours at the county courthouse in hopes of getting a seat inside. As a way of advertising the latest model, a local Cadillac dealer loaned new automobiles to visiting journalists and other important out-of-town visitors so that the streets of Ardmore "were jammed and crowded with them."[54] However, less than three weeks after Smith Hamon's acquittal, the mayor and the board of city commissioners sought to stifle publicity about the case by passing a municipal ordinance forbidding the screening within city limits of any "motion picture film which directly or indirectly portrays or simulates the life or any person or purported person who has lived a life of violence, crime, or immorality or which *directly calls to the mind of the public* or *any immediate audience* such life of any such individual or purported individuals, and this to apply although such motion pictures or exhibits are innocent in themselves if the ultimate effect thereof is to *recall acts or lives of lawlessness or immorality* of any such person or purported person."[55] Given the interest expressed in the ordinance in regulating not only the content of films but the responses of film audiences to particular personalities, it is apparent that its drafters were responding to and taking up the film industry's stated concerns about the deleterious social effects of Smith Hamon's appearance in motion pictures. However, this municipal ordinance became law in Ardmore only after the mayor cast a deciding vote to break a deadlock on the board of commissioners.

The local Ardmore newspaper reported that a group of "eight representative women" had attended the board meeting to protest the showing of any Clara Smith Hamon pictures in the city. One of the women complained that municipal intervention in the situation was long overdue since the whole Hamon affair had been the responsibility of all of Ardmore's citizens who "knew of the conditions which existed [between Jake Hamon and his secretary]—the mayor, the chief of police, everybody." The mayor responded by informing these women that an ordinance to ban the screening of all films featuring immoral persons had already been prepared and was available for the board's vote. After the ordinance was read aloud, one city commissioner stated that, while he would have favored such a prohibition a year ago and while he might now favor the establishment of a board of municipal film censors, he could not support the proposed legislation in its present form "when effort is being made to place the burden on the shoulders of one poor, sinful girl."[56] This particular commissioner felt that such a law was hypocritical since it was obviously motivated by an unjustifiable desire to punish Smith Hamon. The mayor addressed these concerns by pointing out that Ardmore was a center of world attention because of the Hamon case, and he recommended putting an end to this publicity through a definite course of action, just as several women present at the meeting had demanded. According to the local paper, the mayor also sought to counter popular representations of Smith Hamon's film career as an evangelical mission by "attempting to show that the Lord never desired a sinner to go out into the world in an effort to reform others."[57]

During the proceedings, an attorney from the law firm that had defended Smith Hamon addressed the city board and presented them with a copy of her motion picture contract. Over objections raised by "the women's committee," the mayor permitted S. A. George to read specific items from the contract, one of which stated that no scenes of an immoral character were to be depicted in her films, and another that guaranteed that the production would employ only "clean and competent" film personnel. George, who also revealed that he was a stockholder in the company set up to make Smith Hamon films, cautioned that a ban on the exhibition of such films would only play into the hands of the major Hollywood concerns. According to George, Smith Hamon created an independent film production company of her own because the majors would not honor her request to turn over 20 percent of all her films' profits to "a fund administered by a board for the purpose of aiding and assisting unfortunate girls."[58] George was concerned that the passage of the ordinance would inhibit the sale of stock in the new company.

Whether anyone actually believed that a major studio had offered Smith Hamon a contract or that she intended to fund a charitable organization for young women, George's argument against the passage of the ordinance astutely posed Smith Hamon's celebrity in terms of her troubled relation to the social order as an independent working-class woman, a woman who now sought to help "unfortunate girls" like herself. The idea that a "poor, sinful girl" could become a movie star disrupted the easy maintenance of middle-class social ideologies. The idea of a small company taking on the Hollywood corporate oligopoly could be viewed as a noble economic venture, and this, of course, is precisely what George hoped to accomplish. Yet, the driving force behind this particular small company was a woman whose previous success in business matters was too easily connected to prevalent cultural representations of feminine betrayal and violent revolt. Any company promoting Smith Hamon and her life story was endorsing, thereby, not the free-market "return to normalcy" that president Harding had promised America, but rather the perversions of success and social mobility that Smith Hamon's life and her popularity represented. These same financial perversions would soon play a central role in the reform discourses that scrutinized the purported large salaries and lavish lifestyles of more traditional Hollywood film stars. As for Smith Hamon's desire to participate in Progressive-era charitability, any fund or organization made possible by her post-trial success could not properly reproduce those relations of economic dependency and matronly social concern valued by the genteel middle class, who would continue to patronize both the native born and immigrant working poor well into the 1930s. Instead of social uplift, Smith Hamon's popular success as a film personality promised to enact a form of cultural insubordination that must have been quite unsettling to social conservatives in the immediate aftermath of the 1919 Red Scare.[59] The ordinance designed to keep Smith Hamon off the movie screens in Ardmore became law by only a single vote.

Clara Smith Hamon finally got her jury of twelve women after *Fate* opened in San Francisco on September 3, 1921. The film's official producer, W. B. Weathers, was arrested on charges of indecency during a screening of the picture at the College Theater where law officials from the district attorney's office halted the sale of tickets at the box office and interrupted the second afternoon screening to confiscate the film from the projection booth.[60] Weathers was released on $250 bail, and when the case was tried in police court two weeks later, Weathers's attorney requested a jury trial and asked that all eight reels of *Fate* be screened in the courtroom so that the jury might judge for themselves whether or not the film was "adapted to excite vicious and lewd thoughts and acts." The jury of twelve "married women" who viewed the film found the defendant "not guilty."[61] *Fate* would meet its final end not in San Francisco, but in the state of New York where the newly formed New York State Motion Picture Commission (NYSMPC) rejected the film in its entirety, issuing it a "Certificate of Disapproval" on October 14, 1921. *Fate* was only the second feature film to be condemned in toto by the commission, and Weathers immediately exercised his right to appeal the commission's decision by asking for an immediate reexamination of the film with all three members of the NYSMPC present.[62] When the commission responded that the previous decision had been unanimous, Weathers hired a New York law firm to pursue the matter of a reconsideration of the film by the NYSMPC.[63] Weathers's lawyer initially attempted to sway the commission by offering to remove from *Fate* "the only features which might be considered in any way objectionable," specifically, a scene portraying Clara Smith's marriage to Jake Hamon's nephew and the jubilant applause that follows the courtroom announcement of Smith Hamon's acquittal.[64] While the film's promoters and stockholders waited for a license to book the Clara Smith Hamon story in New York's theaters, *Fate* was playing to small-town audiences in Oklahoma.

The first showing of *Fate* in Oklahoma was given in Bristow on November 6, 1921, at the Empress Theater where, according to the local newspaper, "in spite of the fact that the exhibitors over the United States turned thumbs down on the picture, the public has taken a different attitude, if the business done by the Empress during the two-day engagement is any foundation upon which public opinion or interest may be based."[65] Because of continued interest in the picture, *Fate* returned to the Empress on November 16, after which it traveled to the Liberty Theater in Marietta, Oklahoma, for a two-day run, and then on to the Rialto in Wilson.[66] The local press in Bristow claimed that the main exhibitor's organization for Oklahoma was in the process of reversing its previous ban on *Fate*, noting that "the man who drew the resolution condemning Clara's life story telephoned the local representative three times asking for a booking of the film."[67] Contrarily, the national trade publications were reporting that the president of the Theater Owners' and Managers' Association of Oklahoma had requested the state's attorney general to halt all screenings of the film in the wake of *Fate*'s successful Bristow premiere.[68] The historical record of *Fate*'s reception is structured throughout by such disparities. A struggle over the meanings of "popular" and "public interest" is evident in the contradictions between national and local accounts of *Fate*, between institutional and noninstitutional responses to the film and between the corporate and entrepreneurial representations of Smith Hamon's celebrity as a business enterprise. Using the ordinance passed in April, the Ardmore city commissioners officially banned *Fate* on November 24 as inimical to "the welfare of Ardmore," though many city residents had already traveled to see the picture in Marietta and Wilson.[69]

Back in New York, Weathers's lawyer sent the NYSMPC numerous letters from high school teachers, clergymen, and prominent social reformers who had viewed the film at a private screening in October and who found it to be not only unobjectionable but also a profound lesson in temperance with a strong warning to girls and young women about the trap of easy romances with older men. When the NYSMPC still refused to grant the film a license, Weathers and his lawyer received permission to have the commission's decision regarding *Fate* reviewed by the New York State Supreme Court, which in late 1922 finally upheld the commission's original decision. *Fate* had been only the second feature film rejected by the NYSMPC after it began its work in August 1921.

The passage of censorship legislation in New York had been an alarming

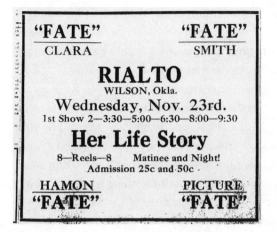

Advertisement from the *Daily Ardmoreite*, November 22, 1921. While *Fate* was banned from the screen in Ardmore, Oklahoma, newspaper advertisements for its upcoming engagements at theaters in neighboring towns were not.

event for the film industry, and the trade journals scrutinized and criticized the commission unceasingly. But while, for example, the trade journals made much of the commission's deletion of a bathing-beauty scene from a Pathé newsreel, they said nothing about its rejection of *Fate* and they gave scant coverage to the protracted legal challenge to the NYSMPC mounted by *Fate*'s producer. In the end, the ban on screenings of *Fate* worked to the benefit of both the film industry and the NYSMPC. The commission had found in *Fate* a film upon which they could demonstrate, with the full blessing of the industry, their unflinching commitment to cleaner pictures. And the ban significantly aided the film industry in regaining regulative control over film personalities.

The NYSMPC contended that its rejection of *Fate* was based solely on the fact that the picture would "corrupt morals and incite crime," while Weathers's attorney argued that the commission's decision was arbitrary and unlawful because it was, at least in part, motivated by a consideration of the lead performer's moral character and was, therefore, in violation of previous court decisions requiring the exclusion of a performer's private life when determining the moral suitability of motion pictures or plays.[70] The commission denied that its action was based on anything other than the film text itself, thereby disavowing the obvious relation between the film's story and the private life of the lead actress, as well as contradicting earlier public statements by members of the NYSMPC.[71] Interestingly, while Pathé was pursuing a case against the NYSMPC for censoring a newsreel, the commission was fighting against any possible understanding of *Fate* as a form of reportage about the Hamon case.

When the New York State deputy attorney general A. E. Rose argued the case on behalf of the NYSMPC before the state supreme court, he referred to the very same model of static spectatorship that NAMPI president Brady had earlier used to distinguish genuine stars from notorious celebrities. According to Rose, the commission's decision to refuse the film an exhibition license was justified since *Fate* "contains nothing new or of wholesome interest to the public. . . . It depicts the same old, old story known to all and read in the newspapers almost daily with its usual consequential result."[72] What was unacceptable about *Fate* to both the film industry and the NYSMPC was its claim to represent the world from the unauthorized position of its main attraction.[73] Just how unauthorized *Fate*'s representation of the world was is revealed succinctly in one of the letters sent to the commission by Weathers's lawyer in support of the film. Elizabeth Grannis, president of the National Christian League, asked the commission to defer to "the woman's voice to speak as to the moral effect which this picture will exert on the mind of the woman who views its portrayals." Grannis praised the film made by Smith Hamon, writing:

> One of the most impressive scenes in the picture is that of leading politicians being entertained by the wealthy seducer who had acquired genuine leadership, if not real statesmanship, even while extending his debauching hospitality to his political guests.
>
> Are our Church leaders remembering the wealthy capitalists in public or private prayers to God in this present day? Are not the souls of heads of family known for advantages of education, blood, and money quite as valuable for eternal and human salvation as the street walking girl, or poor dependent factory girls?[74]

While undoubtedly the three members who sat on the commission would have been made uncomfortable by such sentiments—a former Republican lieutenant governor, a state committeewoman for the Republican Party, and a Republican ward supervisor from New York City—what was ultimately scandalous about *Fate* was that it represented a type of counterdiscourse to the disciplinary moralism and uplift of the genteel middle class. At long last, it was a hardware store clerk's turn to moralize about the abuses and sexism of the wealthy and powerful; at long last, a secretary had become a producer.

NOTES

This project was supported in part by a grant from the Susan B. Anthony Institute for Gender and Women's Studies at the University of Rochester. I presented a shorter version of this essay as part of the panel "A Woman's Business: Manufacturing the Female Star in the 1920s," at the conference of the Society for Cinema Studies, Chicago, March 9–12, 2000. I am grateful to Lynn Arner for her always insightful suggestions and good advice. My research was also aided by the independent film archivist Chistel Schmidt; by Connie S. Green at the Montfort and Alice B. Jones Public Library in Bristow, Oklahoma; by Delbert Amen at the Oklahoma Historical Society in Oklahoma City; and by Mary Ann Clark at the New York State Appellate Court Law Library, Rochester, New York.

1 B. A. Bridgewater, "One Picture for the Films and then the Home Life with Perhaps a Mate—Clara," *Tulsa Daily World*, March 18, 1921, 1.

2 "Fight Films Showing Clara Smith Hamon," *New York Times*, March 25, 1921, 12; "Bumpy Road Awaiting Clara Hamon in Movies," *Moving Picture World*, April 9, 1921, 573; "Clara Hamon for Films," *New York Clipper*, March 23, 1921, 5; and "Clara Hamon Signs L. A. Film Contract," *San Francisco Examiner*, March 22, 1921, 11.

3 Several witnesses testified some three years after Hamon's death that the oil tycoon had purchased his position as national Republican committeeman for Oklahoma at the party's convention in June 1920, and that he subsequently spent hundreds of thousands of dollars to control the newspapers in Oklahoma during the presidential election. Most disturbing to some members of the Senate committee investigating oil industry graft in the Harding administration was the fact that a number of witnesses testified that Hamon had offered his money and his regional influence to any Republican presidential candidate who could promise him the post of secretary of the interior. Of course, Hamon died several weeks before Harding's inauguration and the announcement of his cabinet. See the testimony of Al Jennings, J. E. Dyche, J. B. French, Julius F. Baughn, William H. Miller, Edward J. Costello, Jack Smith, H. W. Ballard, J. C. Clopton, and W. B. Nichols, U.S. Congress, Senate, *Leases Upon Naval Oil Reserves: Hearings Before the Committee on Public Lands and Surveys*, 67th Cong., 2d sess., and 68th Cong., 1st sess., October 22, 1923–May 14, 1924, vol. 3. See also "Oil Men Offered Wood Backing in 1920," *New York Times*, March 8, 1924, 1; and "Says Hamon Fought to Be Interior Chief," *New York Times*, March 15, 1924, 4. Reports at the time of the shooting claimed that president-elect Harding, who was then visiting Panama, inquired into Jake Hamon's condition by telegraph ["Hamon's

Friends Bitter at Accused Slayer," *Tulsa Daily World*, November 27, 1920, 1, 13]. David H. Stratton maintains that Albert Fall wished to leave politics and that he only reluctantly accepted the nomination to secretary of interior. Stratton quotes a letter, though, that Fall wrote to his wife soon after deciding to accept the cabinet post: "I am now trying to look upon the bright side and see the compensations which may offer themselves in that position." Given Fall's long-standing commitment to deregulation and private oil development, those compensations could only include his ability to influence federal policy on resource conservation. See David H. Stratton *Tempest over Teapot Dome: The Story of Albert B. Fall* (Norman: University of Oklahoma Press, 1998), 197.

4 "Jake Hamon: Not a Resident of Oklahoma, So He Swears," political circular, 1920; and "Who Jake L. Hamon, Prominent in Gore's Bribery Charge, Is," unidentified newspaper clipping from Guthrie, Okla., August 10, 1910, Jake Hamon File, Oklahoma Historical Society, Oklahoma City. See also the entry for Hamon in *Men of Affairs and Representative Institutions in Oklahoma* (Tulsa: World Publishing Company, 1916), 187.

5 "Hamon Women to Match Wits at Trial," *San Francisco Examiner*, March 7, 1921, 7.

6 Gilbert L. Robinson, "Transportation in Carter County, 1913–1917," *Chronicles of Oklahoma* 19, no. 4 (December 1941): 368–76. After World War I, Hamon also extended his railroad concerns into Texas. See Ken Swift and and Marg Gordon, "Jake Hamon Railroad," unidentified article in Jake Hamon file, Southwest Collection, Texas Tech University, Lubbock, Texas.

7 "Charge Woman 'Guest' Shot Hamon," *Tulsa Daily World*, November 23, 1920, 1, 12; "Hamon's Pretty Secretary, Charged with Shooting Him, His Protege for Ten Years," *Tulsa Daily World*, November 24, 1920, 1; "Hunt for Woman When Hamon Dies," *New York Times*, November 27, 1920, 6; and "Will Charge Woman with Hamon Murder," *New York Times*, December 1, 1920, 11.

8 Smith Hamon was not formally charged with murder until December 8, when the prospects for her capture and return to Ardmore had increased. "Clara Smith Now Accused of Murder," *New York Times*, December 9, 1920, 6. The adultery charges were eventually dropped against Smith Hamon after she was acquitted of the murder in March 1921.

9 "Says Clara Smith Confesses Killing Hamon; Will Surrender If She Can Be Tried by Women," *New York Times*, December 7, 1920, 1; and "I Shot Hamon, Ex-Secretary Tells Writer," *San Francisco Examiner*, December 7, 1920, 1, 6. Other reports claimed that the San Antonio reporter Penny A. Ross had previously been acquainted with Smith Hamon and recognized her when he encountered her repairing an automobile by the side of the road. See "Locate Clara Smith in Mexican Town," *New York Times*, December 8, 1920, 19; and "Clara Smith Is Found by Newspaper Man," *Tulsa Daily World*, December 7, 1920, 1.

10 "Clippings and Notes Reveal Clara Smith's Life Tragedy," *Tulsa Daily World*,

December 3, 1920, 1; and "Say Clara Smith Is Now in Mexico," *New York Times*, December 3, 1920, 10. Frank L. Hamon and Clara Barton Smith were married on February 17, 1917, in El Paso, Texas. Frank L. Hamon was then granted an unchallenged divorce from his wife on May 23, 1917, in Weatherford, Texas. Copies of their marriage license and the divorce decree can be found in the Jake L. Hamon file, Oklahoma Historical Society, Oklahoma City.

11 "Clara Smith's Dramatic Revelations Continued," *Tulsa Daily World*, December 5, 1920, 1, 9; and "Hamon Girl Depicts 'Crucifixion,'" *San Francisco Examiner*, December 5, 1920, 8.

12 "Why She Killed Hamon!" *Tulsa Daily World*, December 4, 1920, 1; "Diary Bares Heartaches of Clara Hamon," *San Francisco Examiner*, December 4, 1920, 8.

13 Clara Smith could easily have been either a year or two younger (or a year or two older) since her actual age varied from story to story. Early reports suggested she was born in 1893 or 1894, but during the trial and in her statements afterward Smith Hamon maintained she was born in October 1891, thus placing her at the age of consent by the time she met Hamon. Her California death certificate gives her date of birth as October 22, 1891. When Clara Smith Hamon died from a stroke in San Diego on December 30, 1962, she was survived by her husband of thirty years, Charles H. Diggs.

14 See, for example, "Hamon's Pretty Secretary," *Tulsa Daily World*, November 24, 1920, 1; and "Hamon's Friends Bitter," *Tulsa Daily World*, November 27, 1920, 1, 13.

15 "Hamon's Pretty Secretary," *Tulsa Daily World*, November 24, 1924, 1. Some reports maintained that the nephew was paid one hundred dollars by Jake Hamon for marrying Clara Smith. See "'Clara Wronged' Says Her Father," *Tulsa Daily World*, December 10, 1920, 1, 14.

16 "Asks Federal Writ in Hamon Case," *New York Times*, December 6, 1920, 6. In a fashion typical of the news coverage of Smith Hamon's life, this article is immediately followed by a "Special to *The New York Times*" which quotes a private investigator employed by Smith Hamon in the late 1910s to gather information about Jake Hamon's philandering when she was not accompanying him. The investigator reported that his detective agency "procured for Clara Smith Hamon what would be considered absolute divorce evidence in any State in the Union."

17 For summaries of Smith Hamon's testimony, see "Clara Wanted to Die after Shooting Jake," *Tulsa Daily World*, March 16, 1921, 1, 8; and "Girl Denies Intent to Kill Jake Hamon," *New York Times*, March 16, 1921, 3.

18 In her revelations to Sam Blair, the syndicated newspaper correspondent who extensively interviewed Smith Hamon in Chihuahua, Mexico, she claimed to have been crucially involved in Jake Hamon's many successes: "Every dollar he had, every political influence he had, I helped him achieve." See Sam Blair, "Clara Hamon Bares Tragic Romance," *San Francisco Examiner*, December 21, 1920, 4.

19 See Frank Ketch's testimony reported in "Hamon's Widow Testifies at Trial,"
    New York Times, March 15, 1921, 6.

20 "State to Help Try Clara Smith Hamon," *New York Times*, December 24,
    1920, 5.

21 "Clara Hamon Waives Right to Argument," *San Francisco Examiner*, March 17,
    1921, 1–2.

22 "Clara Hamon Freed by Murder Jury," *New York Times*, March 18, 1921, 1, 2.
    Sam Blair compared the courtroom applause for the verdict to "the firing of a
    pack of firecrackers." See "Clara Hamon Is Acquitted of Slaying," *San Francisco
    Examiner*, March 18, 1921, 1, 2.

23 For a brief history of this film's production and censorship, see Kevin Brown-
    low, *Behind the Mask of Innocence: The Social Problem Films of the Silent Era*
    (New York: Knopf, 1990), 153–55. To my knowledge Brownlow is the only film
    historian to have discussed this film in any detail, though his account is full
    of factual inaccuracies—in part because it relies too heavily on information
    taken from *Variety*. For example, Brownlow misreads an item that appeared
    in *Variety* in order to claim that *Fate* was screened in Ardmore, Oklahoma
    ("With Clara Hamon," *Variety* [2 September 1921], 61) an event that, from all
    my research, never occurred since the film had been effectively banned by mu-
    nicipal ordinance in that town since April. Brownlow also incorrectly describes
    Clara Smith Hamon as "shoot[ing] her husband," Jake Hamon, an "unpalat-
    able fact" that, Brownlow says, "caused her so much difficulty when she came
    to make the picture." Clara Smith Hamon did not kill her husband; she killed
    her boss.

24 While the manager of the Jake L. Hamon estate had testified at the trial that
    Clara Smith Hamon owned part of a motion picture concern, he also settled
    her claim on the estate in early May 1921, paying her $10,000 just as *Fate* was
    going into production. See "Clara Hamon Gets Oil Lands," *San Francisco Ex-
    aminer*, May 13, 1921, 5.

25 "Marries Her Director," *Variety*, August 26, 1921, 39. This article reports on
    Smith Hamon's marriage to her director, John Gorman, the most widely re-
    ported incident of *Fate's* production during summer 1921. Smith Hamon di-
    vorced Gorman in 1924, charging him with "cruelty and intoxication." "Clara
    Hamon Seeks Divorce from Mate," *San Francisco Chronicle*, September 3,
    1924, 1. Arbuckle was officially charged only with murder since, according to
    California law at the time, a rape that resulted in death would be subsumed
    under a murder charge but would not constitute separate felony offense. See
    David Y. Yallop, *The Day the Laughter Stopped: The True Story of Fatty Arbuckle*
    (New York: St. Martin's Press, 1976).

26 Brownlow, *Behind the Mask of Innocence*, 154.

27 "California Movie Houses Bar Clara Smith Hamon Films," *New York Times*,
    March 24, 1922, 19. The statement was issued by the Allied Amusement Indus-
    tries of California. For other industry-aligned, state and local motion picture

organizations that made formal statements against Smith Hamon's screen appearance, see "Screen Interests Protest Clara Hamon in Films," *Motion Picture News*, April 9, 1921, 2442; "Bumpy Road Awaiting Clara Hamon in Movies" and "Oppose Undesirable Films," *Moving Picture World*, April 9, 1921, 573 and 574, respectively.

28 "New York Exhibitors Ban Clara Hamon Picture," *Variety*, April 1, 1921, 46.

29 "Fight Films Showing Clara Smith Hamon," *New York Times*, March 25, 1921, 12.

30 "Homespun Hearts," *New York Times*, March 21, 1921, 12. The melodramatic possibilities of the Clara Smith Hamon story are demonstrated by the inclusion of the case in Ione Quinby's true crime collection, *Murder for Love* (New York: Covici Freide Publishers, 1931), 51–89. Quinby's recounting of the case makes for entertaining reading but it is also full of factual errors, not the least of which is her claim that a motion picture starring Smith Hamon "was never produced." That *Fate* could have been so thoroughly suppressed as to be undetectable to a researcher ten years later testifies to the danger that the film posed to the film industry and to the interests of state power. It is more than likely that Clara Smith Hamon influenced the depiction of Lorelei in Anita Loos's popular novel *Gentlemen Prefer Blondes*. In a chapter titled "Fate Keeps on Happening," Lorelei recounts in her diary how she had attended a business college in Little Rock, Arkansas, until a lawyer named Jennings desired her to be his personal stenographer and removed her from school. After a year in his employ, Lorelei eventually discovered that Jennings "was not the kind of a gentleman a young girl is safe with," and she eventually shoots him with a revolver during an argument, the precise details of which she cannot remember. At her trial, everyone was "lovely" to her except the district attorney, and the jury took out only three minutes to pronounce her "not guilty." Lorelei confides to her diary: "I mean it was when Mr. Jennings became shot that I got the idea to go to Hollywood, so Judge Hibbard got me a ticket to Hollywood." Loos's portrayal of Lorelei as a dizzy gold-digger is often vehemently classist and misogynist, with much of the novel's humor produced by Lorelei's shallow pretensions to cultural sophistication. Given Loos's position within the Hollywood corporate structure, her particular satirical approach to the Clara Smith Hamon story is hardly surprising. Anita Loos, *Gentlemen Prefer Blondes* (New York: Boni and Livewright, 1925), 47–49.

31 Smith Hamon's desire to lecture at churches about her life is discussed in several recaps of the trial, as in "Verdict Found in 39 Minutes of Conferring," *Daily Oklahoman*, March 18, 1921, 1, 2. Clara Smith and her sister, Mrs. G. J. James, were baptized in an Ardmore church two days after the acquittal. See "Clara Hamon Joins Church," *Washington Post*, March 21, 1921, 1.

32 The New York State governor Nathan L. Miller had just signed legislation establishing a motion picture censorship commission in his state, an event that was considered a major setback for the industry's anticensorship efforts. See

statements by Gabrielle L. Hess, chairman of the censorship committee of NAMPI, in "Courts Will Pass on Constitutionality of New York Censorship Law, Say Hess," *Moving Picture World*, May 28, 1921, 379.

33 Richard deCordova, *Picture Personalities: The Emergence of the Star System in America* (Urbana: University of Illinois Press, 1990).

34 *Moving Picture World*, April 9, 1921, 573. *Fate*'s producers hardly claimed otherwise; in a public appeal for investors in the film, they claimed that no one had ever "entered motion pictures with an income assured and insured as is Clara Smith Hamon" (*Variety*, April 29, 1921, 46).

35 "Frame-Up Charged by Mrs. Stillman; Letters Revealed," *New York Times*, May 7, 1921, 1, 3.

36 "Mrs. Leeds, Named in Stillman Suit, Century Show Girl," *New York Times*, March 18, 1921, 1, 3.

37 "Rule on Beauvais Film," *New York Times*, December 31, 1921, 5 (my emphasis).

38 For an important examination of how film representations of "immoral" women became acceptable through the transformations of American society and culture during the first decades of the twentieth century, see Janet Staiger, *Bad Women: Regulating Sexuality in Early American Cinema* (Minneapolis: University of Minnesota Press, 1995).

39 "Inside Stuff," *Variety*, June 3, 1921, 44.

40 Sam Blair, "Clara Hamon Waives Right to Argument," *San Francisco Examiner*, March 17, 1921, 1, 2.

41 "Defense Ends Case; Brown Flays Clara," *Tulsa Daily World*, March 17, 1921, 1, 6, 13. See also "Waives Argument for Clara Hamon," *New York Times*, March 17, 1921, 17.

42 Lee Grieveson, "The Thaw-White Scandal, *The Unwritten Law*, and the Scandal of Cinema," in *Headline Hollywood: A Century of Film Scandal*, ed. Adrienne L. McClean and David Cook (New Brunswick, N.J.: Rutgers University Press, 2001), 27–51.

43 For a brief discussion of the social regulation of the fallen woman story in its various literary, theatrical, and film versions in the 1910s and early 1920s, see chapter 1 of Lea Jacobs, *The Wages of Sin: Censorship and the Fallen Woman Film, 1928–1942* (Berkeley: University of California Press, 1995), especially 9–12.

44 Reportedly, NAMPI met in New York in late May 1921 to discuss the possibility of a screen career for Mrs. Stillman, who was rumored to have been offered $100,000 for a year's film contract. See "Mrs. Stillman Bars Exile, Case to Go On," *New York Times*, May 21, 1921, 1. Underneath this story is a report that Fred Beauvais turned down a movie offer of $25,000. The next day, NAMPI president William Brady assured reporters that no member of his organization had made Mrs. Stillman any such an offer. "Stillmans Prepare to Resume Hearings," *New York Times*, May 22, 1921, 1. Flo Leeds and Peggy Hopkins-

Joyce are mentioned as potential film stars in "Notorious Stars as Stock Sale Lure," *Variety*, July 8, 1921, 30. For an example typical of the coverage of the Hopkins-Joyce divorce, see "Assails Joyce as Stage-Door Johnnie," *New York Times*, June 10, 1921, 1.

45 "Capitalizing Indecency," *Daily News* (New York), June 22, 1921, 9.

46 "Brady Demands an Apology for Stigma on Industry," *Motion Picture News*, July 9, 1921, 327.

47 Marshall Neilan, "New Pointers on Pictures from the Trade Schools," *Variety*, July 8, 1921, 30. On Barlatier's dismissal from the ASC, see "Cameraman Disciplined," *Variety*, June 24, 1921, 38.

48 See Sam Stoloff, "Fatty Arbuckle and the Black Sox: The Paranoid Style of American Popular Culture, 1919–1922," in McClean and Cook, eds., *Headline Hollywood*, 52–82.

49 See the judge's instructions to the jury in Blair, "Clara Waives Right to Argument," 2.

50 "How God Works in Oklahoma," *New Republic* 26, no. 330 (March 30, 1921): 159.

51 Walter Benjamin, "The Critique of Violence," in *Reflections*, ed. Peter Demetz; trans. Edmund Jephcott (New York: Harcourt Brace Jovanovich, 1978), 281.

52 "Hundreds Eager to Pay Penalty for Clara," *Tulsa Daily World*, March 17, 1921, 1.

53 "Unilaterally opposed" was used by Brady to describe NAMPI's position on the film. "The clearly voiced opinion of the country" and "justified reception" are phrases used by the *Photoplay* editor James Quirk for the alleged failure of *Fate* to secure an audience at the end of 1921. Of course, with a virtual moratorium imposed on *Fate* by the industry for any and all exhibitors, this failure was anything but the popular expression of the filmgoing public. See Quirk's editorial column "Close-Ups" in *Photoplay*, November 1921, 64, and February 1922, 39.

54 This information is taken from oral histories about the Clara Smith Hamon trial gathered by Robert L. Atkins in 1964 (Jake Hamon file, Oklahoma Historical Society, Oklahoma City).

55 Ardmore Municipal Code, Ordinance 464, approved April 1, 1921 (my emphasis).

56 "By Special Ordinance Ardmore Bans Immoral, Criminal and Indecent Moving Pictures: Board of Censors Created," *Daily Ardmoreite* (Oklahoma), April 3, 1921, 1, 2.

57 Ibid., 2.

58 Ibid.

59 See Robert K. Murray, *Red Scare: A Study in National Hysteria, 1919–1920* (New York: McGraw-Hill, 1964). Interestingly, Brownlow, *Behind the Mask of Innocence*, 153, characterizes the intensity of the purported widespread condemnation of *Fate* by claiming that such anger would be more historically understandable if directed at "an apologia for Bolshevism." Of course, my point

is that *Fate*'s relation to Bolshevism is not as farfetched as Brownlow assumes, since the film in both its story and its production history was thoroughly involved in the immediate class antagonisms of the era.

60 "Clara Hamon Film Stopped," *San Francisco Examiner*, September 4, 1921, 4. It is unclear if this screening was the film's national premiere since some newspaper accounts suggest that *Fate* may have been screened at the Garrick Theater in Los Angeles prior to its September 3 opening at the College Theater in San Francisco. See "Clara Hamon Film in S. F. Protested in Notes to the Police," *San Francisco Examiner*, September 2, 1921, 4. Despite this ambiguity about screening dates, *Fate* was undoubtedly booked into both of these venues and was prevented from being screened at both by the enforcement of municipal ordinances forbidding the display of indecent motion pictures. Neither theater was affiliated with a major exhibitor's organization. *Fate*'s exhibition (or planned exhibition) in Los Angeles apparently led to the drafting of an ordinance to create a censorship board in that city. See "Los Angeles Business Men Uniting in Determined Fight against Censorship," *Moving Picture World*, October 22, 1921, 887–88.

61 "Theater Hearing for Promoter of 'Fate' is Urged," *San Francisco Chronicle*, September 8, 1921, sec. 2, 1. An abridged transcript of the proceedings of Weathers's San Francisco police court trial is included in the papers of the New York appellate court's review of the commission's decision to refuse *Fate* a permit. See petitioner's Exhibit A at 88, "In the Matter of the Petition of William E. Weathers, Petitioner, for a Order of Certiorari to Review a Final Determination of George H. Cobb and Others, as and Constituting the Motion Picture Commission of the State of New York, Respondents," 203 A.D. 896, 197 N.Y.S. 956 (A.D., 1922).

62 The first feature film rejected in its entirety by NYSMPC was the underworld crime drama *The Night Rose* (Goldwyn Pictures 1921) starring Lon Chaney. It was rejected by the commission on September 17, 1921, and Goldwyn appealed for a review of the decision in state court. While the court upheld the original ban on November 18, 1921, Goldwyn quickly worked out a deal with the commission and distributed a revised version of this film in New York in 1922 under the title *Voices of the City*. *Fate* was condemned by the commission on October 14, 1921.

63 Certificate of Disapproval and letter from W. E. Weathers to the Motion Picture Commission of the State of New York, October 12, 1921, Papers of the New York State Motion Picture Division, License application case files, Box 2634, series A1418, New York State Archive, Albany, New York. According to communications sent to the NYSMPC in March 1922, as it prepared a legal response to the appellate division review of their decision, *Fate* had not been submitted to either the Ohio Board of Censorship or the Pennsylvania State Board of Censors.

64 Letter to Joseph Levenson from Samuel Hershenstein, January 5, 1922, Papers

of the New York State Motion Picture Division, License application case files, Box 2634, series A1418, New York State Archive, Albany, New York.

65 "Clara Smith Sans Shank," *Bristow Record* (Oklahoma), November 10, 1921, 3.

66 "Clara Smith Hamon Picture Shows Here," *Marietta Monitor* (Oklahoma), November 25, 1921, 7; "The Clara Smith Picture," *Wilson Gazette* (Oklahoma), December 2, 1921, 2. Because of the successive dates of the Oklahoma screenings, it appears that a single print of the film was traveling in the state. Presumably, only a few prints of *Fate* were ever struck and in circulation, despite *Variety*'s earlier report that the film's promoters estimated "three hundred or more of her first picture to be released simultaneously throughout the United States, as well as a limited number of foreign countries" ("Clara Hamon Film in Raw Stock Deal," *Variety*, April 28, 1921, 46).

67 "Against Hamon Film," *Variety*, November 25, 1921, 44.

68 "Clara Smith Sans Shank," *Bristow Record*, November 10, 1921, 3; "Against Hamon Film," *Variety*, November 25, 1921, 44.

69 "'Fate' Is Barred from Screen in Ardmore Theatre by Order of City Commissioners Today," *Daily Ardmoreite*, November 24, 1921, 1.

70 For example, *Ivan Film Production v. Bell*, 167 N.Y.S., 123–124 (1914). Weathers's lawyer made the argument that the immorality portrayed in the film was no worse than that found in such popularly performed stories as *Madame Butterfly* and *Camille*.

71 For example, one of the trades reported in October 1921 that the NYSMPC member Joseph Levenson claimed to have knowledge of "'benefactors,' who are willing to pay large sums of money to get their 'lady friends' on the screen, but they are not going to be allowed to do it, according to Mr. Levenson, if they cater to what he calls 'the degraded element'" ("Levenson 'Uplifts' Industry with Discourse on 'Lady Friends,'" *Moving Picture World*, October 8, 1921, 648).

72 Respondants' Brief at 2, *Weathers v. Cobb et al.*, 203 A.D. 896, 197 N.Y.S. 956 (A.D., 1922).

73 When the three commissioners of the NYSMPC came up for confirmation before the New York State Senate in January 1922, minority leader James J. Walker attacked the commission as ineffective and wasteful since "censorship has not kept Clara Hamon and Fred Beauvais off the screen." Whether Walker's comments indicate that *Fate* played without a permit in economically marginal venues, or whether he was simply repeating the rumors driving a moral panic, his comments demonstrate that certain legislative positions in the state government understood the powers of censorship and regulation to be necessarily applicable to popular personalities. See the various clippings from New York state newspapers for January 18, 1922, in the papers of the New York State Motion Picture Division, License application case files, Box 2634, series A1418, New York State Archive, Albany, New York. In the NYSMPC's 1923 annual report to the governor, the commissioners specifically requested

the expansion of their powers to include the censoring of films that feature or reference scandalous individuals. While this power was not part of the original 1921 legislation, and while such discretion was never officially granted to the NYSMPC, "the Commission has felt that if the persons involved [in such films] were convicted of a crime or their characters were bad that it would be justified in deciding that the mere exhibition of the film in which they were shown would tend to corrupt morals." See New York Motion Picture Commission, *Annual Report of the Motion Picture Commission for the Year 1923*, Legislative document no. 49 (1924) (Albany, N.Y.: J. B. Lyon Company, 1924), 5.

74 Letter from Elizabeth Grannis to Joseph Levenson, November 2, 1921. Petitioner's request for a writ of certiorari at 74, *Weathers v. Cobb et al.*, 203 A.D. 896, 197 N.Y.S. 956 (A.D., 1922).

THE CRAFTING OF A POLITICAL ICON
Lola Lola on Paper
Andrea Slane

The December 22, 1947, issue of *Paramount News* contains a series of publicity items on the progress of Billy Wilder's *A Foreign Affair*, then in production. One item noted that Marlene Dietrich, one of the film's stars, was rehearsing three songs with the composer Friedrich Holländer, with whom she had worked on the 1930 German film *The Blue Angel*.[1] "Co-incidentally," the article notes, "Marlene played a night club singer in Berlin in that earlier picture and has a similar role in 'A Foreign Affair.'"

Given how conscious the references in *A Foreign Affair* are to *The Blue Angel*, it is highly doubtful that any aspect of the parallel between these two films is "coincidental." A publicity still sent to theaters after the film's completion, for instance, pictures Dietrich with Holländer, along with a ruined bass drum advertising the Hotel Eden, a popular Berlin club in the 1920s, and the Syncopators, a famous Berlin jazz band whose members were backup musicians on the earlier film. The image explicitly extends the time line from Weimar Germany's Blue Angel nightclub to the postwar "Lorelei" club of *A Foreign Affair*—and, by extension, between Lola Lola, the character Dietrich played in the 1930 film, and Erika von Schlütow, the character

Marlene Dietrich as Lola Lola, singing in *The Blue Angel*.

she plays in *A Foreign Affair*. As Bosley Crowther of the *New York Times* wrote in his July 4, 1948, review of *A Foreign Affair*, "It doesn't take much imagination to see in Miss Dietrich's current role the still fascinating night-club charmer whom we saw in that other film—the same indestructible female who presumably rode the Nazi wave, slipped out the side door when it was crashing and is now back in business again."[2]

A Foreign Affair's reprise of Lola Lola, the original "fascinating night-club charmer," is the first in a long series of films that would subsequently reference the character—at first as played by Dietrich herself and eventually by others. Her appearance in *A Foreign Affair* establishes on film the crucial assumption upon which all subsequent appearances rely: that the character Lola Lola, a fiction of the pre–Nazi era, carried on her profession (and romantic exploits) through the Nazi period and beyond. Dietrich's appearance in Wilder's *Witness for the Prosecution* (1957), for instance, calls on English distrust for the German Lola Lola figure in the postwar period, and then subverts it. Stanley Kramer's *Judgment at Nuremberg* (1961) requires Dietrich to age with a version of her character and lend emotional

Marlene Dietrich as Erika von
Schlütow in A Foreign Affair.

complexity to the proceedings pictured. And her role in David Hemmings's
Just a Gigolo (1979) casts her as a Madame in Lola Lola's soon-to-be Nazi
milieu, projecting the aging Dietrich and all of the associations of the character back into the historical moment from whence she came.

Appearances of Lola Lola without Dietrich proliferate after the 1969
screen debut of the drag Lola Lola in Luchino Visconti's *The Damned*, and
then extend through *The Night Porter* (Liliana Cavani, 1974), *Lili Marleen*
(Rainer Werner Fassbinder, 1981), and some of Madonna's music videos
from the early 1990s, to name a few. In each instance, Lola Lola's iconic
resonance is either to the moment just before the Nazis came to power
(and hence she stands for the forces that turn men to fascism) or to the
Nazi period itself (in which case she stands in for the lure of political spectacle, or the commonly theorized psychosexual dynamics of fascism). But
in 1948, when Dietrich embodied the first reprise of Lola Lola on screen,
her fate was still uncertain. Paramount had not yet decided whether it was
in the best interests of the box office to emphasize the connection that
Wilder had in mind when the studio issued the publicity item in *Paramount News* cited above. By the time the film was released, however, publicity materials and advance reviews clearly highlighted the connection

that Dietrich's role afforded. Thus, while *The Blue Angel* is the origin point of the Lola Lola icon, film historians have to find a way to deal with the eighteen-year hiatus before the character makes her first filmic reappearance as a political icon in *A Foreign Affair*.

One approach to dealing with this issue would be to examine the variety of "co-texts" contemporary to the 1948 film, thereby illustrating a discursive resonance between the aging fictional Lola Lola and the larger cultural milieu in which she circulated. In this essay, however, I will primarily analyze texts peripheral to the film. I will look at the archival materials available on *A Foreign Affair*'s production and distribution in order to bridge filmic and extrafilmic discursive domains, and in so doing examine how the people involved in the making and marketing of *A Foreign Affair* saw their product engaging in precisely this sort of dialogue with the larger culture. This cultural intertextuality, in a larger sense, produced images of Nazism that form a significant part of the image-vocabulary through which an array of political issues (both foreign and domestic) are articulated and understood in American culture, especially the political connection between public and private life. The imagined life story of Lola Lola is but one specific example of this larger phenomenon.[3]

The primary evidence for the genesis of the Lola Lola icon cannot be found on film per se, but rather in the documents surrounding *A Foreign Affair*. In this essay I purport to use Lola Lola as a case study for doing film history without films by analyzing reviews and publicity materials published in newspapers and magazines, the correspondence surrounding the production of *A Foreign Affair* found in the Production Code Administration files, and the script revisions made in the course of the production. In this way, I can chart Wilder's idea for Lola Lola's ongoing biography in addition to some of the external influences that dialogue with this idea. Since hers is a retroactive attribution of biography, I will begin at the end of the process with the reviews and publicity materials surrounding *A Foreign Affair*'s release and then work backward through the materials available on the film's production. By following the archival trail back from her first filmic appearance as an icon in the post-Nazi era, I'll show that Lola Lola, whose ongoing presence on film is in itself remarkable, actually began not on film but rather "on paper."

"THE BLUE ANGEL" 2: REVIEWS UPON THE
RELEASE OF *A FOREIGN AFFAIR*

Between Paramount's December publicity item and the film's June 1948 release, the promotional strategy for the film clearly shifted toward acknowledging the connection between Dietrich's 1930 and 1948 roles. In the June 9 issue of *Life* magazine the promotional materials for *A Foreign Affair* make explicit the parallel; as writer Percy Knauth declares, "As a singer in the nightclub, Marlene Dietrich enjoys a triumphant return to the same sexy role that made her famous 18 years ago in the German film *The Blue Angel*—the heartless siren who lures men to degradation and goes on singing."[4] And Crowther admits to nostalgic delight in his July 4 review quoted above, which comes from "our wistful discovery in Miss Dietrich's current role of the girl, now grown older and wiser, whom she played in *The Blue Angel* years ago."

Knauth and Crowther's fondness for Lola Lola and her new incarnation as Erika in *A Foreign Affair* is clearly built upon the direct association of Dietrich with the two roles, an explicit instance of Richard Dyer's theory that a star's appearance in any one film includes the memory of all of his or her previous roles.[5] Due to the intentional similarity of each of the characters' circumstances—as cabaret singers in the German contemporary to each film's setting—*A Foreign Affair* is an especially specific instance of a character/star fusion carried over from Dietrich at the age of twenty-eight (when she appeared in *The Blue Angel*) to Dietrich at a very young forty-six (when she appeared in *A Foreign Affair*). But Dyer further notes that it is not only the screen roles but also the off-screen and publicity persona that the star has cultivated that concatenate into additional appearances. The resulting star image consequently embodies contradictions that the star's multiple appearances manage, resolve, or, in exceptional cases like Dietrich's, embody in an "alternative or oppositional position."[6] Wilder's Erika is indeed not only a reincarnation of Lola Lola but also is influenced by Dietrich's own activities in the intervening years. Publicity materials thus not only made explicit the parallels between Lola Lola and Erika as characters but emphasized Dietrich's wartime anti-Nazi activism: two factors that contribute to Wilder's project in contradictory fashion—much to his assured delight.

Wilder was surely cognizant of the work of the cultural critic and film historian Siegfried Kracauer, who, in the book he published the year before *A Foreign Affair* was released, singled out *The Blue Angel* as an example of the ways in which Weimar cinema betrayed proto-Nazi tendencies. The book, *From Caligari to Hitler*, purports to chart a "psychological history" of the German nation, using films as sociological and psychological evidence. Kracauer views Lola Lola as *The Blue Angel*'s narrative and erotic core, and he states that the two major reasons for the film's international success were Dietrich and what he names as the film's "outright sadism." Kracauer decries the film's popular appeal to "the spectacle of torture and humiliation," and further argues that von Sternberg deepened such a spectacle "by making Lola Lola destroy not only [the film's male protagonist] but his entire environment."[7]

Kracauer argues that in being destroyed by Lola Lola, *The Blue Angel*'s professor is a prototype for the future Nazi, as are his students, whose "sadistic cruelty results from the very immaturity which forces their victim into submission. It is as if the film implied a warning, for these screen figures anticipate what will happen in real life a few years later."[8] Thus, while Knauth and Crowther speak with affection for Lola Lola and seem untroubled by her projected ability to ride "the Nazi wave," as Crowther puts it, Kracauer casts his similar imagined trajectory for the character with much less sympathy. Indeed in Kracauer's logic, Lola Lola is a harbinger of Hitler himself, in that just as both the professor and his students fall for Lola Lola's song, so too will they fall for the fiery oratory of the Führer.[9]

On celluloid, Dietrich's role as Erika in *A Foreign Affair* is the first time the Lola Lola persona is explicitly linked with fascism. But in Kracauer's book she is linked with fascism long before the film began production. Lola Lola became a Nazi before she was rediscovered in the Lorelei club in Wilder's film, in large part because of Kracauer's application of widespread beliefs about the sadomasochistic psychology of Nazism to film narratives.[10] Wilder, on the other hand, reportedly chose Dietrich specifically as a pre-Hitler icon in order to inflect postwar Berlin both with the triumph over Nazism and with sadness over the destruction of the city and the pre-Nazi life that Lola Lola represents.[11] And considering the comedic role that Dietrich's character plays in the film, Dietrich's anti-Nazi activism contributes to the Lola Lola reprise in a way that runs against Kracauer's version of Lola Lola's biography.

Wilder's project in *A Foreign Affair* is not to warn of women like Lola

Lola and to argue that the psychological hold they have over men offers a mirror to fascism. Rather, the film directly lampoons postwar American moralism that would uphold such an association. The film tells the story of an American army captain, Johnny Pringle (John Lund), who is forced to hide his illicit relationship with Erika by a moralistic and prudish congresswoman from Iowa named Phoebe Frost (Jean Arthur). The script affords many opportunities to poke fun at the dowdy Frost, whose fresh-scrubbed wholesomeness is contrasted with Erika's glamour in what clearly becomes a reversal of the associations that conservative rhetoric hoped to forge between decadence and Nazism: that is, it is Frost who most closely resembles Nazi ideals of female beauty while Erika is clearly more Hollywood than anything else.

Again, this role for the "older and wiser" Lola Lola was not lost on some critics, as Crowther points out, "For in Miss Dietrich's restless femininity, in her subtle suggestions of mocking scorn and in her daringly forward singing of . . . two stinging songs, are centered not only the essence of the picture's romantic allure, but also its vagrant cynicism and its unmistakable point." [12] The point that Crowther obliquely refers to here is that any high-handed attempts to associate glamour and sexiness with decadence and fascism, and hence preserve a lackluster wholesomeness for democracy, is a misguided project worthy of ridicule.

In order for Dietrich to embody not only the taint of fascism but also the freedom of Wilder's version of "democratic" sexuality, Dietrich's wartime anti-Nazi record crucially informs her star persona. Reviewers who praised the film and its subversive message thus often noted that Dietrich, as distinct from Lola Lola, had not been chummy with the Nazis. Knauth, in his praise of A Foreign Affair in Life magazine, concedes that Dietrich's "stature in the film world was always strangely paradoxical: her pictures almost always caused outcries and controversies, and although the studios recognized her drawing power sufficiently to pay her, at one time more than any other woman in the world, no one could say whether she was truly 'popular' or not." [13] Knauth immediately mitigates this assertion by adding, "It was not until World War II, in fact, that Marlene won a place of real fondness in the hearts of thousands of her countrymen. A citizen of the U.S. by then, she threw herself into the struggle against the land of her birth with an ardor and abandon unmatched by any big or little star of the screen or radio." [14]

Thus, as illustrated in the publicity-still discussed above, Edith Head's costume designs for *A Foreign Affair* more closely resemble the sorts of gowns Dietrich had come to be known for in her extensive wartime USO shows rather than the skimpy outfits she wore in *The Blue Angel*. And Paramount, in its myriad press releases prior to the film's completion, also stressed Dietrich's anti-Nazi record: a December 8, 1947, item in *Paramount News*, for instance, reported that Dietrich had arrived from Paris to begin working on her role, and that "The glamorous star, usually accustomed to displaying her shapely 'gams' to photographers, this time displayed something she considered more important. This was the Medal of Freedom, highest civilian decoration of the War Department, presented to her recently at ceremonies at West Point in recognition of her outstanding war record in entertaining troops overseas." [15]

Not everyone approved of Wilder's project—least of all the Production Code Administration (PCA), which repeatedly decried as contrary to PCA policy Wilder's duplicitous deployment of Lola Lola/Dietrich. As a review in the *New Statesman and Nation* similarly opines, "Miss Jean Arthur, by wearing spectacles, turns herself into a conventional figure of fun as a Congresswoman abroad, and there, in a night-club cellar called 'Lorelei,' is Miss Marlene Dietrich singing the same old kind of song that used to enslave the dilettantes of 'The Blue Angel.' But the limited success of *A Foreign Affair* is due chiefly to its pair of script-writers, Charles Brackett and Billy Wilder, who have gone in with a gay disregard not only of taste but of accepted American virtues." [16]

Crowther, however, was by far more astute when he wrote that "somehow this fancied projection of [the Lola Lola] character into today enhances appreciation of the tacit ironies in this film. Think, when you're seeing this picture—and when you're hearing Miss Dietrich sing her cynical songs, . . . of that sensual and arrogant creature who lured the pompous [Emil] Jannings to his doom when the Nazis were starting their big putsch and see if it doesn't do something to you." [17] The "tacit ironies" of the film include the doubleness of the Dietrich/Lola Lola figure—Lola Lola as an emblem of Germany, Dietrich as an emblem of American anti-Nazism—that Wilder deploys as a foil for his real target of criticism: a repressive attitude toward sexuality.

The ongoing incarnations of the Lola Lola icon in the decades since likewise invoke this doubleness—usually in order to serve as a marker of ambiguity, both political and sexual, and hence to characterize not just Nazism but late-twentieth-century political culture more generally.[18] Erika's reprise of Lola Lola in *A Foreign Affair* establishes the enduring complication of what Kracauer's line of reasoning would have made a simple demonology. Moving back now to the production of *A Foreign Affair* and looking into the PCA files on the film, the archival evidence points to the PCA's similar efforts to heap only negative associations onto the Lola Lola character, and to the failure of the regulatory body to achieve this aim.

THE POLITICS OF REGULATION

The history of the policies giving rise to the Production Code play a major role in the evolution of the characterization of Lola Lola as a Nazi. The December 1930 release of *The Blue Angel* in the United States occurred in the midst of a struggle between heated censorship campaigns and a Hollywood industry trying to use risqué fare to ward off fears that the Depression would hurt the box office. The Hays Office, the first incarnation of the Production Code Administration, accepted a version of the Production Code in 1930, but it was much more liberally interpreted than it would be after 1934 with the establishment of the PCA itself. The PCA file on *The Blue Angel* indeed reflects the more liberal policies of the Code between 1930 and 1934; Jason Joy, in a letter dated July 23, 1930, notes that the film "has many things in it which could not be undertaken successfully by us in this country," but then he adds that "on the whole it is not as bad as these offensive shots would at first make it appear to be."[19] An official report from December 13, 1930, then concludes that "both from the standpoint of the Code, and that of Censorship, the various suggestive postures of Lola, when she leaves very little to the imagination, were noted," but the film subsequently was released to the state and local censorship boards for their decisions.[20]

In 1935, however, in an effort to bolster Dietrich's somewhat flagging career, Paramount applied to the PCA for a re-release of *The Blue Angel*. The PCA response came in a letter dated October 8, 1935, from Joseph Breen, the much more conservative and more powerful successor to Jason Joy. Needless to say, Breen's response was decidedly negative: "With regard to the picture Blue Angel, I suggest that you withdraw this picture. It is a sordid story based on an illicit sex relationship between the two leading

characters, and contains a great deal of offensive suggestiveness in its portrayal throughout."[21] Breen concluded that the PCA would likely reject the
application for reissue (and as a consequence the film was not re-released
at that time).

Dietrich became a star during the years when Hollywood acted in de-
fiance of the socially conservative censors. And she was among those that
suffered most once the Code became more strict in 1934. The changing
attitudes toward the European exoticism that Dietrich and von Sternberg
had cultivated and the success of conservative forces in getting the industry to agree to more strict enforcement of the Code, while not the only
reasons for Dietrich's lagging popularity after 1934, are certainly key. There
were two significant extrafilmic developments that influenced Dietrich's
role as Erika von Schlütow a decade later: the first is the way in which
the Production Code handled sexually charged material in the context of
World War II, and the second is Dietrich's own anti-Nazi activities during the war. The cooperative relationship that Hollywood developed with
the Office of War Information encouraged the production of many anti-
Nazi films after the United States had officially entered the war in 1941.
Taking the 1942 B-movie *Hitler's Children* as an example, anti-Nazi films
were able to express more sexually risqué material with the blessing of the
PCA than could other sorts of films, so long as it was the Nazis who appeared to be debauched. The PCA file on *Hitler's Children* shows very few
problems with any state censorship boards, and indeed very little wran-
gling over the script in the course of the production, with only minor suggestions such as, "There must, of course, be no unacceptable exposure of
Anna's person in this scene where the blouse is ripped off her back while
she is being lashed."[22] Again revealing the relatively permissive logic of the
otherwise sexually sensitive Code, one member of the review board stated,
in a note written on her ballot approving the screenplay of *Hitler's Children*,
that, "this film must be horrifying and frightening but apparently 'our side'
comes through with 'flying colors.'"[23] What this sort of judgment reflects
is the larger socially conservative anti-Nazi rhetoric also found in popular
wartime journalism, where a binary opposition between democracy and
fascism characterized democracy through heterosexual monogamous marriage and fascism as an attack on traditional morality (hence the images of
Nazi promiscuity, perversion, or homosexuality).

This dynamic opposition between democracy and fascism was also the terrain that Billy Wilder and his production of *A Foreign Affair* tried to navigate, and indeed the PCA file on the film includes a submission cover form, dated March 12, 1948, on which all of the appropriate boxes are checked: the "German Girl Cafe Singer," is checked as "unsympathetic," while the "Congresswoman" and "Army Captain" are checked "sympathetic." From the perspective of the PCA, Dietrich's character, since she was "unsympathetic," was thus free to reenact her early 1930s persona that the Code had helped to banish, so long as she was now marked as a political enemy.

However, because Wilder had a far more politically complex project in mind, the film did meet with quite a few objections from the script's censors: unlike *Hitler's Children*, *A Foreign Affair* poked fun at the very morality that the Code peddled in the name of American nationalism. While craftily conceding Erika as a biographical extension of Lola Lola's story, the butt of most of the film's jokes is actually the "sympathetic" American congresswoman on a moral crusade to clean up Allied-occupied Berlin, and the story revolves around the shenanigans of the likewise "sympathetic" American captain whose affair with the lovely "unsympathetic" Erika interferes with his enforcement of de-Nazification policies. The seductive appeal of Erika, unlike Kracauer's take on Lola Lola, is universalized in Wilder's film: virtually all men, whether Nazis, Communists or patriotic Americans, fall for her charms, and so her seductiveness itself cannot be aligned with any one political orientation.

The PCA file on the film thus further reveals myriad objections to these aspects of the film's plot; as Stephen Jackson of the PCA wrote on December 2, 1947, "We believe this material presents a very serious problem of industry policy with regard to the characterization of the members of the Congressional Committee and of the members of the American Army of Occupation." The review board's complaints mainly center on the many scenes where GIs and eventually the congresswoman herself are shown to indulge in the "decadent" pleasures that Berlin has to offer, and the "excessive passion" evident between Erika and her lover, the American officer Johnny.

In an earlier treatment for the film (before Dietrich was cast), Erika is described as "a big, handsome, beautifully molded woman—a Rhine maiden, a Valkyrie—but a Rhine maiden who had gone off the deep end, and a Valkyrie who had ridden the wrong way."[24] Clearly in this earlier conception of the story, Erika is meant to be the butt of some of the film's jokes: in the revision process, the writers Wilder, Charles Brackett, and Richard Breen shifted the burden of this variant of the Nazi ideal to Frost, and by extension to the soldiers' wives, mothers, and sisters whose interests Frost—and the PCA—purports to protect. Wilder thus takes the complexities of the sexy Nazi icon Lola Lola as his playground by setting her up against a moralist who ultimately succumbs to a universal human hankering for material and sexual pleasures.

In the end, however, most of the illicit material objected to by the censors remained in the film with only minor appeasing script changes. This phenomenon attests to the limited power of the PCA to entirely determine the sexual politics of a film. But the struggle over Erika/Lola Lola's role evidenced by the material in the files of both *The Blue Angel* and *A Foreign Affair* illustrates the changing production climate between Lola Lola's first appearance and her reprise, which Wilder appears hell-bent to lampoon. In 1930 Lola Lola was not a political figure, but by 1948 she had become a political icon—not only in the fictionalized context of Nazi Germany but in the sexual politics of the United States.

CONCLUSION

The film theorist Noël Coward suggests that Aristotelian rhetoric might be a useful way to approach film. As he writes: "While narrative films are not arguments per se, they are rhetorical in that they are structured to lead the audience to fill in certain ideas about human conduct in the process of rendering the story intelligible."[25] This use of "rhetoric" is akin to the notion of ideology elaborated by A. J. Greimas, as it functions through the logically controlled unfolding of possibilities within a given narrative structure.[26] But what I have demonstrated here in the Lola Lola case is that cultural rhetoric might be something other than ideology per se, with the nascent icons of Hollywood, fascism, and sexuality negotiating the variety of rhetorical tendencies at play in the culture at large: in short, Lola Lola served as a focal point for the developing sexual politics that would preoccupy American political culture for the rest of the twentieth century.

Wilder is clearly a master at manipulating the image vocabularies current in the immediate aftermath of the war. But what this exercise in doing "film history without films" reveals for us generally is that film is a negotiated art—both internally and in dialogue with larger cultural tendencies. Concrete archival evidence, as demonstrated above, is able to substantiate and specify what might otherwise be conjecture. The genesis of the imagined biography of Lola Lola between 1930 and 1948 can perhaps be surmised merely by watching the films in which she repeatedly appears, but it is really on paper that her story is told.

NOTES

1 "Dietrich to Warble 3 Tunes in 'Affair,'" *Paramount News*, December 22, 1947. *A Foreign Affair* file, Margaret Herrick Library, Academy of Motion Picture Arts and Sciences, Beverly Hills, California (hereafter AMPAS library).

2 Bosley Crowther, "Remembrance of Things: 'A Foreign Affair' and 'Easter Parade' Stir Fond Memories," *New York Times*, July 4, 1948, 2:1.

3 Similar methodologies have been addressed by historians who have linked individual and collective subjectivities to textual representations and who understand historical documents in literary terms. See, for instance, the exchange between Judith Walkowitz (historian) and Myra Jehlen (literary theorist) transcribed in "Patrolling the Borders: Feminist Historiography and the New Historicism," *Radical History Review* 43 (1989): 23–43.

4 Percy Knauth, "Movie of the Week: Marlene Dietrich Steals the Show in an Uproarious Hollywood Version of Low Life in Postwar Berlin," *Life*, June 9, 1948, 59. The cover of this issue of *Life* also features Dietrich, in which she is given the title "Grandmother Dietrich" since her daughter, Maria, had just had a baby around the time the film was released. Thereafter the young grandmother was often called "The Most Glamourous Grandmother," and even "Gorgeous Grandmarlene." This is one of the many ways that Dietrich's persona defied conventional images of women.

5 Richard Dyer, *Stars* (London: British Film Institute, 1979), 38.

6 Ibid.

7 Siegfried Kracauer, *From Caligari to Hitler: A Psychological History of the German Film* (Princeton, N.J.: Princeton University Press, 1947), 217.

8 Ibid., 218.

9 Judith Mayne, "Marlene Dietrich, *The Blue Angel*, and Female Performance," in *Seduction and Theory: Readings of Gender, Representation, and Rhetoric*, ed. Dianne Hunter (Urbana: University of Illinois Press, 1989), 41.

10 For a full discussion of wartime anti-Nazi psychology, see Ellen Herman, *The Romance of American Psychology: Political Culture in the Age of Experts* (Berkeley: University of California Press, 1995).

11 Wilder had shot footage of bombed-out Berlin right at the end of the war, when he was an officer for the U.S. Army. His duties had been to approve or deny Allied performing licenses required for every German stage performance

during the occupation. Wilder's duties are thus reflected in the plot of *A Foreign Affair*, which centrally revolves around whether Erika should be allowed
to continue to sing in the club.

12 Bosley Crowther, "A Foreign Affair" (review), *New York Times*, July 1, 1948 (*A
    Foreign Affair* file, AMPAS library).

13 Knauth, "Movie of the Week," 64.

14 Ibid.

15 "Dietrich Arrives from France for 'Affair,'" *Paramount News*, December 8, 1947
    (*A Foreign Affair* file, AMPAS library).

16 "The Movies," *New Statesman and Nation*, September 4, 1948 (*A Foreign Affair*
    file, AMPAS library).

17 Crowther, "Remembrance of Things," 2:1.

18 See my *A Not So Foreign Affair: Fascism, Sexuality, and the Cultural Rhetoric of
    American Democracy* (Durham, N.C.: Duke University Press, 2001).

19 Letter from Jason S. Joy to Maurice McKenzie (NYC), July 23, 1930 (*Blue Angel*
    file, AMPAS library).

20 *Blue Angel* file, AMPAS library. *The Blue Angel* was shot at UFA in Berlin in
    November and December 1929, in both German and English. The German
    version of the film premiered on March 31, 1930, at the Gloria Palast in Berlin,
    with a 106 minute running time. The U.S. release of the film was delayed in
    order to allow Dietrich to make her American debut in the Paramount pro-
    duction *Morocco*, which was shot in summer 1930 and premiered on Novem-
    ber 24, 1930, at Grauman's Chinese Theater in Los Angeles. The English ver-
    sion of *The Blue Angel*, distributed by Paramount, was then premiered at the
    Rialto in New York on December 5, 1930, with a running time of ninety-nine
    minutes. The December 13, 1930, note from Joy presages the film's broader re-
    lease.

21 Letter from Joseph Breen to Paramount, October, 8, 1935, in reply to an applica-
    tion for Certificates of Approval for re-issue (*Blue Angel* file, AMPAS library).

22 On August, 21, 1942, Joseph Breen, head of the PCA, sent a letter to the pro-
    ducer Edward Golden as a follow-up to their meeting about the script. In this
    letter he writes, "The basic story seems to meet the requirements of the Pro-
    duction Code. However, there were certain scenes and lines of dialogue that
    seemed to us questionable from the standpoint of political censorship gener-
    ally. We venture to suggest some rewriting of these scenes, and it is our under-
    standing that you are in full agreement with the changes indicated." He then
    concludes by saying, "May I take this opportunity of expressing our apprecia-
    tion of the splendid way in which you have handled this difficult story, and to
    wish you all success in the production of an outstanding picture." Production
    then began on October, 5, 1942, and Breen sent a letter on October 6, 1942, ap-
    proving the script as written thus far. Kansas, Maryland, Massachusetts, New
    York, and Ohio all passed the finished film without changes, with Pennsylva-
    nia asking for minor deletions.

23 Letter to Breen from Miriam Tooley, secretary to Mrs. James F. Looram. On
    the PCA form, the German characters are listed as both sympathetic and un-
    sympathetic, while all of the American characters and the Catholic bishop are
    sympathetic.

24 Second script for *A Foreign Affair*, dated May 31, 1947, by Brackett, Wilder, and
    Harari (*A Foreign Affair* file, AMPAS library).

25 Noël Carroll, "Film, Rhetoric, and Ideology," in *Explanation and Value in the
    Arts*, ed. Salim Kemal and Ivan Gaskell (Cambridge: Cambridge University
    Press, 1993), 215–37. The Aristotelian notion of rhetoric identifies the following
    components: (1) establishing one's good character is key to gaining authority
    as a speaker; (2) example is a crucial form of argument (with major variations
    being fable or allegory, hypothetical scenarios, and anecdotes); and (3) various
    strategies of persuasion, including drawing on common knowledge/maxims,
    and dominant cultural logic by way of the use of enthymemes (a syllogism that
    leaves something out and requires the audience to fill in the missing premise).

26 Fredric Jameson has elaborated Greimas's model to illuminate how dominant
    narratives limit the logical narrative resolution of their plots, to which Jameson
    then proposes a critical practice that uncovers the other narrative possibilities
    that a text contains. See A. J. Greimas, *Structural Semantics: An Attempt at a
    Method*, trans. Daniele McDowell, Ronald Schleifer, and Alan Velie (Lincoln:
    University of Nebraska Press, 1984; originally published in French in 1966);
    Fredric Jameson, *The Political Unconscious: Narrative as a Socially Symbolic Act*
    (Ithaca, N.Y.: Cornell University Press, 1981).

III   REGULATION

GOING HOLLYWOOD SOONER OR LATER
Chinese Censorship and *The Bitter Tea of General Yen*
Eric Smoodin

After a series of complaints from the Chinese vice consul in Los Angeles, Frederick Herron wrote an irritated memo to Willys Peck, the American consul general in Nanking. The Chinese vice consul hoped to make changes in the global version of Frank Capra's 1933 film *The Bitter Tea of General Yen*. As a result, Herron, the foreign manager of the Motion Picture Producers and Distributors Association of America (MPPDA), contacted Peck on May 31, 1933. He claimed that if Capra's studio, Columbia Pictures, acquiesced in this case, then "this Vice Consul just as sure as the sun will rise tomorrow, will 'go Hollywood' sooner or later" and cause no end of trouble. Insisting that the desire to meddle in movie production—to "go Hollywood"—leveled all national differences, Herron went on to say "I don't believe the Chinese are any different from any others in the world," and then he added that if Columbia and the MPPDA recognized the authority of the vice consul, they would simply be "getting ready for a squabble in which we will come off second best."[1]

Herron, a longtime diplomat and friend of the MPPDA president Will Hays, had been the MPPDA foreign manager for ten years, ever since the movie industry trade association had opened a Foreign Department to deal with other countries' complaints about Hollywood movies and economic practices.[2] During that time, he had gotten used to smoothing over a variety of problems relating to Hollywood's international markets. But the *Bitter Tea* incident tested his mettle and his patience, because it was just the latest case in a series of very difficult censorship negotiations with the Chinese government.

By examining Herron's memo and the more than thirty other State Department documents about *Bitter Tea*, all of which are stored in the National Archives in Washington, D.C., we can come to understand the workings of international regulatory practices during this period. The documents explain what we might call an "official" interpretation of Capra's film—that is, by Hollywood officials like Herron but mostly by bureaucrats in the Chinese and U.S. governments as they argue over commercial and political relations between countries. In addition, the *Bitter Tea* papers tell us how Chinese and American officials sought to act upon the film as they tried to produce a version suitable to those locations influenced by China's concerns over representational practices and the political implications of motion pictures. Thus we can combine a diplomatic history of a specific case of international business relations with an examination of censorship practices designed to lessen the impact of American films in foreign markets.

Looking at these documents helps us to rethink the narrative of American film censorship during the silent and early sound periods. That narrative would have it that the Hollywood film industry weathered a period of domestic government censorship, typically from cities and states, that began with the development of the cinema as a commercial enterprise at the end of the nineteenth century. In the "happy end" to the narrative, at least from the standpoint of the film companies, this form of censorship was made more or less obsolete in the 1930s by the industry's adoption of the self-censoring Production Code. In fact, though, at least through the 1930s, the industry confronted intense government censorship, some of it domestic but most of it from the foreign markets on which Hollywood depended for a substantial amount of revenue.[3] At least three aspects of historiographic research seem to be at stake in correcting the prevailing narrative about censorship and the Hollywood cinema. First, on a practical, methodological level, we see the centrality to film history projects of

studying government documents. Second, such a study helps us fully acknowledge and understand the status of many significant national cinemas
as international commodities often dominating global markets while at the
same time subject to those markets' stringent controls.[4] Finally, we realize
the extent of the relationship between national governments and private
industry, which, in the case of *Bitter Tea*, manifested itself in the struggle
over access to audiences around the world.

Through the work of Richard Maltby and others, we know that Hollywood executives were far less concerned with the domestic regulation of
representational practices—censorship—than with the regulation of trade
practices relating to distribution and exhibition.[5] As a result, these executives were pleased to let public discourse through the 1930s emphasize film
content rather than industry practices such as block booking and the major
studios' ownership of most first-run theaters. Foreign censorship, however,
posed very serious problems. Governments—and this was precisely the
case with *Bitter Tea*—might threaten to prevent Hollywood films from
even showing in their countries, thereby eliminating all possibility for revenue. In spite of this, historians have focused largely on considerations of
domestic practices and audiences and have paid relatively little attention to
Hollywood's foreign markets.[6]

Based on a popular novel by Grace Zaring Stone, *The Bitter Tea of General Yen* "reportedly cost about $1 million," according to Capra biographer
Joseph McBride, with Columbia counting on it being the kind of high-
quality, top-grossing film around which the studio could market its other,
lesser films.[7] As a sign of this high profile, *Bitter Tea* was the first film to
play at the newly finished Radio City Music Hall, and in part because of
the novelty of the venue it had an impressive opening at the box office.
Nevertheless, the film proved to be a financial disappointment overall for
Capra and Columbia, although the reasons for this are difficult to pinpoint.[8]

Bitter Tea begins with the "burning of Chapei" in 1931, an event that
the film situates as part of the Chinese "civil war" rather than as an act of
Japanese aggression.[9] An American missionary, played by Barbara Stanwyck, falls in love with a Chinese warlord, played by the white, Swedish
actor Nils Asther, who kidnaps her, and who eventually commits suicide.
Possibly, American audiences had begun to tire of this kind of film, as the
studios certainly had produced a number of movies taking place in China.

There is evidence, as well, that the film may have alienated audiences outside of major urban areas. One theater manager, writing to the *Motion Picture Herald*, lamented that this was "Not a small town picture," while another complained that *Bitter Tea* was "too deep for a small town." Barbara Stanwyck believed that the film's failure was due to its interracial romance; as she noted, "The women's clubs came out very strongly against it, because the white woman was in love with the yellow man and kissed his hand." It is also possible, of course, that a film coming out in the midst of the Depression, as well as in the middle of winter (*Bitter Tea* premiered on 11 January), might naturally have had difficulty drawing an audience. Yet another theater manager, merging concerns about the Depression with those about audiences outside of big cities, complained that despite the quality of *Bitter Tea*, "the low wages and restricted income that is rife in the small towns just won't let even good pictures gross what they would in good times." [10]

Such primary sources as these reports by theater manager provide wonderful anecdotal evidence about the interaction between domestic audiences and the films they enjoyed or disliked, attended in droves or avoided. With recent scholarship, however, a continuing problem in understanding the "success" or "failure" of any movie has been the tendency of textual critics to remove films from the complex systems, both domestic and international, that might go a long way toward determining audience enthusiasm or disinterest. In perhaps the most thorough contemporary reading of *Bitter Tea*, for example, David Palumbo-Liu suggests that the "failure" of the film "may be attributed in part to the fact that it is unable to establish a stable identificatory position," and that the film's apparent inability to negotiate complicated racial, gendered, and class-based subject positions also made it unable to "satisfy the moviegoing public in the 1930's." [11] In very basic terms, this kind of text-based analysis implies that people who saw the film did not like it and, apparently through word of mouth, convinced others to stay away. I would suggest, however, that in addition to the reasons mentioned above, some of the difficulties for the film came from its foreign audiences. More properly, problems arose not so much for the foreign audiences that saw *Bitter Tea* but from the industry officials and government censors who attempted quite actively to prevent people outside of the United States from seeing it at all. In script form and then as a finished film, *Bitter Tea* easily passed muster with the industry's self-censoring Production Code, but it had serious censorship problems in Great Britain and the British Commonwealth because of its interracial romance. Further, in the case that interests me here, not only did the film apparently never play in China, it faced Chinese lobbying efforts against it in several other countries and it was removed from at least one other foreign market, Japan.[12]

FRANK CAPRA, HOLLYWOOD CINEMA,
AND CHINESE MARKETS

Within the context of the director's career, *Bitter Tea* comes from the end of a period that might be called "Capra before Capra." That is, although Capra already had become well known, he had not yet—with the exception perhaps of *American Madness* (1932)—begun making the films that we think of as quintessential Capra: *It Happened One Night*, for instance, would come out the following year. Interestingly, though, for a director known for his "American" themes, Capra made more movies about Far Eastern locales than did most other Hollywood directors from the period: not only *Bitter Tea* but also *Lost Horizon* (1937) and the World War II documentaries *The Battle of China* (1944) and *Know Your Enemy: Japan* (1945). As a product of a major American corporation, *The Bitter Tea of General Yen* and, indeed, the struggle between Chinese censors on the one hand and Columbia Pictures and the State Department on the other, help to explain the relationships between the government and business and between that business and its global audience. In addition, the fight over the film demonstrates the broad efforts on the part of the Chinese government to control its own domestic commercial sphere and to discipline those Western countries seeking to exploit a new, huge market.

By the time of *Bitter Tea*, American businessmen had come to consider China a significant and expanding market for U.S.-made goods.[13] There is, as well, anecdotal evidence that the possibility of converting the Chinese into consumers of U.S. products had become something of an interest to the American public in general. At least two major commercial publishing houses—Macmillan and Harper and Brothers—issued books about the matter: C. F. Remer's *Foreign Investments in China* (1933) and the advertising man Carl Crow's *400 Million Customers* (1937)—the very title of which got quite directly to the point.[14] Crow's book, with its conversational style and amusing illustrations, clearly was marketed for a mass audience, with the author stating early on that "my work has naturally made my point of view that of one who looks on the Chinese as potential customers, to consider what articles they may purchase, how these articles should be packed, and what advertising methods will be most effective in producing sales." Crow also asserted the importance of movies in his line of work, as he wrote that his firm "induced all the Chinese moving-picture stars to use the toilet soap we advertised," and then acquired testimonials from them.[15] For Crow, Chinese stars were more effective salespersons in China than were Hollywood celebrities, but the significance of movies in general, as a product themselves and as a means of selling other goods, could not have been lost on American businessmen.

Indeed, the Hollywood movie studios found China a promising market. Precise figures are difficult to come by, but if American films played no more frequently in China in the early 1930s than they had before, they were almost certainly generating more controversy. In 1931, for example, at the fourth Conference of the Institute of Pacific Relations, held in Hangchow and Shanghai, attendees "urged that a conference round table concern itself with the disruptive influence of Western moving pictures upon the morals and manners of Oriental peoples." This influence, however, could only be assumed rather than proved, and the round table apparently was called off because "it was pointed out that no studies had as yet been made of the exact nature or strength of that influence; and that possibly effects were attributed to it merely because it was the most visible and, indeed, spectacular of many forms of foreign influence upon the indigenous culture."[16]

While these studies seem not to have been conducted, the American government became convinced of the centrality of Hollywood motion pictures in China and of the need to make sure that China remained open to American movies. As a result, in August 1932, just a few months before the State Department became involved in the *Bitter Tea* case, Richard P. Butrick, a member of the American Consulate in Shanghai, supervised the production of a lengthy document called "The Motion Picture Industry in China." The document cautioned that despite Chiang Kai-shek's emergence as a national leader, "the generally unsettled condition of the country, with its numerous bandit-infested provinces, the vast number of illiterate Chinese and the very small purchasing power of the masses," all militated against any expansion of either Chinese or American film interests.[17] Nevertheless, all of the major Hollywood film companies had branch offices in China, with Columbia, which produced Capra's films, sharing one with Paramount.[18] The document insisted, furthermore, that sooner or later there would be a significant expansion in the number of theaters in China, which would "increase the demand for American pictures." Even if Chinese film production itself increased (according to the document, China had produced fifteen sound films in the last eighteen months), theaters still would need American movies, which in 1932 accounted for 75 percent of the footage shown in Chinese theaters.[19]

These theaters stood out as particularly important to American concerns. At this time, there were about 280 movie theaters in China, and some were undoubtedly owned or managed by U.S.-based companies.[20] Even more significant for U.S. business, of the 97 Chinese theaters capable of showing sound films, 70 had been wired with American equipment. Thus, as the number of sound theaters grew, so too would the outlets for American films, and, in addition, the revenues for those American companies supplying sound equipment would only increase.[21]

The highest concentration of these theaters—28 sound and 21 silent—were in Shanghai, with other major cities, such as Canton (20 theaters) and Tientsin (15), also having a significant number of venues for seeing movies.[22] Residents of these cities, in particular those in Shanghai, experienced flourishing film cultures. Along with Chinese films they saw British, French, Italian, and Russian films, but never to the extent that they were exposed to American movies, which in Shanghai and elsewhere in China usually were shown in English accompanied by subtitles.[23] Frederic Wakeman, in his study of Shanghai between 1927 and 1937, has pointed out that "it is difficult to exaggerate the centrality of the cinema" to that city's mass culture, and that "Movie actors and actresses were national celebrities and popular idols." As a means of following these performers, over a million readers regularly read the illustrated newspaper *Dianying huabao* ("Movies illustrated").[24] The Shanghai residents' tastes in movies seem to have been similar to those of American audiences, with Butrick's document extolling the recent successes of such films as Chaplin's *City Lights* and the Eddie Cantor vehicle *Whoopee*, along with Lubitsch's *Love Parade* and Lewis Milestone's version of Erich Maria Remarque's international bestseller *All Quiet on the Western Front*. The State Department document also recorded the star preferences of these viewers, indicating that they were fans of Maurice Chevalier, Laurel and Hardy, Ronald Colman, Jeannette MacDonald, Greta Garbo, and Joan Crawford, among others, with Norma Shearer occupying a special place, having a "large following among the better class Chinese."[25]

Of course, not all of China, and not all Chinese officials, welcomed Hollywood movies or, more generally, Western goods and services. In 1927, the Chinese Nationalists (the Guomindang) began a ten-year period of control marked by almost immediately disaffiliating themselves from the communists who had fought with them and by attempts to establish a party-republic led by Chiang Kai-shek. In trying to carry out the "program of national construction" begun by Sun Yat-sen, who had died in 1925, Chiang Kai-shek emphasized efforts to limit foreign business and culture and to impose Guomindang discipline in Shanghai—on the Chinese there as well as on foreign nationals.[26] Shanghai was the most significant metropolitan area in China, and the site of perhaps the greatest Western influence (the very geography of the city emphasized this influence, as it was divided into the International Settlement, the French Concession, and the Chinese Municipality). As a result, for the new government the city came to signify both the problems and prospects of modernity and also "the westernized world of commerce that now occupied China's shores."[27]

In part as a result, the new regime established a modern police force in the city and sought to crack down on crime and vice. In the latter category came the old standbys—gambling (greyhound racing, for instance) and prostitution. But entertainment also figured prominently, including cabarets and, occasionally, movies. More properly, the authorities, most notably the Public Security Bureau, concerned themselves with movie theaters, which could become locations for gambling and prostitution. Attempts to control the cinema as an institution, however, also applied to film production and representation. Throughout the 1930s, members of the government-approved "New Life Movement" worked to purge communists from the Chinese film industry (which was centered in Shanghai), while the Guomindang government itself, through censors working in Nanking, routinely rejected film scripts and shut down fourteen film studios in 1934 and 1935.[28]

For Chinese officials, though, and especially for the Chinese censors, the American cinema posed a very special problem, with the popularity of Hollywood movies standing out as the surest sign of cultural degeneration in China.[29] As a result, in 1931 the Chinese government passed a national film censorship law mandating that all movies receive clearance from the National Board of Film Censors (also referred to as the Film Censorship Committee) before they could be exhibited in China. The law itself, according to Butrick's document, seems to have been rather cumbersome with its complicated series of fines and permits. The Censorship Committee convened in the capital, Nanking, and all seven of its members were political appointees chosen by the Guomindang leadership of the Ministry of Education and the Ministry of the Interior. The censorship law gave the committee members a good deal of interpretive leeway, requiring them to reject four kinds of films: those "derogatory to the dignity of the Chinese race"; those "injurious to good morals or the public order"; those "tending to foster superstition and heresy"; and those "contrary to the Three People's Principles," which Butrick's document defined rather obliquely as "a complicated code on the political, economic and social development of China."[30]

The committee examined all films, including shorts and newsreels, but naturally it was the feature-length films that received special attention. It is difficult to determine just how many feature films Hollywood studios submitted to the censors, but by July 1, 1932—a full year after the law took effect—the committee had rejected twenty-six American films. Some of these—*Lasca of the Rio Grande* and *Boudoir Diplomat*, for instance—are unknown today. Others, though, are some of the more famous of the studio product from the period: *Dr. Jekyll and Mr. Hyde*, *Dracula*, *The Unholy Three*, and *In Old Arizona* are just a few examples. In addition, *An American Tragedy* also failed to pass the committee, marking just the first of director Josef von Sternberg's problems with the Nanking censors. Most of the banned films, both American and those from other countries, failed to receive exhibition permits because the censors deemed them to be "derogatory to the dignity of the Chinese race." This meant, typically, that they included Chinese characters who clearly conformed to Western racist stereotypes. Even more than banning films, however, the Nanking censors sought to cut them to remove offending scenes or lines of dialogue. Butrick, for instance, "believed that at least fifty per cent of the films submitted are subject to cuts.'"[31]

In setting up its disciplinary practices, the Chinese government did not pretend to be starting from scratch or to be inventing something absolutely different from systems in other countries. For its police force, for instance,

China depended upon Western and Japanese models of command hierarchies, patrol methods, training practices, and weaponry. Particularly in
terms of policing Shanghai, Chinese officials believed that this would be
the best way to compete with the Western and Japanese domination of
the city.[32] Similarly, as their model of film censorship, China looked to the
United States. Apparently believing that the federal government controlled
film censorship practices, in June 1931 the Chinese Censorship Committee
contacted Willys Peck, the American consul general in Nanking who later
would have to deal with Frederick Herron's complaints about the Chinese
vice consul in Los Angeles. The committee informed Peck that it was anxious to "avail itself of the experience of other countries in the censorship of
motion pictures," and sought to "collect copies of laws, etc. relating to the
subject." A member of the committee then asked Peck to get him whatever
material he could from the United States.[33]

Peck related this conversation to the secretary of state, suggesting that
the State Department might act as a liaison between China and the MPPDA,
which administered the self-censoring Production Code. Peck added that
it was his impression that the Chinese were "especially interested in learning the methods employed in censoring films in the United States . . . on a
national scale and . . . locally, and in learning the principles which govern
the condemning of films or portions of films as unfit for exhibition." In the
name of international relations, Peck suggested that the United States cooperate with the Chinese in this request for information.[34] As a result, the
United States, besides at least partially controlling world film markets, also
may have had at least some control over world censorship systems. Rather
than working to the benefit of Hollywood filmmakers, however, their own
regulatory system would work, at least in China, to weaken their hold on
the market.

This situation became abundantly clear to at least one State Department employee, who composed an apparently anonymous memo on the
subject. The memo acknowledged the Chinese request for information on
American censorship laws and also for information, rather mysteriously,
about state censorship regulations in Kansas. While suggesting that the
department cooperate with the Chinese in providing this information, the
memo writer warned that "there is a possibility that the Chinese authorities may include in their censorship regulations the provisions of the . . .
'production code' and laws of the state of Kansas which might make very

difficult an effective protest if such regulations were unreasonably interpreted to the detriment of American films."[35] In other words, the Chinese
may have intended to use American-style censorship regulations precisely
to censor American films, and neither State Department bureaucrats nor
Hollywood officials could complain too loudly if the MPPDA's own regulations were used against the MPPDA's product.

Just as in the United States, censorship in China was never universally
agreed upon or enforced. Even after the institution of the 1931 censorship
law there remained some "independent censorship areas," such as Canton,
Hong Kong, and, in Shanghai, the French Concession and the International Settlement. In addition, independent groups agitated for better
films, with the Shanghai American Women's Club, for instance, printing
a bulletin of "films worth seeing." For the most part, however, the Censorship Committee exercised by far the most power and provided the greatest
irritation for American diplomats and film executives.[36]

CENSORING HOLLYWOOD FILMS IN CHINA

The 1930 Howard Hughes production *Hell's Angels* was the first significant
censorship case in China that seems to have come to the attention not
only of the MPPDA but also of the State Department. The exact grounds
of the objection are difficult to determine, but a complaint seems to have
been lodged by the German Legation in China, probably because of the
manner in which the film interpreted German participation in World
War I.[37] Honoring this objection, Chinese officials refused to grant the
film an exhibition permit unless certain changes were made. After some
negotiations between the Censorship Committee, the State Department,
and an American law firm in Shanghai (presumably representing Hughes's
interests), some cuts in the film were agreed to and an exhibition permit
was granted in June 1932. This constituted business as usual in relations
between China and the Hollywood studios; the latter never seemed too
concerned about making cuts in their films, as long as those films then
could be exhibited. That is, the film studios concerned themselves with
access, and film content became very much a secondary issue.

On a few occasions, however, access itself came to be threatened, and
these cases turned into significant diplomatic events—at least to the extent
that this was possible in the film business. At about the same time as the

amicable resolution of the *Hell's Angels* case, Beh Chuan Peng, a member of the Censorship Committee, complained to Willys Peck about Josef von Sternberg's 1932 film *Shanghai Express*. Chinese students who had seen the film in Germany and in the United States had contacted Chinese officials about the film, with Peng then telling Peck, reasonably enough, that "the plot of the film was objectionable, in that it laid great emphasis on Chinese bandits, prostitutes, and other disreputable characters." He went on to say that "there was reason to believe that [the] Japanese had inspired the film ... with a view to defaming China and thus lowering China in the esteem of Western nations." Paramount, the company that produced *Shanghai Express*, apparently had decided not even to try to exhibit the film in China, probably for some of the reasons Peng had mentioned. But Peng asked that the film be destroyed and thereby removed from all non-U.S. markets.[38]

In response Peck argued with Peng, and their debate both set the ground rules for the *Bitter Tea* case one year later and established the inability of American and Chinese bureaucrats even to use the same terms in their discussions. Peng stressed representational issues—the depiction of the Chinese as bandits, prostitutes, etc. Peck, in his rebuttal, asserted narrative concerns, telling him that "in every exciting plot there must be a conflict, and that the usual conflict was between good and evil." He continued by stating that "to eliminate all bad characters from a movie film would, therefore, destroy the plot of most exciting films," and that the Chinese should not "feel over sensitive if the bad characters in a film were occasionally Chinese, just as they often were Americans and persons of other nationalities."[39] Peck's argument failed to persuade the Censorship Committee, but Paramount hardly felt compelled to withdraw *Shanghai Express* from the global film marketplace.

To get Paramount's attention, however, the committee "passed a resolution barring all Paramount films from exhibition in China unless all copies of *Shanghai Express* throughout the world were destroyed." In other words, the entire output of the studio would be barred, a situation that Paramount's Chinese representative called an "emergency." Paramount finally consented to a token (and soon discontinued) effort to remove prints from international circulation, with the committee then agreeing to censor Paramount films once again, thereby clearing them for exhibition in China. The studio also produced an apology and a promise, which it sent on to the committee: "In producing *Shanghai Express*, Paramount had not the slightest intention to disparage the Chinese people and it regrets that the film has been so interpreted. It is the desire and intention of Paramount to refrain from producing any film which may be regarded as injurious to the dignity of the Chinese people."[40]

Despite having brokered the settlement, the State Department seems to have been convinced that the problem, finally, had more to do with intransigent Chinese attitudes than with reasonable differences between the American film industry and a foreign government. In writing to the secretary of state about the affair, Peck adopted a position of distanced, academic interest, saying that the *Shanghai Express* incident "throws . . . light on modern Chinese official psychology." He then insisted that the case provided "an illustration of the mental attitude which the younger generation of Chinese officials takes toward international relations," an attitude that "may overlook forms of procedure and may display an inherited arrogance," while also exhibiting "hypersensitiveness to real or imagined insult and oppression."[41]

Thus the modern Chinese state of rationalized, Western systems of discipline was being undone by unstable and irrational Chinese bureaucrats.

THE CASE OF BITTÉR TEA

Despite what he called the "mechanical and artistic excellence" of *Bitter Tea*, J. B. Albeck, Columbia Picture's Far Eastern representative, "decided on no account to show it in China, because of the various difficulties which had arisen."[42] He was referring here, of course, to the problems experienced by *Shanghai Express*, as well as to the complaints that Capra's film already had generated in other foreign markets. Objections to the film came to China from Cuba, Batavia, Java, Sumatra, Chicago, and—the site of the most troublesome comments—Los Angeles, and from consul members rather than from students as in the case of *Shanghai Express*. In Havana, for instance, the Chinese consul general had managed to have about a thousand feet of film eliminated from *Bitter Tea*, while the consul general at Chicago lobbied to have "eliminated some sixty-three words of dialogue which . . . [he] considered insulting to China."[43]

The Los Angeles vice consul remained, however, the most intractable of the critics. He had apparently been sent to Los Angeles specifically "to look after films," with Herron complaining, in his memo to Peck, that he had become "pugilistically inclined in his obstreperous approach to the studios," and that "his idea is to demand that he be allowed to do this, that and the other." Herron added that "This attitude, of course, has not been conducive to good relations and it has irritated everyone of our people naturally." Herron complained that if the MPPDA gave in to the vice consul in the case of *Bitter Tea* and other films about China, then the organization would have to give in to representatives from all over the world. "The first thing we would know," Herron concluded rather ominously, "our industry would be run by a lot of foreign representatives."[44]

Just as the Chinese censorship apparatus somewhat mirrored Hollywood's Production Code, Herron, the industry representative, here registered a complaint about foreign influence in the studios that typically had been lodged against the industry itself. Throughout the 1920s and early 1930s, industry critics frequently associated the "salaciousness" of Hollywood films precisely with the influence of foreigners—namely, the Eastern European Jews who ran several studios. As Richard Maltby has pointed out, demands for censorship often came to be "couched in moralistic terms and under the anti-Semitic expectation that a Jewish-dominated industry had to be intimidated into decency."[45] For Herron, however, the problem had nothing to do with the perceived foreignness of any of Hollywood's executives, but rather with staving off the constant foreign pressure for influence. This pressure came from foreign governments, and, according to Herron, acceding to it finally would lead to an industry run not by the Louis B. Mayers, Harry Cohns, and Samuel Goldwyns whose own "Americanism" so often was called into question by U.S.-based critics, but by a hodgepodge of bureaucrats of varying nationalities, speaking various languages, and representing vastly different global interests.

This was bold talk from Herron. The development of sound film had made the censorship of international prints of Hollywood films more difficult; silent films usually only needed to have a title card reworded, but the state of recording and editing technology made the elimination of lines of dialogue more difficult, and it also affected the continuity of scenes. Nevertheless, as Ruth Vasey has pointed out, the Hollywood studios, at least from the end of World War I, typically "adapted [films] for release in overseas markets wherever their potential revenue outweighed the cost of modifying, distributing, and advertising them." In addition, the studios frequently sought the advice of consular representatives and other foreign officials in the planning of films with foreign locales or themes.[46] Regardless of Herron's feelings about the Chinese vice consul, this tendency toward accommodation, when it came to film content, even applied to the case of *Bitter Tea*.

The Los Angeles vice consul wrote to the Censorship Committee that Capra's film "contained situations and dialogues reflecting discredit on the Chinese race." To emphasize the point, the committee itself decided not to censor any further Columbia films, thereby keeping them from playing in China.[47] An alarmed Columbia representative wrote that, as a result, the studio might have to refund $60,000 to Chinese theaters that had already contracted to show the films that would be denied entry. As a sign of the continuing expansion of American film interests in China, the studio also had plans to open a branch office in Shanghai in early 1934, and so hoped not to alienate the Chinese government. Columbia, therefore, quickly volunteered to cut the offensive scenes and to apologize to the Chinese vice consul in Los Angeles, and then requested that the censors once again begin considering Columbia's motion pictures.[48]

The exact nature of the vice consul's objections remains somewhat obscure. One memo from Albeck, Columbia's representative, claimed that they amounted to only "eight sentences."[49] Yet another document, this one a State Department dispatch that quoted rather roughly from the film, detailed something less than two hundred words. According to this document, for example, in the first reel the vice consul complained when a missionary exclaims, "Rain and Fire! What a country! I pity him who devotes himself to China." The vice consul further objected to the same character complaining that some Chinese peasants, whom he had attempted to convert, were nothing but a bunch of "highway robbers," and that they were interested in the story of Christ only to the extent that it inspired them to crucify members of a desert caravan. In the sixth reel, the problem became an American arms merchant who claims with pride that "in the business of raising dough I am a match for any Chinese." This was relatively small change for Columbia, and the studio readily agreed to the cuts.[50]

Of course, neither diplomatic nor business relations ever run so smoothly. The vice consul really could not speak for the Chinese censors, and, for them, the cuts were not enough. Taking the complaints about the film very seriously, and invoking the precedent they set with *Shanghai Express*, the censors informed Albeck that they would "refuse to censor any further films brought to China by Columbia Pictures ... until that firm had agreed to withdraw *Bitter Tea of General Yen* from circulation throughout the world."[51] Just as they had with *Shanghai Express*, the National Board insisted that access to the Chinese market for an entire body of films from one studio depended upon the censors being able to control the global distribution of any individual film from the same studio. This was not lost on the various U.S. government officials and film industry representatives who weighed in on the incident, as they typically commented that the case of *Bitter Tea* served to continue the policy established with *Shanghai Express*.[52]

Compounding this very significant problem, but also somewhat separate from it, were the complaints that still came in from those areas where Columbia claimed that prints of the film already had been altered. The studio insisted that it had shown a re-edited version to the Chinese censors and, for good measure, to those in Batavia. Nevertheless, Chinese consular officials insisted that the offending footage remained in Batavian prints, and also in those showing in Java and Sumatra. Similarly, in Cuba, although the re-edited film had been shown in Havana, a complete, original print circulated in other locales (resulting in a fine being levied by the Cuban authorities against "the persons responsible").[53]

These events demonstrate some of the significant problems with global film markets and the attempts to regulate them. Just as censorship in China might vary between regions (for instance, as noted above, the separate censorship committee in Shanghai), so too might communications from a country's government officials vary considerably, even to the point of contradiction. Columbia apparently felt that by acting on the Chinese vice consul's requests for a re-edited version, the studio would also appease the censors in Nanking. Instead, the censors lobbied for the film's complete withdrawal from the global market. In addition, if it is to be believed that Columbia really did delete several passages from the film, the studio itself apparently could not assure that those new versions actually would be exhibited, or that, in the case of the Havana version, a print tailored for one Cuban city would necessarily be exhibited in another. Even though the Hollywood studios made a limited number of prints and attempted to control their distribution fairly vigorously, the *Bitter Tea* documents indicate that different versions might well have circulated regardless of studio efforts.[54] Further, as Albeck pointed out in Columbia's defense, in some markets the studio sold its films outright rather than renting them, thereby losing any of its ability to enforce cuts and, as a result, its capacity to placate some of the demands of foreign censorship.[55]

The studio also maintained a somewhat loose relationship with its foreign distributors. Charles Roberts, the assistant foreign manager for Columbia, wrote to Albeck, the studio's Far Eastern representative, about the problems of the film in the Dutch East Indies. Columbia had never favored exhibiting the film there precisely because of the possibility of protest, but the studio's distributor in the Dutch East Indies and adjoining territories had insisted on placing the film in the theaters under his purview. He seems to have come to regret this decision, apparently because of Chinese consular objections, but Columbia wanted to wash its hands of him and his problems. "If we are successful in these arrangements we will take Mr. Samuel's print away from him and he will be rid of all his worries," Roberts wrote. He then added, however, "If we are not successful . . . we must leave it up to him to get the situation straightened out." Roberts then insisted that the distributor had acted alone because the studio "never favored the shipment of this picture to the Dutch East Indies," and that it gave in only because of the distributor's "insistence." The global distribution system thus seems to have been a diffuse one, initially coordinated by the studio's foreign office but then very much left in the hands of individual, territorial distributors with the power to act on their own.[56]

When *Bitter Tea* did play in these foreign territories, it faced Chinese lobbying efforts designed to keep people away. In the Dutch East Indies, Batavia, Singapore, Manila, and Calcutta, Chinese consular officials advised Chinese citizens "not to patronize the film in question." The exact nature of this consular advice remains unclear, but it was apparently effective enough, according to Willys Peck, to have "resulted in loss to the American firm." Peck, the State Department official, urged China's Foreign Office to contact their consulates and tell them that *Bitter Tea* indeed had been amended according to consular recommendations, and that the re-edited film had been screened for the National Board of Film Censors in Nanking.[57] Indicating the confusion caused by the case, however, and one that may have been either willful or accidental, the Foreign Office, after contacting the National Board for instructions, "was told that the Board knew nothing about the merits of the film." As a result, "The Foreign Office . . . expressed its inability to take the action requested" by Peck.[58] Here, then, a kind of extragovernmental form of censorship—that is, one organized by individual diplomatic officials rather than by the National Board of Film Censors but nevertheless receiving the Board's tacit approval—seems to have had an impact on the foreign revenues of Capra's film.

The continuing inability of Columbia and the State Department on the one hand, and the Chinese government on the other, to reach an agreement led to some fascinating discussions by all parties to justify their positions. Indeed, these justifications point out certain governmental and corporate notions of film reception and also of national difference. Both Columbia and the State Department invoked a sort of global reception practice to make the film seem harmless to the Chinese. Albeck, the studio's Far Eastern representative, argued that the film "portrayed the Chinese in a favorable light, since a Chinese bandit general was depicted as a hero." He used, as proof of his interpretation, the advice of Columbia's Japanese distributor, who recommended against showing the film in Japan—China's longtime enemy—precisely because of the sympathetic depiction of General Yen.[59] In a subsequent memo to the Board of Censors, Albeck insisted that this constituted absolute proof of the film's fitness: "The fact that Columbia's buyer in Japan has objected to take delivery of this picture, because it shows a Chinese General as a hero and in general gives a friendly picturization of Chinese," Albeck wrote, "will convince you, that the picture in general can not be considered offensive to [the] Chinese."[60]

Again and again, Columbia and the State Department brought up the Japanese in order to make the film acceptable to Chinese officials. Willys Peck, for example, engaged in a lengthy debate with Chaucer Wu of the Chinese Foreign Office about the fitness of *Bitter Tea* and about Wu's objections to the anti-Chinese dialogue in the film. Peck, reprising his logic in the *Shanghai Express* case, wrote that "I called his attention to the fact . . . that every country has its enemies and to represent such enemies in a play as praising the country in question would be ridiculous." He went on to state that "to reduce the matter to its simplest elements, I observed that every Japanese in a motion picture play, if he were to meet the view of the Chinese, must be represented as finding no fault whatever in China." In other words, the imperatives of the dramatic form made it impossible not to insult China in the film, and disregarding this logic would lead to films in which even Japanese characters would be forbidden to criticize China. Peck seems to have felt quite satisfied with this lesson in film appreciation, narrative construction, and character motivation, and he noted that "Mr. Wu admitted the force of this contention."[61]

To underscore the point that the film should be acceptable to the Chinese, both Peck and Albeck shifted from narrative to ideological grounds. In a discussion with Peck, Albeck claimed that, if nothing else, the "one feature of the film that ought to please the Chinese was the denunciation of American missionaries by the Chinese general." Peck then used this interpretation to turn the Chinese censors' argument around by insisting that he "did not think it would be a good idea to show such a film in China, because it would be harmful to American missionary interests, which constituted a very important American interest in China."[62] That is, Peck interpreted Capra's film (which he admitted he had not seen) as being critical of an American religious movement with global aspirations.[63] As a result, Bitter Tea, if shown either in China or in territories with large Chinese populations, would act only to bolster the new Chinese regime's anti-Westernism. By this logic, the Chinese censors should have welcomed the film, and the Chinese consular officials should have urged Chinese nationals to see it.

Practically missing, of course, from these rather thorough readings of the film is any mention of the romance between the white American missionary and the Chinese general. Indeed, in Peck's comments and those of others interested in the case, the relationship can only be hinted at, and then without any judgments being made, or made only obliquely. Neither the National Board of Film Censors nor the various vice consuls seems to have had any problem with this aspect of the film. All of the requests for dialogue cuts, for instance, concerned descriptions of China or the Chinese. In at least one of China's "independent censorship areas," however, the love story may have constituted grounds for banning the film. In Shanghai, censorship regulations clearly reflected the ongoing colonial status of the city, and the attempt of Westerners to maintain power and authority in part by controlling motion pictures. In that city's International Settlement, censors banned films that "prominently" featured "the color question," and also those that were "calculated directly to lower the moral prestige of women (especially white women)."[64] American officials, however, seem to have positioned themselves somewhere between the Chinese censors and those in Shanghai—that is, able to acknowledge the romance as an issue, but unable to state precisely just what kind of issue it may have been.

In his conversation with Peck, Albeck mentioned that "the Chinese general was represented as falling in love with the American heroine, but as deporting himself in an unexceptionable way." Thus, Yen's gentlemanliness—that which the film clearly posits as his European manners—seems, for Albeck, to exempt the film from any exploitation of "the color question." The memo then either recounts the same conversation or indicates that Peck wanted to clarify further the nature of the love story: "Mr. Peck inquired whether the American heroine was represented as falling in love with the Chinese general, and Mr. Albeck said that this phase was touched on very lightly."[65] The men then moved quickly to their very assured discussion of the film's antimissionary zeal. The romance, then, became something of a structuring absence in the official American discourse about the film. It could be mentioned, but without any certainty as to what it might signify in terms of international censorship, and then it must quickly be dismissed. The romance seems, potentially, to have posed problems for both Peck and Albeck, but they were unable to place it within the narrative of the negotiations between the Chinese censors, the Department of State, and Columbia.[66]

The Chinese officials, rather than countering with their own interpretive strategies, instead invoked a desire for efficient, rational international relations. Chaucer Wu of the Chinese Foreign Office, during his own discussion with Peck, "observed that the Chinese Government is often in receipt of requests from different nationalities asking that motion picture films objectionable to them be suppressed, action which the Chinese Government sometimes takes in the interest of the international good relations."[67] Thus, for the Chinese, the request to suppress, from one friendly government to another, should suffice. The Americans countered this assertion of Chinese diplomatic gentlemanliness with their own version of national, governmental superiority, based on film reception. As Albeck wrote in his memo to An Shih Ju of the National Board of Film Censors: "You will be aware, that American films often picturize Americans as all kinds of crooks and murderers and in this particular film the Chinese General Yen is making some very insulting remarks about American missionaries." He then added that all of this took place "without the American Government having raised any objections."[68] Thus while Peck in his debate with

Wu tried to give a lesson in film appreciation, Albeck simply insisted that American authorities had a far more reasonable attitude about representational issues.

Peck himself seems to have come around to Albeck's point of view. After several months of discussions with the Chinese, Peck felt that there was little left that the government could do, and he suggested that Columbia's home office in New York take up the negotiations. He lamented that the censors in "Nanking are genuinely sympathetic with the efforts of Chinese abroad to put an end to what they all consider are insulting references to Chinese in motion picture films." Peck complained that "the Chinese are unreasonable in these matters," and then he invoked his argument from the *Shanghai Express* case that the Chinese simply were different from Americans. Rather than insisting on a kind of modernized, bureaucratic arrogance primarily afflicting younger Chinese, as he had in his dealings with von Sternberg's film, Peck this time claimed that the censors' objections to American representational practices were simply "matters of sentiment" and that, in the case of *Bitter Tea*, "logic" on the part of the Chinese "does not seem to count for very much."[69]

Despite Peck's problems with the Chinese censors, however, the State Department finally found itself limited in its ability to formulate criticism of Chinese censorship policy. Officials could not find fault with Chinese national practice, but rather only with the attempts by the Chinese to manipulate the world market for American films. The acting secretary of state, William Phillips, weighed in here by restating the United States' official policy of and support for self-determining national markets. According to Phillips, the United States "does not question the right of any government to prevent within that government's jurisdiction the exhibition of any motion picture which it may regard as contrary to its interests." Indeed, Phillips, who seems to have been the highest-ranking official to offer an opinion in the case, went so far as to assert the possibility of aligning the United States with Chinese efforts to ban all of a studio's product—as had been threatened with both Paramount and Columbia—pending the removal from global distribution of a single film. The assistant secretary of state wrote that the government would not "be disposed to object if permission to exhibit pictures of any particular company were made conditional on the suppression" of a specific film. In making this statement of policy, Phillips proposed a theory of the absolute readability of any film and of the possibility of scientific certainty about the meaning of a movie. A foreign government could only be justified in making demands similar to China's when, "following a dispassionate and unbiased study thereof, [a film] is found to contain features which vilify or hold up to ridicule the people or government of a friendly power or which are likely to affect adversely international relations."[70]

Thus the government both acknowledged the disruptive potential of motion pictures in the global market and also established limits as to how much it would assist any American business enterprise. Nevertheless, Phillips established an extremely difficult standard for any foreign government to meet in the assessment of film content. As he wrote: "Such extreme measures on the part of any government, however, would be warranted only when there could be no reasonable doubt as to the seriously objectionable character of the picture and when the picture could not be revised so as to remove its objectionable elements, or when the producer refused to make such a revision."[71] Columbia, of course, had passed this test, and so, by Phillips's calculation the studio could count on at least some government support.

As a further sign of the government's willingness to help, and as an indication of the compatibility between national and business interests, Phillips insisted on the right of the United States to protect commercial access to what might be considered "neutral" territories. In response to China's demand that *Bitter Tea* be removed from the global market, Phillips insisted that "this Government could not admit the right of any government to demand the suppression of an American picture outside the jurisdiction of the government making the demand, and any attempt to coerce American producers by unreasonable demands should be firmly opposed."[72] Almost certainly, Phillips stressed Chinese jurisdiction over its own markets in order to justify the same for the United States. For the movie business, in regard to the United States, this meant access to most of the world.

These, then, were the two battles being fought between Columbia and the State Department on one side, and the Chinese government on the other: the first, determining national rights in domestic markets and in global ones, and the second, ascertaining control of representational practice and interpretation. In terms of the latter, the State Department and Columbia argued for logical, "dispassionate" systems of film reception. Japanese disapproval must lead to Chinese approval, and the critique of

American missionaries in the film must soften any of the movie's criticism of the Chinese. The Chinese censors and consular officials were no less rigorous and narrow, despite the State Department's claim of their sentimentality. They argued, simultaneously, to ban the film and to delete sections of dialogue, with Columbia gladly agreeing to make the proposed cuts.

The Chinese government also seems to have proposed the most acceptable solution to the "problem" of the film, and it did so in such a way that would make *Bitter Tea* readable, finally, as a kind of literary fantasy, with all of the disclaimers usually associated with Western historical novels. Chaucer Wu of the Chinese Foreign Office, who had had to submit to Willys Peck's lectures on film appreciation, alerted Peck that "the Foreign Office had devised a means to meet the needs of the situation." Wu proposed that Columbia add a prologue to the beginning of the international prints of *Bitter Tea*, one that would read: "The picture represents a mere literary fancy devised by its author, and it does not in any way pretend to depict actual conditions in the real life of China. Its setting is introduced merely to promote the story of the sentimental conflicts of two civilizations symbolized by a Chinese warrior and an American girl."[73] Thus Wu wanted to create a reception context, through the prologue, in which the film must be read as allegory, or only as melodrama, rather than as faithfully reproducing current events. In the battle over the regulation and reception of the film, and over the representation of Chinese events, Wu and the other Chinese officials wanted a final version of *Bitter Tea* that emphasized the sentimental narrative and not the political one.

Peck liked the idea, calling it "ingenious," and also appreciated its literary quality, likening it to the prologues that preceded so many novels about "contemporary politics" and that denied the likeness of any characters to persons living or dead.[74] He passed the idea on to Albeck, who forwarded it to the Columbia home office, "asking them to get such [a] 'prologue' prepared for insertion in all the prints." Albeck added that he hoped this would "clear up any misunderstandings which may exist with regard to this picture." Columbia apparently viewed this solution as the most practical one, and although the studio cautioned Peck that preparing prologues for all prints worldwide might take awhile, it decided to implement Wu's idea. The studio further asked Peck to issue an apology, on its behalf, to the Chinese. Expressing its "desire to continue to do business in China," the studio asked Peck to "point out to the Chinese authorities that Columbia is doing everything possible to avoid in . . . future productions any scenes or dialogues which may be considered offensive to the Chinese."[75]

This seems to have solved the *Bitter Tea* crisis, and in somewhat the same way—in part through a formal apology and an assurance that the studio would not allow this to happen again—that Paramount brought closure to the case of *Shanghai Express*. Columbia issued the apology and began inserting prologues in December 1933, and the following month the State Department closed its file on the case.[76] It is difficult to determine how many prints with prologues actually played throughout the world, and also the expediency with which the Chinese censors once again began reviewing Columbia's films. In a struggle over the international film market, however, the Chinese government appears to have won the battle over the "final cut" of *Bitter Tea*, thereby amply demonstrating that even as late as the 1930s a studio's control over its own product was never as absolute as perhaps has been perceived.

THE CASE OF BITTER TEA AND FILM HISTORY

The incidents surrounding *The Bitter Tea of General Yen* might provide a way to rethink the manner in which audiences understood the films they saw, as well as the logic on the part of studio executives that went into production decisions. First and most narrowly, we can start to imagine an international regulatory and reception context in which Josef von Sternberg, the director of *Shanghai Express*, and Capra, the director of *Bitter Tea*, might be placed together as filmmakers. Such a pairing makes little sense in terms of most modern auteurist practices, with Sternberg the director of European and orientalist exotica, and Capra the purveyor par excellence of homespun Americana. But their films about China were both interpreted and handled in almost identical ways by the Chinese censors. More broadly, scholars might also be able to chart in increasingly complex terms the development of genres. Although it would take more research to be sure, Hollywood studios apparently slowed down their production of films about China in the latter part of the 1930s. The lavish version of *The Good Earth* released by MGM in 1937 may well have been one of the final movies in the cycle, while in terms of international diplomacy such films as *Oil for the Lamps of China* (1935) and *The General Died at Dawn* (1936) seem to have been among the last American movies to raise the ire of Chinese censors in the manner of *Shanghai Express* and *Bitter Tea*.[77] This lessening of interest on the part of producers may have had to do with a small cycle of films running its course with the American audience, or with a shift toward movies related to World War II, or with an inability to find the dramatic interest, for domestic viewers at least, in the Sino-Japanese war that began in 1937. But the end of the cycle of films about China also may have been influenced quite significantly by the headache of dealing with Chinese censorship.

Understanding the issues of international censorship also helps us to understand, or at least to extend the possibilities for understanding, the "success" or "failure" of a film at the box office. *Bitter Tea* has been labeled, with some justification, a failure. There may well have been reasons for this in the domestic market, but the imposition of foreign censorship restrictions, the threat of such restrictions, the lobbying efforts by foreign officials, and the unavailability of certain markets also may help to explain the film's performance. China itself counted for a relatively small percentage of foreign income for Hollywood studios, but the Chinese censors' ability to slow down the distribution of Capra's film throughout the world (by insisting on cuts and adding a prologue), consular efforts to keep audiences away in Cuba and other territories, and Columbia's inability to show the film in Japan certainly could not have helped the film's financial prospects.[78]

Most significantly, the case of *Bitter Tea* shows that, at least in the 1930s, individual Hollywood films did not take shape solely from discussions between the studios and the Hays Office, which administered the Production Code, or from debates between the MPPDA and American censors in various states and localities. Instead, these films also were the product of negotiations between studio officials, the federal government, and foreign governments. The global market also becomes more complex through a consideration of the *Bitter Tea* documents. The American film industry may have controlled this market, but the Hollywood studios simply could not impose their will on foreign theaters and viewers. Indeed, the studios might willingly avoid parts of this market (Columbia never intended to exhibit *Bitter Tea* in China), they might enter other parts of it only unwillingly (as in the case of the Dutch East Indies), or they may have been kept out of some sectors as a result of a rather diffuse chain of command (the Columbia distributor who decided not to show *Bitter Tea* in Japan). And often, unless the studios acquiesced to their demands, foreign censors at least could threaten to ban a film company's entire output. This is not to discount Hollywood hegemony, but instead to call for a more nuanced understanding of the place of American movies in the world. By explicating the complex relation of Hollywood to the global market we can understand the connections between American film corporations and the American government, and we also can understand the relationships between governments—in this case the United States and China—that finally helped to determine Hollywood's business practices and representational strategies.

NOTES

1 Frederick L. Herron to Willys R. Peck, May 31, 1933, State Department file 893.4061 (Motion Pictures), document no. 76, National Archives, Washington, D.C. (hereafter 893.4061 Motion Pictures/76).

2 Ruth Vasey discusses Herron's appointment in *The World According to Hollywood, 1918–1939* (Madison: University of Wisconsin Press, 1997), 38.

3 For a case study of local censorship in the United States during the 1930s, by both government and independent interests, see Greg M. Smith, "Blocking *Blockade*: Partisan Protest, Popular Debate, and Encapsulated Texts," *Cinema Journal* 36, no. 1 (fall 1996): 18–38. Some form of federal censorship extended at least into the 1940s. For a study of how the Office of War Information influenced film production, see Rick Worland, "OWI Meets the Monsters: Hollywood Horror Films and War Propaganda, 1942 to 1945," *Cinema Journal* 37, no. 1 (fall 1997): 47–65.

4 The American cinema is not the only one so affected. Other national cinemas, especially during times of market dominance, have had to contend with international regulatory practices. Richard Abel discusses this issue in regard to pre–World War I French cinema in *The Red Rooster Scare: Making Cinema American, 1900–1910* (Berkeley: University of California Press, 1999).

5 Maltby discusses the studios' responses to censorship debates in Tino Balio's *Grand Design: Hollywood as a Modern Business Enterprise, 1930–1939* (Berkeley: University of California Press, 1995), see chapter 3, "The Production Code and the Hays Office," 37–72. Other useful histories of Hollywood movie censorship include Gregory D. Black, *Hollywood Censored: Morality Codes, Catholics, and the Movies* (Cambridge: Cambridge University Press, 1994); Garth Jowett, *Film: The Democratic Art* (Boston: Little, Brown, 1976); and Francis G. Couvares, ed., *Movie Censorship and American Culture* (Washington, D.C.: Smithsonian Institution Press, 1996).

6 Ruth Vasey, Kristin Thompson, Ian Jarvie, and Thomas J. Saunders are among the few scholars who have written exemplary studies of Hollywood's relations

with foreign markets. See Vasey, *The World According to Hollywood, 1918–1939;* Thompson, *Exporting Entertainment: America in the World Film Market, 1907–1934* (London: British Film Institute, 1985); Jarvie, *Hollywood's Overseas Campaign: The North Atlantic Movie Trade, 1920–1950* (Cambridge: Cambridge University Press, 1992); and Saunders, *Hollywood in Berlin: American Cinema and Weimar Germany* (Berkeley: University of California Press, 1994).

7 Joseph McBride, *Frank Capra: The Catastrophe of Success* (New York: Simon and Schuster, 1992), 281.

8 In its first eight days at Radio City *Bitter Tea* made $80,000, an extraordinary amount of money for the period. The next highest-grossing film in New York, for instance, during the same period (in this case only seven days) was *A Farewell to Arms,* which earned $52,500. Much of the earnings of Capra's film, however, might be attributable to the opening of Radio City and to the relatively high ticket prices, which ranged from $0.35 to $1.65 (patrons of the Paramount, where *Farewell* played, paid only $0.35 to $0.99). That same week, in Chicago and Los Angeles, Capra's film earned, respectively, 30 percent and 8 percent less than the films playing the previous week (*Motion Picture Herald,* January 28, 1933, 32, 34). At Radio City Music Hall, the week after *Bitter Tea* played there, *The King's Vacation* earned $88,000 in seven days (*Motion Picture Herald,* February 4. 1933, 42).

9 For a review of the historical events that form the context for the film, see David Palumbo-Liu, "The *Bitter Tea* of Frank Capra," *positions* 3, no. 3 (winter 1995): 759–89.

10 One theater manager complained that the film contained too much "war, Chinese and horrible things our patrons have had too much of," indicating that at least some audiences in the United States may have been tired not only of films about China, but of events taking place in China (*Motion Picture Herald,* July 1, 1933, 49). For the analysis of small town movie tastes, see *Motion Picture Herald,* May 20, 1933, 45, and June 24, 1933, 45. Stanwyck is quoted in McBride, *Frank Capra,* 281. I have found no evidence to support her claim, but it seems plausible that some of the groups (e.g., those led by women, teachers, parents, etc.) that judged the suitability of films for young audiences would have objected to the interracial romance in *Bitter Tea.* For the theater manager's report on small towns during the Depression, see *Motion Picture Herald,* July 1, 1933, 49.

11 Palumbo-Liu, "The *Bitter Tea* of Frank Capra," 766, 767. For a superb analysis of the film as a captivity narrative, see Gina Marchetti, *Romance and the "Yellow Peril"* (Berkeley: University of California Press, 1993), 49–57.

12 There is, to my knowledge, no extended scholarship on the film's problems with British censors. For brief discussions, see McBride, *Frank Capra,* 282, and Vasey, *The World According to Hollywood,* 150. In his autobiography, Capra claimed that the film indeed had been "banned in Great Britain and in the British Commonwealth countries, due to the shocking implications of a love

affair between a yellow man and a white woman" (Capra, *The Name above the Title: An Autobiography* [New York: Macmillan, 1971], 141–42). The existing Hays Office files, housed at the Academy of Motion Pictures' Margaret Herrick Library, indicate very smooth sailing with the Hays Office. On July 11, 1932, Jason Joy, in charge of the Hays Office's Studio Relations Committee, wrote to the Columbia Pictures studio head Harry Cohn: "We have read with very much pleasure Script no. 3, *The Bitter Tea of General Yen* and believe that it is satisfactory from the standpoint of the [Production] Code and that it is free of any reasonable censorship worries." On November 4, 1932, James Wingate, who had succeeded Joy, also wrote to Cohn: "Recently we had the pleasure of reviewing the Columbia picture, *The Bitter Tea of General Yen*. We found it to be an excellent picture, free from elements to which official censorship could take serious objection . . . We had no suggestions whatever to make to the studio as regards any necessity for prerelease cuts." Columbia did, however, have to make some cuts in the film for showings in New York, Pennsylvania, Ohio, and Massachusetts (for the latter, sequences only needed to be cut for Sunday showings of the film, but it is doubtful that theaters showed one print six days of the week and another print on Sundays).

13 By the end of the nineteenth century and the beginning of the twentieth, the United States had moved from the position of primarily a buyer of Chinese goods—silk and tea, for instance—to selling American goods in China. See Mira Wilkins, "The Impacts of American Multinational Enterprise on American-Chinese Economic Relations, 1786–1949," in *America's China Trade in Historical Perspective: The Chinese and American Performance*, ed. Ernest R. May and John K. Fairbank (Cambridge, Mass.: Harvard University Press, 1986), 259–88. As just one example of American business involvement, in 1921 Henry Ford became interested in China, and by 1928, as Wilkins notes, he had "decided to open a sales and service branch in Shanghai to cover China, French Indochina and the Philippines" (275–76). As Wilkins points out, though, there were a variety of American investors in China during the period: "Not all U.S. investors in Chinese industry were part of multinational enterprises. There were also individual American businessmen resident in China" (279).

14 C. F. Remer, *Foreign Investments in China* (New York: Macmillan, 1933); Carl Crow, *Four Hundred Million Customers: The Experiences—Some Happy, Some Sad—of an American in China* (New York: Harper and Brothers, 1937). For an additional view of American business interests in China from this period, see *China through the American Window*, compiled by Julean Arnold, the commercial attaché in China for the U.S. Department of Commerce (Shanghai: American Chamber of Commerce, 1932). According to Arnold: "I believe I echo the sentiments of our American business public in China in expressing the ardent hope that as modern means of communications bring these two great Pacific countries into closer and more intimate contact and as the ever expanding interchange of commodities accentuate their interdependence, the

urge to intelligent mutual understanding may lead to the development of enduring foundations of good will and friendship" (14).

15 Crow, *Four Hundred Million Customers*, 12, 33.

16 Bruno Lasker, ed., *Problems of the Pacific 1931: Proceedings of the Fourth Conference of the Institute of Pacific Relations, Hangchow and Shanghai, China, October 21 to November 2* (Chicago: University of Chicago Press, 1932), 467.

17 "The Motion Picture Industry in China," 21, completed October 4, 1932, 893.4061, Motion Pictures/69.

18 Ibid., 52.

19 Ibid., 20–23.

20 Ibid., 22.

21 Ibid., 72.

22 Ibid., 28–29.

23 For a discussion of the national cinemas that were popular in Shanghai, see "The Motion Picture Industry in China," 47. For information on the Hollywood practices of subtitling and dubbing, see Vasey, *The World According to Hollywood*, 63–99.

24 Frederic Wakeman Jr., *Policing Shanghai 1927–1937* (Berkeley: University of California Press, 1996), 10–11.

25 "The Motion Picture Industry in China," 25.

26 For information on the "party-republic" and on "national construction," see Wakeman, *Policing Shanghai*, xv.

27 Wakeman, *Policing Shanghai*, 8. Throughout this section on Shanghai, I am indebted to Wakeman's exemplary study. Other very useful studies of China during this period include Albert Feuerwerker, *The Chinese Economy, 1912–1949* (Ann Arbor: University of Michigan Press, 1968); Edwin E. Moise, *Modern China: A History* (London: Longman Group, 1986); and May and Fairbank, eds., *America's China Trade in Historical Perspective*.

28 Wakeman discusses the crackdown on "vice" in *Policing Shanghai*, 97–115 (see pp. 238–39 for a discussion of the efforts to police the film industry).

29 Wakeman, *Policing Shanghai*, 11.

30 "The Motion Picture Industry in China," 2–4, examines the formation of, and rules governing, the Censorship Committee (a definition of the "Three People's Principles" is given on p. 2).

31 "The Motion Picture Industry in China," 4, mentions the banned films, and the reason why most films were banned. Butrick's estimate of the percentage of films that needed to be re-edited is on p. 5.

32 Wakeman, *Policing Shanghai*, 58.

33 Peck related this conversation in a memo to the Secretary of State, April 15, 1932, 893.4061, Motion Pictures/59.

34 Ibid.

35 See memo, June 24, 1932, from the State Department, Division of Far Eastern Affairs, 893.4061, Motion Pictures/61.

36 For a discussion of other forms of film censorship in China, see "The Motion Picture Industry in China," 9. For a discussion of the Shanghai American Women's Club, see p. 14.

37 Peck discusses the objections of the Chinese students in Germany in a memo to the Secretary of State, August 9, 1932, no. D-318, 893.4061, Motion Pictures/64.

38 Peck mentions the complaint from Chinese students in Germany in a memo to Nelson Trusler Johnson, American Minister, Peiping, June 21, 1932, Despatch no. 1592. An anonymous memo from the State Department, Division of Far Eastern Affairs, August 10, 1932, mentions the complaint from Chinese students in the United States.

39 Ibid.

40 Peck to Secretary of State Henry L. Stimson, August 9, 1932.

41 Ibid.

42 Memorandum of Conversation, Johs. Albeck, Representative for the Far East of the Columbia Pictures Distributing Company, Inc., on "Objection of the Chinese National Board of Film Censors to the Film *Bitter Tea of General Yen*," May 23, 1933, 893.4061 Motion Pictures/74.

43 For the complaints from Batavia, Sumatra, and Java, see J. H. Seidelman, Foreign Manager, to Mr. Kiang, Chinese Consulate, Los Angeles, October 6, 1933, 893.4061 Motion Pictures/101. The objections from Cuba are described by Willys R. Peck in a memo to Nelson Trusler Johnson, American Minister in Peiping, October 12, 1933, 893.4061 Motion Pictures/89. For Chicago objections, see Peck to Johnson, June 20, 1933, 893.4061 Motion Pictures/80.

44 Herron to Peck, May 31, 1933.

45 Maltby, in Balio, *Grand Design*, 49.

46 Vasey, *The World According to Hollywood*, 84, 80.

47 Memorandum of Conversation, Johs. Albeck and Willys Peck, May 23, 1933, 893.4061, Motion Pictures/74.

48 Albeck and Peck discussed the $60,000 investment in the May 23, 1933, Memorandum of Conversation. Albeck mentioned the proposed branch office in Shanghai in a memo to Peck, November 24, 1933, 893.4061, Motion Pictures/97. For the agreement to make the cuts, and the apology to the Chinese government, see Albeck to Peck, May 25, 1933, and Albeck to An Shih Ju, Chairman of the National Board of Censors, Nanking, May 25, 1933. Both documents are numbered 893.4061, Motion Pictures/76.

49 Albeck to An Shih Ju, May 25, 1933.

50 For the dialogue to which the Chinese censors objected, see Despatch to the American Legation no. L-36 Diplomatic, from Nanking, China.

51 Peck to Johnson, May 31, 1933, 893.4061, Motion Pictures/74.

52 See, for instance, Herron to Peck, May 31, 1933. Also, Peck to Johnson, June 7, 1933, 893.4061, Motion Pictures/76.

53 Seidelman to Kiang, Los Angeles, October 6, 1933. Peck to Johnson, October 12, 1933.

54 Douglas Gomery has written that during the 1930s studios typically made about four hundred prints of a film, although it is not clear if Gomery is speaking here only of domestic prints or of global prints as well. See Gomery, *The Hollywood Studio System* (New York: St. Martin's Press, 1986), 18.

55 Albeck to Puma Films Ltd., Shanghai, December 11, 1933, 893.4061, Motion Pictures/101.

56 Charles Roberts to Albeck, October 10, 1933, 893.4061, Motion Pictures/101.

57 Peck to Dr. Louis N. Tchou, Director of Department of International Affairs, Waichiaopu, Nanking, October 3, 1933, 893.4061, Motion Pictures/88. For the report on the Dutch East Indies, Singapore, Manila, and Calcutta, as well as Batavia, see Peck to Johnson, October 6, 1933, 893.4061, Motion Pictures/88.

58 Despatch to Legation no. L-34, from Nanking. Subject: *The Bitter Tea of General Yen*, October 6, 1933, 893.4061, Motion Pictures/88.

59 Memorandum of Conversation, Albeck and Peck, May 23, 1933.

60 Albeck to An Shih Ju, May 25, 1933.

61 Peck to Johnson, October 12, 1933, 893.4061, Motion Pictures/89.

62 Memorandum of Conversation, Albeck and Peck, May 23, 1933.

63 Peck acknowledges not having seen the film in the memo to Johnson recording his meeting with Chaucer H. Wu of the Chinese Foreign Office, October 12, 1933, 893.4061, Motion Pictures/101 (in fact, at this time Wu also had not seen the film).

64 "The Motion Picture Industry in China," 10.

65 Memorandum of Conversation, Albeck and Peck, May 23, 1933.

66 It is precisely this "structuring absence" of the romance that has been of primary interest to contemporary scholars. For the best analysis of the relationship between Megan and General Yen, see Marchetti, *Romance and the Yellow Peril*, 46–57.

67 Peck to Johnson, October 12, 1933.

68 Albeck to An Shih Ju, May 25, 1933.

69 Peck to Albeck, December 1, 1933 893.4061, Motion Pictures/97.

70 William Phillips to Johnson, August 3, 1933, 893.4061, Motion Pictures/74.

71 Ibid.

72 Ibid.

73 Peck to Johnson, October 12, 1933.

74 Peck to Nelson Trusler Johnson, October 12, 1933.

75 Peck expressed his admiration for the prologue solution in his memo to Johnson, October 12, 1933. For Albeck forwarding the idea to Columbia, cautioning about the time that implementation might take and also stressing Columbia's pledge for future productions, see Albeck to Peck, December 12, 1933, 893.4061, Motion Pictures/101.

76 The last document in the file is dated February 1, 1934.

77 Some of the documents relating to *Oil for the Lamps of China* and *The General Died at Dawn* have been published in *Foreign Relations of the United States:*

Diplomatic Papers, 1936, vol. 4, *The Far East* (Washington, D.C.: Government Printing Office, 1936), 670–85.

78 In 1927, the last year for which I have found figures, China accounted for only 0.8 percent of Hollywood's foreign income (Japan accounted for 3.1 percent; Cuba for 1.25 percent). Great Britain, where *Bitter Tea* also experienced severe censorship problems, accounted for 30.5 percent of foreign income, by far the largest percentage of any foreign territory. See Vasey, *The World According to Hollywood*, 84.

PLAIN BROWN WRAPPER
Adult Films for the Home Market, 1930–1969
Eric Schaefer

A few years ago, a staff member where I work called me into his office. His grandfather had died recently and had left him a box of 8mm home movies that the old man had made. Mixed in with the home movies were some reels of commercial films—Castle newsreel digests, sports films, and Blackhawk prints of Laurel and Hardy. And then there was the coffee can that contained, along with a brochure for "Candid Cinema," several reels of Joe Bonica's *Movie of the Month*, with titles like "Atomic Bomb" and "Underwater Ballet." The staffer was surprised not only that Gramps had owned a stash of nudie movies but also that such movies had been made and distributed in the 1940s and 1950s when his grandfather had participated in the 8mm hobby.

Much of the received wisdom today is that home video and cable television served to "domesticate" adult films by moving them from urban grindhouses and the basements of VFW halls into the living rooms and bedrooms of Mr. and Mrs. America in the 1980s. Certainly when we think about adult movies in the prevideo era, whether "adults only" exploitation films or even "smokers" featuring stag films, we have an image of material that was consumed in a social setting, whether in a theater or in the "private" space of a lodge or fraternity hall. In any event it was not in the home, the province of "dirty" books, French postcards, spicy pulps, nudist magazines, and later *Playboy* and its progeny. But the adult film was domesticated decades before home video arrived on the scene, a fact that is often overlooked by those who study pornography as well as those who campaign against it.

Adult movies that were made for the home market are certainly not "lost" films. They exist in abundance in video collections (e.g., Something Weird Video's series "Nudie Cuties Shorts, Loops and Peeps" among many others) and in caches at flea markets and yard sales. It's common to see dozens of 8mm movies up for bid at any given time on Internet auction sites such as eBay, often commanding sums that seem outrageous for a "dead" medium. While the actual movies may be abundant—if not well catalogued or documented—what is lacking is systematic information about who made the films and how they were made, how they were advertised and distributed, and how they were used. These movies, which probably number in the tens of thousands, have remained invisible due to their borderline legal status at various points in history and because they were usually used in the home, away from the prying eyes of friends and neighbors, law enforcement officials, and moral crusaders.

Moving image archivists, who are slowly being joined by film scholars and social historians, have come to champion "small gauge" and "orphan" films in recognizing their historical, and occasionally aesthetic, value.[1] Small gauge films represent a fascinating intersection between the movies, technology, and everyday life, and they are only now being mined for the insights they contain on life in the twentieth century.[2] But adult films continue to be seen as problematic. The sexual nature of the material, whether coy and teasing or flagrant, appears to be at odds with the content of much of small gauge film: celebrations of middle-class family life in the form of children's birthday parties, holiday revelry, vacation pictures, and the like. Even the commercial movies available for the home market—cartoons, comedies, historical events and newsreels, sports films—could give the appearance of a wholesome addition to the domestic entertainment diet.

Adult films for the home market have, then, been doubly orphaned by their substandard gauge and by their dubious status. But it is possible to put together a provisional history of this form by casting a wide net—using articles from the mainstream press, business correspondence, government documents, interviews, and advertising materials. Patterns of manufacture, distribution, sales, and use begin to emerge from the period of the early 1930s—the point from which the earliest documents date—to 1969, when the U.S. Supreme Court handed down its decision in *Stanley v. Georgia*. That decision effectively said that "a State has no business telling a man, sitting alone in his own house, what books he may read or what films he may watch."[3]

What follows is a brief account of this hidden industry. First, it serves as an introduction to the history of adult movies made for consumption in the home. Second, it provides a basis on which to launch further investigations into the aesthetics, industrial practices, and reception of such films. Finally, it indicates that the middle-class American home at midcentury was not the sexually sterile environment we often imagine it to be, thanks to the home movie hobby and these down-and-dirty little films.

THE BUSINESS OF ADULT MOVIES FOR THE HOME

Amateur movie equipment was available from the earliest days of cinema, but "home movies" began in earnest with the introduction of 16mm and 8mm equipment in the 1920s. Even though various substandard gauges had been around for years, Eastman Kodak's introduction of the 16mm Ciné-Kodak camera and projector in 1923 attracted the "leisure classes" to the hobby of home movies.[4] Bell & Howell and Victor Animatograph quickly moved into the 16mm market and as the collector and historian Alan Kattelle notes, the May 1928 issue of *American Photography* reported "amateur as the fastest growing branch of the motion picture industry" with over 125,000 amateur cameras in use."[5]

From the start 16mm was an expensive proposition: Kattelle states that "a typical 16mm camera in the early '30s sold for over $100, and a roll of film cost $6."[6] With almost a quarter of the population unemployed, most people were focused on their next meal, not the eyepiece of a pricey 16mm camera. In 1932 Kodak introduced a new format that was substantially less expensive than 16mm—the Ciné-Kodak 8 Model 20 camera could be purchased for $29.50, the Kodascope 8 projector for $22.50, and a twenty-five-foot reel of film went for $2.25.[7] The new 8mm format gained in popularity through the 1930s, eventually supplanting 16mm as the home movie format of choice.

With the development of movie outfits for home use came film rental libraries and movies that were sold directly to consumers. Camera stores, magazines such as *Movie Makers* and *Home Movies*, and Kodak itself— which in major cities operated rental units called Kodascope Libraries— spread the word about rental movies.[8] Not surprisingly, it was only a short time before adult films were manufactured and sold to home movie enthusiasts. In an interview in 1969 with investigators for the Commission on Obscenity and Pornography, Ted Paramore, himself a producer of mail order movies and theatrical sexploitation films, indicated that in the years prior to World War II the mail order adult film business involved just a handful of people.[9] Southern California became the center of production and distribution for adult mail order movies. And at least some of the individuals who made adult films were attached to the mainstream film industry. For instance, Elmer Dyer, who began his career at Universal in 1915, became a freelance aerial cameraman who worked on films such as *Wings* (1927), *The Winged Horseman* (1929) with Hoot Gibson, *Hell's Angels* (1930), *Night Flight* (1934), and *Air Force* (1943).[10] In addition to his work as a cinematographer, Dyer wrote articles for *Travel*, *International Photographer*, and *American Cinematographer* and made films for a nontheatrical company called NuArt Productions. NuArt made and distributed 16mm films such as "Dare Devil's of the Air," a 400-foot film "featuring world famous aviators from many nations in the greatest array of daring stunts ever assembled in a single picture!"[11] NuArt also produced and distributed 100-foot and 200-foot adult films such as "September Morn," "Glimpses in a Nudist Colony," and "The Artist's Model," which featured nude women in various settings. For instance, the description of "September Morn" in a promotional flier reads: "In this secluded nook, created by the wonders of nature, our artist finds a living 'September Morn.' She proves a very agreeable model and as he sketches we are able to obtain many beautiful scenes, where the wonders of nature and the sheer beauty of this lady vie for each other for your admiration."[12] If the brochure's copy stressed beauty and taste, the pictures in it give little doubt that it was "T&A" that was moving the merchandise.

One of the most active producers during the late 1930s was Pacific Ciné Films, which was operated in Hollywood by Robert I. Lee. Around 1935 Lee bought a featurettes company called Hollywood Ciné Film Distributors for $2,500. He then merged it with two other small companies and

Brochures such as these were used to sell 8mm and 16mm prints of "adult" films to the home movie enthusiast in the 1930s and early 1940s.

changed the name to Pacific Ciné Films. Working with a regular staff of four secretaries, along with models and technicians hired on a per-film basis, Lee cranked out several new films every three or four months. In the late 1930s cameramen received $125 for shooting and editing the scenarios that Lee developed, and models recruited from art schools and nightclubs were paid around $50 each—with most films featuring two girls. Exposed 35mm film in lengths of 1,000 feet usually resulted in a full series of up to fourteen movies, reduced to 16mm and 8mm for sale to the home market. The series generally included a 400-foot featurette, several 100-foot films, and a half dozen or more 50-foot and 20-foot reels, ranging in price from $25.00 for the featurette to $1.00 for 20-foot quickies.[13]

NuArt, Pacific Ciné Films, and similar outfits generated direct mailing lists by placing ads in magazines such as *Film Fun*, *High Heels*, and *Camera Craft*. Advertising constituted one of their largest operating expenses. According to the journalist Thomas Wood, Pacific Ciné Films spent over $1,000 in 1937 on mailing announcements and placing ads in magazines. Lee purportedly had developed a mailing list of fifteen thousand names by that time. In addition to direct mail sales, which were the most profitable transactions, the companies also wholesaled films. Pacific Ciné dealt with jobbers who distributed the films to an estimated fifteen hundred dealers—usually camera supply stores—across the country. For instance, in New York City the Camera Specialties Company served Pacific Ciné films to around one hundred camera stores within the city limits.

At the time that Elmer Dyer was working with NuArt, the company did not use jobbers but instead had a sales manager, W. W. Bell, who with Dyer sold directly to camera stores, radio shops, optical shops, and film libraries. NuArt gave dealers one-third off the price of single orders, and 50 percent off lots of twelve.[14] While some of these retailers sold films outright to their customers, others placed them in their libraries and then rented them to individuals, much like videotapes and DVDs are rented today. Depending on the locality, rentals may have been handled under the counter, with loyal customers being informed about products with brochures or lists. A December 31, 1936, letter from Church and School Film Service in Cincinnati to NuArt requested, "Will you kindly send us 1,000 of your attractive circulars on the Screen Classic Nudist material? Will be glad to pay cost of same."[15] Dyer sent an accommodating reply.

Evidence indicates that companies like NuArt and Pacific Ciné Films toed a careful line with regard to the law. In a letter to Alan Benjamin's Film Craft in Brooklyn, NuArt described the content of its Screen Classics series saying that "while these pictures contain nude models, the pictures have been made in such a way that they are not vulgar in the least.... nothing objectionable shows." But then the letter went on to indicate, "we are of the opinion that you would not encounter any trouble in letting them be shown, naturally we cannot advise you what your local police may say, since such regulations may vary in different places."[16] If some retailers may have been concerned about the content of the films, others were clearly looking for something more daring. A letter from The Radio Shop in Hanover, Pennsylvania, stated that the company found the NuArt product "OK," but suggested "we would be interested in something a little bit spicier."[17] A general contractor in Fort Worth, Texas, requested a discount and also wanted to know "if you could tell me where I may purchase something out of the ordinary—to be used at a stag party . . . or something."[18] NuArt replied by noting that "state authorities are very strict about shipping stag films either by express or mail, and so many concerns here have met with difficulties we do not handle them." The letter went on to state that "there is nothing smutty about our films and I could not say they would [be] entirely suited for a stag party."[19]

Indeed, the films made by NuArt and Pacific Ciné might not have been suitable for a stag party if we consider that stag films featured unobstructed views of sexual activity.[20] Stag films and their distributors would have been pursued aggressively by postal authorities or local law enforcement officials when, and if, they were identified. At the same time, it is probably not too cynical to suggest that most viewers of mail order films were not sitting in their homes in front of the screen with a sketch pad or an easel and paints. Such films were no doubt used as fodder for sexual fantasies and, much like pinups, spicy pulp magazines, and French postcards, they were probably used as visual stimulus for masturbation. The films would have been purchased and viewed primarily by middle-class and wealthier men who could afford the home movie hobby. They seldom would have fallen into the hands of children, minorities, or those of lesser economic means—the very groups around which American sexual anxieties usually flourished— and thus they attracted relatively little attention from censors and prosecutors during the 1930s and 1940s.

In addition to NuArt and Pacific Ciné Films, other companies or individuals making films during this period included William H. Door, Vanity Productions, Peerless Productions, Ciné Varieties, and Standard Pictures Corporation. The vast majority of films were undated, and thus only rough assessments can be made about the date of productions based on the styles of clothing (when worn), hairstyles, and the look of interiors and other surroundings. Most of these short films are remarkably simple in concept and execution, akin to moving pinups, and as such are precursors to the nudie-cutie features of the early 1960s. At their most basic, the films featured several shots of static models, sometimes slowly rotating in front of the camera on a turntable. In other instances the model or models engage in simple activities such as walking, sitting, climbing ladders, and so on. Activities were often dictated by the location, so that films shot outdoors at beaches or in parks might find models skinny-dipping, walking on the beach, or thrusting their arms and faces up to the sun. Sometimes, in an effort to show an interesting action, things got decidedly odd. Take, for instance, the short film "Old Fashioned," which probably was produced in the late 1940s. A woman outdoors in high heels, panties, and bra, peels off the bra and then proceeds to pick up a hatchet and make several lame attempts at chopping wood—the process of which is made difficult by her efforts to maintain balance on her high heels.

Films shot indoors—usually in photo studios, apartments, or the occa-

Efforts to show nude or seminude women in unusual situations could turn out rather odd, as this frame enlargement from "Old Fashioned" indicates.

sional motel room—were more often than not limited to models lounging around on couches, chairs, or beds. In some films the models appear to have been caught by the camera, stretching as if waking from a nap, a sub-genre that the archivist Stephen Parr refers to as "cheese-nappers"—that is, cheesecake shots of napping women. In some films models engage in routine domestic activities—dressing or undressing, putting on makeup, cleaning house, or just puttering around. In some instances they engage in dances for the camera or act out simple scenarios, such as in "Christmas Eve," a not altogether accurately titled short. Four women wake up on Christmas morning and then cavort in a living room in the nude, opening packages and playing with the presents such as a target shooting game and so on. Others employ odd fantasy elements such as "Row Row Row," which finds a young woman in a living room pretending to get into a boat, rowing to an island, and then sending a message in a bottle. An evidently smaller number of films from the 1930s and 1940s, such as "Let's Make Mary Moan," do not have nudity but include fetish material—in this case two women in nylons engaging in spanking and light bondage.

Films including full-frontal nudity were generally accompanied by a square-up (caveat) that they were intended strictly for the use of artists and art students who could not afford to work from live figure models.[21] For example, the NuArt brochure for the "Screen Classics" series noted, "Many schools, colleges and private art classes are not fortunate enough to obtain, or cannot afford living models. Such institutions will immediately recognize the value of this series of motion pictures."[22] The square-ups, ad-

This frame enlargement from *Goldilocks Goes Glamorous* is typical of a "cheesenapper." The film would have been spiced up by the inclusion of narration filled with double entendres.

vertising, and the content of the films attempted to align them with fine art nudes and distance them from charges of obscenity. Films featuring full-frontal nudity ranged from more "natural" scenes of women sunbathing or swimming, to films shot on sets in which the camera travels up and down their bodies, often isolating body parts. While the manufacturers might have claimed that this afforded the would-be art student to concentrate on the details of the body, it must have also given the covert masturbator shots of pubic areas not seen in most erotica readily available at newsstands during the period.

Like most aspects of daily life, World War II also affected amateur filmmaking. In 1942 the War Production Board "directed Kodak to cut its production of amateur film to 50 percent of 1941 levels."[23] In addition to the restrictions on raw materials, we might also assume that at least some of the customer base for adult films went into military service where their hobby would have been curtailed. The postwar years, however, saw a reinvigorated market for home movies. Spurred by the baby boom and increased travel and leisure time, amateur moviemaking reached a "watershed" in 1958 as 1,108,000 8mm cameras were shipped.[24] Along with a general growth in the home movie hobby, the field of adult mail order films grew tremendously following World War II.[25]

In the years after the war, advertisements for a number of companies began to appear in hobby magazines such as *Home Movies*—a trend that increased as the 1950s wore on. The growth in the number of men's magazines like *Playboy, Flirt, Eyeful, Beauty Parade, Laff, Titter,* and *Chicks and Chuckles* meant more opportunities to advertise. Some companies at-

tempted to cover all possible outlets for their films. W. Merle Connell's
Quality Pictures produced one-reel striptease films such as "Dances That
Thrill," "Night Club Girls," and "Sweethearts of Burlesque" that played in
theaters, peep machines, and also in the expanding home market. Other
companies restricted their distribution to the home screen. Joe Bonica
launched his Movie-of-the-Month-Club, probably in 1947, which mailed
cheesecake footage on a monthly basis. Much like book-of-the-month
services, which grew in popularity in the postwar years, charter members of Bonica's club could view the films when they arrived, then choose
whether to purchase or return them.[26] The former dancer and nightclub
owner Klaytan W. Kirby, who had started a mail order cheesecake company around 1943, followed in Bonica's footsteps with the Best Film-of-
the-Month Club ("Don't confuse with any other club" warned the advertisements). Kirby's ads promised "a PROFESSIONALLY produced major
studio style film selected as THE BEST FILM OF THE MONTH for your
feature show."[27] The first film offered was "How Females (and Males) Win
Beauty Contests." Seaside Films promised "Hilarious Hits for Your Next
Party!" and National's "exclusive" movies were "Party Films—The Kind
Men Like!"[28]

Parties and professionalism were two important tropes in the advertising of postwar adult home movies. References to "parties" were evidently an
attempt to create a connection in the mind of the buyer between the softer
mail order films with their hardcore stag counterparts that were usually
shown in some sort of fraternal party atmosphere, whether at a fraternity
house, an Elk's Lodge, or a VFW hall. Furthermore, the use of the terms
"party" and "parties" amplified the connections between sex and leisure that
were becoming increasingly central to postwar consumer culture. Every
day was a party for Hugh Hefner and his Playboy bunnies, so why couldn't
Harold Homeowner re-create some of the same fun with a shaker of mar-
tinis and an 8mm projector in his basement rathskeller?

A number of companies frequently invoked "professionalism" in their
advertising as a criterion that set their films apart from other mail order
operations. As home movies became part of the "do-it-yourself" movement
of the postwar period there was clearly an effort to distance the films purchased for use in the home from those actually made by the home movie
enthusiast. We can assume that despite all the advice from professionals on
how to make home movies look more polished, many, if not most, still featured shaky camera work, poor framing and lighting, and a variety of other

problems. Indeed, a whole class of jokes and cartoons developed around the threat of being invited over to watch the neighbors' vacation films.[29] Ads for adult movies that touted their "professionalism" were designed to reassure the purchaser that the films he bought would be of higher quality than the movies that he, or his neighbor, made—and that lighting and careful camera work would actually allow him see what he was paying for.

The films themselves were issued in different ways. Some companies released their films as individual units. For instance, the movies from Seaside were brief black-and-white narratives with sound that featured narration laced with double entendres. In "Goldilocks Goes Glamorous" a shapely blonde investigates the Three Bears' swimming pool, trying out several bathing suits before settling on Baby's Bear's bikini, in which she is displayed in loving detail. Other companies issued their films serially. Each of William Door's series of films of women "from around the world" started with title art indicating an exotic locale such as "Rome," "Singapore," "Bali," and "Saigon." A few of the films actually begin with stock shots of the city or country referred to in the title, before cutting to shots of the "local" beauty. Virtually all the films were shot in and around Southern California, often at the beach. The only concession to the place in the title was in props or costumes—usually little more than a hat or a scarf so as not to obstruct the T&A that composed the films' stock and trade. Other series were given a blanket title, such as Vanity Films's "Artists Studio Models," and then given numbers to differentiate one film from the next.

PROTECTING THE NEST

Adults-only films in theatrical settings had to deal with a web of state and local censors, zealous crusaders, district attorneys, and police departments, as well as the Hays Office and representatives of the organized motion picture industry. Those who dealt in 8mm and 16mm films for the home market had only one major obstacle to contend with: the Post Office. The Comstock Act of 1873 prohibited the mailing of "every obscene, lewd, lascivious, indecent, filthy or vile article, matter, thing, device or substance; and—Every article or thing designed, adapted, or intended for preventing conception or producing abortion, or for any indecent or immoral use."[30] The list of items prohibited in the mails actually grew at the turn of the century as cheaper printing and photographic processes proliferated.

To keep the mails clean the Post Office employed two methods that, as described by James Paul and Murray Schwartz, were dependent on complaints received or on the diligence of mail carriers or postal inspectors. The first was the "confiscation of obscene publications discovered in transit—the so-called non-mailability ruling." The second was "non-delivery of mail addressed to persons using the mails to sell objectionable materials—the 'unlawful order' or 'mail block.' Mail blocks were the sanction when inspectors uncovered the operation of commercial purveyors of noxious books or pictures." The last, criminal prosecution of individuals found disseminating obscene material, was in the hands of the Justice Department and was fairly rare due to the time and effort involved. Therefore, most of the policing of the mails fell to the Post Office. Stoppage "depended very much on local policing" while mail blocks usually resulted from "more deliberate investigation by the Postal Inspection Service."[31] The postal enforcement of antiobscenity statutes was handled by the department's legal staff, which was alerted to questionable material either through a complaint or through an accident in which a package came open in the presence of a postal worker. According to Paul and Schwartz, "The lawyers assigned to this work would simply inspect the challenged item and make up their minds." When it came to the revocation of mailing permits, there was no obligation for adversarial hearings nor were there challenges in the form of expert testimony. The courts were an option for those whose mail was confiscated or blocked, but most courts deferred "to the Postal 'experts.'"[32] It was only during the 1950s, some years after Congress had passed the Administrative Procedure Act, that the Post Office was forced to stop judging the cases it had both investigated and prosecuted.[33]

The market for adult material expanded during the 1950s. Increasingly, Klaytan Kirby, Irving Klaw, the glamour photographer Bernard of Hollywood, and others used photo sessions to shoot both motion pictures and still photographs. Buyers could purchase films or stills of favorite models, and the producers—who retained the rights to the photos—had an additional market available to them by selling spreads to men's magazines. Beyond the films and the men's magazines, there was a proliferation of other adult material: nudist magazines, calendar pinups, and mass market paperbacks, all of which overlapped to some extent with confession and true crime publications in purveying sexually oriented entertainment. The proliferation of "pornography"[34] caught the attention of congressmen, journalists, and parents in the 1950s.

In 1952 the House Select Committee, under Representative Ezekiel Gathings, endeavored to expose the amount of "obscenity" that circulated on newsstands and in the mails. A letter to the Gathings Committee from John B. Keenan, director of the Newark Department of Public Safety, recounted two raids, one of a local newsstand that netted 209 reels of "completely obscene" film and a list of 1,385 renters representing "all trades and professions." The second bust, this time on a bookstore, netted "28 filthy films and a large number of duplicates" as well as 10,000 still photos. Keenan claimed that "in all cases we have evidence that juveniles had access to the films and stills."[35] While comic books have become the most famous victim of the panic surrounding juvenile delinquency in the 1950s, pornography was also at the heart of the frenzy. Senator Estes Kefauver's 1955 hearings into delinquency determined that pornography was a "modern" industry, "utilizing the latest technological developments of the graphic arts." The hearings discursively linked pornography to traffic in narcotics. Teenagers were branded as "the biggest market for pornographic materials," and it was further alleged that teens were "widely used to 'push' dirty pictures, films, and books."[36]

Among the targets of the Kefauver hearings were the fetish materials produced by "the King of the Pin-Ups," Irving Klaw. Klaw, whose *Movie Star News* had purveyed stills of screen stars, had gradually moved into producing bondage and spanking photos and 8mm films. The cult figure Betty Page was the subject of the most popular Klaw photos and films. Because Page and the other models were always dressed in underwear or lingerie, the material would have been difficult, if not impossible, to classify as obscene. But during the hearings the material was linked to sex crimes perpetrated by teenagers.[37] One result of the hearings was the passage of a law that made it illegal to transport pornography over state lines—thus bringing the FBI, which had been largely on the sidelines, more fully into the porn wars.[38]

Adult films and images were moving beyond mere cheesecake into the realm of the "perverse." In 1959 Harry Kursh—evidently a concerned reader—wrote a letter to the *Ladies' Home Journal*. As Kursh recounted, "Recently, my wife and I were called in by upset neighbor friends for an evening of "shocking" home movies. We left their living room stunned and embarrassed. The movies turned out to be several small rolls of 8mm film containing indescribable sex filth. It had arrived via the mails, in a plainly wrapped package addressed to one of their young sons and was inadvertently opened by the father. Thanks to our friends' warning, my wife and I are now guarding our mailbox like a pair of outraged hawks."[39] From the second decade of the twentieth century to the 1950s the vast majority of the hardcore stag movie business had been the province of the purveyors of traveling road shows. These showmen, who usually traveled with a 16mm projector and a suitcase full of films, were generally hired for $40 or $50 to provide a one- or two-hour program to fifty to two hundred people in those fabled smoke-filled lodge halls and fraternity houses.[40] But the transition to 8mm had killed the traveling road show.

During the postwar period 8mm stags became available through "bars, gas stations, photography shops, delicatessens, insurance agencies, auto junkyards, industrial catering services, industrial tool rooms, barber shops" and eventually through the mail.[41] "Mr. X" sold both soft- and hardcore films in this way from approximately 1953 to 1965. He would begin by placing a call to an associate in an eastern U.S. city who would then ask a middleman to contact him. These two would then arrange to meet at the counter of a local coffee shop, each with an identical handled shopping bag, topped with cabbage and lettuce. In the bottom of the middleman's bag were the films. The bottom of Mr. X's bag was filled with empty boxes. After they had coffee, he would offer to "buy the coffee" and hand over the amount for the films. They would then surreptitiously take each other's shopping bag and then go their separate ways. Mr. X would buy the 8mm reels for $5 each and then sell them for $25, as part of a sideline business, retailing between sixty and one hundred films a year to individuals in the western United States.[42] As a small retailer Mr. X would have gone largely unnoticed by authorities, which were on the lookout for larger operations. For instance, a New York Times article in April 1959 recounted the seizure of 2,100 reels of film and the arrest of a "ring" of seven men who were allegedly selling $25,000 worth of films a week—most probably destined for retailers such as Mr. X.[43]

The information exposed in the Kefauver hearings about mail drops, aliases, and efforts to infect American youth hit a chord because the discourse on mail order porn was so similar to that of communist spies and other supposedly subversive elements operating in the United States at this time. People like Mr. Kursh were not only guarding their mailboxes—ergo their families—like hawks, they were guarding their country from corrosive influences. By the time the Granahan Committee launched its investigation into mail order obscenity in 1959, there seemed to be no question that the spread of pornography was part of a conspiracy to subvert American youth: "The committee does not believe it unreasonable," its report stated, "to suspect that there is a connection between pornographic literature and subversive elements in this country." The report went on to quote Dr. Carl F. Reuss, the executive secretary of the Board for Christian Social Action of the American Lutheran Church, who stated that "it seems possible, indeed, that these interests catering to the warped, unbalanced, immature attitudes of many Americans toward sex can be used by the communist conspiracy to undermine the foundations of our national life."[44] The Cincinnati-based Citizens for Decent Literature went so far as to suggest in its report *Is the Flood of Pornographic Material a Communist Plot?* that hundreds of sex criminals, perverts, and prostitutes had been shipped to a Polish town where they were "turned loose in front of scores of Red movie photographers with thousands of feet of film."[45]

Theories about communist conspiracies may have sent law enforcement officials, postal inspectors, and hawk-eyed moms and dads to the mailboxes with a sense of dread, but it was good old-fashioned capitalism and the promise of easy money that turned average people into pornographers. In April 1959 the postmaster general, Arthur E. Summerfield, described mail order pornography as a $500 million business.[46] Just five months later, Senator Kefauver estimated that the business was between $500 million and $3 billion and that the bulk of the business was from "youths between the ages of 12 and 18."[47] A breathless 1964 *Reader's Digest* article described the ease with which individuals moved from peddling a few pictures of a wife or girlfriend into full-scale mail order operations with profits in the thousands of dollars: "A Knoxville dealer was arrested only eight months after going into business. Even so, he had already cleared $20,000, and had 100,000 new circulars ready for mailing."[48] The increase in the amount of material in the mails, coupled with concerns about its allegedly devastating impact on young people, prompted increased efforts to control the flow of pornography on the part of the Post Office. The *Reader's Digest* article described how "youngsters, a major target of mail order pornography, have sometimes found themselves deluged with offers of filth after merely answering an ad for camera equipment, acne pills or rare coins."[49] In 1961 there were 377 convictions on charges of using the mail to carry obscenity.

By 1965 the number of convictions reached 874. The number of "suppressions"—an inspector notifying a sender that what he or she was mailing was considered illegal—jumped nearly tenfold, from just over one thousand in 1961 to just under ten thousand in 1965.[50]

UPPING THE ANTE

In the December 1960 edition of *Chicks and Chuckles*, a hundred-page digest of risqué cartoons and cheesecake photos, three of the five full-page advertisements were for 8mm films. And among the smaller ads for books, photo sets, gambling advice, and the "Vibra-Finger" ("allows localized massage in needed areas") were another five ads for movies. The relatively high volume of these ads is indicative of the expanding segment that small gauge film had in the pornographic marketplace. Moreover, movies were becoming more competitively priced: the photo sets and books advertised in *Chicks and Chuckles* ranged between $1 and $3, and copies of 8mm movies ran from $0.80 (in quantity) to $3. The fact that movies could be had cheaply meant that adult films were within reach of teenagers and those who did not have vast amounts of expendable income. For those who did not have an 8mm projector, simple hand-held viewers could be purchased for around $5, often as a package deal with films. The battery-powered viewers could be operated by one hand, thus keeping the other hand free to handle pressing tasks that might arise. It was during this same period that movies appealing to gay men—namely physique and wrestling films—began to become available from companies such as Apollo Productions, Zenith Productions, and the Athletic Model Guild.[51]

Up until 1960 most of the manufacturers that made mail order adult films were lone individuals operating out of their homes, garages, or small offices. But the business was poised for growth. Michael Milner, in his 1964 book *Sex on Celluloid*, cited as an example the American Photo Company, which printed one thousand reels of pornographic film in April 1959. "From their New York store-front laboratory, [the company] sold some three thousand, two hundred and fifty reels during a similar period. In bulk lots of five hundred reels and up, they received three to four dollars apiece."[52] From approximately 1960 onward, the operations, while still small by most industrial standards, were becoming considerably more sophisticated. There were several companies operating out of New York

City and no fewer than twenty with Los Angeles as a base of operation. Most of these companies had multiple dba's (names under which an individual is "doing business as") as well as multiple post office boxes, mail drops, or addresses. A 1967 report to the California legislature by the state attorney general, Thomas C. Lynch, and his chief deputy indicated that Southern California was "a production center for 'homemade' girlie films and still photos of varying sexual content." The report indicated that "some individuals have even set themselves up as one-man studios, handling all operations from the photography to the final procession [*sic*] and printing of the films and photos. Such an operator usually branches into mail order sales." The report went on to claim that the films that producers sold directly to bookstores or other outlets tended to be stronger than those sold through the mails.[53]

Among the companies operating in the late 1960s were some that had started in the postwar years. William Door had bequeathed his concerns upon his death, which were in turn sold to Robert Thorpe who continued to operate under names such as International Imports and Diamond Films. Joe Bonica continued to operate as Variety Movie Club and Movie Newsreels, while Klaytan W. Kirby (who sold his businesses in 1969) used no fewer than twenty DBA's, including O.K. Jackson, Rancho Tongo, and Art Film Guild. The larger operators in the mail order film business in the Los Angeles area included John Lamb (DBA Pacifica, Horizon Productions, Shangri-La Productions, Brigette Productions, ASEF, Art Films International, etc.), Ted Paramore (DBA Mondo Film Corp., Producer Film Guild), Armand V. Garcia (DBA Cinema Products), and Myron Griffin (DBA Laurel View, Crystal Co., The Canyon Co., Centro Co., Sonic, Fortune Films, Margin Films, Frenzy Films, Excitement Films).[54] At the end of 1969 the *Los Angeles Times* estimated that two hundred or more companies operated in the Los Angeles region—but noted that "many are under the same ownership." The article went on to cite figures from postal authorities suggesting that "about 15 dealers are responsible for almost 95% of America's mail-order erotica, and local estimates indicate that most of those dealers are based in the Los Angeles area."[55]

In 1969 and 1970 investigators for the Commission on Obscenity and Pornography interviewed several individuals who manufactured and sold 8mm adult movies, including Paramore, Saul Resnick, Norm Arno, and Chris Warfield. Based on information from the interviews and other sources, a "hypothetical" mail order operation was described that included a production shot on 16mm featuring three women and one man, which was then used to create four 200-foot segments. Production costs were put at $700. A mailing composed of 30,000 names (20,000 of the hypothetical operator's own names, plus 10,000 additional names rented at $30 per thousand) prompted a response of 2.5 percent, with the average order resulting in a purchase of $20. Gross sales of $15,000 (750 x $20) minus expenses netted a profit of approximately $6,550 from a single mailing. As the report concluded: "Although an individual operator can live quite comfortable [sic] on the profits to be made in 8mm home movie film mailings, it is doubtful that many exceed an annual income in excess of $30,000 or $40,000. The mean net income for more than 100 operators dealing in 8mm home movie films is probably not more than $20,000 to $25,000 . . . certainly not mere pittances . . . [but it] will not make many millionaires overnight."[56] Even if the business in mail order adult movies wasn't making millionaires, it was easy to conclude that it was making a number of people a great deal of money.

The business was also making more customers. The films themselves were becoming more explicit, often mimicking the "beaver" films that were starting to appear in storefront theaters in major cities. Customers responded to ever more sophisticated come-ons. Barney Rosset's Grove Press, which published Henry Miller, Anaïs Nin, and William S. Burroughs, as well as distributing theatrical films such as *I Am Curious (Yellow)* (1967), started the Evergreen Club. The club, named after the publisher's controversial magazine, functioned as a kind of dirty-book-of-the-month club by offering members reprinted Victorian erotica, collections of explicit etchings, and photographic sex manuals. The Evergreen Club also offered 8mm film selections such as Stan Brakhage's "Lovemaking" (1969), Phyllis and Eberhard Kronhausen's "Psychomontage" (1962) and digest portions of their feature *Freedom to Love* (1969), as well as other movies.[57] The club maintained an aura of urbanity and sophistication—in sharp contrast to the lustier ads that filled men's magazines. The May 1968 issue of *Adam*, a popular *Playboy* clone, contained three dozen ads for 8mm films. A close examination and comparison with the Commission on Obscenity and Pornography lists of dba's reveals that at least a few of the ads were for individuals using different company names. Chris Warfield advertised as Kingston on page 65 ("2 Brutal Females!") and as Vixen Enterprises on page 69 ("the

Magazine advertisements, such as this one from 1968, promised an array of sample subjects for a low price as a ploy to get the respondent on mailing lists.

unrepressed intimacies of a couple in love"). Evelyn Louise Miller had ads as Eve Miller on page 64 ("I'm lonely too, Mister") and as Louise Miller and Friends on page 82 ("Enjoy Our *Uninhibited* Way of Life!"). Many ads promised "samples" for a dollar, which put the respondent on a mailing list (often rented or traded with other dealers) of potential buyers. Along with the samples came more detailed fliers or brochures.

Some fliers advertised a single film or series. Some focused on the display of individual models while others sold rudimentary narratives. Athena Productions served up Marie, Kathy, Dene, Linda, Diana, Janet, and Janice, along with other models in films and photo sets.[58] An illustrated brochure for "The Newlyweds" ("Don't ask *how* this film was made . . . just be glad that it *was!*") indicated that the film was available in two 200-foot segments, "The Discovery" and "The Experience," at $20 for black-and-white prints or $35 for color. Some ads attempted to lure buyers with promises that they would be getting hardcore material, such as the brochure for "Honey Bee" with the headline, "California Court Says: The Film 'Honey Bee' Is 'Hard-Core Pornography!' You be the Judge!" Others gave buyers the opportunity to select their film from illustrated lists of models. And in the polymorphously perverse atmosphere of the sexual revolution, other companies such as Nu-Day, John Amslow, and Central Distributors included both gay and straight material in their fliers.[59]

Evelyn Louise Miller, who used a number of different dba's, took a more personal approach to her fliers. Miller's pitch often took the form of a "personal" letter—in many instances with words "scratched out" with colored ink and "handwritten" notes scrawled in the margins ("Nudists are just about the friendliest people ever!"). These "letters" offering special 8mm films often relayed "personal" stories, such as that of "Rosita Escobar" who, in fractured English, relays how she had a child out of wedlock and was forced to "leave my hacienda" and make her living as a prostitute. "The picture of my life and experience in Tijuana is now of completion and ready for your pleasure."[60]

Finally, other brochures made reference to recent events and court cases, both to titillate potential customers and to stay within the law. In 1969 the *Los Angeles Times* described one of the "well-worked approaches" to mail-order erotica as "the medical—artistic—scientific—literary gambit."[61] By claiming that their products had some sort of social relevance, producers and distributors hoped to stay within boundaries of the law, which continued to be fluid. For instance, a discreet flier picturing only a reel of 8mm film claimed 0–7 as "the film that rocked the nation! the film that is in the center of controversy in the appointment of Justice Abe Fortas as Chief Justice of the U.S. Supreme Court. Is '0–7' pornographic? You be the judge! You can now receive this precedent-shattering film, available exclusively from Raymond C."[62] D. G. Sales, yet another Los Angeles outfit, included with its flier a "confidential mailing" that stated: "Because you have the right to view, in the privacy of your home, any and all films dealing with sex, I am enclosing this folder, leaving nothing to the imagination, that also includes well-endowed, vigorous male performers."[63] The statement in this ad refers to *Stanley v. Georgia*—a case that permanently altered the status of adult movies for the home.

Robert Eli Stanley was prosecuted and convicted of possessing obscene material after law enforcement officials, holding a warrant to seize evidence on a bookmaking prosecution, found at Stanley's home several reels of "obscene" 8mm film. The Supreme Court's 1969 ruling overturned the lower court's decision that found Stanley guilty. "If the First Amendment means anything," Justice Thurgood Marshall wrote, "it means that a State has no business telling a man, sitting alone in his own house, what books he may read or what films he may watch."[64] In his 1969 book *The Porno Shops*, Roger Blake speculated that many people "seem to have a 'feeling' that the mere possession of such films can get them into trouble, whereas books and magazines and photo displays enjoy some special sort of immunity."[65] But by the end of that year, whatever legal reservations individuals might have had about possessing porn movies seemed to evaporate as the market for adult home movies exploded. As a full-page ad in the New York sex tabloid *Screw* urged, "This weekend, see real, live 8mm love-making on your bedroom wall! Turn off Carson! Turn on your libido!" Yet still taking care to cover all bases on the constantly shifting legal ground, the ad demurred, "We wish to emphasize, on the advice of our lawyers, that these are educational films—for adults only. They are NOT to be regarded as stag film."[66]

Some of the smaller companies hung on for a while, but as the 1970s progressed most were displaced by a few larger, and considerably slicker, operations. While they still made short films—virtually always in color and sometimes with sound—they often employed stars from the burgeoning hardcore feature arena and supplemented their films with glossy, full-color magazines and fliers. Among the companies with the most widely circulated home movies of the 1970s and early 1980s were Blazing Films, Lasse Braun, Collection, Color Climax, Diplomat Films, Expo Film, Limited Edition, Pretty Girls, Swedish Erotica, and The VIP Collection. But before most of these outfits cranked out their first reel, and before features such as *Deep Throat* ever hit the screens, the demise of 8mm adult films was in the works. As Addison Verrill reported in *Variety* in 1971, "Producers and distributors of sex-art, sexploitation and hardcore theatrical features are currently being blitzed with offers to sell the rights to such material for videocassette market.... The availability of sex features for private home viewing on a rental or ownership basis is seen as one of the most exploitable and potentially profitable aspects of the videocassette business, despite all the public relations chatter about Grand Opera and Ballet."[67]

Hardcore videocassettes paved the way for the video revolution in the late 1970s and early 1980s.[68] As video penetrated the market, home movies—both legitimate and adult—were quickly buried. Today adult home movies continue to reach new audiences on the format that killed them, as video (and now DVD) packages of adult films from the 1930s through the 1970s that were designed for home use are peddled amid the steady stream of shot-on-video porn. Not only do these works stand as an alternative for the porn purchaser bored with contemporary offerings or as a bit of erotic nostalgia, they remain as a reminder that the "innocence" of the past was not quite as innocent as we sometimes imagine it to have been.

NOTES

For materials, information, and advice used in the preparation of this essay my thanks go to the following: Scott Curtis and the Margaret Herrick Library of the Academy of Motion Picture Arts and Sciences; Tina Houston and Bob Tissing of the Lyndon Baines Johnson Library in Austin, Texas; Karan Sheldon, David Weiss, and Dwight Swanson of Northeast Historic Film; 8martini8; Stephen Parr of Oddball Film + Video; Geoff Alexander of the Academic Film Archive of North America; the staff of the Institute for the Advanced Study of Human Sexuality; Ivan Stormgart, Mike Vraney and Lisa Petrucci of Something Weird Video; and, as always, Eithne Johnson.

1 "Small gauge" or "substandard" film generally refers to motion pictures of less than 35mm: namely, 16mm, 8mm and Super-8mm, as well as more obscure formats such as 17.5mm and 28mm. "Orphan" films are those films that were independently produced and have not been preserved by commercial interests. Among the most common types of orphan films are home movies and amateur productions, educational films, industrial films, and pornography.

2 Aiding in this recognition is the fact that several small gauge films (home movies, in fact) have been added to the National Film Registry—the list of "culturally, historically or aesthetically significant films" chosen annually by the Library of Congress. Among those films are "Topaz" (1943–1945), footage from a Japanese American internment camp, the "Zapruder film" (1963) of John F. Kennedy's assassination in Dallas, and "Multiple Sidosis" (1970) by the amateur moviemaker Sid Laverents.

3 The decision in *Stanley v. Georgia* was delivered in April 1969. Police, who had received a warrant to search Stanley's home for evidence of bookmaking, seized several films in the process of the search. Stanley was charged with possession of obscene material, something not part of the original warrant. As Edward de Grazia and Roger K. Newman note, "*Stanley* held that a man's possession and enjoyment of obscenity—the right to read and observe what he pleases—at home, was *included* within the protections of the First Amendment and a constitutionally derived 'right of privacy'" de Grazia and Newman, *Banned Films: Movies, Censors and the First Amendment* [New York: Bowker, 1982], 114; emphasis in the original).

4 See Alan D. Kattelle, *Home Movies: A History of the American Industry, 1897–1979* (Hudson, Mass.: self-published, 2000), 82–83. Kattelle, who has what may be the largest collection of home movie equipment in the United States, provides a fine overview of the industrial aspects of the home movie business from its origins to the 1970s.

5 Ibid., 84.

6 Ibid., 94.

7 Ibid., 96.

8 For a brief discussion of the Kodascope Libraries, see Kattelle, *Home Movies*, 83–84.

9 Ted Paramore interview, Folder: "Mail Order—8mm Film," Box 64, Commission on Obscenity and Pornography Records, Lyndon Baines Johnson Library, Austin, Texas (hereafter LBJ Library).

10 "Flying Cameraman Missing in Canyon," *Hollywood Citizen News*, June 9, 1947, 1.

11 Flier, Elmer Dyer Collection (folder 9), Margaret Herrick Library, Academy of Motion Picture Arts and Sciences (hereafter AMPAS).

12 "Screen Classics in Sixteen Millimeter," Flier, Elmer Dyer Collection (folder 17), AMPAS.

13 Thomas Wood, "For Art Lovers Everywhere," *Coast*, October 1938, 19.

14 Letter from NuArt to Church and School Films Service, April 18, 1937, Elmer Dyer Collection (folder 75, NuArt orders), AMPAS.

15 Letter from Church and School Films Service to NuArt, December 31, 1936, Elmer Dyer Collection (folder 75, NuArt orders), AMPAS.

16 Letter from NuArt to Alan Benjamin's Film Craft, October 20, 1936, Elmer Dyer Collection (folder 75, NuArt orders), AMPAS.

17 Letter from E. J. J. Gombrecht, The Radio Shop, Hanover, Pennsylvania, to NuArt, November 7, 1936, Elmer Dyer Collection (folder 75, NuArt orders), AMPAS.

18 Letter from A. M. Stone, Fort Worth, Texas, to NuArt, January 2, 1937, Elmer Dyer Collection (folder 75, NuArt orders), AMPAS.

19 Letter from NuArt to A. M. Stone, Fort Worth, Texas, January 5, 1937, Elmer Dyer Collection (folder 75, NuArt orders), AMPAS.

20 For information on the stag film, see Al Di Lauro and Gerald Rabkin. *Dirty Movies: An Illustrated History of the Stag Film, 1915–1970* (New York: Chelsea House, 1976); and Linda Williams, *Hard Core: Power, Pleasure and the "Frenzy of the Visible,"* expanded ed. (Berkeley: University of California Press, 1999).

21 A square-up is a prefatory moral statement that justifies through the exposure of some social ill or moral ill images of nudity or other forbidden sights. See Eric Schaefer, *"Bold! Daring! Shocking! True!" A History of Exploitation Films, 1919–1959* (Durham, N.C.: Duke University Press, 1999), 69–71.

22 Flier, "Screen Classics in Sixteen Millimeter," collection of the author.

23 Kattelle, *Home* Movies, 100.

24 Ibid., 106, 128. See also Patricia R. Zimmermann, *Reel Families: A Social History of Amateur Film* (Bloomington: Indiana University Press, 1995), 114–21. Compared to Kattelle's industrial take on the history of home movies in the United States, Zimmermann offers a more theoretically nuanced account.

25 Ted Paramore interview, LBJ Library.

26 Advertisement, "Movie-of-the-Month-Club" *Home Movies*, March 1947, 167.

27 Florence Kirby, letter to the author, February 13, 1992; advertisement, "Best Film-of-the-Month Club, *Home Movies*, October 1949, 506.

28 Advertisement, Seaside Films, *Home Movies*, September 1951, 321; advertisement, National, *Home Movies*, May 1952, 164.

29 For an example of "professional" advice to amateurs, see "How Can an Amateur Become a Good Movie Maker?" in *Home Movie Making: A Popular Photography Annual*, 1959, 11–15, 60–61. The magazine symposium contained advice from the avant-garde filmmaker Maya Deren, the screenwriter Carl Foreman, the actor Anthony Quinn, and the directors Elia Kazan and David Lean, among others. See also Zimmermann's discussion of professionalism and amateurism throughout *Reel Families*.

30 The Comstock Act, quoted in James C. N. Paul and Murray L. Schwartz, *Federal Censorship: Obscenity in the Mail* (Westport, Conn.: Greenwood Press, 1977 [1961], 343). The Comstock Act was passed by Congress without debate in 1873 and then was subsequently tinkered with and strengthened over the years. It was named after Anthony Comstock (1844–1915), the founder of the New York Society for the Suppression of Vice, and the nineteenth century's most successful—and zealous—self-appointed censor. As an unpaid "special agent" of the U.S. Post Office, Comstock boasted that he was responsible for destroying "more than fifty tons of indecent books, 28,425 pounds of plates for the printing of such books, almost four million obscene pictures, and 16,900 negatives for such pictures. He also credited himself with the dubious distinction of having driven fifteen people to suicide" (Robert W. Haney, *Comstockery in America: Patterns of Censorship and Control* [New York: De Capo Press, 1974], 20).

31 Paul and Schwartz, *Federal Censorship: Obscenity in the Mail*, 91–93.

32 Ibid., 38–39.

33 Ibid., 95, 96.

34 I put the word pornography in quotes in this instance because much of what was cited as pornographic at the time would probably not be considered pornographic by even the most zealous antipornography crusader today.

35 John B. Keenan to E. C. Gathings, December 8, 1952. In U.S. Congress, House of Representatives, Select Committee on Current Pornographic Materials. Hearings, December 1, 2, 3, 4, and 5, 1952, Eighty-Second Congress, Second Session, 365.

36 "The Wages of Sin," *Newsweek*, June 6, 1955, 29.

37 See Greg Theakston, "The Case of the Missing Pin Up Queen," *The Betty Pages*, spring 1989, 16.

38 See "The Wages of Sin," *Newsweek*, June 6, 1955; and J. Edgar Hoover, "Combating Merchants of Filth: The Role of the FBI," *University of Pittsburgh Law Review* 25, no. 3 (March 1964): 469–78. Hoover claimed that prior to the passage of the law it was illegal to transport obscene matter by common carrier

(commercial truck, railroad), but it was not an offense to use a personal automobile or truck (471).

39 Harry Kursh, letter to the Editor, *Ladies' Home Journal*, February 1959, 4.

40 "'Under-the-Counter' or 'Hard-Core Pornography,'" *Technical Report of the Commission on Obscenity and Pornography* (Washington, D.C.: U.S. Government Printing Office, 1970), 190.

41 Ibid., 194.

42 "Mr. X," e-mail interview with Geoff Alexander (conducted for the author), April 15, 2003. According to Alexander, Mr. X was not overly worried about the possibility of arrest, but he was concerned that his family might find out about his "sideline" business. This concern persists to this day, and so he is identified here as Mr. X in order to maintain his anonymity.

43 "7 Held in Smut Ring," *New York Times*, April 23, 1959, 7:2.

44 U.S. Congress, House of Representatives, Subcommittee on Postal Operations, "Obscene Matter Sent Through the Mail: Report to the Committee on Post Office and Civil Service," September 1959. Eighty-Sixth Congress, First Session, 14.

45 Cited in Michael Milner, *Sex on Celluloid* (New York: Macfadden, 1964), 14–15.

46 "Obscene Mail Earnings Placed at Half Billion," *New York Times*, 24 April 1959, 12:1.

47 "3 Faiths Attack Mailing of Smut," *New York Times*, August 29, 1959, 15:8.

48 Don Wharton, "The Battle Against Mail-Order Pornography," *Reader's Digest*, February 1964, 151.

49 Ibid., 152.

50 Edwin A. Roberts Jr., *The Smut Rakers: A Report in Depth on Obscenity and the Censors* (Silver Springs, Md.: National Observer, 1966), 64.

51 For an overview of movies made for the gay market, see Thomas Waugh, *Hard to Imagine: Gay Male Eroticism in Photography and Film from Their Beginnings to Stonewall* (New York: Columbia University Press, 1996), especially 253–69. Waugh notes that the earliest commercial gay films—usually consisting of solo models posing for the camera wearing "straps" over their genitals—date from about 1949. The number of companies producing films with gay interest was quite small in the pre-Stonewall period.

52 Milner, *Sex on Celluloid*, 16.

53 Thomas C. Lynch and Charles A. O'Brien, "Obscenity: The Law and the Nature of the Business," report to the California legislature, April 6, 1967, 91. Box 33, Commission on Obscenity and Pornography Records, LBJ Library.

54 Traffic and Distribution Panel: Card File of Distributors. Box 134 B, Commission on Obscenity and Pornography Records, LBJ Library.

55 Noel Greenwood, "L.A.—Capital of Mail-Order Erotica Firms," *Los Angeles Times*, November 3, 1969, 1.

56 "K. Hypothetical Mail Order Operators; 1. 8mm Films." Box 127, File: Final

First Draft (Before Editing), Commission on Obscenity and Pornography Records, LBJ Library.

57 The Evergreen Club, various brochures ca. 1969–1970, collection of the author.

58 Various brochures. Box 66, Commission on Obscenity and Pornography Records, LBJ Library.

59 Various brochures. Mail Order Files. Institute for the Advanced Study of Human Sexuality, San Francisco, California (hereafter, IASHS).

60 Various brochures. File: Evelyn Louise Miller. Box 66, Commission on Obscenity and Pornography Records, LBJ Library.

61 Greenwood, "L.A.—Capital of Mail-Order Erotica Firms," 20.

62 Horizon Productions Brochure. Mail Order Files, IASHS. Senator Strom Thurmond (Republican of South Carolina) had shown films freed by the Supreme Court to senators and the press in an effort to torpedo Fortas's nomination as chief justice.

63 D. G. Sales Brochure. Mail Order Files, IASHS.

64 "Home Movies, Anybody?" Newsweek, April 21, 1969, 36.

65 Roger Blake, The Porno Shops (Cleveland, Ohio: Century Books, 1969), 46–47.

66 Advertisement, John Merriweather, Screw 38, November 24, 1969, 31. Evidently the ad writers weren't terribly concerned that their copy sent some confusing signals, since they advised readers to have fun on the weekend by turning off a program that ran on weeknights—The Tonight Show with Johnny Carson.

67 Addison Verrill, "TV Cassettes Bid for Sex Pix," Variety, January 27, 1971, 1, 54.

68 See Frederick Wasser, Veni, Vidi, Video: The Hollywood Empire and the VCR (Austin: University of Texas Press, 2001), especially 92–95. Wasser notes that Noel Bloom, a key figure in the rise of video, parlayed the Swedish Erotica home movie line into Caballero Control, a major adult video production/distribution company. Bloom later diversified—creating companies to carry mainstream and children's video lines—before giving up participation in Caballero in 1986.

IV   RECEPTION

ETHNOGRAPHY AND EXHIBITION
The Child Audience, the Hays Office,
and Saturday Matinees
Richard deCordova

Everybody is talking about the movies, about what is wrong with them, what is right with them; whether they are moral or immoral. There are many who say they are the one and just as many who say they are the other, and in between there are those who say they are both and those who say they are neither. And there is always much talking and a very great deal of walking up and down on the platform.

These are grown folks.

They are talking about movies, especially about children and movies.

I listened a long time and then slipped away and went in search of the children to ask them what they thought about it all — about children and movies.

And this book tells you what the children told me about movies.[1]

So began Alice Miller Mitchell's 1929 book *Children and Movies*. Oddly enough, an article today might plausibly, or even predictably, start with much the same lines. It would only need to substitute "emancipatory" and "oppressive" for "moral" and "immoral" and stress other subordinate groups (women, workers, "ordinary fans") over children as the topic of all of the talk. Indeed, after years of a text-based criticism dedicated to determining the ideological effectivity of films, scholars are beginning to step off "the platform" in search of the concrete audiences that consume and make sense of those films.

This has all of the characteristics of a departure, but it is perhaps also, by some unexplored route, a return—a return to a set of interests and methods (though perhaps not goals) that characterized early research on film. Audience studies proliferated in the 1920s and 1930s, particularly those focused on children. Statistical studies of various sorts measured childhood attendance at the movies and the broad film preferences of boys and girls.[2] More properly ethnographic studies such as Mitchell's and Herbert Blumer and Philip Hauser's *Movies, Delinquency and Crime* attempted to gauge the broad meanings children ascribed to the movies and moviegoing.[3] And more narrowly statistical and ethnographic studies of reading such as *Children's Responses to the Motion Picture "The Thief of Baghdad"* attempted to record and assess the meanings produced by a single film.[4] Although groups other than children occasionally fell under the researcher's gaze, the child's encounter with the moving picture constituted the primal scene of early audience research and, for that matter, social criticism of the movies. Film scholars have tended to ignore this scene, perhaps in order to distance themselves from the disreputable forms of research it engendered. However, an investigation of the practices through which researchers attempted to understand the child audience may tell us something about audience research today and the various power relations that subtend it.

The ethnographic impulse in recent cultural studies has arisen largely as a way of countering or complicating theories of spectatorship put forward in much of 1970s film theory. Within that theory an abstract, psychoanalytically inflected notion of the textual subject served to account for the role of the spectator. In effect, the textual subject permitted a way of theorizing spectatorship without straying from what was largely a theory of textual determinism. Textual processes placed a pliant spectator in a position from which sense could emerge.[5]

Ethnographic work has held a particular promise for contemporary researchers as a way of challenging this abstract and deterministic view with the concrete evidence of the ways audiences make sense of texts.[6] It has tended to shift the presumed source of meaning away from the text to the spectator and the social matrices within which she or he is inscribed. In doing so, it has stressed the variety of ways that people interpret texts and their activity in the work of interpretation. One of the avowed aims of this research has been the empowerment of spectators, not only by conceptualizing and stressing their activity, but also by allowing them to speak for themselves within academic discourse and escape their status as mere objects of research. The democratic, anti-elitist, non-paternalistic goals of this work exist in marked contrast to those implicit in traditional mass-culture research in this country, including, of course, most of the work on children and movies produced during the 1920s and 1930s.

However, as much recent anthropological writing suggests, the methods that allow ethnographers to pursue these goals also militate against them to some degree by placing limits and posing a set of problems that are not, in any simple way, overcome.[7] Simply put, the researcher cannot have unmediated access to the readings of other groups; one is, from the start, involved in the interpretation of these readings as texts from a particular institutionally and culturally prescribed (and often privileged) position. It is not necessarily damning to say that these texts must themselves be interpreted. However, the point does raise certain questions about the extent to which the subjects of this research can escape becoming its object, constituted in an interpretive gesture by the researcher in relation to his or her agenda, identity, and desires. If identity is always, as psychoanalysis claims, "secured" on the rather difficult terrain of the other, then the ethnographer, whose task has historically been the explanation of "other" cultures, is involved in no small way in an act of cultural self-definition—and perhaps self-legitimation. Such processes as displacement, transference, and projection are thus not simply unscientific aberrations but constitutive of the ethnographic act itself. These concerns have, of course, been central to the postcolonial critique of ethnography in recent years; a critique that has pointed to the complex ways in which the ethnographer's construction of an image of a native other has been implicated in the history of colonialism. At some level, this image has had more to do with the Western ethnographer's identity than with that of the subject whose identity and culture are ostensibly being explained. And, of course, the West had to construct a certain image of itself in relation to the other to make the colonialist venture possible.

I point to the constructedness of the ethnographer's subject not to ascribe any similar motives to recent work on the ethnography of media audiences, but to call attention to an inescapable condition of audience (ethnographic) research. Mitchell seems to assume naively that the child's response to movies is transparently available to her and that she can make them transparently available to the reader of her book. That naiveté is perhaps misnamed, however; the illusion of transparency is what gives such work its authority, the sense that the researcher's interpretive role has become minimized and that the subjects are simply speaking for themselves.

Studies on the cinema and children in the 1920s and 1930s provide ample evidence with which to question such claims to transparency. The audience research of the day hardly existed in the realm of disinterested knowledge; it was connected to broader social and political imperatives, ones which in fact depended upon a certain conceptualization of the (child) audience as a necessary support. It is that connection which interests me here—the ways that the construction of the child audience in research was linked to efforts to construct the "real" child audience through the regulation of production, distribution, and exhibition, and linked more broadly still to efforts to construct children—childhood—in the society at large. If I focus on the constructedness of the child audience here, it is not to deny the unruliness of real audiences but to stress the researchers' and reformers' allied attempts—which were neither wholly successful nor wholly unsuccessful—to produce and place the audience in a certain way.

The problem of understanding and controlling the child was obviously not confined to the cinema. Indeed, the construction of children extends well beyond the bounds of audience research to the broader social and cultural processes through which notions of childhood are constituted and maintained. Historians such as Philippe Ariès have demonstrated that childhood is not an essence but a historical construction, a period of life defined differentially in relation to other periods of life by particular societies at particular times.[8] And Freud, in his investigations of fantasy structures, argued that childhood was not only the source of the psychic dynamics of adult identity but also something that the adult is always reworking, reimagining and refabricating according to the demands of repression.[9] Whether we take a socio-historical or a psychoanalytic approach, the process of representing the child audience is always overdetermined by the analyst's frame of reference. What does it mean for us (adults) to understand the child at the moving pictures, to produce a particular image of him or her? In what complex ways and through what processes (displacement, projection, disavowal) is that image linked to adult identity? What, in short, is at stake in the system of differences through which our society attempts to constitute a boundary between child and adult?

Such questions are still with us today and are important in considering the continuing viability of arguments about the mass media's effects on children. Although these arguments did not begin in the 1910s and 1920s, it is during this period that they were put forward most forcefully and were most closely tied to political and social action. Even the most cursory look at popular writing about the cinema during this time reveals the obsessiveness with which writers approached the problem of children and movies. Everyone with a complaint about the movies found references to the victimization of children to be their most powerful rhetorical tool. Denouncing the movies' harmful influence on children was a way of venting one's spleen on any number of perceived social ills—ills that in many cases extended well beyond the issue of childhood per se. So, for instance, as Robert Sklar has argued, references to children were often veiled attempts to deal with the problem of class—the immigrants and workers who were also enthusiastically embracing the movies.[10]

The concern over children and the movies was not merely a displacement of other concerns, however. To some significant degree, what was at issue in writing on the cinema in the 1910s and 1920s was the preservation of a particular image of childhood that had its roots in the nineteenth century. During this time, childhood was set apart as a distinct stage of the life cycle and was sentimentalized. Children were no longer encouraged to imitate adults so much as they were encouraged to behave like children, to exhibit precisely their difference from adults—their innocence and their disingenuous charm. Childhood became a period of life to be protected and preserved at all costs, and the supervision of childhood became much more rationalized as the church, the state, the schools, and families implemented changes to further order the child's life and establish a greater degree of control over it. As the family's economic and educational functions dwindled, its remaining function in the nurturing and maintenance of children was ascribed more importance. The family and the home themselves became sentimentalized and idealized, in Joseph Kett's words, as a "total environment united by ties of warmth and intimacy."[11]

This image of childhood was a historical construction. The writers and reformers in the 1910s and 1920s undoubtedly viewed childhood as an essence at some level, but they also clearly realized that it was subject to historical forces; that definitions of childhood and the experience of childhood could change and, from their perspective, change for the worse. An article in *Playground* posed the question implicit in much writing of the period: "Are we trying to abolish childhood?"[12] Such writing revealed an intense interest in preserving a certain image of children, and it followed from the claim that this image was in crisis.

This brief sketch provides a context through which to understand how people of the time could have conceived the cinema as a threat to definitions of childhood. First, in an era which increasingly worked to separate children from adults through institutions such as children's hospitals, juvenile court systems, and reform schools, the cinema mixed ages indiscriminately, providing the same entertainment for adults and children alike. The ideal of preserving childhood by maintaining a childhood culture distinct from adult culture was disrupted by the cinema as the boundaries between children's films and adult films became blurred. The fact that many children seemed to prefer the films aimed at their parents to the films made for them was particularly troubling because it called into question the difference between adult and child desire. Virtually everyone who wrote on the subject was interested in maintaining a traditional system of differences between child and adult. The cinema, because of its mixed audiences and adult films, was viewed as a threat to that system.

A second threat the cinema posed to the traditional image of the child revolved around the family's role in the supervision of the child's leisure. The view of the family as a "total environment" for the nurturing and supervision of children was no doubt a comforting one, but it was increasingly challenged by the changes of the nineteenth and early twentieth centuries. City life provided the child with a broader range of contacts, while parks, school activities, automobiles and movies increasingly drew children away from the home. As Robert Lynd and Helen Lynd noted in their study of Muncie, Indiana, "The family was declining as a unit of leisure time pursuits."[13]

Around this perceived crisis, a veritable industry arose to "place" the child both symbolically and physically at the movies; to give children a particular way of looking at films that satisfied adult conceptions of childhood innocence. This attempt at placement took several forms—from the ethnographies previously mentioned, to debates and initiatives surrounding what would today be called the textual subject, to attempts to define and regulate the body of the child at the movies. An account of the full range of these forms and practices is well beyond the scope of this study. What I would like to focus on here is a specific set of initiatives that attempted to

"place" the child at the movies—the children's matinee movements of the
1910s and 1920s, and particularly the Hays Office efforts of 1925.

A number of solutions to the problem of childhood movie attendance
were in fact offered during these years. Many writers and reformers called
for the censorship of all films that included scenes deemed harmful to
children. The National Board of Censorship, and later the Hays Office,
countered this argument by claiming that such a measure would reduce all
adult entertainment to the level of "childish intelligence."[14] The prospect
of child-like adults was perhaps as threatening as that of adult-like children; it was precisely the difference between the two that most were trying
to maintain. Others called for laws prohibiting children from attending
pictures unaccompanied by an adult. By the late 1920s, New York and New
Jersey had such laws on the books, and six other states had slightly less
stringent laws that restricted children's attendance at certain hours.[15] The
difficulty of enforcing these laws was widely noted. A few states and cities
had laws that prohibited children from attending certain films identified
as harmful by censorship boards. There were calls for a specialized movie
industry devoted exclusively to the production and exhibition of films for
children; there were requests for special family shows that children and
parents could attend together; and there were pleas to parents to reassert
control over their children's leisure and restrict their moviegoing to only
the most wholesome fare.

Children's matinees were thus among the least radical solutions offered
to solve the problem of children and movies. Matinees involved no state
censorship, no laws restricting children's access to films, and no change in
the basic structure of production and exhibition. They were preferred most
by those who believed that the power of the movies could be harnessed for
the good of children. They were also favored by those most closely aligned
with the industry, and, at least by 1925, by the industry itself.

It was in that year that the Motion Picture Producer and Distributors
Association (MPPDA) began its campaign for Saturday morning movies.
On April 25, 1925, approximately 2,700 children paid their dimes and
entered the Eastman theater in Rochester, New York, for a Saturday matinee. They had seen in their classrooms the posters advertising the show, and
their parents had been encouraged, through the newspapers and through
the local activities of such organizations as the PTA, the Federation of
Women's Clubs, and the Daughters of the American Revolution, to have

them attend it. The children were escorted to their seats by Boy Scouts, sang "America the Beautiful," and then viewed a film program made up of a short health talk, a Fleischer cartoon, a scenic short, an animal picture, and the feature presentation, *The Hottentot*. The program was, by all accounts, a great success—not surprisingly given the fact that the considerable forces of the MPPDA were behind it. The Rochester screening was carefully planned to inaugurate publicly the Hays Office drive for Saturday morning movies for children.[16]

Long before the Hays Office involvement, as early as 1913, children's matinees were a visible component of urban culture. In 1913, an organization called the Children's Motion Picture League began to organize children's matinees in six theaters in New York City. Although their efforts were almost certainly not the first, they drew national attention and, according to an article in *Outlook*, served as a model for similar ventures in the South, Southwest, and Puerto Rico.[17] At the beginning of the same year, a theater manager in Davenport, Iowa, had organized a series of matinees that continued successfully for at least five years. By 1915, there were regular matinees in Boston, Louisville, New Orleans, Grand Rapids, New Rochelle, and probably many other cities in the country. The matinees during these early years were largely local efforts, initiated by community leaders as a way of dealing with the specific problems they sensed in their own neighborhoods. They were rarely organized by individual theater managers; in fact, writers contended that matinees would not be successful without the broad support of the civic and religious organizations of the community. So, the organization of matinees was almost always conducted by local reformers, under the auspices of the PTA, the Board of Education, local women's clubs, or special committees formed from ad hoc groups of concerned citizens. In fact, it is probably fair to say that matinees remained local efforts through most of their history. However, in 1916, the National Board of Review's Committee on Films for Young People (formerly the Committee on Children's Pictures and Programs and later the National Committee for Better Films) began a concerted effort to organize the various local activities into a national movement.[18] Local groups active in promoting children's matinees and family programs were joined together as the Affiliated Committees for Better Films under the umbrella of the National Committee. The National Committee coordinated and organized the movement through four types of activity. First, they worked to recruit new affiliated committees. Mary Peck, a former University of Minnesota professor, was sent on a speaking tour in late 1916 and early 1917 toward this end. The committee solicited national publicity and wrote letters to local groups throughout the country to encourage involvement. By October 1917, there were ninety-nine affiliated committees spread throughout the country. Second, the National Committee published and distributed pamphlets and lists of suitable films for matinees and for family shows. These included "Principles Governing the Selection of Motion Pictures for Young People Under 16," "Films! Fine Films! Films for Youngsters!" and "A Garden of American Motion Pictures." Third, the committee published the monthly *Committee for Better Films Bulletin*, which served as a clearinghouse for information on community involvement in moving pictures, particularly special programs. Finally, the National Committee encouraged motion picture companies to produce films suitable for children and to keep in distribution those films that had already been produced.

The growth of the matinee movement during the mid-1910s is impressive, though the matinees did not always reflect the tastes of the child audience. The problems reported at a large New York City theater were not unusual:

> The program was planned for clean entertainment, making education secondary to the amusement that children need on Saturdays . . . [It] included *Pigs Is Pigs*, featuring John Bunny, Bostock's wild animals and a fine production of *Alice in Wonderland*.
>
> It seemed as if it would be a morning of rare pleasure for the boys and girls who were accustomed to attend the usual program of motion pictures.
>
> But the children would not attend on Saturday morning, nor on succeeding Saturday mornings. They wanted to pay more and see a sensational adult picture thrown on the screen. As one little girl of twelve expressed it: "We like to see them making love and going off in automobiles." And a boy explained, "There won't be any shooting or dynamiting in those kid pictures. What's the use of seeing them?" [19]

Despite such objections, the children's matinee became both a common and highly conventionalized form of exhibition during the 1910s. Local organizations publicized the shows and encouraged their members to have their children attend; some organizations and businesses bought up blocks of tickets to give to poor children or to their employees. Within the theater, Boy Scouts, Girl Scouts, or college women in caps and gowns served as ushers, and one or more matrons watched over the children. Stage presentations prior to the films often showcased local child talent or an adult storyteller. It was quite common to award a five dollar gold piece or a season pass to the matinees for the best essay written about the film viewed that day. And, in some cities, Public Library tie-ins encouraged children to read books related to the films. By 1925, a substantial body of knowledge had been developed about the conduct of children's matinees.

The Hays Office drive for Saturday morning movies was launched by the Committee for Public Relations, an advisory board that Will Hays had formed shortly after assuming his duties as head of the MPPDA in 1922. The Committee for Public Relations was made up of the leaders of over sixty national civic and religious organizations, including the National Council of Women, the American Legion, the National Council of Catholic Women, the Boy Scouts of America, the YMCA, and the American Civic Association. The committee thus had access to and influence over most of the local organizations that had traditionally produced matinees in their communities.

During 1924 and early 1925, the committee completed a survey of the films in the vaults of the MPPDA's member companies. They identified those films that were suitable for children to view and constructed a series of thirty-six programs for special matinees. By the fall of 1925, fifty-two programs were available to any organization or theater—a full year's supply of movies for weekly matinees. Each program consisted of a feature film, a two-reel comedy, and what was referred to as a semi-educational short, usually a scenic or industrial film.

The films were re-edited and often re-titled to make them appropriate for the child's psychological needs. *The Hottentot*, the feature shown at the Rochester matinee, was cut by 1,500 feet. According to *Motion Picture News*, it was cut "not because of its objectionable business in its action, but because the reel in its original form was considered too long to sustain the interest of the young audience."[20] However, the *Pasadena Post* noted that the editing was also meant to have a moral function: "There has been an effort to cut out everything that would puzzle or mislead the youthful spectator. Simpler captions have been substituted. Nothing tending to imply impropriety in the conduct of any character has been retained. If curiosity is aroused in the young mind, it is hoped that it shall be an entirely wholesome curiosity, the answering of it useful to the youngster."[21] Apparently, the curiosity aroused by 1,500 feet in plot gaps was considered of the wholesome kind.

The films were shipped in "special metal containers" that held all eight reels, and exhibitors, in signing the standard contracts for the films, promised to show nothing but the movies included therein. This policy was designed to ensure that films appropriate for children would not be paired with inappropriate ones. But it also greatly reduced the burden on the citizens and theater managers interested in organizing children's matinees by providing a full ready-made program of films. Those who organized matinees frequently commented on the many difficulties involved in securing a program of films. There was never enough children's fare produced to fill a regular schedule of matinees with current releases. Thus, organizers had to depend primarily on films that had long since had their first run, and because such films had often dropped out of distribution entirely, organizers had to write a number of exchanges to locate prints, which then were usually in poor condition. Moreover, to put together a single show they often had to deal with two or three exchanges, potentially a different one for each of the films to be used. One of the most significant aspects of the Hays plan was that it reduced the labor of choosing, locating, and securing prints by devising an incredibly streamlined system of national distribution for children's films. Organizers of matinees only had to deal with one exchange for a steady supply of ready-made programs of such films.

In the late summer and early fall, the plan was set in motion on a national scale when thirty-two of the largest cities in the country began to exhibit the MPPDA-sponsored weekly matinees. When Hays announced the plan, he said that he expected it to extend everywhere, and in fact by the fall a number of smaller cities had also implemented the idea. Hays proclaimed that the arrangement was "the complete answer to the situation. Any really interested group anywhere, cooperating with the local exhibitor, may now obtain pictures proper for this purpose."[22]

The children's matinee movement was motivated by a number of goals. For the MPPDA, of course, the primary goal was always the protection of the economic interests of the industry. And, as always, to protect the industry from more extreme adversaries whose agendas would lead to a reduction in industry profits. Censorship and child attendance laws were definite threats during the 1920s, and the MPPDA drive for Saturday matinees was an effective and apparently constructive way of countering those threats. However, the industry had other, related motives. Critics charged that Hays was interested only in turning children into movie fans. Little probably had to be done to accomplish that, but there is no doubt some truth to this claim. The matinee drive coincided with a broader drive called the Greater Movie Season, an elaborately planned set of festivities and gimmicks planned to foster further goodwill and involvement in the cinema. Additionally, the industry was concerned with what Hays called the "Free Movie Menace." Civic, religious, and educational organizations were increasingly showing films in auditoriums and courtyard squares, often without charging admission. Thus, an alternative mode of exhibition had arisen that bypassed the theaters and presumably hurt their business. Many of the early matinees were run precisely this way. In Hays's 1925 annual report, he noted the efforts of the MPPDA's Film Board of Trade to control this menace, while Jason Joy, in an early statement on the matinee plan, argued that it was unwise to show movies to children for free because it had the effect of lessening the child's estimation of the show's value.[23] In one sense, then, the matinee plan was an attempt to gain back a significant portion of this alternative business. However, there was also a more direct pecuniary interest in the industry's cooperation. Although Hays's publicity always claimed that the matinees were not money-making ventures but acts of goodwill on the part of the industry, the plan was, from the beginning, designed to earn profits. A plan submitted to Hays by Ward Wooldridge, the secretary of the Public Relations Committee, claimed that in the most conservative estimate, exhibitors would gross $1,620,000 and member companies $405,000 in the venture over a three-year period. Most of the latter figure would be eaten up by print costs and publicity, but for the member companies any profit on these older films appeared as a windfall. The exhibitors, meanwhile, could make a tidy profit during a time of day when the theater was usually dead.[24]

But civic organizations and reform groups were not simply being duped by the industry. They had their own complex set of goals, and the matinee movement appeared as a practical way to achieve them. First, the matinee movement addressed the widespread concerns that the mass media and modern life were destroying childhood; matinees were one means of attempting to reassert traditional distinctions between child and adult by identifying, producing, and preserving a children's culture within the cinema itself. The desire to segregate children from adults in the cinema was a strong one, and reformers felt that if provided their own Saturday movies, children would be less likely to go to the movies during the rest of the week. One study in Asheville, North Carolina, reportedly found that the percentage of children in general audiences had been reduced from 28 percent to 3 percent since the establishment of Saturday matinees.[25] Reformers also hoped that the matinees would instill in children a heightened appreciation of films and a greater ability to distinguish the good from the bad, the wholesome from the unwholesome, and the highbrow from the lowbrow. The essay contests that were so frequently conducted through the matinees were certainly a part of this effort; they rewarded children for responding to movies along lines valued by reform-minded middle-class adults.[26] In addition, the matinee movement was designed to address certain fears about the relationship between the child and the space of the movie theater. The MPPDA matinees were placed largely in the theaters of "preferred exhibitors"—theaters that were large, lavish, well ventilated, and well lit. Thus, unlike the small, dark theaters that were seen as bad for both the health and the morals of the young, the matinees placed children in a healthy environment under the watchful eye of a matron—a surrogate of parental authority.

The Hays Office drive for Saturday morning movies was abandoned in 1926, and the work of organizing and promoting matinees fell back into the hands of local organizations and the National Committee for Better Films. This drive was only a small part of a much broader history, a history not only of matinees but of social concern over the movies and children. But the Hays Office efforts were emblematic in certain ways, particularly in the ways in which they positioned the child at the moving pictures. First, through the selection and editing of films they attempted to produce a particular kind of textual subject, a symbolic position and mode of address that would ideally produce the spectator as a true child. Second, through essay contests, organizers tried to gauge the actual response of real children to the films of the week. If this was not exactly ethnography, it was only because of the explicitness of the aim of shaping that response; the response rewarded was the one deemed best from an adult perspective. Finally, the matinees exerted a power over the child's body, both through the ways in which it worked systematically to separate the child from the adult and through the ways it placed the child in a system of surveillance within the space of the theater itself.

The concept of audience was relevant only in two general contexts in the

1910s and 1920s. First, it was used as a way of criticizing the cinema or some aspect of it. Those who did not like the cinema argued their cases most forcefully when they located a victim among those who did, and, as in all good melodrama, the villain's villainy rose in direct proportion to the victim's helplessness, gullibility and lack of awareness. The cinema was evil because of what it was doing to a particular audience, and in such arguments children often if not always made the best victims. Second, the concept of audience was relevant as part of broader efforts to survey and circumscribe the activities and attitudes of particular groups within society—groups such as women, immigrant workers, and children, who were marked both by their "otherness" and by their relative lack of social power. Attention to these audiences may have followed from a good-hearted concern for the victimized and helpless, but it was also inseparably linked to a form of surveillance designed to assure effects of power such as those described by Michel Foucault in *Discipline and Punish*. Ironically, in a world of surveillance, the darkened movie theater afforded the possibility of escape, and, insofar as it intensified the spectator's power to see without being seen, even reversal. Audience research and a set of related efforts attempted to combat this—to pierce the darkness of the theater, to place the spectator under the steady gaze of social scientists, reformers, and policymakers. Certain groups of spectators would not simply watch movies; they would be watched while watching them.

It seems odd that with the exception of Robert Sklar and Garth Jowett, film history has so completely ignored the obsession with the child audience, particularly if we admit that it was the dominant feature of critical approaches to the cinema at the time. We might say more—that the image of the child at the movies has functioned as a precondition of audience research generally. If mass-culture research has historically been paternalistic, it is because it has been modeled on that image, an image that remains largely unexamined. An understanding of such attempts to constitute and control the child audience during the 1910s and 1920s might give us a keener sense of the stakes of audience research today.

One might object that we are already beyond that now, that the paternalistic view of the audience has been discredited and cast aside and that we now finally have the opportunity to see how real audiences read and react. But in fact, I would argue, we are still firmly within the problematic established in debates around the cinema and children in the early part of the century. Recent work in film and cultural studies has certainly not yet dislodged this traditional view from dominance. And furthermore, that work, which relies increasingly on ethnography, remains stuck within the terms of this traditional debate, condemned to what may be a strategically important but conceptually limiting reversal of its terms. Where the audience was once passive, it is now active; where once gullible, now critical; where once manipulated, now manipulative, etc. I offer no way out of this bind, but I do suggest that a genealogy of the concept of media audiences and a consideration of the child's significance as the privileged site of audience research might give us a better sense of the present situation. Foucault asked "What matter who is speaking?" in order to call attention to the ways the concept of the author functions in a given society at a given time to limit, manage, and contain the proliferation of discourse.[27] "What matter who is viewing?" might be asked in a similar spirit, not as a way of denying the real experience of spectators but as a way of calling into question the conditions under which concepts of audience have entered into public discourse.

NOTES

1 Alice Miller Mitchell, *Children and Movies* (Chicago: University of Chicago Press, 1929), xvii.

2 See, for instance, Harold O. Berg, "One Week's Attendance of Children at Motion Picture Entertainments," *Playground* (June 1923): 165; Harvey C. Lehman and Paul A. Witty, "Education and the Moving Picture Show," *Education* (September 1926): 39–47; Clarence Arthur Perry, "Frequency of Attendance of High-School Students at the Movies," *School Review* (October 1923): 573–87; and "The Child, the Movies and the Censor," *Sunset* (July 1916): 31.

3 Herbert Blumer and Philip M. Hauser, *Movies, Delinquency and Crime* (New York: Macmillan, 1933).

4 Mary Allen Abbott, *Children's Responses to the Motion Picture "The Thief of Baghdad"* (Rome: International Educational Cinematographic Institute, League of Nations, 1931).

5 See John Fiske, *Television Culture* (New York: Methuen, 1987) for a useful elaboration of this point.

6 Prominent examples of this work include David Morley, *The Nationwide Audience: Structure and Decoding* (London: BFI, 1980); and Ien Ang, *Watching Dallas* (London: Methuen, 1985).

7 See, for instance, James Clifford and George E. Marcus, eds., *Writing Culture: The Poetics and Politics of Ethnography* (Berkeley: University of Califor-

nia Press, 1986); George E. Marcus, "Rhetoric and the Ethnographic Genre in Anthropological Research," *Current Anthropology* 21 (1980): 507–10; George E. Marcus and James Clifford, "The Making of Ethnographic Texts: A Preliminary Report," *Current Anthropology* 26 (1985): 267–71; Vincent Crapanzano, "On the Writing of Ethnography," *Dialectical Anthropology* 2 (1977): 69–73; and George E. Marcus and Dick Cushman, "Ethnographies as Texts," *Annual Review of Anthropology* (1982): 25–69.

8   Philippe Ariès, *Centuries of Childhood: A Social History of Family Life*, trans. Robert Baldick (New York: Vintage, 1962).

9   For an excellent account and application of psychoanalysis to the question of childhood, see Jacqueline Rose, *The Case of Peter Pan: Or, The Impossibility of Children's Fiction* (London: Macmillan, 1984).

10 Robert Sklar, *Movie-Made America: A Cultural History of the Movies* (New York: Basic, 1975), 122–40.

11 Joseph F. Kett, *Rites of Passage: Adolescence in America, 1790 to the Present* (New York: Basic, 1977), 138. Another particularly strong account of the new status of childhood in the late nineteenth century is Viviana A. Zelizer, *Pricing the Priceless Child: The Changing Social Value of Children* (New York: Basic, 1985). Related work in this area includes Bruce Bellingham, "Institution and Family: An Alternative View of Nineteenth Century Child Saving," *Social Problems* 33, no. 6 (1986): 533–57; Philip Greven, *The Protestant Temperament: Patterns of Child-Rearing, Religious Experience and the Self in Early America* (New York: Knopf, 1977); Hilary Russell, "Training, Restraining and Sustaining: Infant and Child Care in the Late 19th Century," *Material History Bulletin* 21 (1985): 35–49; Robert Wells, "Family History and the Demographic Transition," in *The American Family in Social Historical Perspective*, ed. Michael Gordon (New York: St. Martin's, 1983): 372–92; and Bernard Wishy, *The Child and the Republic: The Dawn of Modern American Child Nurture* (Philadelphia: University of Pennsylvania Press, 1968).

12 "Are We Trying to Abolish Childhood?" *Playground* (April 1923): 32.

13 Robert Lynd and Helen Merrell Lynd, *Middletown: A Study in American Culture* (New York: Harcourt, 1956), 272.

14 Lawrence A. Averill, "The Motion Picture and Child Development," *Educational Review* (May 1918): 398–409.

15 Roy F. Woodbury, "Children and Movies," *Survey* (May 15, 1929): 253–54.

16 *Motion Picture News*, October 16 1925; *Rochester Times Union*, April 17, 1925, April 22, 1925, October 2, 1925; *Rochester Herald*, April 17, 1925, April 20, 1925, April 25, 1925; *Rochester Democrat Chronicle*, April 18, 1925; unpaginated clippings, Will Hays Papers, Indiana State Library.

17 "The Children's Motion Picture League," *Outlook*, July 26, 1913, 643.

18 For general accounts of the activities of the National Board of Review, see Charles Matthew Feldman, *The National Board of Censorship (Review) of Motion Pictures: 1909–1922* (New York: Arno, 1977); Garth Jowett, *Film: The*

Democratic Art (Boston: Little, Brown, 1976), 108–39; Nancy J. Rosenbloom, "Between Reform and Regulation: The Struggle over Film Censorship in Progressive America, 1909–1922," *Film History* 1 (1987): 307–25.

19 "Motion Pictures Specially for Children," *Rutland Evening News*, October 31, 1916, unpaginated clipping, Theater Arts Collection, New York Public Library, New York.

20 "Hays Morning Show Tried Out," *Motion Picture News*, May 16, 1925, unpaginated clipping, Will Hays Papers.

21 *Pasadena Post*, November 9, 1925, unpaginated clipping, Will Hays Papers.

22 Will Hays, "Motion Pictures and the Public," address to the Women's City Club of Philadelphia, April 20, 1925, Will Hays Papers.

23 MPPDA, *Annual Report, 1925*, Will Hays Papers; *Playground* (September 1925): 345.

24 Ward Wooldridge, memo to Will Hays, April 28, 1925, Will Hays Papers.

25 *Schenectady Gazette*, October 3, 1925; *San Mateo News Leader*, January 29, 1925, unpaginated clippings, Will Hays Papers.

26 As Jason Joy said in one of the announcements of the matinee plan, "Best of all, the young people are taught to appreciate the really high-class sort of picture—and having acquired that taste in their youth will continue it as they grow up" (*The American City* [September 1924]: 246). Lea Jacobs discusses the related aesthetic ideology of the film education movement in "Reformers and Spectators: The Film Education Movement in the Thirties," *Camera Obscura* 22 (January 1990): 22–49.

27 Michel Foucault, "What Is an Author?" in *Textual Strategies: Perspectives in Post-Structuralist Criticism*, ed. Josue V. Harari (Ithaca, N.Y.: Cornell University Press, 1979), 141–60.

DISH NIGHT AT THE MOVIES
Exhibitor Promotions and Female Audiences during the Great Depression
Kathryn H. Fuller-Seeley

The Great Depression, the worst economic downturn ever experienced in the United States, began in October 1929 with the stock market crash. Conditions then continued to spiral downward to terrible lows in 1932 and 1933. To some panicked observers, it looked like the entire consumer economy was collapsing. With the unemployment rate over 25 percent and a further quarter of the country's labor force working only part-time, cash-strapped families cut their purchasing to the bone. One of the first nonessential expenses trimmed by working- and middle-class households was money spent on entertainment. Attendance at sporting events turned dismal—the National League saw baseball game receipts drop 40 percent, and the minor leagues were nearly wiped out. Two-thirds of all Broadway theaters closed, and federal tax revenue from theater and concert entertainments across the country plummeted by more than 65 percent. Seasonal hotels saw a 75 percent drop in business.[1] Instead of going out, families sat at home and listened to the radio, which at least was free after they had paid for the receiver.

Even America's favorite pastime, going to the movies, was gravely affected. In the kind of news story that appeared all over the nation in summer 1932, a headline in Virginia's *Richmond News Leader* stated, "100 Movie Houses in State Suspend Operations." The article further reported that fully one-third of the state's three hundred movie theaters had closed, and that "the number of theaters in the large cities of the state have been appreciably reduced in number ... but the greatest reduction has been in the smaller towns, where a great many have closed down. In a number of the smaller places, as well, theaters which had formerly showed pictures two or three times a week have cut their programs to once a week. Motion picture addicts, who formerly took in a picture five or six nights a week in the cities, have cut their movie sprees to one or two nights."[2]

Small town and neighborhood movie theaters across America during the early Depression years faced a tremendous drop in ticket sales. Exhibitors had to find the means to stem their losses and find profit in difficult times or else face widespread bankruptcy. Theater managers, whose options were significantly limited by block-booking and other aspects of the studio control of film product, often focused their efforts less on which features they could play and more on the nonfilmic elements of their program—the advertising and promotional events that they could control on a local level.

Dish Night giveaway promotions were one of the most successful solutions to exhibitors' problem of bringing movie patrons back to the theater in the 1930s. Merchandise giveaways and cash-award contests filled movie theaters in the Depression with as much drama, elation, desire, disappointment, and anguish as anything that was shown on their silver screens. Yet while these promotions boosted box office receipts at a crucial time, critics feared that they also opened a Pandora's box of woes. The seemingly benign "one free to each lady" plates, cups, and bowls could become dangerous weapons in the hands of film exhibitors locked in lethal competition with each other to remain in business, let alone in the hands of rioting movie audiences.

In this essay I examine film exhibitors' use of "premiums" or free giveaway promotions directed at women. I focus especially on Dish Night, which we now look back on as a quintessential Depression-era movie theater event. By investigating the publicity material surrounding these giveaway programs, I note how the persuasive arguments that chinaware companies provided to exhibitors, and the discord that Dish Night provoked between exhibitors trying to rebuild box office business in tough times, reveals several aspects of the film exhibitors' contentious relationship with their patrons. In analyzing the variety of responses of exhibitors and the public to Dish Night and its even more volatile rival, Bank Night, I provide new insights into the fears of social mayhem that haunted American businessmen and authorities, as well as into the hopes they cherished that an expanded consumer economy would restore calm, order, and control.

THE SUDDEN END OF PROSPERITY

The film exhibition business had experienced an unprecedented boom in 1929, due to the astonishing popularity of the new talking pictures and the opening of sumptuous picture palaces in cities across the nation. Movie attendance had nearly doubled in four years, skyrocketing from 55 million admissions weekly in 1925 to 110 million in 1929, if industry estimates can be believed. Executives had a more utilitarian purpose than mere public relations puffery for inflating attendance totals, for optimistic attendance figures would help boost film companies' stock prices and reputations among investors during the massive studio merger deals that were taking place in 1929.[3]

Initially, the movie business was not greatly affected by the downturn that followed the October 1929 stock market crash, and film producers and exhibitors thought they would be immune to any ills of an economic downturn. While small town and neighborhood theaters in the hard-hit textile centers in New England had seen box office declines since the beginning of the recession there in 1927, exhibitors elsewhere had assumed that this was merely a regional slump. By the end of 1930, however, movie theater weekly admissions across the country had declined by 28 percent to 80 million. A year and a half after the stock market crash, movie theater business began to tumble rapidly. Box office receipts fell from $732 million in 1930 to $482 million in 1933, a drop of nearly 34 percent. Weekly attendance plummeted from its 1929 high by 45 percent, down to only 50 million. "The winter of 1932–1933 was just about the toughest year in the history of the amusement business," recalled one reporter. When President Franklin Roosevelt closed the nation's banks for several weeks in March 1933 so that the financial system could be stabilized, cash became nonexistent. The film exhibitors' trade papers reported that movie attendance plummeted (albeit temporarily) by yet another 45 percent.[4]

It is probable that the actual declines were even more precipitous than these estimates, for, as Tom Doherty and Tino Balio point out, the film industry was known for inflating all of its statistics, from attendance figures and box office revenues to production costs. Doherty notes that the *Film Daily Yearbook* initially reported that weekly movie attendance had collapsed from 100 million to fewer than 40 million. But by 1939, the *Yearbook* editors had revised their story by boosting the Depression low figure by 50 percent; now they reported that theater attendance had only declined to 60 million at its lowest point. In 1939, the film industry trumpeted that attendance had risen to about 90 million a week, but again the numbers are suspect—Balio cites a Gallup Poll report in 1940 showing actual weekly movie attendance to be only about 54 million. The movie business had a lot at stake in these numbers—nearly all of the studios faced bankruptcy, and the disastrous box office figures might make financial support for their reorganization impossible to obtain. Flamboyantly boastful in good times but secretive in bad times, the film industry was loath to reveal exactly how low its attendance figures had sunk.[5]

While few hard numbers exist to chart the decline of business at movie houses in the Depression, evidence suggests that small town and neighborhood theaters were hit harder than urban picture palaces. One of the few tangible figures that show the Depression's impact on smaller theaters was the percentage of movie houses that were forced to close. The number of open movie theaters declined by 35 percent, from about 23,000 to fewer than 15,000.[6] In 1933, 30.5 percent of all theaters were still closed, and 25 percent remained shuttered in 1934. The number of theater employees dropped by one third, from 129,600 in 1929 to just 86,937 in 1932.[7] Contributing to the problem was the overabundance of older theaters in small towns, where exhibitors had far smaller populations to draw from than their urban counterparts.[8] It was difficult for the theaters in nonmetropolitan areas to draw in new patrons or to achieve the economies of scale upon which the corporately owned urban theater chains and picture palaces could count. A great many small town and rural theaters could not withstand the one-two punch of the expense of switching to "talkies" and the loss of ticket sales. Thus they closed by the thousands.[9]

A *Motion Picture Herald* survey in January 1934 showed that the theater closings impacted some of the nation's thirty-one film distribution districts (which were roughly equal in population) far more severely than others. Large cities fared relatively well. Only 11 percent of the New York

City district's movie houses were closed. Five other urban districts fared well, including Philadelphia with 6.8 percent closed, Detroit 9.4 percent, Seattle 10 percent, and New Haven 10.8 percent closed. Eight other districts, mainly in the South and Pacific West, saw only 15 to 20 percent of their movie houses closed, while seven districts in the mid-Atlantic and in the industrial Midwest had 22 to 32 percent of their theaters shuttered.

At the same time, other film distribution districts across the nation were hit disproportionately hard by Depression-era movie theater closings—the largely rural and small town Albany, New York, district saw 33.6 percent of its theaters closed; New Orleans and Indianapolis both lost 35 percent, Omaha 37.1 percent, Boston 37.7 percent, and Salt Lake City 43.2 percent. In the Cincinnati district, which included most of rural Kentucky, West Virginia, and southern Ohio, a shocking 47.7 percent of all movie houses were closed.[10]

Across the nation, even the movie theaters that already had been wired for sound took a beating—12.6 percent of them were shut down. But again, the decline was not distributed equally across the country. Despite the high unemployment in America's largest cities, eight major urban districts saw only 9 percent or fewer sound theaters closed in January 1934. The more-rural areas experienced significantly higher closure percentages of their wired theaters: the Albany district had 20 percent shuttered, Boston 22 percent, Cincinnati 15 percent, Kansas City 20.7 percent, Memphis 18 percent, St. Louis 16.5 percent, and in Salt Lake City 21 percent of the wired theaters were closed.[11]

The less-affected film distribution districts not only tended to have more areas of urban concentration, they were also dominated by large theater chains, which could absorb the box-office losses of individual theaters. On the other hand, the hardest-hit districts tended to have larger numbers of rural areas and small towns, where independently owned theaters and smaller chains were more common—such as in New England, upstate New York, Appalachia, and the Mississippi Valley. The independently owned theaters accounted for only 40 percent of theaters in New York City, 65 percent in Philadelphia, and 73 percent in Detroit; however, independents represented 86 percent of theaters in Cincinnati and in Salt Lake City and 91 percent in Omaha. The seven healthiest film distribution districts in 1934 accounted for 26 percent of the national market, according to figures from the *Motion Picture Herald*, but the seven worst-off districts could not be easily dismissed, for they accounted for 21 percent of the national total. The full impact of the Depression on film exhibition, particularly on independently owned theaters in districts comprised of small towns and agricultural areas, may never be precisely known but it was devastating, indeed.[12]

DISH NIGHT AND OTHER THEATER PROMOTIONAL PLANS

"The movies have been hit just like jewelry and other luxury trades," despaired an exhibitor in Muncie, Indiana, in 1933.[13] The decline of moviegoing from an inexpensive, thrice-weekly habit to an unaffordable luxury was a sudden, painful shock for audiences and exhibitors alike. The great fear among all film exhibitors, both urban and small town, was that Americans were permanently falling out of the moviegoing habit. Small exhibitors looked for any scheme to restore the flow of regular, twice-weekly patrons. Their focus shifted away from the screen toward nonfilmic ways to make a profit, for with block-booking they had very little control over which films they could schedule.[14] Even a few blockbuster films that drew large audiences, such as *King Kong* or *Grand Hotel*, could not significantly help theaters that changed programs every three days.[15]

Instead, exhibitors began playing double features, which offered their patrons more show for the money (even though the second film was often a mediocre B-grade picture). They cut ticket prices from a boom-time average of 50 cents for the best seats at evening shows back to 35 or 25 cents, or even as low as 10 cents for "bargain nights."[16] They slashed theater-operating expenses by laying off musicians, ushers, and projectionists. They increased their promotions and advertising, undertaking all manner of attention-getting stunts, contests, amateur nights, and local business booster and charity events to keep themselves in the public eye. They held SCREENO nights (a form of bingo), which offered prizes, groceries, or money to winning audience members. Theater owners also gave away everything from toys, postcards, pocket mirrors, and beauty aids to groceries and coal. Some exhibitors arranged "country store nights" in which patrons who had accumulated "dollars" by attending the theater regularly could "spend" or bid them for goods displayed on stage.

While most of these promotions addressed the movie audience as an undifferentiated mass that could be attracted back to the movies by rational appeals to economics, exhibitors moved further to tailor their promotional campaigns to reach target audiences. Teenage girls and adult women made up 55 to 60 percent or more of the small independent theater's audience; children under twelve represented about 20 to 25 percent, and teenage boys and adult males accounted for 20 to 25 percent. Women formed the core of the neighborhood theater market, whereas men represented a larger percentage of the audiences at downtown picture palaces and the "action houses" that specialized in cowboy and horror films. Savvy film exhibitors knew that women usually made the decisions for the whole family about what films they might see together and which neighborhood theater they might attend.[17]

Appealing to women was thus essential to luring audiences back to the small independent theaters in hard times. But what promotions might bring them in? As times got harder and housewives had little spare change left in the family budget to indulge in movie shows, exhibitors searched for a different type of free gift (or premium, as they were known in the retail trade) for their female patrons, something that was useful and practical yet attractive and appealing. The more that female patrons desired these products, the more necessary it would be for them to attend the theater each week in order to acquire them. Exhibitors thus found a solution in dishware, which was a perfect premium for Depression times.

The humorist Jean Shepherd, in his 1965 short story "Leopold Doppler and the Great Orpheum Theater Gravy Boat Riot," captured the bittersweet memories of his Depression-era childhood in Hohman (actually Hammond), Indiana. His stories detailed the thousand small absurdities that working- and middle-class families faced in hard times. He emphasized how the desire for consumer goods and sensual pleasures continued to gnaw at people, and how in a world of reduced means everyone was hungry to have something to call their own. Hohman's housewives stoked those acquisitive desires at the movie theater; as Shepherd describes:

> A spectacular display in a gleaming case appeared without warning in the Neo-Mosque lobby of the beloved Orpheum. Row on row of radiant, magnificent works of pure beauty lay displayed before them, cushioned on dark, blood-red velvet and setting each observer's soul on fire with instant desire. . . . "FREE! FREE! Beginning next Friday, one piece of this magnificent set of Artistic De-Luxe Pearleen Tableware, the Dinner Service of the Stars, will be presented

FREE to each adult woman in attendance. . . ." The effect of the Orpheum's incredible offer was galvanic. The word spread like the bubonic plague. . . . Red, chapped, water-wrinkled hands paused on clothes wringers and washboards; bathrobe clad figures hunched over sinks nodded in amazement. . . . By the end of the week of waiting the air had become tense and fretful. It was as though the whole town was waiting for Christmas morning. . . . Dish Night had come to Hohman, Indiana.[18]

Dish Night was not a frivolous matter for Hohman's middle- and working-class housewives, for dishes were a tangible symbol of social status in the 1930s. A young woman engaged to be married eagerly selected a china pattern to register at the local department store; she and her mother collected dinnerware, utensils, and linens to "go to housekeeping" in the proper manner, just as surely as they assembled her trousseau. The young bride faced the social challenges of setting a dinner table that would be admired when her husband's boss—or the minister, or the in-laws—came to dinner. Mismatched, chipped, and cracked old plates could cause a woman as much shame in front of her guests as holes in her Sunday dress.[19]

Most entertaining was done in the home, and many women, like the wives of Middletown or Carol Kennicott and her Sauk Center neighbors in Sinclair Lewis's novel *Main Street*, invested much energy and pride in competing to throw the loveliest tea parties and the most stylish bridge club luncheons, Saturday night buffets, and Sunday dinners. The guests expected not only good food but also the elegant presentation of meals on delicate chinaware, and they leveled critical judgments on the hostess's skills.

How humiliating it was, then, for homemakers in the Depression to see their dishes wear and break and not be able to afford to replace them. What would the neighbors think if no two plates or cups matched? What if the family were reduced to drinking out of empty pickle jars, or if a woman owned neither casserole nor platter to take to the church covered-dish supper? The neighborhood's best serving dishes thus might be loaned from one woman to the next to keep up appearances at social gatherings.[20]

Cultural historians such as Studs Terkel, Robert McIlvaine, Steven Mintz, and Susan Kellogg have noted how personally most people took their losses in the Great Depression. People blamed themselves, not the collapsing capitalist system, for poverty and failure. Families suffered psychological blows from job layoffs and reduced economic status. For homemakers, the loss of status was painfully visible—in their children's worn clothing, in their own best overcoats, frayed and twenty years old, and even in the boiled vegetable suppers they had to serve when they could not pay the butcher's bill. Stung with humiliation that neighbors might see their distress, some women stopped entertaining, dropped out of clubs, and hid at home in their shabbiness.[21]

Under these circumstances, a shiny new dinner plate was a marvelous gift for a Depression-era housewife. Many women denied themselves pleasures and slighted their own needs during hard times in order to provide for their families. Not all women were selfless, by any means, but there are thousands of Depression family stories about mothers pinching pennies by refusing to buy anything new for themselves, and by making do or doing without so that their children could have shoes for school, a Christmas gift, or the rent could be paid.

With pretty dishes on the table, a woman could have at least a few new consumer items in the house. Further, she got to know them well as she washed them up every night. Plates, cups, and bowls were useful items, but they could also be beautiful objects, desirable enough to collect. For a poor woman, a matched set of new dishes could symbolize a return of the family's former prosperity, or a step up the ladder toward gentility. Although for some of the lucky middle-class families less affected by the Depression the free dishes might have held little value, the genteel status made visible in a well-set dinner table, was something that struggling working- and middle-class women, fearful of slipping further down the social ladder, might desperately desire to hang on to.[22]

Giving away gifts to female patrons was nothing new at movie theaters; since the days of nickelodeons, exhibitors had used premiums to build loyal patronage. Most giveaways were in the form of picture postcards of movie stars, but small gifts to women and children, like handkerchiefs, beauty aids, stuffed bears, booklets, and small toys also were also popular. Yet these items were handed out only at occasional giveaway events, and many of the items were worth only a penny or two. In hard times, however, people were attracted to items with more utility and value, and giveaways of practical china and kitchenware filled the bill.[23]

Film exhibitors planned to hold Dish Nights to boost attendance on the slowest nights of the week, usually Mondays and Tuesdays, when they otherwise showed films to empty houses. On Dish Night, what film a

theater played mattered little, so theater owners saved money by showing cheap "poverty row" features. Female movie patrons were sometimes
even involved in selecting the night of the week for the program: a display placed in the lobby of the New Fruitvale Theater in Oakland, California, announced: "Ladies! You choose which night will be Dish Nite"; in
that community, Tuesday, Wednesday, and Thursday split the vote for the
favorite night.[24] Once established at a theater, Dish Night could seemingly
go on forever, as exhibitors lured in women once or twice a week for a solid
year to collect all of the pieces of a 54- or 104-piece china set.

On average, each "free" dish cost the exhibitor a dime, so how was the
exhibitor able to make up this expense to gain profits at the box office?
As a *Business Week* article on movie house premiums explained: "Prior
to the giveaway, a certain house took in $50 on Monday. By distributing
1,000 pieces of china costing $110, Monday business increased to $300. Net
boost from premiums, $140."[25]

The Salem China Company was one of dozens of potteries in the Ohio
River Valley devastated by the downturn in retail product sales. Like other
firms that survived the Great Depression, Salem sold inexpensive dinnerware in bulk as advertising stunts to thousands of banks, furniture stores,
groceries, and food product marketers. Prior to the 1930s, consumers had
saved box tops from products, or collected "points" at drug stores to purchase dishes at deep discount, while banks offered dishware with new accounts and furniture stores gave away dish sets with dining room purchases.
As the Salem sales manager Floyd McKee noted in a company history, in
the 1920s, "Peoples Drug used over 150,000 32-piece sets from Salem, the
housewife playing $2.98 for a set costing about $2.72 at the factory." The
American Stores grocery chain in Philadelphia used about 130 railroad car-
loads of Salem dinnerware in another promotion.[26]

Salem quickly got on the Dish Night bandwagon; their sales literature
even claims that they invented the movie theater program in 1927. Salem's
Theater Sales Department offered exhibitors bulk prices on dishes such as
their distinctively art deco triangular-patterned Tricorne dishware, which
ranged from 14 cents for a nine-inch dinner plate to 10 cents for the tea-
cup and 7 cents for the saucer. For a minimal investment of five cents per
head, exhibitors could get ceramic coasters or ashtrays. As special event
premiums, creamers and sugar bowls were available for 20 cents each and
sandwich trays were 30 cents.[27]

Salem's theater sales department captured the opening night scenes of Dish Night promotions in advertising photographs, which show long lines of patrons passing under theater marquees announcing "Dish Night Tonight!" Other photos show auditoriums crammed with plain-clothed, worn-faced women brandishing dinner plates for the cameraman. The caption for one such photo states: "A Full House. Opening China Night June 2, 1932 Roosevelt Theater, San Francisco, California. Original contract 700-sets of Square Golden Pheasant China. Seating capacity 1,005. Attendance first China Night 1,230 paid admissions. Distributed first China Night 702 pieces. Second China Night 800 pieces. Now planning to hold China Night twice each week to accommodate the crowds." The 702 women in attendance that night had brought 528 men and boys along with them, further filling the Roosevelt Theater's coffers. The caption of the Salem publicity photograph showing the jam-packed interior of the Parkway Theater in Oakland, California, stated, "Showing 73rd consecutive China Nite."[28] The photographs of big crowds of happy movie theater patrons must have made very persuasive advertising for the Salem China Company.

As *Business Week* commented on 1933's Dish Night boom, "Here is a business worth the battle." The report estimated that on the national level, pottery sales to theaters topped $25 million. This success caused severe price cutting and competition among the potteries in attempts to secure Dish Night orders. Further, Dish Night's success at some theaters bred adverse reaction at others, for *Business Week* also noted that "part of the [theater] industry is trying to abolish them."[29]

Although many film exhibitors were using giveaway programs in the early 1930s, the trade journals *Motion Picture News*, *Exhibitors Herald*, and *Film Daily Yearbook* were adamantly opposed to the practice. They followed the lead of film producers who disliked any movie theater activity that diverted money normally spent for picture rental to go toward promotional expenses.[30] While reports of closed and failing theaters filled each issue, the trade journal columnists preached that what exhibitors needed to do was to increase their ballyhoo. They claimed that suffering local exhibitors just weren't trying hard enough, and that good showmanship would bring patrons back to the box office. "Study your situation!" a typical story instructed, "Are you posting enough paper? Is it the right kind? Is it going on the best location obtainable?" "Show is Lure, Not Premiums," warned

Motion Picture News, "A theater sells entertainment. If the sales argument is proper, if your schedules, prices and programs are right—then you don't need premiums or prizes."[31] Yet the columnists' words rang more hollow with each more disastrous month, and soon few exhibitors could afford to listen only to trade journals' dictums.

Most large urban theater chains hated premium giveaways because they felt forced to participate to stay in competition at the box office. In 1934 neighborhood theaters gained a few percentage points over their dismal 1933 figures, and as such they were reported to be doing better than the picture palaces; in response, jealous picture palace exhibitors charged that Dish Nights were the reason why.[32] Small town exhibitors defended their use of premiums not as underhanded competition but as a service to the industry to revive America's moviegoing habit.[33] They argued that premiums (and the idea of value added to the movie ticket being sold) were a better sales stimulant than straight price cuts in Depression times, for angry consumers resented attempts to raise prices once they had been lowered.[34] Their explanations fell on deaf ears, for theater corporations wanted to abolish giveaways, and they looked to the new National Recovery Act (NRA) codes being drawn up by the federal government to give them the power to do it.

Film exhibition was just one of sixteen hundred industries that came under Roosevelt's sweeping plan to stabilize American business through the New Deal's National Recovery Act. Each industry had to create a "Code of Fair Conduct," prohibiting destructive competition and (supposedly) curtailing unfair labor practices in factories and stores. Critics complained that the major film producers, distributors, and exhibitors dominated the code-writing process to guarantee their advantage at the expense of independent exhibitors and studio and theater workers. Thus, if the big boys got their way, movie ticket prices were to be kept as high as possible and giveaways and prizes would be abolished.[35]

Much of the contentious debate at the film exhibitors' NRA code-writing hearings, held in Washington, D.C., in September 1933, revolved around labor issues—theater owners did not want to give projectionists guaranteed employment, higher wages, or better working conditions. However, Dish Night was also on the table in discussions of how the Code of Fair Conduct could prevent ruinous competition and unfair advertising. The seriousness of the Dish Night dilemma brought pottery manufacturers to testify before the NRA code-writing committee. As Terry Ramsaye reported the scene in the *Motion Picture Herald*:

> Manufacturers of chinaware and other premiums distributed in motion picture theaters registered vigorous protests against the code's prohibition of the practice. At the same time, it became known that RKO Theaters was the first large circuit to outlaw this form of merchandising. Charging they will be driven out of the business, therefore defeating the very purpose of the NRA, pleas were made on behalf of premiums and giveaways by Michael Flynn, National Brotherhood of Operating Potters, Charles Sebring, of Sebring Pottery Company [and Salem China Company], and W. E. Wells of the United States Potters' Association. . . . Mr. Sebring declared that 20 percent of his business comes from theaters, adding that this percentage applied to all others in his field.
>
> Sebring warned that 100 skilled potters would lose their own jobs if Dish Night was banned.[36]

The potters' pleas only slightly softened the hearts of the corporate theater powers. The final draft of the NRA code for film exhibitors stated that if 75 percent of a community's theater owners voted to ban Dish Night in their district, then it was illegal; each theater had one vote. In cities with a large chain-theater presence, small exhibitors wishing to hold Dish Nights were outmaneuvered, outvoted, and out of luck. The NRA administrators had their hands full from the moment the motion picture code went into effect, making sure that exhibitors properly followed the rules of allowable competition. The regional grievance boards were swamped in 1934 with 548 complaints by exhibitors against one another for giving away premiums, running cash prize contests, and reducing ticket prices in places where local exhibitor groups had decreed such practices illegal. In fact, 52 percent of all complaints filed in the first eight months were about giveaway programs.[37]

Dish Night remained popular with theater owners but unsanctioned by the film exhibition industry. The trade journals contained virtually no information for exhibitors on Dish Night, nor were there any advertisements from giveaway product distributors. Some dishware manufacturers like the Salem China and Homer Laughlin companies along with other premium product makers contacted theater owners directly through their own sales forces. Other middlemen, like Playhouse Premiums in New York and the

Price Company in Chicago, set themselves up as distributors of giveaway merchandise to movie theaters; the Stetson Company, for example, sold through premium wholesalers almost all of the dinnerware it manufactured.[38] Both potteries and distributors promised to school novice theater managers in the art of the giveaway by providing Dish Night promotional kits complete with posters, banners, theater displays, handbills, newspaper advertising, and special "talkie" promotional film trailers.[39]

THE DEPRESSION APPEALS OF SALEM'S DISHWARE PREMIUMS

The Salem China Company attempted to associate its dishes with the allure of Hollywood glamour and celebrity; its sales and marketing department arranged for stars from Warner Bros. to pose for advertising and publicity photographs taking their tea with Salem's distinctive triangular-patterned Tricorne dishware. Glenda Farrell and Ruby Keeler, for example, were shown on the set between scenes of the First National/Warner Bros. 1935 feature Go into Your Dance. Another photo in the Salem Company files showed "Joan Blondell, William Gargan and Dick Powell between scenes of Warner Brothers forthcoming production Broadway Gondolier, 'enjoying a little bite.'"[40]

The cultural historian Roland Marchand uses the phrase "the democracy of goods" to explain the particular appeal that such promotions would have for Depression movie audiences. A poor woman could eat from the same elegant Salem china that the movie stars did, so she could share some essential part of their glamour. Richard deCordova and Charles Eckert have shown how widespread this hope was among manufacturers in the early 1930s—that is, that the notion of "tying up" or linking their goods to the movies would help boost their product sales in the Depression as well as enhance the consumption ideal's appeal for wary American families. Both authors show, however, that these appeals to Hollywood celebrity and style were only partially successful.[41]

The Salem China Company did not merely associate its dishes with the movies in the hope that film popularity would increase interest in its products; instead, the company slyly insinuated in its theater sales literature that the Salem dishware itself was superior to the movies and more reliable than star power to pull in the patrons to their movie theaters on a regular basis. In its advertising letters sent to exhibitors, Salem argued that "only occasionally can you feature a star that jams the aisles. But when you add Salem China Nites to your bill, you have a string of features week after week that draw the crowds in all seasons, all weathers."[42]

In sales fliers like "Salem China Nite Pleases the Ladies—Packs Your House," Salem's general manager Floyd McKee developed themes for selling Dish Night to exhibitors that centered on women and what they want, the question that so befuddled male film exhibitors. McKee's sales rhetoric touched on the Depression's humiliating impact on housewives: "Remember, they are always wanting new dishes in every home. . . . It gives them something they need and prize."[43] But the hard facts of hard times were not the key to the real appeal of dishes. Perhaps unconsciously, McKee and the Salem sales literature writers drew on imagery of addiction and uncontrollable desires. "Chinaware as premium has more appeal to the house wife than most articles. Since she never has the idea that she has enough chinaware already."[44] Salem further told exhibitors that, with the help of Dish Night products, they could condition their female patrons to keep returning to fetch another piece of the china set: "Salem Dinnerware has the color, the sparkle, the year-round usefulness that makes women glad to come and get it, and bring their men and children with them."[45] "Give them a chance to build up a dinner set by offering it as an attendance prize and you will see the crowds coming your way, and they will keep on coming week after week, steadily, surely, with big profit to you."[46] McKee also hinted at chinaware's potent symbolism of women's attachment to consumer goods and their homemaking ability: "The housewife can always remember where she secured each particular dish, much more so than with other items which she does not identify with the source."[47] Even a reply postcard that Salem sent to theater owners, which featured a smiling Mickey Mouse jauntily waving a greeting, offered a response that could be read as a hint about dishware's addictive power, "Sure Mickey, send me the dope on Salem's China Night plan for my theater!"[48]

Salem counseled exhibitors as one concerned man to another about their female problem: "Year in and year out, Salem China Nites have proved to be the most reliable attendance builders theater men have ever found."[49] The company also suggested it would deliver to the exhibitor an audience of women so mesmerized by the free dinnerware in their hands that they would be oblivious to the fact that the movie they paid to see was third rate, or that the theater had never reduced its ticket prices. "If you cut your retail price to move an over-stock, it is hard to go back to the original price, as the public have appraised the article at the reduced price. With a premium offer, you can set a date or fix a quantity limit and when that has been met, there is no criticism of the deal."[50]

Yet these spellbound female patrons were only partially under the exhibitor's control; if angered, they could turn and bite at any moment. To disappoint a woman was to make her unhappy, to earn her rancor and make her the enemy of the theater owner. "The ladies go for it because they do not need to guess or gamble to win. Every woman who attends goes home happy with a piece of high-grade dinnerware that she is proud to own and use." As McKee assured the exhibitors, "You take no risk" with Dish Nite's democratic handing out of prizes; with this type of promotion there was no chance to offend and anger the women.[51] Salem's marketing materials reassured women of their good intentions and reminded them of how other giveaway programs might infuriate them: as a sign on the Salem lobby display at the Lincoln Theater in Decatur, Illinois, announced, "Ladies Free! Free! Attend this theater every Tuesday and receive a piece of Mandarin Tricorne China! No raffles or drawing."

Salem even drew on the same arguments put forth by the exhibitor's trade journals. *Motion Picture News* had warned readers in 1930 of the smoldering anger that could build from audience members' disappointment in losing big prize contests: "One thing you must remember. For one person that benefits through a theater contest where prizes are given, there are many hundreds that get nothing for their effort. One person boosts for you, the others hold a grudge because they did not win."[52] Dish Night giveaways had a democratic inclusiveness based on plain jealousy—women hated a situation where other women got something they did not have. But the women's anger at losing games could be turned to the exhibitors' advantage when they offered Dish Night. As Salem stated: "Because every woman wins, it creates good will and steadily growing business."[53]

Although Salem's advertising rhetoric might at times seem amusing, McKee and the Salem Company marketing staff were familiar with the desires and preferences of their customers. They knew from firsthand experience about the emotional connections between women's consumer desires and the pleasures of pretty-but-utilitarian dinnerware. However, if women's consumer desires were as easily controlled as was claimed by Salem and other advertisers in the 1930s, then wouldn't the economy have improved much more quickly? As Marchand explains, consumer product advertisers in the 1930s had a love-hate relationship with female purchasers. No matter how much they cajoled or whipped women into a frenzy of desire, no matter how enticingly they presented their goods, no matter what horrible threats about the health of their children, rejection by potential mates or other judgmental women if the advertised products like Listerine were not used religiously, women might still not buy the product. Advertisers continually railed about the perfidy, inconstancy, stubbornness, and stupidity of the female consumer, but this disdainful attitude often masked how fearful they were. In despair, advertisers sometimes admitted that they did not really understand women and what women wanted.[54]

Film exhibitors were as frustrated as advertisers in 1936 when Dish Night ticket sales began to sag. Merchants groused about the success of movie theater Dish Night (Chicago retailers claimed to have lost $6 million in dish and kitchenware sales),[55] and the effectiveness of dishware's seductive appeal seemingly had worn off. The film exhibitor's trade press continued to warn theater owners away from Dish Night by asserting that premium programs would inevitably fail. Giveaway schemes that lasted twenty-six or fifty-two weeks dragged on so long that they bored the housewives; an extended dishware promotion offered little variety, little drama, and prizes of relatively low value. Trade journal columnists anticipated with growing trepidation, however, that Dish Night would be swept aside by a flood of new cash prize programs at theaters, and that a bad situation would be replaced with one that was infinitely worse.[56]

BANK NIGHT AND DISORDER IN THE THEATERS

Far more controversial and contentious than Dish Night was the Bank Night cash giveaway program, which swept through American movie theaters between 1935 and 1940. Charles Yaeger, a young entrepreneur who worked his way up through his father's movie theaters in small town New Mexico and Colorado, invented a simple yet highly effective scheme. In a Bank Night promotion, townspeople registered their names each week at the movie theater; on the same dead Monday or Tuesday evening that previously had been brightened with dinnerware, the theater manager held a drawing on stage for an enticingly large cash prize—often $100 to $500 or more, a sum that could make a great difference to most families in the Depression. The winner of the drawing had to rush to the stage to claim the money within sixty seconds or the prize was forfeited and the pot grew larger at the next drawing.[57] Unlike Dish Night, Bank Night allowed for only one lucky winner and many empty-handed losers.

Small towns across America came to a standstill on Bank Night because everyone was in the theater or was standing outside the packed house, straining to hear the winner announced over a loudspeaker attached to the marquee. It did not matter what picture was showing at the theater on Bank Night because people came for the drawing, not the film. A cartoon in *Esquire Magazine* (reprinted in the *Literary Digest*) depicts a movie theater draped with huge Bank Night banners; at the box office a man turning away remarks to his companion, "He says they've stopped having pictures." Ira Parkhill, who examined the Bank Nite frenzy in a lengthy *Saturday Evening Post* article, noted that the practice "has profoundly affected the social life of America, especially in the small town, although movie audiences of the largest cities have gone equally mad over it."[58]

Yaeger devised the program in 1931, and when he took Bank Night nationwide, a thousand theaters quickly joined up. The participating exhibitors paid Yaeger a license fee of $5 to $50 per week or a percentage of box office receipts, depending on seating capacity.[59] In September 1933 Bank Night was totally prohibited by the film exhibitors' NRA code, although Yaeger campaigned to have it reclassified from a lottery to a premium program.[60] The Supreme Court declared the NRA unconstitutional on June 1, 1935, however, and the Motion Picture Code's restrictions were voided.[61] Immediately, thousands of theaters plunged into the previously restricted giveaway schemes. Of the 15,000 operating movie theaters in 1935, an estimated 4,000 played Bank Night, a figure that swelled to 5,600 in late 1936, then to 6,000. Although an estimated 10,000 exhibitors (two-thirds of all theaters) had been hosting Dish Nights, the number of pottery giveaway programs dropped as theaters switched to the flashier cash games.[62] By 1937, Parkhill estimated that 10,000 of the nation's theaters were either playing Bank Night or one of its imitation games, and Yaeger was earning $30,000 to 65,000 per week in licensing fees.[63]

Many observers expressed concern about the frenzy of anticipation that Bank Night aroused in the crowds who jammed theaters and spilled outside onto the sidewalks. "It is a headache to the traffic squads," one com-

mented.[64] The palpable excitement and frustration of the throngs antici-
pating a win or regretting their loss could lead, local authorities feared, to
pushing and shoving or outright riots. *Time* magazine reported that, in
Des Moines, "Bank Night has been so popular that police and fire departments had to be called out sometimes to control theater crowds."[65]

Bank Night was unsettling to some social critics because it disrupted
traditional social activities. Choir rehearsals in one Long Island community, along with high school sporting events in Perryopolis, Pennsylvania,
were canceled because so many people insisted on going to Bank Night
instead. The *Literary Digest* reported that hoodlums in the Midwest had
attended a Bank Night drawing and then mugged the winner on his way
home.[66] As one civic leader complained, "It's got to the point where no-
body can schedule a basketball game, a church social or a contract [bridge]
party on Tuesday night, because everybody is down at the Gem hoping to
cop a cash prize."[67] To stop the drawings, the town of Pittsfield, Massachusetts, threatened to withdraw the Sunday showing permits of any theater that ran Bank Night.[68] The four major newspapers in New Orleans
banned movie theater advertising that made any mention of Bank Night.[69]
The wildly popular cash promotion faced court hearings in Maine, New
Hampshire, Texas, Massachusetts, New York, Illinois, and Iowa (where
three hundred theaters had suspended Bank Night for five months waiting
for the decision on its legality to be handed down).[70]

The appeal of Bank Night was significantly different from that of Dish
Night. The game was not specifically geared toward women, for women
may have preferred that everyone should share in the gift receiving. However, in hard times the attraction of large sums of money knew few gender restrictions. Both women and men would scramble for cash, and the
competition could provoke disorder. Unrest lay just under the surface of
Yaeger's giveaway scheme, as the *Literary Digest* hinted in a Bank Night
report: "Mrs. Joseph Sebastian Phau, an adult white citizen of the United
States, went to a motion picture theater last Monday night. She paid a desperate quarter for an admission ticket, squared her ample shoulders and
began the violent task of thrusting her way through 2000 other citizens
fired by a similar zeal. No portentous film was to be screened that night.
Indeed, the picture to be shown was of inferior quality, But Mrs. Phau
didn't mind. It is doubtful if she ever knew what the picture was about, or
cared, what brought her there was a 200-to-1 chance of going home with
$150. It was Bank Nite."[71]

The rivals of a game-playing theater feared Bank Night perhaps most of all. In Kansas City, where 68 percent of neighborhood theaters were said to be giving away premiums,[72] Mrs. Abe Baier, owner of the Lindbergh Theater, lobbied the U.S. Post Office (which banned lottery materials from traveling through the mail) to help exterminate Bank Night at her rival theaters. As her legal brief stated:

> At the present time, practically all suburban theaters in Kansas City are giving away dishes, silverware, running children's bargain shows, using trading stamps, etc. If Bank Night at the Prospect and Belmont Theaters is allowed to continue, it is reasonable to assume that at least 75 percent of the theaters in Kansas City will adopt the scheme. This will lead to a most disastrous condition not only for my theater and a few others which do not wish to cheapen their operation by running lotteries, but will grow until all first run theaters will be compelled to resort to similar tactics to protect their huge investments.[73]

The intense competition among film exhibitors over premium programs could even turn openly violent, as the *Motion Picture Herald* reported in September 1935: "Minneapolis recently was the scene of considerable excitement when the Northtown [theater], operated by Harry Dickerman, was bombed. Exhibitors have been protesting what they termed Mr. Dickerman's 'unethical' practices in giveaways, and it is understood he has agreed to discontinue a combined gift night plan at three of his houses." While this level of open warfare was rarely reached, the trade journals routinely described the struggle between exhibitors as a "Chance Games 'War.'"[74]

Historians have examined the potential for anger, violence, and revolt that the collapse of the consumer economy caused in the Great Depression. The Bonus Army's march on Washington in summer 1932, one of the most public episodes of protest and disorder, greatly alarmed authorities like President Herbert Hoover, FBI head J. Edgar Hoover, and General Douglas MacArthur, who saw too much potential for unrest in allowing the veterans and their families to remain camped in the city, despite the fact that participants and most observers saw the march and occupation as a peaceful gathering. Much of the nation worried that the intensity of the violence with which the U.S. army routed the veterans out of Washington, as well as the resulting chaos and fear, were harbingers of things to come across the nation.[75]

Social critics and local authorities in the 1930s were quite frightened by the potential for mob action. Film exhibitors were among the most worried of the Main Street merchants, for they feared that movie audiences could erupt into violence upon viewing incendiary films. A radical call to revolution, a long shot panning across a garbage-dump Hooverville, or even a picture of Hoover himself might generate an uproar in their auditoriums. Rioting audiences might first tear up the theater then surge out to rampage up and down Main Street, and theater owners could be held responsible. Tom Doherty's examination of newsreels and fiction films in the early years of the Depression finds that both producers and exhibitors strove to keep unvarnished reality off their screens and avoided showing anything that might upset their audience. Theater managers edited out anything questionable that had slipped unawares into their newsreels from the producers. Yet while exhibitors were keeping patrons distracted and amused with films that portrayed nothing of the Depression's suffering and disorder, with Bank Night drawings they were stirring up dangerous passions among their patrons in the theater. Jammed together inside a movie theater or overflowing the Main Street sidewalks after the prize announcement, angry groups of Bank Night losers were situated at the heart of commercial districts with the plate glass windows of nearby stores ready to smash.

As noted above, in the advertising fliers of the Salem China Company there was a sly appeal to exhibitors' worries —"Women hate to be disappointed . . . they hate lotteries. . . . They hate going away empty handed." Salem argued that women patrons would not like the intense competition and the slim chance of winning that Bank Night entailed. Was this part of the calculated appeal of Dish Night to movie theater managers— to avoid the potential for violence and social disorder that Bank Night's big jackpots could provoke? Many people assumed that white middle- and working-class women did not like gambling, and that they were less competitive and less given to anger than were men. Theater managers thus felt that the "equality" of dish night—something for every woman—would be much more congenial to the average female patron. There is no evidence, however, to suggest that women avoided or were significantly less attracted to Bank Nights; female names are mentioned as winners about half of the time in 1930s news articles on Bank Night games. Social critics knew that angry women could cause as much destruction as rioting men, but American culture assumed that women as a whole were less prone to violence and disorder.

As Marchand argues, the genius of the "Democracy of Goods" advertising appeal was that if producers could offer the public some minimally
expensive items that were equally available to everyone (and everyone, including movie stars, smoked cigarettes and ate off dishes), then even the
lowest people on the economic scale would feel they had something in
common with the privileged. The less fortunate would be more likely to
subordinate their differences rather than gather together in class conflict
and revolt against the rich, or at least the advertisers hoped so.[76]

Despite this cultural assumption of women's controllability and even
passivity that may have led authorities and movie theater managers to
think that female movie patrons would be kept quiet by the present of
a small consumer item, even the benign Dish Night could be a source of
friction for audience members. Many women became impatient with the
seemingly endless length of the promotion; Gussie Seidenberg recalls that
"it took *forever* to assemble the whole set of dishes." Women could feel
fiercely entitled to their "free" gifts, and once they had made a "contract"
with a film exhibitor that they would get a whole set of china if they purchased weekly tickets to the movies, they could become agitated when that
agreement was tampered with.

Jean Shepherd's short story "Leopold Doppler and the Great Orpheum
Theater Gravy Boat Riot" explored women's anger over thwarted consumer desires in the Depression, as well as the eternal battle of the sexes.
The moviegoing housewives of Hohman anxiously awaited the arrival of
each lovely new plate and bowl so that they could complete the entire set
of Dish Night free china. They attended every giveaway performance for
months without fail in order to get their "due" promised to them by the
manager of the Orpheum Theater.

In the story's climax, through a terrible turn of events a shipping mix-
up with the dinnerware distributor meant that for several weeks in a row
Mr. Doppler had only gravy boats to hand out to his increasingly agitated
female patrons. One gravy boat might symbolize the elegance of a formal
dinner, and a second boat still had usefulness for holding salad dressing,
perhaps, but a third and a fourth were totally superfluous—worse, even,
than getting nothing. Increasingly restless and hungry to consume, the
frustrated women felt it was their right to have all the different pieces of
the set. In response the nervous Doppler attempted to defuse his patrons'
anger by promising to trade extra gravy boats for useful cups, saucers, and
serving bowls if the women brought the extras back to the theater the next

week. On the fifth week, however, the gangly teenaged ushers, with down-cast eyes, handed out yet another gravy boat to the furious homemakers:

> Each gravy boat was received in stony silence, quietly stuffed into shopping bag or hatbox completing a set of four carried hopelessly for exchange. The feature that night was "The Bride of Frankenstein," the story of a man-made monster that returned to pursue and crush his creator. . . . On this night no gay music played through the theater loudspeakers. No Coming Attractions. The candy counter was dark and untended, as though Mr. Doppler himself felt the impending end near. The mothers waited. A sudden blinding spotlight made a big circle on the maroon curtain next to the cold, silent screen, then out of the wings stepped Mr. Doppler to face his Moment of Truth.
>
> "Ladies," he began plaintively, "I have to apologize for tonight's Gravy Boat." A lone feminine laugh, mirthless and arid, mocking, punctuated his pause. He went on as though unhearing. "I give you my personal Guarantee that next week . . ." At this point a low, subdued hissing arose spontaneously. The sound of cold venom landing on boiling lava began to rise from the depths of the void. Doppler, his voice bravely raised, continued: "Next week I personally guarantee we will exchange ALL gravy boats for . . ."
>
> And then it happened. A dark shadow sliced through the hot beam of the spotlight, turning over and over and casting upon the screen an enormous mag-nified outline of a great Gravy Boat. Spinning over and over, it crashed with a startling suddenness on the stage at Doppler's feet. Instantly a blizzard of Gravy Boats filled the air. Doppler's voice rose to a wail. "Ladies! Please! We will Exchange . . . !" A great crash of Gravy Boats like the breaking of surf on an alien shore drowned out his words. And then, spreading to all corners of the house, shopping bags were emptied as the arms rose and fell in the darkness, maniacal female cackles and obscenities driving Doppler from the stage.[77]

CONCLUSION

The sociologist Jesse Steiner, studying the impact of the Depression on commercial amusements toward the end of the decade, found that the response by movie exhibitors to the economic crisis had been the key to the recovery of the film business from the disastrous situation of the early 1930s: "Equally if not more significant than the changes in attendance, are the steps taken by the moving picture industry to stimulate increased popular support."[78]

Dish Night and other premium promotions had been important elements of independent neighborhood and small town theaters' campaigns
to bring patrons back to the theater in the 1930s. Merchandise giveaways
and cash-award contests filled Depression-era movie theaters with patrons
anxious for the winning number to be drawn, dreaming of what they could
do with a sudden windfall of cash, a shiny bicycle, or a house full of new
furniture, and then deflated when yet again their luck failed them. At least
for women, their acquisitive desires could be mollified somewhat by the
experience of seeming to get "something for nothing."

Yet while these promotions boosted movie theater box office receipts
and propped up the business of American potteries at a crucial time, they
also created numerous problems and concerns. Dish Nights and giveaways
were used by rival film exhibitors to intensify local competition and to capture patrons from each other and from alternative forms of entertainment
and leisure. The death of vaudeville, theatrical stock, and road show companies and concert groups across the nation was hastened by the public's
turn to the movies and radio, both of which used technologies of mass
production and mass communication to undercut the viability of the expensive performances of live performers in local theaters. The cutthroat
competition between film exhibitors meant that thousands of small, independently owned theaters in the poorer, more rural portions of the country could not continue to eke out a profit, and a quarter to a third of small
town silent theaters closed and never reopened.

Bank Night in particular also raised concerns among conservative social critics that traditional social habits were being pushed aside as theaters lured all the impressionable and penny-pinched townspeople to the
movies with cruelly unrealistic hopes of winning sudden riches. Like their
suspicions of New Deal relief payments to the poor and unemployed,
some critics claimed that the dreams of "easy wealth" engendered by Bank
Night made people lazy and too dependent on "handouts," and made them
feel "entitled" to receive such largess permanently. Social critics feared that
this sense of entitlement and dependency urged disappointed losers on
toward disorder and mob violence. Thus the crowds of moviegoers filling
theaters to the rafters in pursuit of big cash prizes, or brandishing their free
plates and cups, looked very threatening to outside observers. Yet concurrently, other critics hoped that the further spread of inexpensive consumer
products into the economy, a "democracy of goods" in practice, would do

much to diffuse class antagonisms and social unrest among the poor. Thus presents of pretty dishes from sympathetic film exhibitors might bond working- and middle-class housewives more loyally to the movies, even in hard times.

Nevertheless, as the *Motion Picture News* had warned theater managers, "All the crockery, silverware and china ever made won't do you lasting good if your entertainment isn't what the people want."[79] It is doubtful that the small independent theaters, or the urban picture palaces for that matter, could have survived the Depression decade if the Hollywood studios had not been turning out good product. Indeed, it was only because of audiences' enduring interest in the movies that giveaway promotions could succeed. The resilience of movie theaters and the film industry in the face of the Depression crisis is significant. Although families cut back moviegoing from four or five times a week to once or twice, they increasingly considered the movies a necessary recreation, and they cut back much further on other amusements in order to afford an occasional movie. During the Depression the American people put a higher percentage of their amusement dollars into the movies than they had done in previous years.[80]

Dish Night and Bank Night did help movie theaters recover from the Depression's ravages. By propping up the moviegoing habit in the hardest times, these promotions ensured that the movies would become even more popular and further entrenched as America's favorite pastime. By the late 1930s, movie theaters would run in the black again and they had regained their former attendance figures. It would take World War II prosperity, however, to return theater income to a level as high as it had been in the late 1920s; during the war years, movie attendance would reach its highest levels ever. The practice of giving premiums at smaller neighborhood movie theaters would continue sporadically among theaters throughout the 1940s and 1950s. However, due to the movement of the population to the suburbs and the devastating competition from television, ultimately such attempts to stem the loss of patrons were unsuccessful.

NOTES

1 Jesse Steiner, *Research Memorandum on Recreation in the Depression* (New York: Social Science Research Council, 1937), 94.
2 "100 Movie Houses in State Suspend Their Operations," *Richmond News Leader*, July 15, 1932.

3　On film exhibition in the 1930s, see Douglas Gomery, *Shared Pleasures: A History of Film Presentation in the United States* (Madison: University of Wisconsin Press, 1992); Tino Balio, *Grand Design: Hollywood as a Modern Business Enterprise, 1930–1939* (New York: Charles Scribner's Sons, 1993); Donald Crafton, *The Talkies: American Cinema's Transition to Sound, 1926–1931* (New York: Charles Scribner's Sons, 1997); and Thomas Doherty, *Pre-Code Hollywood: Sex, Immorality, and Insurrection in American Cinema, 1930–1934* (New York: Columbia University Press, 1999).

4　Balio, *Grand Design*, 15.

5　*Film Daily Yearbook*, 1939, 43; Doherty, *Pre-Code Hollywood*, 28–29.

6　Andrew Neff, "Slump-Proof? Not Films: Depression Figures on Profits, Payroll, Sites," *Variety*, April 2, 1980, 6; A. D. Murphy, "Trace Recession's Impact on Pix: Data Puts Sluggish B.O. in Perspective," *Variety*, August 6, 1980, 1.

7　"National Income in the United States, 1929–1935," Division of Economic Research, U.S. Department of Commerce, 1936, table 200, reprinted in Steiner, *Research Memorandum on Recreation in the Depression*, 107.

8　*International Motion Picture Almanac 1934*, 889.

9　Ibid.; Gomery, *Shared Pleasures*, 70. On rural and small town film exhibition, see Gregory Waller, *Main Street Amusements: Movies and Commercial Entertainment in a Southern City, 1896–1930* (Washington, D.C.: Smithsonian Institution Press, 1995); Kathryn Fuller, *At the Picture Show: Small Town Audiences and the Creation of Movie Fan Culture* (Charlottesville: University Press of Virginia, 2001 [1996]); George Potamianos, *Film Exhibition in Sacramento and Placerville* (Berkeley: University of California Press, forthcoming); and Fuller-Seeley, ed., *Movie-Going History in Small-Town America* (Berkeley: University of California Press, 2007).

10　"Theaters in the United States," *Motion Picture Herald*, January 20, 1934. Eight other districts that saw 15 to 20 percent of their movie houses closed were Atlanta, Charlotte, Denver, Memphis, Minneapolis, Portland, St. Louis, and San Francisco. A number of districts had between 22 and 32 percent of their theaters shut, including Buffalo, Chicago, Cleveland, Dallas, Milwaukee, Pittsburgh, and Washington, D.C.

11　"Theaters in the United States."

12　Ibid.

13　Robert Lynd and Helen Lynd, *Middletown in Transition: A Study in Cultural Conflicts* (New York: Harcourt Brace, 1937), 260–61.

14　Crafton, *The Talkies*, 256–65.

15　Doherty, *Pre-Code Hollywood*; Gomery, *Shared Pleasures*.

16　"Small Town Showmen Pruning Prices," *Motion Picture News*, June 28, 1930, 46; Steiner, *Research Memorandum on Recreation in the Depression*, 107; Crafton, *The Talkies*, 264.

17　On the history of the dishware industry, see Regina Blaszczyk, *Imagining Consumers: Design and Innovation from Wedgwood to Corning* (Baltimore, Md.:

Johns Hopkins University Press, 2000). On the importance of women in the movie audience, see Shelly Stamp, *Movie-Struck Girls: Women and Motion Picture Culture after the Nickelodeon* (Princeton, N.J.: Princeton University Press, 2000); Miriam Hansen, *Babel and Babylon: Spectatorship in American Silent Film* (Cambridge, Mass.: Harvard University Press, 1991); Nan Enstad, *Ladies of Labor, Girls of Adventure: Working Women, Popular Culture, and Labor Politics at the Turn of the Twentieth Century* (New York: Columbia University Press, 1999); Fuller, *At the Picture Show*.

18 Jean Shepherd, "Leopold Doppler and the Great Orpheum Theater Gravy Boat Riot," in *In God We Trust, All Others Pay Cash* (New York: Doubleday, 1966), 252–53.

19 On women and their households in the 1920s and 1930s, see Blaszczyk, *Imagining Consumers*; Robert Lynd and Helen Lynd, *Middletown: A Study in Contemporary American Culture* (New York: Harcourt, Brace, 1929); Lynd and Lynd, *Middletown in Transition*; Ruth Schwartz Cowan, *More Work for Mother: The Ironies of Household Technology from the Open Hearth to the Microwave* (New York: Basic Books, 1983); Susan Strasser, *Never Done: A History of American Housework* (New York: Pantheon Books, 1982).

20 Shepherd, "Leopold Doppler and the Great Orpheum Theater Gravy Boat Riot."

21 On the impact of the Depression on American families, see Studs Terkel, *Hard Times: An Oral History of the Great Depression* (New York: Avon, 1970); Robert McElvaine, *The Great Depression: America, 1929–1941* (New York: Times Books, 1984); Robert McElvaine, ed., *Down and Out in the Great Depression: Letters from the "Forgotten Man"* (Chapel Hill: University of North Carolina Press, 1983); T. H. Watkins, *The Great Depression: America in the 1930s* (Boston: Little, Brown, 1993); Steven Mintz and Susan Kellogg, *Domestic Revolutions: A Social History of American Family Life* (New York: Free Press, 1988).

22 Blaszczyk, *Imagining Consumers*.

23 Stamp, *Movie-Struck Girls*; Fuller, *At the Picture Show*.

24 Photograph of lobby display at New Fruitvale Theater, Salem China Company papers, The National Museum of American History Archives, Washington, D.C. (hereafter, Salem China Company papers).

25 "Premium Thriller," *Business Week*, December 8, 1934, 24; Gomery, *Shared Pleasures*, 70–71.

26 Floyd McKee, "History of USA Pottery Industry," n.d., Salem China Company papers.

27 List prices for Tricorne ware for theaters, January 24, 1935, Salem China Company papers. The noted ceramics designer Don Schreckengost created the now-famous Tricorne pattern in 1934 when he was a nineteen-year-old local art college student on a summer internship at the firm (interview with Don Schreckengost, August 2001).

28 All photographs from Salem China Company papers.

29 "Premium Thriller"; "The Unconquerable Premium," *Business Week,* January 5, 1935, 16; "Give Aways—Premium Men Look Forward to 500 Million Sales of 'Free' Merchandise," *Literary Digest,* October 10, 1936, 44–46.

30 Forbes Parkhill, "Bank Night Tonight," *Saturday Evening Post,* December 4, 1937, 82.

31 "Danger to Theater in Prize Contests," *Motion Picture News,* June 7, 1930, 107.

32 "Neighborhood Theaters are Getting Most of the New Business," *Motion Picture Herald,* June 16, 1934, 9.

33 "Small Town Showmen Pruning Prices," *Motion Picture News,* June 28, 1930, 46.

34 "Something for Nothing," *Business Week,* March 1, 1933, 9.

35 On the NRA, see Watkins, *The Great Depression;* McElvaine, *The Great Depression,* Balio, *Grand Design.*

36 Terry Ramsaye, "Problem of Labor Leads Debate at Capital's Hearing on Code," *Motion Picture Herald,* September 16, 1933, 22.

37 Louis Nizer, "1934 and the Motion Picture Code," *Film Daily Yearbook* 1935, 618.

38 Some entrepreneurs even vertically integrated from distribution only to an integrated manufacturing-distribution arrangement. One well-known example was that of Beatrice Miller who, after working for a premium distributor, purchased the old E. H. Sebring dinnerware plant and created the Royal China Company. The company went on to become a prominent manufacturer and distributor of dinnerware in the 1940s and 1950s. Jo Cunningham, *Collector's Encyclopedia of American Dinnerware* (Paducah, KY: Collector Books, 1982), 246–47.

39 E-mail interview with Phil Stetson, April 2001; Cunningham, *Collector's Encyclopedia of American Dinnerware,* 272.

40 Photographs, Salem China Company papers. Salem's triangular Tricorne design, introduced in 1934, was used in movie theater premium sales between 1935 and 1937.

41 Roland Marchand, *Advertising the American Dream: Making Way for Modernity, 1920–1940* (Berkeley: University of California Press, 1985); Richard deCordova, "The Mickey in Macy's Window: Childhood, Consumerism and Disney Animation," in *Disney Discourse: Producing the Magic Kingdom,* ed. Eric Smoodin (New York: Routledge, 1994), 203–13; Charles Eckert, "The Carole Lombard in Macy's Window," in *Fabrications,* ed. Jane Gaines and Charlotte Herzog (New York: Routledge 1990), 100–21.

42 DeCordova, "The Mickey in Macy's Window"; Eckert, "The Carole Lombard in Macy's Window"; "Salem China Nites Give Star Performances," n.d., Salem China Company papers.

43 "Salem China Nite Pleases the Ladies—Packs Your House," n.d., Salem China Company papers.

44 Floyd McKee, "Dinnerware as Premiums" n.d., Salem China Company papers.

45 "Salem China Nites Give Star Performances."

46 "Lovely Dinnerware," n.d., Salem China Company papers.

47 McKee, "Dinnerware as Premiums."

48 Mickey Mouse sales postcard design, July 17, 1934, Salem China Company papers.

49 "Lovely Dinnerware."

50 McKee, "Dinnerware as Premiums."

51 "Lovely Dinnerware."

52 "Danger to Theaters in Prize Contest," *Motion Picture News*, June 7, 1930, 107.

53 "Salem China Nite Pleases the Ladies."

54 Marchand, *Advertising the American Dream*.

55 "The Unconquerable Premium."

56 *Motion Picture Herald*, August 10, 1935, 59–60.

57 On the history of Bank Night, see Paige Reynolds, "'Something for Nothing': Bank Night and the Refashioning of the American Dream," in Fuller-Seeley, ed., *Movie-Going History in Small-Town America*; and Gomery, *Shared Pleasures*, 70–71. "It evades most state lottery laws because the patron does not pay for his number and may conceivably win the prize without buying a ticket to the theater, by waiting outside while the winning number is announced by a loudspeaker in the lobby, then running in to claim his prize" ("Bank Night," *Time*, February 3, 1936, 56).

58 "'Bingo!—Aw! Nuts!': Movie Temples Lure Monday, Tuesday Patrons with Prize-Money," *Literary Digest*, March 6, 1937, 36; Parkhill, "Bank Night Tonight," 20.

59 Parkhill, "Bank Night Tonight," 82.

60 James Cunningham, "The Code Question Box," *Motion Picture Herald*, October 6, 1934.

61 "Film Code Machine Jams at Collapse of the NRA," *Motion Picture Herald*, June 1, 1935, 9.

62 "Exhibitors Spend $13 Million Yearly on Chance Game Awards," *Motion Picture Herald*, September 21, 1935, 23. It noted that in the Chicago area, "since the inception of prize giveaways, free chinaware to patrons has fallen off sharply, more than 60 percent of the houses using the plan have abandoned it for the cash award idea, and the percentage is growing" ("Chicago Stores Fight $6 Million Chance Games," *Motion Picture Herald*, December 5, 1936, 13).

63 Parkhill, "Bank Night Tonight," 20–21.

64 Ibid., 20.

65 "Bank Night," *Time*, February 3, 1936, 57.

66 "'Bingo!—Aw! Nuts!'"

67 Parkhill, "Bank Night Tonight," 20.

68 "'Bingo!—Aw! Nuts!'"

69 "Bank Night," 57–58.

70 "Bank Night," 56–57; Parkhill, "Bank Night Tonight," 82; "Exhibition," *Film Daily Yearbook*, 1937, 755.

71 "'Bingo!—Aw! Nuts!'"

72 "Exhibitors Spend $13 Million."

73 "US Mail Bars Ads on Bank Night 'Lottery,'" *Motion Picture Herald*, May 4, 1935, 9.

74 "Exhibitors Spend $13 Million"; "Chance Games 'War,'" *Motion Picture Herald*, September 14, 1935, 72.

75 Lynd and Lynd, *Middletown in Transition*. On the Bonus March, see McElvaine, *The Great Depression*; Terkel, *Hard Times*; and Watkins, *The Great Depression*.

76 Marchand, *Advertising the American Dream*.

77 Shepherd, "Leopold Doppler and the Great Orpheum Theater Gravy Boat Riot," 258–60.

78 Steiner, *Research Memorandum on Recreation in the Depression*, 99.

79 "Poor Losers Big Element in Stunts," *Motion Picture News*, June 7, 1930, 108.

80 Steiner, *Research Memorandum on Recreation in the Depression*, 92.

"A TREATISE ON DECAY"

Liberal and Leftist Critics and Their Queer Readings of Depression-Era U.S. Film

David M. Lugowski

L ong before the "in-your-face" Showtime cable series *Queer as Folk* generated controversy through preview publicity about the show's racy content—or commentators spoke admiringly on its representation of a gay sexual public sphere, or disparagingly for its emphasis on gay white men obsessed with sex—queer representation flourished in the media.[1] Queer historical readers, whether they were gays doing campy, subversive takes on mainstream films or censorious media hawks like Jerry Falwell deciding that the purple, triangle-sporting T V Teletubby character Tinky Winky was gay, developed a remarkable range of interpretations suited to their own political ends. Here I am particularly interested in a period in which queer content, considered quite daring and open for its time, proliferated in media fictions, namely the Great Depression. As I will show, the politics of queer interpretation were no less contentious then than they are now.

Beginning in 1929–1930 gay, lesbian, and otherwise "queer" gender performances, sexual innuendoes, and also representations of "perverse" behaviors, social identity, and even minority communities exploded in U.S. film to a greater extent than ever before. Most of

these performances were based on popular, widely disseminated stereotypes, derived from quasi-scientific sexological discourses, of gender inversion, that is, "effeminate" men and "mannish" women, to use terms of the
day. (In some cases, though, representations of same-sex desire appear as
well, in the form of kisses, looks, and touches, signaling the shifts then
taking place in mass conceptions of homosexuality.)

Many factors made 1930s cinema very rich in queer content: the full-
blown emergence of sound cinema, with its capacity for spoken, risqué
dialogue; the emergence or growth of such genres as the horror film, the
sophisticated comedy, and the musical, all focusing on urban eccentrics or
exotic outsiders; the influx of "adult" stage plays easily turned into screenplays and the stage-trained actors and directors of the Roaring Twenties
who came with them; the avid moviegoing habits of residents of New
York and Los Angeles in particular, both cities with large and surprisingly
open gay communities; and the need for titillating content to lure the all-
important urban filmgoer once attendance began to drop.[2] And yet the
notion of "content" being queer is a debated one, often more so than with
other types of cinematic discourse deemed to be more "obvious" in their
meaning. Representations of "visible" minorities rarely provoke any doubt
that issues of race are present and relevant, yet queer readings of texts from
bygone days (or even today) are frequently doubted as to their historical
validity and specificity. Is something queer actually "present" in the text?
Those afraid of queer readings tend to argue that the people of the time
could not possibly have read effeminate men, mannish women, or comi-
cally accidental same-sex kisses as homosexual; how, therefore, can we do
so now? Thus, the extratextual "evidence" that people made such interpretations then is essential in helping to historically anchor queer readings.[3]
Furthermore, it is largely through extratextual resources that a larger picture of queer readings in this period emerges, particularly when considering the multivalenced political struggles waged over queer imagery.

Chon Noriega, writing about films based on plays with fairly overt queer
content (*The Children's Hour* and *Cat on a Hot Tin Roof*), suggests that the
film reviews between 1936 and the early 1960s that mention these plays
cued queer readings that the more muted film adaptations themselves did
not. However, as with other scholars attempting to historicize queer discourse in U.S. film, Noriega suggests that this representation had disappeared completely after Hollywood set up the Production Code Adminis-

tration (PCA) in 1934 to more strongly enforce the code that was written in 1930. Since the films themselves were no longer queer, he argues, audiences needed the reviews to produce queer readings. I completely agree that these reviews could have promoted queer readings; I myself will be using film reviews, among other sources, to suggest the historically specific nature of such readings. The issue emerges with the "coming out" of the problematic term "subtext." Noriega writes that "like the Code's authors, film critics tend to examine the film itself, and not the discursive acts that surround a film and play a sometimes central role in shaping its meaning(s). Contemporary gay and lesbian film criticism of Production Code era films operates on the same principle, with the added limitation that historical evidence and homosexual 'images' either do not exist or were censored. Thus, in order to ensure 'the survival of subcultural identity within an oppressive society,' gay and lesbian film critics have employed a wide range of interpretive strategies to recuperate a history of homosexual images from the censored screen. The emphasis, therefore, has been on 'subtexting' censored films from a singular presentist perspective."[4]

Noriega also writes that "these strategies do not differentiate between the sensibilities and cinematic codes or iconography that existed during the Production Code era and those that are specific to the present."[5] While rightly emphasizing the importance of historical specificity, these remarks also hint that queer "images" and discourse "do not exist" in the films of this period. I would counter that evidence proves that queer discourse thrives even after 1934; indeed, what is remarkable is how often censorship and Hollywood's attempts at self-regulation failed.

Furthermore, queer extratextual readings help make images queer, just as other reading positions similarly aid in creating the meaning of images. Arguments such as Noriega's suggest that today's queer critics and queer cultures exist so far apart from the sensibilities, codes, and cultures of an earlier era that we cannot share and understand them. I would contend, instead, that contemporary reading positions and debates over queerness in culture have been constituted to a large extent by these very sensibilities, codes, and cultures from our past. Richard Dyer argues that "audiences cannot make media images mean anything they want to, but they can select from the complexity of the image the meanings and feelings, the variations, inflections and contradictions, that work for them."[6] Assigning queer discourse to the untheorized miasma of "subtext" draws too sharp a distinction between readers and texts. Indeed, readers and texts are not fully separate and separable, and meaning is only created where they overlap. The charge that some meanings exist only in the subtext polices reading strategies and the limits of (queer) intelligibility, closeting reader-text interactions then and now, as if cinematic discourse were historically self-evident. What Noriega is calling subtext I would rather read as a series of extratexts and intertexts, some of which primarily work to historically and politically operationalize reading strategies.

In doing so, it is important that I avoid what Alexander Doty has called the "closet of connotation," as my queer readings of Depression-era films do find historical anchorage in extant writings from that period.[7]

Studio publicists, film reviews, and magazine profiles talk about "pansies" (the most commonly used phrase), "nances," "fairies," "Amazons," and "mannish women," and the PCA, although very homophobic, reads a great deal of "sex perversion," "lesbianism," "effeminacy," and "pansy humor" in films, a content that it was often unable to eliminate. For instance, the PCA head Joseph Breen wrote to Jack Warner complaining about the Joe E. Brown comedy *Circus Clown* (1934), specifically "the running gag in which La Tour masquerades as a woman and leads the hero on to make love to him . . . We believe this gag runs serious danger of being offensive . . . as well as being inherently a violation of the spirit of the Code." The PCA read the female vampire's attacks upon women in *Dracula's Daughter* (1936) as lesbian in nature and feared (correctly) that a scene where Fred Astaire teaches his sailor buddies to dance in *Follow the Fleet* (1936) by having them partner each other would be "pansy" in nature. (Even the U.S. Navy tried to have the scene removed!) Critics got into the act as well. A reviewer of *Carefree* (1938) for *Variety* noted the queer nature of the most prolific of the "pansy" character comedians by using both gay slang and a reference to a famously flamboyant fashion designer: "Franklin Pangborn's usual nance is dragged in by the Schiaparelli."[8]

Following a Foucauldian line of argument, it should not be surprising that the PCA's attempts at censorship should have failed so often. Talking about sexuality, categorizing it, had become essential in our culture, and one of the hypocrisies of such censorship is that it necessarily speaks the very discourses that it attempts to contain.[9] Various versions of the Production Code were widely disseminated during the Depression. Many readers would have been familiar with the line of the Production Code dealing with homosexuality and other queerness: "Sex perversion or any inference to it is forbidden." Far from being a never-discussed topic in a more "innocent" era that only recent critics with an "agenda" are reading subtextually, this knowledge of the Code and the wealth of popular references denoted an area of importance and interest, even fascination.

Among other readers and producers of meaning outside of the PCA and the mainstream industry-related publicity and review media, we can find other commentators on the widely discussed subject of representation. The PCA files, for instance, contain letters, typically from conservative church and social groups and individuals, condemning queer content in films. Alternative media writers spotted queer imagery and disseminated queer readings as well. In this essay I will focus upon independent, and especially liberal, leftist and communist commentators who produced queer readings of Depression-era cinema. Sometimes their readings differ from those of, say, the PCA in being fairly neutral and nonpejorative, or even somewhat "liberal" in self-congratulatory ways. Sometimes, though, their readings are equally homophobic (and bigoted in other ways) but also critical in very different ways and for diametrically opposed political ends. Queer representation, in other words, often faced scorn from both the right and the left. The PCA, local censor boards, and conservative church and women's groups read queerness as a sign of the decline of morality and Americanism that manifested itself particularly in the 1920s, and for which people in the 1930s were supposedly paying the price. By contrast, some leftist writers saw queerness as an indication of the decadence of U.S. capitalism and a sign of nascent fascism.

Communist critics were certainly aware of Hollywood's self-imposed Production Code, and they were very willing to be critical of it. Note the scornful tone, for instance, in *New Theater*'s words: "And only last September he [Will Hays] issued his latest set of taboo words: 'alley cat,' 'bloody,' 'dump,' 'sex appeal,' 'skirt,' 'house-broken,' 'guts,' '*fairy*,' '*nance*,' 'mistress,' 'chippie,' 'cocotte,' 'courtesan,' 'eunuch,' 'floozy,' 'goose,' 'nuts,' 'nerts,' 'louse,' 'broad' and 'in your hat.'"[10] Yet we can also see signs of a certain desire to avoid the subject, as if some on the left believed in being enlightened about discussing sexuality, but were unwilling to stretch outside of certain heterocentric parameters, especially if they could not see immediate connections with the possibility of revolution. In a review of *Men and Women* by the pioneering gay activist and sexologist Magnus Hirschfeld, for instance, one writer complains that "too great an emphasis is put on the hypothesis and deviations of sexuality—on those things that make one say 'How very strange' with the result that the main current, sex as a part of the total life and its intimate relation to the structure of society is obscured and often drops out of sight."[11] For this writer, then, sex can only really mean heterosexuality insofar as it has any connections to the structure of society.

And yet queerness clearly played a key role in U.S. culture during the Depression. It was popular in forms from drag balls to gossipy tabloids and "pansy" humor in nightclubs and films. Its importance is also indicated in the increasing crackdown on gay bars, on other areas of queer culture, and on pants-wearing single working women as poor economic conditions lingered. That said, queerness survived in media representation, in transitory social spaces such as bathhouses and cafeterias, and in the same-sex communal living arrangements so common during the crisis.[12] A film dealing with the latter subject, Stage Door (1937), demonstrates just how irresistible queer readings could be during this time, even when an author is not fully comfortable with the implications of his reading. The film, Gregory La Cava's brilliant and fondly remembered seriocomic study of women living at a theatrical boardinghouse, has, of course, long had a large gay following for its parade of cult divas in both leading roles (Ginger Rogers, Katharine Hepburn) and supporting ones (Lucille Ball, Eve Arden, Ann Miller), its highly quotable wisecracks, and its successful mix of screwball comedy and emotional melodrama. The presence of two typecast pansy/sissy character actors (Franklin Pangborn and Grady Sutton) in supporting roles, and the fact that the leading female characters, Jean and Terry, both dismiss the lecherous producer Anthony Powell (Adolphe Menjou) in favor of their life together at the Footlights Club, lends the film a decidedly queer tang.[13] Indeed, it was some of these factors, plus the nature of the female stars and the progress of the film's melodrama, that enabled a queer reading not only by later generations of gays but also by a communist critic in 1937.

The left was evidently quite used to queer readings of melodramas about women's lives and loves. One critic writing about the French film Club des Femmes (1937), also set at a women's boardinghouse, calls it "a well-made and slightly sensational essay on illicit love affairs, illegitimate babies, Lesbianism and other by-products of the genre."[14] Writing in the same publication, the critic David Wolff proffers his queer reading of Stage

Ginger Rogers and Katharine
Hepburn in *Stage Door*
(RKO, 1937).

Door within the context of a highly favorable review of the film, which he
calls "rather sensitive and intelligent."[15] He admires the rich characterizations of the film and he describes the dialogue as "very clever, hard and
funny." Wolff also sees, in vaguely leftist terms relating to the economic exploitation of women as critiqued in the film, the "real successes of the film,
the despair, the shallow and incomplete lives, the empty and casual cruel-
ties of people to one another." He hints at a queer reading in taking notice
of Pangborn as the "slimy and exquisite butler Harcourt." "Exquisite" was,
along with "stunning," "divine," and the obsolete "divoon" one of the coded
words often used by, and hence associated with, the flamboyant gay male
stereotypes of the period. Furthermore, butlers, indicating effete British
manners and class structures, were often read as queer.

   More importantly, Wolff calls the developing relationship between Jean
(Rogers) and Terry (Hepburn) a "love affair" in the film. His characterization of the film's central relationship in this manner is not disapproving
and, as per the era's dominant ideas about queerness, it rests in his perception of gender reversal. Both Hepburn (especially in *Little Women, Christo-
pher Strong* [both 1933], and *Sylvia Scarlett* [1936]) and Rogers (especially in

42nd Street [1933], *Finishing School* [1934] and in "mannish" drag in several of her films with Fred Astaire) had been associated with tomboyish roles and male garb with queer connotations. Wolff seems to have been aware of this intertext. Thus, immediately after characterizing Jean and Terry's relationship in this way, Wolff notes: "Hepburn's hard, beautiful face and cold crisp habit of movement, flashing through doorways or forward past the camera with a kind of *masculine* energy—all her acting serves especially this point."[16] The "point" is, of course, that a lesbian or bisexual reading of the film and its two central characters is possible.

What is also interesting is how Wolff, after reading Hepburn as "masculine," does the same with Rogers by comparing her with a *male* star: "Ginger Rogers reproduces in Jean a type of woman peculiarly American—harsh, tight, wise-cracking, tender, with the wry romanticism stimulated by good clothes (borrowed) or too much champagne (with a price) . . . Jean is a new character for the American screen, a kind of parallel to Jimmie Cagney's portraits of taxi-men or aviators." In reading Rogers as, in essence, a "female James Cagney," Wolff reinvokes the left's great fondness for Cagney (to some degree because of the actor's leftist sympathies, but primarily for his tough working-class persona, the quintessential example of what Robert Sklar has termed the "city boy"). As the definitive screen embodiment of the 1930s female proletariat, Rogers's persona understandably appealed to the left as well. Beyond that, however, it is worth noting that Cagney's persona fits what Sklar calls "the roughneck sissy," a young, pugilistic mama's boy—a type with strong queer connotations. Thus, if the left's appreciation of Cagney included his queerly feminized masculinity (think of his use of eye makeup during this period), what Wolff admires in Rogers would seem to be a queerly masculinized femininity.[17]

Certain conceptions of masculinity and femininity were, however, as valued by the left as by more conservative readers. The Depression precipitated a gender crisis since, as Robert McElvaine notes in his discussion of the "feminization" of U.S. culture at this time, men were made "dependent in ways that women had been thought to be."[18] Or to put it in Margaret McFadden's words, men "experienced their inability to provide adequate family support as a failure of masculinity."[19] Michael Denning notes the limitations of the left in terms of both the symbolic representation of women and the actual roles that women could perform in socialist and antifascist activism. He argues that "symbolic systems of the Popular Front

drew on a traditional iconography and rhetoric of manhood and womanhood that was at odds with the utopian and emancipatory hopes of the
movement." Referring to "the belligerent masculinism of the proletarian
avant-garde," Denning continues by stating that "the cult of the virile male
working-class body is without a doubt a major element" of this cultural
and political faction, "which, like many of the modernist avant-gardes, invoked masculinist metaphors of sexual conflict in their manifestoes."[20]

As a vivid example of the politicization of effeminacy, queer readings,
and homophobia by the left, note the illustration from the communist journal *New Masses*. One of the most important leftist artists of the period, the
painter and cartoonist William Gropper, wittily attacks the archconserva-
tive William Randolph Hearst by presenting him as a Nazi conducting the
"Music of Hitler." In this image Hearst is leading a number of feminized
men, including such prominent leftist and unionizing figures as Matthew
Woll. Gropper, along with many others at the time, was willing to attack
those on the left whose work was becoming potentially compromised. The
cartoon also typifies the gender politics of the era where queerness is concerned. One woman, Emma Goldman (who had spoken in favor of homosexual rights as early as 1915) is placed among the men; notably, she appears
butch and unattractive, as unsuccessful in her gender performance as her
effeminate comrades. Capitalist media leaders feminize (i.e., weaken) political struggle.

In many published responses to Hollywood film, we can note a homophobia similar to that expressed by the PCA. For example, a critic was displeased at finding the dancing of Paul Draper, as Ruby Keeler's partner in
several numbers in the musical *Colleen* (1936), "even slightly effeminate."[21]

Lesbianism, by contrast, could provoke different reactions. Lesbian representation was less prevalent because sexuality not based on male desire
questions the very boundaries of patriarchal representation. In a capitalistic system, where sexuality is rendered in economic terms, and vice versa,
"mannish" women wearing pants were despised more than sissies as a symbolic transposition of the threat of independent working women. Women
in male drag in films were sometimes used to provoke laughter, but unlike the easily ridiculed effeminate men they were often played, and taken,
rather more seriously. In this respect, they could seem very threatening.
In other cases, however, mannish women could seem less controversial
and more acceptable because some degree of tomboyishness can be seen

William Gropper, *Music of Hitler*, 1935. (Courtesy of Heritage Gallery, Los Angeles, for the estate of William Gropper)

as youthful strength and support in a time of crisis. The reviewer of *Stage Door* could feel comfortable because the women do have some heterosexual involvements and their often desperate economic straits and subordinate status are made clear in the film. Furthermore, while Paul Draper's light dancing in *Colleen* can receive a quick, glancing nod of disapproval, Wolff's review of *Stage Door* puts the term "love affair" in quotation marks. He explains that Jean and Terry's trajectory from combative beginnings to shared suffering and final loving acceptance is a love affair only "in the sense of a human relationship which is close, fiery, which undergoes shifts and revulsions." In other words, his review works to contain to some extent the lesbian reading that it has itself generated.

Liberal and leftist writers, whether writing for communist art journals or small independent film magazines, typically championed avant-garde film, political documentary, and other alternative modes of production. Critics liked to distinguish such product as much as possible from Hollywood fare, sometimes praising experimentation as politically progressive, defending it as art, or drawing distinctions between documentary "reality" (read in terms of "straight" social realism) and Hollywood's escapist (and queer) "fantasy." Yet alternative cinemas have often been a haven for queer representation, some of it different from and more explicit than Hollywood's but also much of it quite similar—drawing as it did on commonly held beliefs and longstanding archetypes. At any rate, given the pervasiveness and indeed the *necessity* of queer dynamics in cultural reading practices—in order to provide entertainment, or to maintain ideologically loaded social distinctions between "normal" and "deviant"—liberal and leftist readers continued to produce queer discourse.

A brief but instructive example can be found in one critic's response to *Pie in the Sky* (1935), a silent short made by the leftist filmmaking collective Nykino. The film, an amusing satirical swipe at organized charities and religion and the widespread acceptance of poverty that these institutions encouraged, opens with two hobos (Ellman Koolish and Elia "Gadget" Kazan, as he is billed) awaiting thin slices of pie doled out at a condescending charity house. They are the only two not served when the pie runs out and, snubbing a pompous preacher, they take refuge in a junkyard. Indulging in comic horseplay with various props, they end with a mock-singalong montage of tableaux, ridiculing the oft-heard religious message that stoic endurance of social conditions will yield eternal rewards: "There'll be pie in the sky when you die." Ray Ludlow, giving *Pie in the Sky* some of the only press coverage it received, acknowledged its departure from other leftist filmmaking, mostly on-the-street guerrilla-style labor documentaries. Unfortunately, he also denies its connections to mainstream film: "While [the film] is essentially experimental, Nykino feels that the film is nevertheless a contribution and an advance step toward the creation of a highly developed American revolutionary film, that has nothing in common with Hollywood or the Hollywood product."[22] We find, to be sure, reflexive aspects to the film's shooting, editing, and performance styles and a sharp critique of religion alien to Hollywood product, but these qualities coexist with a fairly clear and linear narrative along with campy burlesque akin to the antics of comedian "buddy" films. Ironically, however, it is Ludlow's interpretation of a seemingly throwaway moment that also historically anchors the film as queer in a way similar to the gags in Hollywood comedy. At one point the men find small cigarette butts and put them into their mouths. One of the men manages to light his. Without any interchange of how best to share their resources, the two light the second butt by bringing their mouths together. Though Ludlow does not pursue the implications of his observation, he specifically reads this action as "a kiss."[23] The film and Ludlow are thus fairly blasé about something well known but rarely acknowledged by the left—that the homosocial conditions of the Depression engendered a "situational homosexuality" for thousands of itinerant male and female hobo couples.[24] Finally, when Kazan embraces a mannequin that he dubs "Mae West," *Pie in the Sky* refers to a figure who, as we shall see, had a special connection in the eyes of the left to queerness in Hollywood film.

While many spectators in the 1930s were doubtless able to ignore, deny, or not notice the queerness of *Stage Door*, *Colleen*, and *Pie in the Sky*, critics from the left, middle, and right alike were less able to deny the queer representation in James Watson's and Melville Webber's experimental rendering of a famous Bible story in their short film *Lot in Sodom* (1930–1933). Writings of the time typically make mention of the film's all-male Sodomites in terms of their "inversion" or comparable expressions; "Sodomite" euphemistically meant homosexual for many in that era. Various journals of cinema praised the film's striking visuals and the filmmakers' use of slow motion, multiple exposures, and symbolic imagery. They also tried to rationalize some of its transgressions, especially the male orgy scenes that are far more sensuous and lengthy than their narrative purpose would seem to justify, by referring to the film's visual beauty, its status as an "art film" or "experimental film," or its "moral lesson."[25] Norman Wilson uses the timely phrase of the Production Code when he describes "Watson and Webber in their interpretation of the Bible episode of Lot's travail in the city of perversion" before concluding, with slightly more coded words, that "it must be welcomed as an attempt at experiment, even though we deplore the choice of theme and the decadent artiness of its treatment."[26] Indeed, even my observation that the film's sensuous visuals conflict with its apparent narrative trajectory of the punishment of sin along the ideological axis of queer visibility finds historical support in the various reactions of the era. The poet Marianne Moore, writing favorably on the film, nonetheless criticizes precisely how the queer visuals seem to undermine the moral message of the film. Note, too, how what may be taken as homophobia is linked with an ethnic prejudice, both "justified" by recourse to the story's biblical origins: "The film is a thing of great strength and one has no wish, nor a very good chance, to pick flaws; but to an imagination based on the Child's Bible, the men of Sodom do not look quite so responsibly sinister as they might, nor fully oriental."²⁷ As we shall see, certain ethnic codings were linked with queerness, to complex political effect.

Despite the evident failure of *Lot in Sodom* to sufficiently vilify its queer Sodomites, many critics on both the right and the left tried to justify or disavow the "excessive" queerness of the film. Even for more liberal factions, however, there were obviously limits. Consider this response by the critic Donald Nash to queer representation in culture:

> The legitimate theater, if it is going to have even one leg to stand on in its refined superiority to the low standards of Hollywood, had better rush to sweep out its own stables. Two little numbers befouled the New York scene last week with truck which the films might have charitably concealed deep in the horse-opera houses. One was Allan Scott's *In Clover*, all about the crazy things that happen when you go and buy a country place. This was picked up by the white wings after its third performance. The other was Stephen Powys's *Wise Tomorrow*, in which a middle-aged Lesbian actress tries to relive her youth by ensnaring Gloria Dickson of *They Won't Forget*. When homosexuality is backgrounded, as in *The Children's Hour*, it has as much legitimate interest as any other theme; when it is presented strictly for its own sensational sake, as in the Powys effort, it gives off an odor such as sent hordes of people scurrying onto the sidewalks long before the end of the play. Nobody seems to be sure whether there is really a Stephen Powys; very soon (as soon as you have ended this sentence, maybe) nobody will be sure there was ever really a play called *Wise Tomorrow*.²⁸

Nash uses an example of what he finds egregious, prominent, and evidently "sensational" queerness to suggest that the New York theater is in danger of approaching the "low standards" of mainstream Hollywood cinema. Indeed, he implicitly strengthens his connections that it has already begun by his reference to the film actress Gloria Dickson and his discussion of *The Children's Hour*, which had recently been adapted to film as *These Three* (1936), with the lesbianism in the story altered to adulterous heterosexuality. Compared to the PCA, Nash appears to be somewhat more accepting of the lesbian angle in Lillian Hellmann's play. In many ways, though, the tone is similar to that of the devoted PCA secretary Olga Martin: "These 'smart alecks' try to hold that nothing artistic has come out of Hollywood since the enforcement of the Production Code ... Yet it was only because of the PCA that the play *The Children's Hour*, with its implications of sex perversion, was recast into a natural love story."[29] The difference is one of the degree to which lesbianism would be tolerated, not whether it was suitable as the main subject matter of a play. *Wise Tomorrow* might have displeased Nash partly because it might not have been as homophobic as he would have liked. Lesbians in the early decades of this century often took men's names or used them pseudonymously. Given that the heroine of Radclyffe Hall's landmark novel *The Well of Loneliness* was also named Stephen, and that Nash found the lesbianism to be so gratuitous, one could postulate an intriguing case of lesbian authorship at work here. Note that Nash wonders, possibly even hopes, that the author's name is a pseudonym.[30]

While Nash's review deals with a stage play, I have brought it up for reasons beyond its dig at the low standards of queer Hollywood. *They Won't Forget* (1937) is mentioned as a point of reference that the reviewer assumes readers might know, and indeed they might, given that it was a late entry in Warners's series of "social protest" films. Earlier examples of these films, strong if sometimes compromised in their indictment of authority, often found considerable respect among communists and other leftists. In the case of *They Won't Forget*, the film was an indictment of unjust local court practice and lynching, in a semidisguised telling of the famous Leo Frank case where southern anti-Semitism led to a man's arrest for murder and his subsequent execution. The film, even more so than *The Life of Emile Zola* (which deals with Zola's involvement in the Dreyfus affair) the same year, muted the Jewish angle to the story, which could not have endeared the film to New York's Jewish communists. Ethnic and religious angles, and the naming of identities are important here, with the charge of being "queer" a slur with powerful political implications.

As I have argued elsewhere, queer representation was often part of a stigma directed at various urban-based ethnic and minority groups, many of them "orientalized," as well as those perceived to be "too liberal" or "dangerous" in their political orientations.[31] In terms of acceptable versus queer gender performance in film, Italians and Latinos are often represented as too emotionally florid, the English are too mannered and prissy, Asians are too inscrutable, certain African-based peoples are too exotic, cowardly, or servile, and Jews, like gays, are the urban outsiders who can pass for what they are not. Just as some African Americans and especially Asians, Italians, Latinos, the British and Irish, and Jews are linked with queerness, so too was queerness stigmatized in the mainstream as un-American. Hollywood films like *Call Her Savage* (1932), *Broadway Melody of 1938* (1937), *Marie Antoinette* (1938), Elsa Maxwell's *Public Deb No. 1* (1940), and even the cartoon short *Wake Up the Gypsy in Me* (1933) lumped together "communists," "radicals," "revolutionaries," and "anarchists" and gave them a queerly effeminate or mannish spin, and often certain ethnic codings as well.

To take an example from another realm of cultural production, the gay painter Paul Cadmus's "sailors and floozies" trilogy (in which pansies are shown making liaisons with sailors) was criticized as the work of a "communist Jew," when in fact Cadmus was neither.[32] Such charges made the American left, very active among urban African Americans and containing notable Italian, Irish, and especially Eastern European and Jewish contingents, very defensive about charges of queerness.[33] Indeed, many minorities, regardless of their political orientation, were leery of such labels.[34] The connection among members of these groups, of course, is one of "whiteness" and assimilation; of discarding certain "dirty" ethnicities and the queer gender and sexual behavior associated with them and moving into the "American" mainstream—white, conservative, Protestant (or at least Christian), and I would argue, "straight."[35] Richard Maltby argues that the Depression-era workings of the PCA are an example of how "an increasingly insecure Protestant provincial middle class sought to defend its cultural hegemony from the incursions of a modernist, metropolitan culture that the provincials regarded as alien—a word that was often, but not always, a synonym for Jewish."[36] Although I agree, I would contend that "modernist," "metropolitan," and "alien" might also aptly describe the intellectual, the leftist, and the queer, as well as the Jew. Thus, while ethnic and religious minorities were asked to assimilate, prodded partially by charges of queerness, leftists and queers were pushed into the same closet as well.

Of course the American left also went on the offensive with its own charges of queerness, as noted in the essay on theater plays discussed above. Perversely enough, the vehicle that one vehemently homophobic writer uses is none other than Mae West, the indirect and rather queer object of desire in *Pie in the Sky* and a unique figure whose highly controversial stage plays openly represented queerness with sympathy and outrageous humor. Several of West's plays, such as *Sex*, *The Drag*, and *Pleasure Man*, feature homosexuality, so it is no surprise that queerness is quite common in her films as well. For example, we see two men arm in arm in a prison cell in *She Done Him Wrong* (1933); West dubs them "the Cherry sisters." There's the fawning, sharply dressed Jewish lawyer in *I'm No Angel* (1933) whose name West begins to spell, "Pinkowitz . . . P, like in pansy," and the Charles Butterworth character in *Every Day's a Holiday* (1938) who spends a great deal of time in drag.[37]

The perversity of the left's use of Mae West in the case I want to explore, however, comes not from a critic's attack but rather from an overtly politicized reading of queerness as a welcome index of decadent capitalism. What Nash condemns about prominent queer representation, another critic seems to praise. The irony is that Nash, the critic of "excessive" queerness, is tolerant to a point, whereas the admirer of Mae West I next examine is much more homophobic. These points are important to note lest I be prone to suggesting that the U.S. left held a completely monolithic attitude toward homosexuality. In general my research has suggested that, to a large extent, the left's liberalism did not particularly extend to homosexuality. Nonetheless, it is vital for me to reiterate here that I want to evaluate some discourses to suggest the politicized nature of the debate at various ends of the political spectrum. Simple binary models are equally inadequate to locating homophobia solely or without contradiction in the writings of the PCA or those of communist critics.

In a fascinating essay titled "Mae West: A Treatise on Decay," Robert Forsythe, a regular contributor to *New Masses*, refuses to condemn West for the salaciousness that many conservatives perceived in her work. In fact, he notes that "it is plain that on any basis of comparison she belongs to the great line."[38] His praise, however, is qualified before it begins with his initial comparison of West to the likes of Madame du Barry and Nell Gwynne. Forsythe's praise suggests that West's influence would operate along solely sexual lines: "Granted that a woman of her intelligence could be prevailed upon to favor a Congressman or a Secretary of War, the spectacle of Miss West affecting state policy as well as private temperatures is something which no future historian could afford to overlook." Having established the parameters of West's merit, he continues his sardonic tone by revealing his thesis argument regarding her real value in American culture:

> There are so many indications of the breakdown of capitalistic civilization that we are inclined to become tender and sympathetic in the midst of the debacle, much in the manner of "don't cheer, boys; the poor devils are dying," but it is obvious that Miss West, more than any of her associates, symbolizes

the end of an epoch. Her stage plays, *Sex* and *The Drag*, uncovered such a horrifying picture of homosexuals, Lesbians and ordinary degenerates that Miss
West was sentenced to the workhouse for ten days as a way of restoring the
faith of the populace in the great city. Her motives in presenting the plays were
undoubtedly mercenary, but her attorneys overlooked a great opportunity of
establishing her as a sociologist and humanitarian, moved solely by her concern
for reform.

Forsythe even references the Production Code, the Catholic Legion of
Decency, and the controversies West caused: "The Christian fathers are
quite correct in worrying about Miss West. Whether the success of her
bawdiness is a sign that we have conquered Puritanism and are a mature
people at last or whether it represents a complete collapse of morality, it is
evident that it reveals the lack of authority of religion. The Catholic campaigns for clean films succeeded in changing the title of the latest West film
from *It Ain't No Sin* to the *Belle of the Nineties*, but it is still Mae West in *It
Ain't No Sin.*"

Forsythe then continues by stating: "If we judged alone from her screen
comedies we should be tempted to say that she represented sexual honesty
in a world given over much too completely to the antics of the fairy. I refer
to the world of the theatre and to the race of people known as perverts."
As with the queer representation in Hollywood film itself, the connection
among theatricality, the public sphere of the theater, and queerness also
emerges through Forsythe's readings of West's work and the overlapping
theater and film communities. One irony resides in his labeling of fairies
and other perverts as a "race" of people, given the stigmatizing links of
queerness with the minorities noted above. The labeling of Jews, linked to
queerness as one slur, as a "race" would have tragic results in a few years.
Without knowing it, Forsythe later makes a connection himself with the
Holocaust to come, but, as we shall see, his rendition of history and his
predictions are dangerously skewed.

Forsythe then introduces a leftist class critique of queerness based on
an image of the decadence of the wealthy present in many Hollywood
representations. Although he misuses "introversion" in place of the intended psychoanalytic term "inversion," he links his superficial class analysis of queerness with fascism in a manner that prefigures the much more
complex but still problematic analyses of the Frankfurt school and later
writers.[39] Forsythe writes that introversion is essentially a class ailment

Mae West in *Belle of the Nineties*
(Paramount, 1934).

and the direct result of a sybaritic life that finally results in profound bore-dom for lack of any further possible stimulus and titillation. It is invariably associated with those twin elements of perversion, sadism and masoch-ism, and generally reveals itself among the thinned-out representatives of a decaying class. The sadistic cruelty of Hitlerism is no accident. It is the unmistakable symptom of an incurable malady.

Although Forsythe states "I am not a psychologist and what I have to say about the coincidences of history in this regard are not to be taken as gospel from the scientific archangels," to argue his case he links his homo-phobic class analysis to several famous historical examples. He thus moves from Mae West to a vest-pocket tour through late-nineteenth and early-twentieth-century European history that begins with the Oscar Wilde trials. Wilde, however, was not an isolated figure in Forsythe's estimation, but instead was a metonym for the corruption of another cultural and po-litical system. He contends that "the wave of indignation swept Wilde to jail, but it also revealed the fact that sexual debauchery was so common among the nobility that Frank Harris could report, without legal action being taken against him, that seventy-five members of the House of Lords were notorious perverts." Forsythe's reading in many ways mimics only too well Hollywood's take on the queerness of English culture.

Forsythe next moves to pre–World War I Germany by drawing comparisons between the Wilde trials and the Eulenberg case of "unnatural vice," which he reads as "evidence . . . that conditions [at the Kaiser's Imperial court] were generally bad." His whirlwind tour through history continues with the war and the rise of Hitler, both of which he reads queerly. Like the PCA censors, Forsythe seems eager to find queerness everywhere— he is simply more open in making political connections: "The War came along several years later to place the world's attention on other forms of perversion such as mass slaughter and it was only with the advent of the Fuehrer that homosexuality was raised to the rank of statesmanship." Certain conceptions of masculinity, as conservative on the left as they were on the right, are thus preserved by suggesting that Hitler himself was queer. Via his use of the umbrella term "perversion"—the same very general term employed in the wording of the Production Code—Forsythe links homosexuality with mass slaughter, an ironic stance given the many similarities among the fates of gays, communists, and Jews alike during the Holocaust. After he makes brief references to a scandal in Russia as World War I broke out (unspecified, perhaps, so as not to queer too much the time and place of the Bolshevik revolution) and to a murder case in France, Forsythe finally completes his bizarre historical survey by returning to Mae West. He argues that "What Mae West did in the plays I have mentioned and what she does in her motion pictures is to show in her frank cynical way the depths to which capitalistic morality has come. There is an honesty in her playing which is even more devastating. It is not the bouncing lechery of Ben Jonson but the mean piddling lewdness of the middle classes getting their little hour of sin before the end."

It might seem at times that Forsythe is praising West with faint damnation, but I can agree with something at least implied in his reading— namely that West is a satirist of many aspects of middle-class morality and its hypocrisies. What he doesn't realize are the ways he is complicit in such ideologies, especially where certain sexist conceptions of gender roles and the homo/hetero binary are concerned. Forsythe was not alone, of course, in displaying a misogyny in reading practices that had homophobic implications when it came to considering popular media like the cinema. Denning notes that even such leading leftist intellectual "figures like Michael Gold and Philip Rahv saw themselves threatened by both a 'feminine' genteel tradition and a 'feminine' mass culture."[40]

One of the results was that, as Wendy Kozol writes, "American radicalism remained a guardian of male sexual authority."[41] As with his earlier uncertainty about whether West represents a "mature" society or an "immoral" one, so too does Forsythe finish with seemingly contradictory praise about her status in a capitalistic culture. He both admires her theatrical "grand manner" and sees her seductive entreaties as reminiscent of a "cheap pathetic romance." Ultimately, however, Forsythe values West as the ideal symptom of American culture and he closes with both his double-edged highest praise and an equally odd prediction: "Because she epitomizes so completely the middle class matron in her hour of license I feel that Miss West has never been properly appreciated as the First Artist of the Republic. It is palpable nonsense to be concerned about such children as Katherine [sic] Hepburn, who will be as forgotten as Mary Miles Minter in a few years' time, when we possess a lady who could assume her position now as the Statue of Liberty and who so obviously represents bourgeois culture at its apex that she will enter history as a complete treatise on decay."[42]

Thus we can see how at least one very prominent trend of thought on the left was reading both homophobically and queerly at the same time. Such queer readings, rife with contradiction and error, were part of the terrain of political struggle in ways very comparable to what was going on with the PCA. As conservative censors and other viewers condemned queerness as immoral, un-American, "ethnic," and anarchist or communist, the left condemned it as decadently capitalistic and dangerously fascistic. Both sides, however, were vigorous readers of queerness; they seemed to find it everywhere and their passions suggest a certain fascination with the enemy within, who after all is so very useful for their projects. Homophobia leads such readers to speak out for the purpose of political gain. In Forsythe's case, however, we are perhaps lucky that his authority seems undercut in retrospect by the gross inaccuracy of his final prediction. More than once in her career, Mae West did impersonate the Statue of Liberty. Where Forsythe turned out to be wrong was that the career of Katharine Hepburn (as well as her queerness, and that of West, Ginger Rogers, Franklin Pangborn, and others) has survived more than a few years' time, thanks to Stage Door and other queer films.

NOTES

1 On *Queer as Folk* as suggesting that gay male sex plays a role in friendship networks and community formation, see Richard Goldstein, "Learning from *Queer as Folk*," *Village Voice*, January 23, 2001, 61. For a more negative evaluation of the show, see Nancy Franklin, "Unbuttoned," *New Yorker*, January 15, 2001, 94–96.

2 See my "Queering the (New) Deal: Lesbian and Gay Representation and the Depression-Era Cultural Politics of Hollywood's Production Code," *Cinema Journal* 38, no. 2 (winter 1999): 3–35.

3 I am, of course, not arguing that we must "prove" that images were read queerly in past times in order to suggest that they can be read queerly now. Every age makes texts its own in new ways, so I do not need the permission of long-dead readers to find things that strike me queerly now. I raise this point so that readers will be clear about the nature of my intervention. I am not trying to justify my own readings now so much as I am arguing that these texts *were* read queerly then, and that those queer readings were part of larger struggles about gender, sexuality, and politics during the Depression.

4 Chon Noriega, "SOMETHING'S MISSING HERE! Homosexuality and Film Reviews during the Production Code Era, 1934–62," *Cinema Journal* 30, no. 1 (fall 1990): 20–21.

5 Ibid.

6 Richard Dyer, *Heavenly Bodies: Film Stars and Society* (New York: St. Martin's Press, 1986), 5.

7 Alexander Doty, *Making Things Perfectly Queer: Interpreting Mass Culture* (Minneapolis: University of Minnesota Press, 1993), xii.

8 The PCA files are held by the Academy of Motion Picture Arts and Sciences. For *Circus Clown*, see letter, Breen to Warner, February 7, 1934; on *Dracula's Daughter*, see letter, Breen to Harry Zehner, January 15, 1936; for *Follow the Fleet*, see letter, Breen to B. B. Kahane, October 7, 1935. On *Carefree*, see *Variety* review, August 31, 1938. For further examples, see my "Queering the (New) Deal: Lesbian, Gay and Queer Representation in U.S. Cinema, 1929–1941," Ph.D. dissertation, New York University, 1999.

9 Michel Foucault, *The History of Sexuality. Volume 1: An Introduction*, trans. Robert Hurley (New York: Vintage, 1980); see especially 3–49.

10 *New Theater*, December 1935, 18, n.p. (emphasis mine). Hays was head of the Motion Picture Producers and Distributors of America (MPPDA), a lobbying, regulation, and public relations organization set up by the Hollywood film industry. Joseph Breen's PCA office, which reported to Hays, did clarify these "offensive" terms, such that "skirt" and "broad" were unacceptable as vulgar descriptions of women but acceptable as words designating, respectively, an article of clothing or an evaluation of width. "Goose" was intended to refer to "goosing" someone's posterior; the PCA never went on record as being against birds.

11 Emanual Gluck, "Men and Women," (review) *New Masses*, July 16, 1935.

12 See George Chauncey, *Gay New York: Gender, Urban Culture and the Making of the Gay Male World, 1890–1940* (New York: HarperCollins, 1994); Lillian Faderman, *Odd Girls and Twilight Lovers: A History of Lesbian Life in Twentieth-Century America* (New York: Columbia University Press, 1991); Andrea Friedman, "'The Habitats of Sex-Crazed Perverts': Campaigns against Burlesque in Depression-Era New York City," *Journal of the History of Sexuality* 7, no. 2 (October 1996): 203–38; and Donald Furthman Wickets, "Why Sex Crimes Increase," *Physical Culture* 78, no. 1 (July 1937): 18–19, 73–74.

13 Some contemporary extratextual "evidence" of the film's formidable queer reputation is provided by a survey from the gay magazine *The Advocate*. Video stores in the famously gay neighborhood of West Hollywood were polled to determine their all-time most popular rentals, and *Stage Door* enjoyed pride of place among the top twenty-five, alongside the likes of *The Women* (1939), *All About Eve* (1950), *Gentlemen Prefer Blondes* (1953), *Mildred Pierce* (1945), and others ("Top 30 Rental Classics," *The Advocate* August 20, 1996, 102). I can provide further extratextual evidence myself, having heard the film quoted in gay bars.

14 Peter Ellis, "Sights and Sounds," *New Masses*, November 2, 1937, 29.

15 David Wolff, "Sights and Sounds," *New Masses*, October 19, 1937, 28. Further citations are from the same text.

16 Ibid. (emphasis mine).

17 For Sklar's discussion of Cagney as a favorite of the left and as "roughneck sissy," see his *City Boys: Cagney, Bogart, Garfield* (Princeton, N.J.: Princeton University Press, 1992), 12–17.

18 Robert McElvaine, *The Great Depression: America 1929–1941* (New York: Times Books, 1984), 340.

19 Margaret McFadden, "'America's Boy Friend Who Couldn't Get a Date': Gender, Race and the Cultural Work of the Jack Benny Program, 1932–1946," *Journal of American History* 80, no. 1 (June 1993): 119.

20 Michael Denning, *The Cultural Front: The Laboring of American Culture in the Twentieth Century* (London: Verso, 1996): 136–37.

21 *New Theater*, April 1936, 34. This reading comes in the context of a slightly more developed queerness to Draper's character. He plays Ruby Keeler's dancing partner, which, given the intertext of the Rogers-Astaire musicals, might have signaled him as a rival for her hand. But instead he is presented as simply a pal. As a prelude to one number, he responds to Dick Powell's endearment to Keeler as if it were meant for him. Then, during a number, Keeler steps aside as a joke, and the two men almost end up arm in arm. Thus, the charge of effeminacy, euphemistic for queerness, is textually based in a manner beyond the dancing—one the critic, however, does not admit to or explore. The criticism is limited to the more abstract, and hence "safer," domain of Draper's dancing style.

22 Ray Ludlow, "Pie in the Sky," *New Theater*, May 1935, 19–20.

23 Ibid., 20.

24 On same-sex hobo couples, see Holly Marie Allen, "Fallen Women and For-
    gotten Men: Gendered Concepts of Community, Home and Nation, 1932–
    1945," Ph.D. dissertation, Yale University, 1996, 36, 85–87. I place "situational
    homosexuality" in quotation marks because although the term is an old one
    from psychiatry that is used to explain away homosexual behavior in gender-
    segregated settings, queer theory has demonstrated that the social contextu-
    ality and contingency of sexuality makes *all* homosexuality—and *all* hetero-
    sexuality—"situational."

25 Similarly, the more mainstream critic Otis Ferguson has argued that "the story
    makes sin very sinful, heartily repellent. A person could say, in fact: For God's
    sake go see *Lot in Sodom* and be literally justified" (Ferguson, "Genesis, 19:8,"
    New Republic, March 21, 1934; reprinted in *The Film Criticism of Otis Ferguson*,
    ed. Robert Wilson [Philadelphia: Temple University Press, 1971], 32–33). To
    his credit, Herman Weinberg seems more comfortable with the film's content,
    though his praise is aimed primarily at the film's formal beauty: "I have never
    seen light manipulated so eloquently as in these expressive lights and shad-
    ows which sometimes form men or fragments of a body" (Weinberg, "*Lot in
    Sodom*," *Close-Up* 10, no. 3 [September 1933]: 268).

26 Norman Wilson, "*Lot in Sodom*," *Cinema Quarterly* 3, no. 1 (autumn 1934): 52
    (emphasis mine).

27 Marianne Moore, "*Lot in Sodom*," *Close Up* 10, no. 4 (December 1933): 318. In
    terms of the "responsibility" of the filmmakers to make the Sodomites suffi-
    ciently sinister, several scholars have recently read *Lot in Sodom* as considerably
    more ambiguous, and even pro-queer, than the bible story inspiration would
    suggest. See my "Queering the (New) Deal," 366–70; see also Richard Dyer,
    Now You See It: Studies on Lesbian and Gay Film (New York: Routledge, 1990),
    109–10; Lisa Cartwright, "U.S. Modernism and the Emergence of 'The Right
    Wing of Film Art': The Films of James Sibley Watson Jr. and Melville Web-
    ber," in *Lovers of Cinema: The First American Avant-Garde, 1919–1945*, ed. Jan-
    Christopher Horak (Madison: University of Wisconsin Press, 1995), 156–79.

28 Donald Nash, "The Theater," *New Masses*, October 26, 1937, 28.

29 Olga J. Martin, *Hollywood's Movie Commandments* (New York: H. M. Wilson,
    1937), 42.

30 One also wonders whether the Allan Scott who wrote the other play of which
    Nash disapproved so strongly was the same Allan Scott who penned several
    of the queerest films of the period, namely RKO's musicals starring Ginger
    Rogers and Fred Astaire.

31 See my "Race, Ethnicity and Sexuality: A Note on Their Intersection in Film
    of the 1930s," Society for Cinema Studies conference presentation, Washing-
    ton, D.C., 2001, which develops the work in my "Queering the (New) Deal,"
    118–46.

32 See the interview material in the feature documentary *Paul Cadmus: Enfant*

Terrible at 80 (1984), in which Cadmus reads the bigoted response his work received. He also gives an example of the ironic failures of censorship when he notes that he owed the start of his career to the publicity that his paintings received when a U.S. Navy admiral tried to suppress his work.

33 For a study of the left in New York's African American community, see Mark Naison, *Communists in Harlem during the Depression* (New York: Grove Press, 1983). Many works have examined the Jewish presence in the American Communist Party or have studied prominent Jewish, Italian, and other minority liberals, leftists, and communists. See, for example, Denning, *The Cultural Front*; Richard Pells, *Radical Visions and American Dreams: Cultural and Social Thought in the Depression Years* (Middletown, Conn.: Wesleyan University Press, 1973); and Howard M. Sachar, *A History of the Jews in America* (New York: Random House, 1992).

34 On the lengthy history of the nationalist intermingling of anti-Semitism and homophobia in Europe, see George Mosse, *The Image of Man: The Creation of Modern Masculinity* (New York: Oxford University Press, 1996). In terms of film history, the anti-Semitism and other ethnic prejudices of the PCA are well documented. See Gregory Black, *Hollywood Censored: Morality Codes, Catholics and the Movies* (Cambridge: Cambridge University Press, 1994); and Thomas Doherty, *Pre-Code Hollywood: Sex, Immorality, and Insurrection in American Cinema, 1930–1934* (New York: Columbia University Press, 1999). See also Daniel Boyarin, *Unheroic Conduct: The Rise of Heterosexuality and the Invention of the Jewish Man* (Berkeley: University of California Press, 1997). Boyarin is interested in rescuing the maligned figure of the "Jewish sissy," the nerdy, scholarly figure in rabbinic Jewish culture who is dedicated to teaching and to the study of the Torah and the Talmud, and who is heterosexual and attractive to women but decidedly not macho in nature. In Depression-era U.S. Yiddish cinema, we find this likably queer figure in such films as *Grine Felder/Green Fields* (1936). Indeed, some post-Zionist scholars of Jewish history and culture, such as Mosse and Boyarin, have been critiquing the Zionist movement in recent revisionist studies for its adoption of Aryan paradigms of masculinity (i.e., the "muscle Jew") in order to appear "manly enough" to win back "the homeland."

35 See Noel Ignatiev, *How the Irish Became White* (New York: Routledge, 1995); Matthew Frye Jacobson, *Whiteness of a Different Color: European Immigrants and the Alchemy of Race* (Cambridge, Mass.: Harvard University Press, 1999); and Karen Brodkin, *How Jews Became White Folks and What That Says about Race in America* (New Brunswick, N.J.: Rutgers University Press, 1999). The connection of homophobia and PCA discourses is made by G. Thomas Poe in "'Disinfecting Hollywood: The Cultural Logics of 'Dirt' in the Rhetoric of the Catholic Legion of Decency" (paper presented at the annual meeting of the Society for Cinema Studies, Syracuse, 1994).

36 Richard Maltby, "The Production Code and the Hays Office," in Tino Balio,

Grand Design: Hollywood as a Modern Business Industry, 1930–1939 (New York: Charles Scribner's Sons, 1993), 41.

37 West's prominence in the history of queer representation through her writing and performances and in her role in gay culture are well known. Recall Parker Tyler's famous labeling of West as "Mother Superior of the Faggots" in *Screening the Sexes: Homosexuality in the Movies* (Garden City, N.Y.: Doubleday, 1973), 1–15. A study that gives considerable attention to gender and queer issues in West's image, oeuvre, and in various reading communities is Ramona Curry, *Too Much of a Good Thing: Mae West as Cultural Icon* (Minneapolis: University of Minnesota Press, 1996).

38 Robert Forsythe, "Mae West: A Treatise on Decay," *New Masses* 13, no. 2 (1934), 29; all further citations are from this text.

39 Despite the many penetrating insights of the Frankfurt school, the writings of Theodor Adorno and his colleagues are marred by their reliance upon homosexuality as stock villain in a manner very like that of Forsythe here. See, for example, Adorno, "Freudian Theory and the Pattern of Fascist Propaganda," originally written in 1951 and reprinted in Andrew Arato and Eike Gebhardt, eds., *The Essential Frankfurt School Reader* (New York: Continuum, 1982), 118–37. See especially the footnote on 177–78: "Under German fascism . . . the borderline between overt and repressed homosexuality, just as that between overt and repressed sadism, was much more fluent than in liberal middle-class society."

40 Denning, *The Cultural Front*, 137. Denning does note, however, that later in the decade, there was some contestation of this "masculinist rhetoric" and that "new representations of women began to emerge" as the Popular Front progressed and got closer to the days of World War II, even if these images were limited by a focus on "militant motherhood."

41 Wendy Kozol, "Madonnas of the Fields: Photography, Gender and 1930s Farm Relief," *Genders* 2 (summer 1988): 15.

42 Forsythe's reference to West as the Statue of Liberty probably cites her appearance as such in her "My American Beauty" number in *Belle of the Nineties* (1934). The critic George Jean Nathan would famously dub West "the Statue of Libido."

V   PRODUCTION

MURNAU IN AMERICA
Chronicle of Lost Films (4 Devils, City Girl)
Janet Bergstrom

This summer I should like to make a picture named: "OUR DAILY BREAD"—a
story that will tell a tale about "WHEAT"—about the "sacredness of bread"—
about the estrangement of the modern metropolitans from—and their ignorance about Nature's sources of sustenance. . . .
　　　　　　　—F. W. Murnau to William Fox, December 22, 1927 [1]

Suggestions of changes for "OUR DAILY BREAD": I would suggest the following
changes which I would have made myself if I had worked longer on the picture.
. . . If talk should be added to the picture, I would suggest it start at the beginning of the final night sequence.
　　　　　　　—F. W. Murnau to William Fox (circa late February 1929) [2]

"IF I HAD WORKED LONGER
ON THE PICTURE . . ."

1928, the year that separates the first of these statements from the second, was the critical period for F. W.
Murnau in America. Between chapters devoted to *Sunrise* and *Tabu*, Lotte Eisner, in her invaluable study of
Murnau, assigned the equivocal title "Compromise in
Hollywood?" to the chapter on *4 Devils* and *Our Daily
Bread*. [3] Was Murnau forced to compromise to such an
extent on *Our Daily Bread* that he left the production
even before the silent version had been completed? In

July 1926, Murnau's arrival in New York from Germany, on his way to Hollywood and *Sunrise*, was publicized in grand style. William Fox held a banquet in his honor on July 7 at the Ritz Carlton Hotel, which was "attended by one hundred members of Manhattan society and broadcast to thousands of others over radio station WNYC."[4] Fox's journal for exhibitors reported: "Mr. Murnau will have his own technical staff and cameraman and all the vast facilities of the Fox company at his command. [...] He is a recognized genius, placed by many capable critics at the very top of the directorial field, and his innovations are certain to go far in bringing something distinctly new to the Fox program and in establishing new standards in the American Studios."[5]

For *Sunrise*, William Fox authorized Murnau freedom from studio constraints that became legendary. In January 1928, at the time he began shooting his next film, *4 Devils*, Murnau wrote with confidence: "Everything is subordinated to my picture, and just as I do not permit myself to be influenced away from what I think is the right thing to do and the right person to use, I will not do a picture that is based on a theme not to my liking or conviction."[6] But only one year later Murnau's situation had reversed. Changing a film's title before release was routine practice in Hollywood. Retitling *Our Daily Bread* to *City Girl*, however, coincided with Murnau's departure not only from that project, but from Fox and from Hollywood. *City Girl* was finished while Murnau was in Tahiti working with Robert Flaherty on the film that would become *Tabu*.

Although we are not able to see *4 Devils*—it remains a famous lost film—and the status of the silent print of *City Girl* has been disputed, we do have access to rich materials documenting the production and reception of both films. These documents can help us understand what we refer to as Murnau's American period, meaning the three films he made for Fox between 1926 and February 23, 1929, when his early termination agreement took effect.[7]

It is particularly surprising that *City Girl* has received so little critical attention considering that, after having been considered a lost film for decades, a complete 35mm print of the silent release version was located in 1969 in the Twentieth Century-Fox studio vaults.[8] It was screened publicly the following year, and since then it has been shown around the world and is currently available on video. The rediscovered print corresponds to the American and French non-dialogue release version, judging from detailed plot summaries provided with Fox's publicity materials for exhibitors. Murnau's letter to William Fox, cited earlier, makes it clear that he left *Our Daily Bread / City Girl* before the production was finished (Murnau's statement was taken from a memo recommending changes), but it is not known how much of the silent version had been finalized at that point. For some, the rediscovered print is simply Murnau's film retitled *City Girl* before it was brutally transformed into the sixty-eight minute release version, nearly half of which had been reshot with dialogue by another director. (No copy of the "part-talking version" is known to exist today.) But Eisner (and others) judge the silent print to correspond to Murnau's version only in certain passages: "There remain in it many traces of Murnau's unique visual style and lighting, mutilated as it is, with much of its nuance eliminated."[9]

That opinion seems too harsh. While we still cannot say exactly how the silent release version of *City Girl* that we know corresponded to the cut Murnau supervised, we can come much closer to understanding what "studio interference" meant for this production, formulate a hypothesis about why Murnau left when he did, and get a fairly good picture of the interests that prevailed in completing the silent version. *City Girl*, as we know it, is still a remarkable film within the context of Murnau's work. Along with *Tabu*, which is more classically balanced and "finished," *City Girl* is the most modern of all Murnau's films, the most directly appealing to audiences today.

WILLIAM FOX AS NAPOLEON

What can the histories of these two films tell us about Murnau in America? Or rather, how can we assemble the pieces of the puzzle at our disposal to try to make sense of them? First, we need to take a big step back, for if we look at Murnau's rapid loss of relative autonomy at Fox from a broader framework, we can see how his rise and fall in Hollywood are closely aligned with the rise and (not very long after Murnau's departure) the fall of William Fox himself.

William Fox's aggressive campaign to expand his studio into an international empire in a few short years (1927–1929) was predicated on forcing theater owners to adapt to his Movietone sound-on-film process (the competitor to Vitaphone, Warners's sound-on-disk process), first through newsreels, then feature films with musical soundtracks, then "part-talkies," and finally "all-talking" films. The "part-talkie" was originally planned to be released as a silent film, or with a synchronized musical soundtrack that might include some sound effects, but usually the ending (perhaps the last two reels) was reshot with dialogue to cash in on the market strength of the "stampede toward sound." A silent version was also made for American theaters not yet equipped for sound projection and for foreign distribution. The "part-talkie" phenomenon has received scant attention, especially concerning specific cases aside from Warners's *Jazz Singer*.

The "part-talkie" had a disastrous impact on Murnau, which was much more serious than a simple resistance to sound film per se on his part. Both *4 Devils* and *City Girl* were shot silent, to be accompanied by synchronized Movietone scores, and were subsequently partly reshot with dialogue and released as "talkies." *4 Devils*, in fact, had two separate premieres and reviews in the trade journals eight months apart: the silent (non-dialogue) version opened in New York on October 3, 1928, and the part-talking version premiered in Los Angeles on June 10, 1929. The dialogue sections of both films were substantial (25 percent of *4 Devils*, half of *City Girl*) and Murnau had nothing to do with them. They were scripted by different writers, photographed by different cameramen, and "staged by" other directors. Nonetheless, the films were reviewed as his. "Staged by" was a new term to designate that the "talking" segments were handled by experienced theater directors, preferably from Broadway, since they were judged experts on directing the actors' delivery of spoken dialogue. The "talking" sections of *4 Devils* and *City Girl* were staged by Broadway expert A. H. Van Buren working with Murnau's former assistant director, A. F. (Buddy) Erickson. Although we cannot know the full effect of these substitutions of key personnel and language in the absence of the films, transcripts in the Fox story files titled "Dialogue as Taken from the Screen" for both *4 Devils* and *City Girl* show us how the style and abundance of talking worked against the mood, rhythm, and characterizations that had been established up until the point when the actors began to speak. Moreover, far more radical changes were made than substituting "talking" for titles: the narrative events of both films were altered—for the worse—and not simply by substituting a happier ending for *4 Devils*, as has been suggested until now.[10] *City Girl*, significantly later in the swing toward all-talking films in America, nearly became unreleasable.

At the same time that William Fox was expanding through Movietone, he was also fully engaged in the "merger mania" of the pre-Wall Street Crash period. In his goal to dominate lucrative first-run theater exhibition from coast to coast, throughout 1928 and 1929 Fox distinguished himself by buying theater chains, not just individual cinemas. At the very time that Murnau most needed his personal intervention, Fox was devoting all his attention to high-stakes financial maneuvers. That meant, effectively, that Murnau, like the other directors at the studio, became primarily answerable to Winfield Sheehan, head of West Coast Production. Sheehan was actively present in Los Angeles, unlike William Fox, whose office was located in his company's flagship Roxy Theater building in New York. On March 19, 1929, *Variety* headlined five different stories on the same page that featured Fox, soon after Fox had bought out his competitor, Loew's theater chain, and acquired MGM, a Loew's subsidiary: "Fox-Schenck on Coast" announced that William Fox was coming to Los Angeles and stationing himself at MGM, not at his own studio, to work out a new plan for MGM under Fox; "Mayer, Thalberg and Rubin Stick with MG" affirmed that the former studio heads would maintain a separate production unit under "the new Fox regime"; "Fox May Buy Great States" predicted the next Fox acquisition of a major theater chain in the Midwest; "U Drops Sound Newsreel Idea" reported that the Fox-Loew merger had caused Universal to abandon its plans for sound newsreels; and finally, the smallest item of the five, "Murnau-Fox Through."

Murnau had already negotiated an early end to his contract with Fox on February 4, weeks before the announcement in *Variety*. For the record, this was Murnau's second contract with Fox, dated July 8, 1926, to commence over a year later "in or about the months of July or August 1927." The terms of this contract are partly cited by Eisner and repeated in countless other places: she believed this was Murnau's first and only contract with Fox and therefore that *Our Daily Bread* was the third of four films covered by the agreement. In fact, Murnau had signed a previous contract with Fox on January 24, 1925, to commence in spring 1926, for one film, which turned out to be *Sunrise*. A payment schedule prepared for Murnau's termination agreement makes it clear that *4 Devils* and *Our Daily Bread* were the first two of four films covered by the second contract. Murnau's legal history with Fox was made to appear even more confusing by the fact that when Fox signed Murnau to his new contract after he had finished shooting *Sun-*

rise, the studio advertised the four-year agreement in glowing terms as a five-year contract.[11]

William Fox was aware of his place in history, or in any event, of the place to which he aspired. For a time, Murnau played an important role in this scenario. When Fox was finally satisfied that Movietone was ready for the public—long after his engineering team at the Fox-Case studio in New York wanted to begin regular production—milestones in American film exhibition, not only in Fox's history, were established in quick succession. Fox began modestly on February 24, 1927, with a screening of Movietone short subjects for fifty members of the New York press. The writers also had the opportunity to be "movietoned" that day so that soon afterward they could see and hear themselves on the big screen and judge the veracity of the experiment. The Fox engineering team then answered questions put to them by the lively reporters.[12] The week before, Fox had announced that two specially designed "talking picture and acoustical stages" were being constructed in Los Angeles and that William Fox had placed the largest order on record for equipment he intended to install in all of his theaters that would enable them to project both Movietone and Vitaphone films.[13] On April 30, the first regularly scheduled theatrical exhibition of Movietone (the Cadets at West Point) was advertised: "First Time 'Movietone': William Fox News Weekly with Actual Sound Reproduction."[14] Both the press and audiences reacted very favorably to this four-minute segment (placed within Fox's regular silent newsreel) and wondered when Fox would produce more.[15]

Soon after Movietone sound trucks were on the spot to record sound along with the images of news events that captured the world's imagination. At daybreak on May 20 the Movietone team recorded Charles Lindbergh taking off from Long Island in the *Spirit of St. Louis*, as he began his solo transatlantic flight. Silent newsreels drew crowds into every movie theater that night, but at the Roxy, along with silent footage, the public could see Lindbergh's departure with sound. The 6,200-seat theater was sold out in anticipation, and the audience reacted to the lifelike "you are there" presentation, thanks to Movietone, with a ten-minute standing ovation.[16] Lindbergh's takeoff was reviewed as Fox's second Movietone newsreel and the first to capture a news event as it was breaking.[17] The event was also promoted by the Fox organization to show that they could "win the race" to deliver high-quality audio prints quickly to theaters across the country, a key point for exhibitors who were eager to capitalize on the timeliness of the Fox coup.

A few weeks later, on June 4, aviators Clarence Chamberlin and Charles Levine took off from Long Island for Germany hoping to break the world's distance record. That night, New York audiences at Fox's Harris and Roxy theaters were thrilled anew by the vividness of the Movietone newsreel "accompanied by the roar of the plane and the cheering of the crowd." The Movietone crew had taken the extra step of filming Chamberlin speaking to them before the flight. "The audience has the illusion of actually being present. Following the successful recording of the Lindbergh takeoff, this Movietone newsreel gave convincing proof of the practicability of the Fox-Case talking pictures in recording news happenings."[18]

In mid-June, Lindbergh returned to America as the most popular figure of his age. His reception by President Coolidge was "movietoned" in Washington, D.C., where both men spoke before the camera. This news feature, too, drew record crowds to movie theaters. *Variety's* reviewer, at the Roxy, observed how it built up to "a sensational burst of enthusiasm from the audience. The reproduction of the speeches brought wild enthusiasm such as was reflected in the views about the grandstand in the screen shots."[19] Lindberg plus Movietone dwarfed the feature film on the program.

In retrospect, the chronology of Movietone news seemed to lead directly to the premiere of *Sunrise* on September 23, 1927, at Fox's new Times Square theater in New York. This event was credited by Earl Sponable, one of the engineers responsible for developing Movietone, as the first all-Movietone program, from the prologue to the feature. (*Sunrise* was the first feature released by Fox with an original synchronized score.)[20] Murnau's film was preceded by a multipart Movietone news film that had been shot in Italy exclusively for Fox. It climaxed with Mussolini addressing the camera, speaking in Italian and in English about international friendship. Once again, the spectacular news event risked overshadowing what was supposed to be the principal attraction, except that this was no ordinary feature. *Sunrise* was William Fox's much-heralded super special, designed to prove his studio's artistic excellence. The news division, however, saw the occasion as the next big opportunity to prove the superiority of the Movietone process itself. The press was invited to an advance screening of the twenty-seven-minute news feature a few days before the opening, with Winfield Sheehan presiding. *Variety* responded on September 21 with a front-page banner headline as if it were breaking a momentous news story, not describing a film: "MUSSOLINI'S HOPE IN SCREEN; 'This Can Bring World Together and End War,' Says Italian Dictator Upon Viewing Own Image and Hearing Record of Movietone."[21] In addition to the front-page story, *Variety* ran a long article on the "Mussolini Movietone" in the section for film reviews, which raved about the perfection that Movietone sound had achieved.[22]

Regular weekly releases of Movietone Newsreel began on December 3.[23] "When the record of accomplishment for 1927 is written," *Film Daily* predicted, "the Movietone newsreel, by every right, will be found making a formidable bid for first honors."[24] William Fox recognized the historical importance of this achievement, and, with publicity in mind as well, he offered to donate newsreels to the National Archives.[25] At the height of Fox Movietone Newsreel's powers at the end of 1929, four separate newsreels were shown every week, which were produced by seventy crews around the world.[26]

In 1927, sound with newsreels had proven to be a financial success, but Fox was reluctant to switch to all-talking feature films, thinking (with others) that they might be a short-lived curiosity. (The part-talking *Jazz Singer* had premiered on October 6, 1927.) 1928 proved to be the year in which opinions turned around quickly on that subject. On July 22 *Film Daily* reported: "Overnight and like a tidal wave, sound pictures have stepped to the fore."[27] Fox opened the much-publicized Movietone City on October 28. A monumental commitment to the future of sound cinema, this $10,000,000 production facility had been constructed in only four months by 1,500 people working around the clock, seven days a week.[28] By the end of 1928, "Mr. Fox had risen to a position of prominence among the Big Four of Cinema (Warner Brothers, Paramount, Fox, Loew)," according to the business journal *Fortune*.[29]

Eisner (and many others subsequently) gives the impression that Murnau communicated exclusively with William Fox about important matters. The trade journals, on the other hand, credit Winfield Sheehan for decisions involving production—his office issued the press announcements. William Fox made statements personally only when it came to epoch-making moves, such as hiring Murnau or buying the Roxy, the biggest, most sumptuous theater in the world that finally gave him a picture palace in New York City, or the acquisition of Loew's theater chain and MGM.

However, William Fox himself had appeared with Murnau before a notary in New York on July 8, 1926 when he signed his second contract. And the following year, on March 25, 1927, after *Sunrise* had been completed but not yet released and Murnau was about to sail back to Europe from New York, "William Fox did the for-him-unusual thing of seeing his guest-director off, going to the pier with fifty dollars' worth of flowers and twenty-five dollar's worth of fruit. Not usually loquacious, Fox said— and this, remember, was only a few days after he had put over the fifteen-million-dollar Roxy theater deal—'Signing Murnau for the five-year contract is one of the finest deals in my moving-picture career; he is, from the artistic and technical view-point, I think, the greatest moving-picture director in the world today.'"[30]

The caption prepared for the publicity photo of the two men (reputedly one of the few in which William Fox can be seen smiling) read: "William Fox bidding F. W. Murnau bon voyage as he sailed aboard the S.S. Olympic on his way back to Germany after completing *Sunrise* for Fox Films. If this photograph is not sufficient evidence of mutual affection and esteem, Murnau's new five-year contract is. He will return next October to resume work with Fox."[31]

Five days later, Fox gave a lecture at the Harvard School of Business in a series devoted to motion pictures, which was organized by alumnus Joseph P. Kennedy. (Kennedy had acquired and become president of FBO Pictures Corporation, forerunner of RKO, in January 1926.) Fox referred to Murnau's *The Last Laugh* as "the greatest motion picture of all time," to "Dr. Murnau" as "the genius of this age," and he also endorsed Murnau's idea that "the motion picture must tell its story by picture and not by reading matter," describing how Murnau had eliminated titles successfully in that film. Fox was not discouraged by the failure of *The Last Laugh* in America (it was distributed by Universal), but he explained to his audience of future businessmen that he wanted to study why it had failed, given its huge success abroad. He believed that the research he conducted helped him understand differences among national audiences.[32]

In July 1927, still before *Sunrise* had been released, *Motion Picture Classic* reported on the unusual bond between the two men that had led Murnau to sign a new contract with Fox despite reputedly higher offers from other studios. Murnau's reason was simple: "William Fox had kept his word." He did not interfere in any way with the production of *Sunrise*.

The few letters between Murnau and Fox that have come to light attest to a close relationship between them without an intermediary such as Sheehan. Murnau wrote to Fox on December 22, 1927, and outlined his plans for 4 *Devils*: "I shall mail you a copy of the script and I certainly would like to hear from you and Mrs. Fox, as to your opinions about the story, and suggestions.... Shortly after starting production, I shall forward to you a reel of tests of my principal cast, so that you will see the faces and contrasts of the types that I have selected for my story." Thinking ahead to the film he planned to make after 4 *Devils*, he remarked, "I would like to hear about the progress of the Grandeur Film camera, whether I could use it this summer." (Grandeur Film was a 70mm widescreen process that Fox was eager to debut.) He then described his idea for *Our Daily Bread*, concluding: "I believe that this theme would be a great starting vehicle for the Grandeur Film." William Fox's four-page reply on December 27 included such comments as:

> After my talk with you in New York, I felt sure that you would make this picture at a reasonable cost, as expressed by you at that time.... I look forward to receiving a copy of your completed scenario which I will read promptly and will also have Mrs. Fox read it, after which I will send you our comment.... Some time between April and May we should have in our possession the Grandeur Film Color [camera] and projection machine. We are working on it day and night and just as soon as it is delivered to us it will be sent to Los Angeles and promptly shown to you so that you may use it in your next picture.... I showed Mrs. Fox your letter. She was pleased to read it and joins me in sending our very kindest and best regards and hopes for your continued good health and success.

Bringing Murnau to his studio was part of Fox's bid for a place in history. Fox had always been a "hands-on" studio head. His admiration for Murnau was personal, as well as part of his business strategy to upgrade the quality of his studio's productions. Richard Koszarski described the influence that Murnau had during a few years of amazing productions at Fox— and through those films, on the American cinema of the period—because William Fox stood behind him: "That Murnau's *The Last Laugh* had been a catastrophe at the American box office failed to daunt Fox, who not only allowed Murnau a free hand in the production of *Sunrise* but encouraged the studio's other contract directors—solid American types like John Ford, Raoul Walsh, and Frank Borzage—to study Murnau's style and take from it what they could. The results were such brilliant amalgams of German and American style as *Seventh Heaven, Street Angel, The Red Dance, Hangman's House* and *The River* [all of them 1927–1928]."[33]

At the zenith of William Fox's career, he succeeded in bringing his studio to a position of leadership in artistic excellence in feature films, gained prominence in sound newsreels, and, after taking over Loew's, owned the largest film production and distribution business in the world, with over one thousand theaters. Fox then expanded internationally, buying the Gaumont British Pictures Corporation, which added some three hundred theaters in the United Kingdom. *Fortune* saw 1929 as "the period of Mr. Fox's greatest glory" and the year that led to his downfall: "Comparing him (probably not to his displeasure) with Napoleon, 1929 might be termed his Moscow year, although Mr. Fox was not nearly as reckless as Napoleon and won a far more complete victory. He did, however, embark upon an expedition a bit too expensive for his resources, and he certainly retreated from it in extremely bad order."[34]

Caught up in the heady days of expansion, Fox became overextended financially, not only because of his expensive theater acquisitions and construction of elaborate picture palaces but also because of his twin strategy of equipping them for dual sound projection. When the stock market crashed in late October, Fox lacked short-term capital. He ended up selling a controlling interest in his companies to his partners with a verbal understanding, according to Fox, that he could buy back his shares when he was able to refinance his loans to his advantage. But when he tried to do so, his partners refused to sell. Winfield Sheehan sided with Fox's enemies. Moreover, the Justice Department filed an antitrust suit against Fox on November 27, which ended in a consent decree according to which the Fox combined company agreed to divest itself of Loew's stock.[35] On April 8, 1930, William Fox sold his voting shares to General Theaters Equipment, thereby putting an end to his litigation, and resigned as president of his companies.[36] William Fox's empire had crumbled, but not his sense of history. He engaged an author no less worthy of the task than Upton Sinclair to write the story of how he had been swindled by the East Coast banking establishment.[37]

Nothing could be more evident than that William Fox had his hands full with other matters at the strange transitional time of the part-talkie when Murnau lost the degree of independence he had known before.

4 DEVILS: DEATH-SPRING
THROUGH A CIRCLE OF FIRE

> Now follows the mad drama of the air, to be worked out to the least detail.
> Fritz's recklessness is the recklessness of a drunken man, before whom the
> amphitheatre, the apparatus, the mighty building with its thousands of
> occupants, faces, heads, lights turn and twist in wild distortion, the faces
> emerge and fade away. . . . Now: The Death-spring!!! A thousand eyes mea-
> sure the awful height, this time the arena is not covered by a net.
> —Murnau's "Treatment" for 4 Devils, October 12, 1927[38]

The production history of 4 Devils, from first-person accounts, the sequence of scripts, and the reviews following the New York premiere in
October 1928, would all lead us to believe that Murnau was continuing a
successful career at Fox and in America. Only two indicators run counter
to this impression: first, after previews in early July, he was obliged to re-
shoot the ending to make it less tragic, and second, according to the shot
list filed with the Library of Congress for copyright purposes, the finished
film had no fewer than 120 titles, not counting the credits or handwritten
notes, posters, electric signs and the like that incorporated words into the
images.[39] That meant an average of one title per minute, which was an
enormous number for the man who had famously made *The Last Laugh*
with only one intertitle, and who worked toward perfecting a form of
silent cinema that could eliminate titles completely. At the time he began
shooting 4 Devils, Murnau published an essay on that very subject: "The
Ideal Picture Needs No Titles: By Its Very Nature the Art of the Screen
Should Tell a Complete Story Pictorially."[40] In this essay and in "Films of
the Future," which was written while working on "a circus picture" but held
for publication until just before 4 Devils premiered, Murnau expressed his
views about the cinema in terms of the innovations he had been led to
create for his latest film and his plans for the film he intended to make
next.[41] These essays convey the stature that Murnau had attained before
and continued after *Sunrise*: he was an authority on the art of the film, a
major director whose opinion counted.

At Christmastime in 1927, the exchange of letters between Murnau and
William Fox was warm (including the practical reassurances or reminders
on both sides), optimistic, and full of plans for the future. Murnau wrote:
"I am sure it will also be good news to you to hear that the estimated cost
of the picture is reasonable, since exorbitant settings like in *Sunrise* are not

required, and since I have also tried my utmost, in order not to be subjected to California weather-whims, to have all my settings on the Hollywood stages, with only a very, very few exterior shots."[42] He added: "I am
glad that a Movietone recording truck has arrived here. I shall make use of
it for some of my circus scenes." Fox replied: "I was happy to learn that you
are enthusiastic about your production and your cast. I am sure you understand that my hopes run high for this production which, when completed,
I feel will be the outstanding picture of the year. Your ability and genius
will make this certain."[43]

The studio advertised 4 Devils as a Fox super-production, and Murnau
was featured prominently throughout the promotional materials in terms
similar to those used for Sunrise: a genius, a master of visualization. Murnau had been given "carte blanche. The entire resources of the company
were placed at his disposal."[44] Fox's Pressbook announced: "The creator of
Sunrise, Faust and The Last Laugh achieves another triumph in his current
Fox production, 4 Devils. In every Murnau picture there is always revealed
something new in treatment, in photography, in lighting and in unique
shooting. It is for this reason that his productions attract and amaze the
public." Similar quotations from early reviews were provided for potential exhibitors or journalists: "The genius of Murnau has wrought another
film of simplicity, of eloquence and of enormous emotional appeal," wrote
Quinn Martin in the New York World. According to Life, "Murnau has directed 4 Devils with the same originality and the same genius for pictorial
work that distinguished his previous works. . . ." A feature article in Picture
Play added a bit more than fact warranted, but it was in keeping with the
spirit of Fox's original presentation of Murnau to the press and the public: "William Fox, in the sincerity of his desire to raise the standard of his
productions, has given Murnau absolute freedom of rein in the inexorable
black and white of his contract. . . . From the moment of [the studio's] final
O.K. [of the script], before shooting has begun, complete control of production is in Murnau's hands. No changes can be made in the scenario, no
supervision permitted over any slightest detail of procedure. The little god
of the Fox lot, Murnau has the best of everything for his work."[45]

The "Final Script" was written by Carl Mayer, Berthold Viertel, and
Marion Orth, although only Viertel received screen credit.[46] Eisner discusses many key passages in the script where visualizations were indicated
that one would expect of the director of Sunrise. She was surely mistaken,

however, in attributing the entire script and so many of these ideas to Carl Mayer alone. We have every reason to believe that Murnau was involved with developing the script, along with Viertel and, at a later stage, Orth, who must have helped to Americanize it. The first treatment in the Fox Story File was written by Murnau. It already contained, in miniature, the visual logic of the film, which is based on strongly marked shifts in point of view and optical effects such as montage sequences and superimpositions combined with the realistic details of the circus.

In "Films of the Future," Murnau wrote that the camera "must gallop after the equestrienne, it must pick out the painted tears of the clown and jump from him to a high box to show the face of the rich lady thinking about the clown. So I have had them build me a sort of travelling crane with a platform swung at one end for the camera."[47] This must be how Murnau could give the impression, during the spectacular first entrance of the 4 Devils into the circus ring, that we are seeing through the eyes of a galloping horse, as if it had a camera attached to it (the script reads: "a camera is fixed on a horse's head").[48] Fox's Pressbook described this device, referred to as the "Go-Devil," as "a gigantic apparatus in the center of the arena, devised by Murnau. . . . This consisted of a large steel upright, from which swung a big steel boom, on the end of which was a car carrying batteries of lights and cameras, capable of revolving at various heights and at dizzy speeds. This framework, which weighed twenty tons, was designed by the director to shoot the young players as they whirled through the air in their acrobatic feats."[49]

An annotated copy of the first part of the script held in Deutsche Kinemathek shows, as do Murnau's other annotated scripts, that shots were added, deleted, or modified during shooting.[50] The "Ring of Fire" that the star trapeze artist dives through during his Leap of Death (the dangerous triple somersault, the *salto mortale*) does not appear in the typed script (the annotated script is missing everything between the prologue, when the performers are still children, and the epilogue), but drawings of it appear in Fox's Pressbook among the advertisements offered to exhibitors. One of them bears a slogan like a circus poster: "The Leap of Death alone is worth the price of admission." The "Ring of Fire" is also mentioned in the shot list filed with the Library of Congress Copyright Office; in the cue sheet for music to accompany the silent version; and in the comments on a preview questionnaire reprinted by Eisner.[51] This effect would correspond well to another that she describes, namely the presentation of the unnamed Lady (the femme fatale) in a "magic circle of light."[52] Moreover, firsthand accounts testify, as Eisner herself wanted to demonstrate, that Murnau was making decisions about how to shoot scenes (or how to visualize them) as he went along, regardless of the difficulties, particularly for the camera team.

Cinematographer Ernest Palmer remembered the challenges:

> Murnau had no mercy on the cinematographer. We had shots of the audience in the arena, and we would shoot 360 degrees, all around, boom! Where would anyone light a thing like that? Because about the second shot after that, he'd say, "I want a shot here."
>
> I'll tell you what I had to do with that enormous set, the inside of the circus. I used arc lights on the pan to give a general exposure light all over. There was an electrician who had improved and invented, so to speak, a long-barrelled, high-intensity light. The carbon revolved at 2000 revolutions. It would spin and make a noise, but it would make a light that could burn a hole right through the set, almost. Such a powerful light. And I used to have to use those as spotlights, in among all those front arcs. To place those lights in such a way that I could go right by them and you wouldn't see the source, that was the problem. He had no mercy on the cinematographer. He'd just say, "That's it, let's shoot!"[53]

Paul Ivano, part of the camera team, described how he made it possible for Murnau to get two of the visual effects he wanted:

> Ernie Palmer, who was in charge, was busy on something, and we had the nets for the acrobats in the circus. Murnau said, "I want one shadow of the net on the ground." In those days, there was only one lamp that could do it. An electrician by the name of Hyde had designed one and we bought it. And when Janet Gaynor falls off a trapeze, I dropped the camera from the top of the stage on a special track and it bounced on springs and things. But to set it up, I had to ride on that track. It was sort of curved, and everything was hooked up so that nothing could fall off. It was not just a flat track, it was an L-shaped track.[54]

Janet Gaynor explained Murnau's rationale for the mechanism that Ivano invented to allow the camera to appear to drop, remembering the first ending that was shot in which both trapeze artists die:

> There was one scene which was supposed to be the scene where we fell. Murnau had the camera on a dolly, but it was high in the tent, and he was photo-

graphing the other people, the spectators. He did not tell them what they were seeing, only that they were seeing people doing an aerial act. Then at a given moment the camera came shooting down this trap at full speed. People fell back, women fainted—it was absolute pandemonium—because they thought that the camera was loose and was coming down upon them. Of course, this was the reaction he wanted. That's the way he directed it.[55]

Fox's Pressbook claimed that the circus audience was composed of more than 1,300 extras, and that six cameras recorded their reactions.

4 Devils may not have been as extravagant a production as Sunrise, but it was not cheap. Shooting began on January 3. On May 1, Murnau was 18 days behind schedule, after 116 days of "actual shooting time," and it took two more weeks to finish. Variety reported that the film "will cost more than $1,000,000."[56] When editor Harold Schuster was asked whether Murnau had complete control over 4 Devils, he replied yes, and then he described what that meant to him:

> I had a cutting room that was about as long as this garage, with two girls, nega-tive cutters. It's the only time I've ever worked that way, two girls and two assis-tant cutters. We'd go into the projection room and he'd have printed 40 or 50 takes. Each one would have to be put into a separate can so sometimes you'd have as many as 40 or 50 cans piled high. We'd spend a whole evening just run-ning one [scene]—picking maybe four takes out of the 40 or 50. They would have to be segregated by the assistants and maybe the next night we'd look at those four again. We'd run them over and over. Berthold Viertel was always in there with him and [Herman] Bing.[57]

Janet Gaynor remembered the same thing about the number of retakes for Sunrise.[58] Up to this point, it seemed, Murnau was able to work the way he was used to. What was important was the final effect that he wanted (perfection, said Gaynor) rather than economy.

The prologue of 4 Devils introduces us to four children: the brothers Fritz and Adolf, orphaned by the tragic fall of their famous parents in a trapeze act, and the two sisters, Aimee and Louise, also circus orphans, who are living with a sadistic circus trainer Cecchi and a kindly clown (J. Farrell MacDonald). Cecchi agrees to take in the boys, and he trains the four children to become acrobats. To save them from his drunken rages, the clown leads them away. Ellipsis. "The Four Devils" enter a Parisian circus ring, each one standing astride a pair of magnificent white horses.

"Murnau," said *Variety*, "has given [them] a ring entrance that will set every acrobat in the world on fire when seeing it. In flowing devilish wraps, they ride into the ring, each on a white horse, with the clowns preceding them. Their trapezes are lowered. As each of the quartet rides under it, they are taken aloft, their wraps falling off on the way up to the aerial pedestals."[59] The climax of their act is the Leap of Death: Fritz (Charles Morton) dives from his trapeze through a ring of fire, executes a triple-somersault and finishes by catching a trapeze that Aimee (Janet Gaynor) sends him.[60] A glamorous Lady (Mary Duncan) lures the young acrobat from his circus family. His sleepless nights of champagne and passion cut him off from the rhythms of his daily life. Every evening she comes to the performance and, after his Leap of Death, she tosses a rose into the ring with a note to Fritz designating their rendezvous after the show. Fritz becomes increasingly distracted. For the first time, he falls into the safety net during a rehearsal. His confidence is shaken, and he sees visions, premonitions of falling during their final performance when they will not use the net. Aimee is heartbroken. She sets out to bring Fritz back from his night visit to the Lady's villa, but she fails.

The climax of the film leads to four different endings. In Murnau's "Treatment," Fritz arrives at the circus for the final performance at the last minute because of the machinations of the vamp to prevent him from going. He is confused, drunk, and reckless. After the Leap of Death, he misses the trapeze that Aimee throws him and falls to the ground. Panic breaks out. He must be dead. But Murnau added another section, which he titled *The Solution of the Drama*. The circus manager announces that Fritz will live and the show will go on. Aimee approaches Fritz, who "lies stretched out, covered up to the throat. . . . Aimee sees it all through a mist of tears, tears of gratitude, because a miracle has happened, because this body is breathing—because these eyes are opening and looking at her: and what this gaze tells her is redemption from all suffering." The film ends there: Fritz falls, his own recklessness is to blame (with the help of the Lady), and he lives.

In the "Final Script" both Fritz and Aimee die, but not because of an accident. When Aimee fails to bring Fritz back to her and their communal life, she resolves that death is better than letting him remain with the Lady. Aimee is called a "nemesis" several times after this. She becomes Fritz's second femme fatale, effectively the Lady's double in ruining him. This is an interesting twist on a theme familiar from Weimar cinema, as is the passive, helpless Fritz at the end of Murnau's treatment. The night they perform without the safety net, instead of throwing Fritz the trapeze at the end of his Leap of Death, Aimee swings on the trapeze toward him. Therefore, he has nothing to catch after his somersault but her body. When she can no longer hold on, they both fall. This is the ending that Murnau decided to shoot, an experience that Janet Gaynor could not forget:

> I was hanging on the trapeze, and [Fritz] was to hang with his legs around my legs and his head down. So Murnau went to Alfredo Codona and said this is what he wanted. Alfredo said, "This is impossible, Mr. Murnau, because no woman can hold her weight and a man's weight with her hands. This is impossible. I can't do it, no one can do that." Mr. Murnau said, "This is what we're going to do."
>
> We were all in little pink tights, and pink satin shorts. They wired me. They put underneath something like a little leather pair of pants, and wires were attached to the leather, run up my back and arms, and attached to the trapeze and to Charles Morton, who was the man. But when they got me up on the trapeze, he was so heavy that even those wires did not take his weight. It still pulled at me so I was nearly cut in two with this leather harness.
>
> They let us go, up in the middle of this tent, as high as a real circus tent. I was in absolute agony with this weight, and there I was wired. I couldn't move, and he was swinging. I was stretched out there, and of course I screamed and I cried and I was almost hysterical. Finally they cut us down and I said, "But Mr. Murnau, you didn't tell me anything . . . !" He said, "You did just what I wanted you to do. You were in agony and that's what I wanted." That's the way he directed. This was realism.[61]

This script, like Murnau's "Treatment," added a brief epilogue to offset the tragedy, but Aimee and Fritz do not come back to life. Instead, the younger brother and sister decide to start over as a married couple, taking the clown with them.

After preview screenings in early July 1928, a new ending was shot that was a curious variation of Murnau's original "Treatment." Instead of Fritz falling accidentally, because of his own recklessness, it is Aimee who falls. She deliberately lets go of her trapeze out of despair. She is assumed dead, but she revives and tells the repentant Fritz that she loves him. This is the ending that was used when 4 Devils premiered in October 1928 with a synchronized Movietone score. Aimee was renamed Marion (the title of the film's theme song) and Fritz became the more American-sounding Charles.

A letter from cinematographer Ernest Palmer to Sol Wurtzel, general superintendent of the studio, shows that the "new ending" of 4 *Devils* was not anticipated and gives us another glimpse of the consequences that Murnau's perfectionism could have on his coworkers.

> Dear Sir:
>
> I can't feel that when you agreed to my being taken off the payroll, which was the day after I was operated on, that you had taken into consideration the amount of work and effort I had put into the productions I have photographed since *Seventh Heaven*, having photographed all of Mr. Borzage's pictures, except his present one, and all of Mr. Murnau's pictures since that time, and as you must know the Murnau productions were big and killing ones for a cameraman, with all the overtime they entailed and irregular hours for meals.
>
> You could say that my contract reads that when I am incapacitated my salary stops, true enough, but my contract doesn't read that I should work days on one production and nights on another, as I did when I was photographing with Mr. Borzage in the day time on *The River* and for a couple of weeks, worked until two and three every morning with Mr. Murnau photographing the new ending on *The Four Devils* . . . . Now that I have had the ulcers removed from my stomach I will be a much better man and should be alright and quite strong again very shortly.
>
> I am,
>
> Yours Truly,
>
> Ernest Palmer[62]

Although Palmer's letter was written in April 1929 after Murnau had left Fox, the ending he refers to can only be the silent release version because of the production dates of Borzage's *The River*.

All of the variations on a "happy ending" to an inherently tragic story undercut its force, at least on paper, although the version Murnau wanted to release was the darkest of the three (Aimee as nemesis, how couple dies). But they were nothing compared to the changes imposed on 4 *Devils* when the studio decided to re-release it with a different ending and dialogue. Two aspects of this operation are significant: first, the absurdity of the story solution and the inappropriateness of the dialogue; second, that by

the time it was shot, Murnau had already run into insurmountable problems with *Our Daily Bread* and had ended his employment at Fox. In the
late spring of 1929, with the studio in Los Angeles already transformed by
the opening of Movietone City and with William Fox absorbed in monumental takeovers (he bought Loew's in February), Murnau had nothing to
do with the "talking sequences."[63]

On February 18, 1929, the first Academy Awards were announced, honoring the films from the 1927–1928 season. *Sunrise* won in three categories: best actress (Janet Gaynor for her combined performances in *Sunrise*, *Street Angel*, and *Seventh Heaven*); cinematography (Charles Rosher
and Karl Struss); and "unique and artistic picture" (Fox Films). Rochus
Gliese won honorable mention for art direction. But at the time of the
announcement, Murnau had only five days left until his contract with Fox
ended. The ceremony took place on May 18, without Murnau and without William Fox: Sheehan accepted the award for the studio.[64] In March,
Murnau and Robert Flaherty had formed a production company, and on
May 12 Murnau set sail on his yacht from San Pedro, the port of Los Angeles, for French Polynesia and a filmmaking venture far from studio interference.[65]

A Fox Story document dated May 22, 1929, is titled: "'4 Devils' Directed by F. W. Murnau. Photographed by L. W. O'Connell. Dialog as
taken from the screen. Talking Sequences. 2047 feet."[66] Doubtless Murnau never saw it. His secretary, Rose Kearin, wrote to him the day after
she attended the gala Los Angeles premiere of the new version on June 10:
"It's quite changed from your story and Mary startles everyone when she
suddenly speaks after almost an entire evening of silence."[67] The program
announced "Miss Gaynor's First Movietone Dialogue Triumph in which
The Public will hear for the first time from the screen 'the voice with a
soul.'" A few credits had been added since the film's first release: "Staged by
A. H. Van Buren and A. F. Erickson, Dialogue by John Hunter Booth."[68]
Fox's publicity stressed that Van Buren and Booth had years of experience
working on Broadway and were well qualified to handle dialogue. Erickson
had previously been Murnau's assistant. Another credit went to cinematographer L. W. O'Connell, who worked alongside Ernest Palmer on the
original production. These were the men responsible for creating the new
ending before the film went into general release.[69]

What was "quite changed" from Murnau's silent *4 Devils*? Adding dialogue and replacing the director, writer, and chief cinematographer were bound to make a difference, but that was not all. In this version, Marion (Janet Gaynor) succeeds in speaking to Charles (Charles Morton) after she follows him to the vamp's home, and, in his presence, she is treated disparagingly by the rich Lady (Mary Duncan).[70] (Unlike the script indications, the characters retain their names from the first release.) After Marion leaves, Charles turns against the vamp and leaves her definitively, but in order to maintain the story structure whereby Charles doesn't arrive at the circus until the moment before his act is supposed to begin, rather than succumbing to champagne and sex, he is hit by a car and knocked unconscious. He wakes up in a hospital just in time to run to the circus as his performance is about to begin. The rest seems to correspond to the first version: Marion falls from her trapeze, but she lives and tells Charles that she loves him. The quality of the dialogue, however, is exactly as Hervé Dumont characterized the talking scenes added to Borzage's *Lucky Star*, released by Fox at the end of 1929: "Not only does the dialogue add nothing, its overexplicitness works against and reduces the metaphorical dimension of the story. There are moments when the banality of what is said paralyzes the spectator's imagination."[71] Strangely, the reviews didn't mention any story changes: they commented almost exclusively on the quality of the sound recording of the principal actors' voices. The main selling point of the second release was "Janet Gaynor Talks." Perhaps eliminating the final seduction scene and thereby reducing Mary Duncan's screen time was a response to the critics who had complained that she played the vamp in an outmoded, exaggerated manner. Or maybe newcomer Duncan had stolen the show, as *Variety*'s reviewer of the silent version believed: "All you see or think of in the picture is Mary Duncan. . . . Janet Gaynor has nothing and does nothing to stand out here; she and the others are completely submerged by Miss Duncan."[72] The same review gave Murnau high praise, even though *4 Devils* was characterized as another film, like *Sunrise*, that probably would not earn the profits expected of such an expensive production. It came close, though, to being "box office" for the American market, and the sets, photography, and direction were superior. "It looks as though there is a big picture in Murnau. Maybe it will be his next, and if one, then more. For he classes among the big directors."

FROM *OUR DAILY BREAD* TO *CITY GIRL*

> Nothing suits a director any better than to hop on a train with his company
> and go somewhere, no matter where it is, as long as he can get away from
> the studio.
>
> —William Fox, December 27, 1917 [73]

The first record we have of Murnau's involvement with *Our Daily Bread*
is his letter to William Fox of December 22, 1927. In August and September of the previous year, the studio had acquired the rights to the source
play, "The Mud Turtle" by Elliott Lester, after a positive reader's report and
a script adaptation by Willis Goldbeck had been submitted. The project
was revived in March 1928 with a new synopsis and positive recommendation. Herman Bing translated the play into German, and, beginning in the
spring of 1928, Berthold Viertel began to write a series of three drafts of
the script, with some contributions by Marion Orth. The first script with a
shot breakdown is dated July 7, 1928, and carries Marion Orth's name. The
final script, by Viertel and Orth, is undated. [74]

Evidently the studio was considering sending Murnau to shoot *Our
Daily Bread* on location (Chicago and a wheat farm in Minnesota). In
April a company scout, Tommy Tomlinson, went to Minneapolis and
Duluth, sending back word that he had "all the dope on grain elevators,
milling methods and shipping of grain operations. I also took some pretty
good pictures of locations Murnau might want. I will be in Chicago and
vicinity for at least a week longer, as I want to be fully prepared on locations and data for Sheehan and Murnau." At his request, International
Harvester sent Fox a promotional film that Tomlinson thought "might be
of interest to Murnau" and a note drawing attention to "five scenes showing
our McCormick-Deering tractor pulling our different types of harvester-
threshers." [75] But Oregon had wheat fields too, and it was much closer to
Los Angeles. Only two months after Tomlinson's memos, arrangements
had been made for the farm scenes to be shot in Oregon. The city realism
of contemporary Chicago would be sacrificed to studio sets.

While legend has it that Murnau bought a farm in Oregon to make
Our Daily Bread—taken as a sign of his extravagance as well as his desire
for authenticity—in fact the studio purchased a large field of standing
wheat, which it would sell after the harvest, along with the use of the
house and barn on the premises and the right to tear down and remove

everything else in sight—buildings (the chicken house was to be moved intact), trees, any "nature" growing there, and rubbish.[76] Cinematographer L. W. O'Connell recalled, "We took a whole apple orchard out and planted it in wheat. You'd take stubs of wheat and put them in plaster of Paris all around the house. The old man was so wheat hungry that he planted the wheat right up to the door. . . . Such a perfectionist we had [in Murnau], everything had to be so real."[77] The location was transformed into Murnau's image of an endless expanse of wheat, without any space wasted, to show the obsessional character of the story's patriarch, the farmer Tustine. Two or three small additional structures must have been constructed to Murnau's taste by set designer Harry Oliver. Instead of using a modern tractor to pull the harvester, Murnau got an impressive team of mules. The machinery, sixty to seventy, and a farm crew were leased to cut the wheat on August 20, or soon after, but the schedule was changed to September 11 because Murnau had an emergency operation for appendicitis at the end of July.[78] The start date for the production was revised accordingly to August 30.[79] Two houses in the town of Pendleton to be used as residences were leased through November 1 (originally October 1), as was the property with the wheat field. By September 27, the wheat had been harvested and sold.[80]

Ernest Palmer's stories about the demands that Murnau made on his skills when shooting Our Daily Bread do not sound so different from his 4 Devils experiences, except that the scale of the production was much smaller. Murnau would have ideas for visualization as he went along that he wanted put into action right away: "Murnau was always putting his eyes through the camera. . . . He was very, very particular about [working with the photography]. I used to have the effects man quite frequently with me when I was shooting because he'd spring some hot ones sometimes, and I had to take a quick revamping of something in order to get the effect he had in his mind. Murnau was inclined to set up [a scene] knowing that he was going to use some kind of effect to cut to. He would be sure to make it perfect all the way through. . . ."[81]

The first part of the film, which takes place in Chicago, was shot in the studio after returning from Oregon (The waitresses' contracts begin November 26.) There, too, Palmer recalled that Murnau wanted a particular effect that was difficult to achieve: "For one scene where we had an elevated train going by the windows at the back, I had to fix up a thing revolving with openings in it, and [put] a very strong arc [light] in it, so that when the elevated was supposed to go by, we'd see these lights flash. A fellow like Borzage wouldn't bother too much with a thing like that, whereas Murnau would concentrate on it to get realism."[82] This effect was created for one of the most unforgettable scenes in the film, when Kate (Mary Duncan) returns from the drudgery of work to her hot, barren room with a half-dead geranium that she tries to keep alive and a wind-up mechanical bird that comforts her. As she looks out the window, where no bit of nature can be seen, the lights from the passing El reflect off her face, emphasizing her longing for what she imagines life in the country must be like. Perhaps Murnau also wanted this subtle visual effect to help keep the focus on Duncan and away from the obviously fake high-rise buildings visible through her windows.

Compared to the elaborate special effects and camera pyrotechnics in *Faust* and *Sunrise*, which seem to have been important in *4 Devils* too, the look of *City Girl* is spare and simple. The visual effects that Palmer describes are subdued. Was this the result of studio interference? Probably Viertel's first draft had begun with an elaborate parallel montage between the farm and the city, where Tustine has sent his inexperienced son to sell the season's wheat.

Heavy farmer's hands open a bible at the Gospel of Matthew: "Behold, a sower went forth to sow. . . ." A picture moves through the pages of the Bible. . . . A peasant toiling up an incline behind his plow, as in olden days. His vigorous back indicates the heavy labor . . . and we see him walking and seeding the soil. We cannot distinguish his features, but we see him wipe the perspiration from his brow with his sleeve. . . . Glaring contrast: Modern machines appear in long rows, machines which turn the earth and distribute the seeds in one operation. . . .

And the Bible further reads that: "some of it fell upon stony places . . . But other fell into good ground, and brought forth fruit, some a hundred-fold, some sixty-fold, some thirty-fold. . . ." We see the grain shooting up from the ground, waving wheatfields, near the time of the harvest. Yes, sixty-fold and thirty-fold!

Suddenly men appear, shouting, perspiring, gesticulating men on the Chicago Board of Trade. The electric lights are more glaring than the sunlight. Giant electric fans whirl madly, and upon the wall there appears a Menetekel-like writing, the traveling lettering, announcing the market prices. Giant telegram tapes, the one fading into the other. Wheat prices are falling! An exciting forenoon on the Board—falling prices!

Up on the visitors' gallery, leaning over the balustrade, stands the country yokel Lem Tustine, staring at the writing on the wall. By his side is the foxy little broker with the perspiring bald spot. He roars into Lem's ear: "Sell! Sell—wheat is dropping!" "WHEAT IS DROPPING—" a chorus of madmen is yelling below. No Movietone on earth has ever recorded such a bedlam of voices.[83]

Viertel and Orth's scripts contain scenes intended to convey subjective states or less personalized impressions through elaborate visualizations (dreams, mental images, superimpositions, montage sequences) as well as passages that are closer to the spare linearity of the film as we know it. In this example, verses from the Bible appear to generate the wheat, and the most rudimentary methods of farming are contrasted with modern machines, efficient and impersonal, rows of them, which provide a link with the dehumanizing modernity of the city, where the Chicago Board of Trade translates grain into money. Viertel moves from these general impressions into Lem's bombarded subjectivity when the broker shouts at him, amidst the "chorus of madmen yelling below" (conveyed through Movietone), to sell before wheat prices fall any lower.

Eventually the story was cut to its essential elements, and the visual effects were scaled back. (Viertel was with Murnau during the shoot in Oregon.)[84] In the film as we know it, the only montage sequence left is all too brief, showing the phases of the harvest. (Several shots taken from this montage also run under the opening credits.) Lem (Charles Farrell) takes the train from his family's farm in Minnesota to sell the wheat at the price his father has named, but the wheat market suddenly begins to collapse and he is forced to sell at a loss. In the meantime he falls in love with Kate, a waitress he has gotten to know at the diner where he eats every day. They say goodbye, painfully, but then they find each other again (an exquisitely moving scene) and Lem broaches marriage indirectly. The next thing we know, they are leaning against each other happily in inexpensive upright seats on the night train going back to the farm. Secondary characters who were present in the script have been eliminated, such as Lem's broker, and scenes showing more of the grain futures market, the shock of the city's modernity as Lem experienced it, the marriage at City Hall, and Lem's chaste visit to Kate's room to help her pack. At the farm in the black of night, a boy rides up to the open kitchen window on a bicycle and hands Tustine a telegram (a stunning shot) with the news that Lem is returning with a bride. The farmer's disgust is conveyed by the word "WAITRESS" that floats up from the message to fill the screen.

The couple's arrival in the sunshine of the next day is the most lyrically beautiful scene in *City Girl*. They run after each other through the tall wheat, the camera gliding along with them until they fall down out of sight, caught up in passion for a moment. If this fits the dream of the country that Kate had in her mind, it won't last long. No sooner are they greeted with warmth by Lem's mother and little sister than the stern Tustine walks in and, refusing to acknowledge Kate, abruptly asks Lem the price he got for the wheat. As his father reads the receipt, Lem deteriorates into a fearful boy. Tustine berates him harshly, blames Kate, and summarily orders Lem to get dressed for work. Alone with Kate, Tustine implies menacingly that she is nothing but a streetwalker. She talks back to him with spirit and, when he grabs her wrists angrily and twists them, she struggles against him, finally biting his hand to free herself. Furious, he slaps her face so hard that she is knocked back against the wall. When Kate tells Lem that his father struck her, he seems ready to have it out with Tustine. But his mother's eyes plead with her son, and Lem, looking helpless, tells Kate he cannot strike his own father. Kate retreats from him, forcing Lem to sleep in the attic on the night their marriage should be consummated.

The next day, reapers come to harvest the wheat. Kate finds herself back in the thankless servant role she has just escaped in the city: serving food to men who measure her up sexually and make jokes about her. In the original play and in early versions of the script, Kate plots revenge to get even with Tustine, but in the film the slightest thing that might cast a negative light on her character has been eliminated. Duncan's performance endows Kate with depth and complexity: she understands the ways of the city, but she is pure of heart and no schemer. Jean George Auriol's tribute to the actress after seeing this version of the film in 1930 was exactly right: "I think Mary Duncan is the most intelligent woman in the cinema. She has the gift of exceptional insight, intensified at times by troubled intuitions."[85] She is an ideal match for Lem, for he is just as true, but he is simpler, inexperienced in every respect, and sees no way out of the stand-off between his father and his already-estranged wife. Kate goes about helping Lem's sympathetic mother and sister, trying to ignore Lem until he will stand up for her and for his own independence.

During the night a rising hailstorm threatens to destroy the wheat. Tustine wakens the men and promises to pay overtime to save the crop. When he becomes desperate, he vows to shoot anyone who attempts to leave. One of the reapers, Mac, makes a play for Kate. Tustine walks into the house from the dark as she is bandaging a wound on Mac's arm and assumes the worst. He announces spitefully that he is going to tell Lem what kind of woman she is. Later, Mac enters Kate's bedroom to tell her he has settled her score with Tustine. The reapers are leaving and the wheat will be ruined. She refuses him, but Mac threatens to tell Tustine that getting the men to leave was her idea. Afraid, she pretends to agree to go away with him, and then she writes a note of explanation for Lem—she is going back to the city alone because he believed his father's lies. Lem finds it and, realizing his injustices and his loss, he challenges Mac, who is already on the buckboard with the reapers. The two men begin fighting, the others scatter, and the horses take off at a gallop. Lem wins and reins in the horses so that he can go after Kate, but Tustine mistakes him for a reaper trying to leave the farm and he raises his rifle. Lem sees him, but Tustine doesn't hear Lem's urgent call, conveyed to us by the title growing bigger and bigger to fill the screen: "FATHER." Tustine shoots just as he realizes that he is aiming at his own son. His shot hits the buckboard's lantern and the screen goes black. Tustine breaks down, and then holds Lem, untouched by the gunfire, who makes him understand the harm he has caused him and Kate. Tustine offers to let the men leave, but they decide to stay and bring in the wheat. Lem finds Kate and persuades her to return, Tustine welcomes her gratefully into the family, and everyone is reconciled at the end.

Studio interference is easier to picture when we correlate the sequence of events in the production of Murnau's last two films for Fox with the studio's increasing involvement with sound. 4 Devils had a long production schedule. Shooting began on January 3, 1928, the film was previewed at the beginning of July, and it premiered in New York with a new ending, a synchronized score, and no dialogue on October 3, nine months after the start date. This was the same month that Movietone City opened, dedicated to Fox's future as the preeminent sound studio. On February 4, 1929, Murnau signed his termination agreement with Sheehan. It took effect two weeks later, about the same time that William Fox bought Loew's. The dialogue ending was shot in May,[86] and the part-talkie version of 4 Devils was released in June.

In comparison, the production of Our Daily Bread was almost interminable—literally. Nineteen months passed from the beginning of shooting (August 30, 1928) until it was screened for a few days, without a premiere, in April 1930 as the 50 percent dialogue *City Girl* in a New York theater described as a "home of double features and a 16-hour grind."[87] Murnau's loss of control over the film and his career at Fox was underscored by the timing of the second Academy Awards ceremony only a few weeks later: Ernest Palmer had been nominated for *4 Devils*. One cannot help but suspect that *City Girl* had been delayed so much by indecision about how to add dialogue and change the story structure to make it more commercial, and that the attempts to patch together scenes reshot on the Fox lot with what Murnau had already finished were so awkward (according to the Pressbook, wheatfields were re-created in the studio) that it might have seemed more cost effective to shelve it.

Murnau's production began a good month before the first version of *4 Devils* opened. The original plan was to shoot *Our Daily Bread* silent and release it with a synchronized score. But by late 1928 (the city sequences were shot at the end of November), that option seemed less and less viable. William Fox, Murnau's former champion, was tied up with aggressive expansion deals. Murnau moved down the chain of command to Sheehan and then even lower, to Sol Wurtzel—men who were not convinced that the directors who had brought Fox to prominence with quality productions would be able to make the transition to sound effectively. In any event, sound was the road to Fox's new horizons, the studio already had prestige. Murnau's plans for *Our Daily Bread* were undoubtedly cut back for budgetary reasons—not only special visual effects but also the realism he wanted for the scenes set in Chicago and, in all probability, the amount of time showing the daytime harvesting scenes and the emergency harvest at night by the light of lanterns (only a few shots remain).

The silent version, made for foreign markets, was not finalized until a full year after shooting began, at the end of August 1929.[88] This was six months after Murnau had stopped working for Fox and over three months after he had left the country. The part-talkie version—like *4 Devils* it was "staged by" A. H. Van Buren and A. F. Erickson and most likely photographed by L. W. O'Connell—was completed on November 19 according to a Fox memo, but even if adjustments were still being made (the document for *City Girl* titled "Dialogue as Taken from the Screen" is dated November 30), the film didn't appear in New York and Los Angeles until

April 1930, five months later.[89] *Variety* commented that it had been listed on Fox's production schedule two years earlier as a Murnau silent super-production: "Then they called it 'Bread' and it was to have been an epic of the wheat fields. . . . 'City Girl' is mediocre material for the second runs. The grinds, of course, can use it."[90]

Was Murnau, perfectionist that he was, capable of overlooking the fact that a second ending was going to be shot for *4 Devils* without him, a new version that would still carry his name as director? Or had he refused to participate in it? Was this part of his decision to leave Fox? Although it would seem from the outset that the production of *Our Daily Bread* began too late to be released by Fox in America without dialogue, that issue must not have been decided absolutely while Murnau was still working on the film, because he prefaced one of the points of a memo listing seven rec-ommendations for changes to be made after his departure: "If talk should be added to the picture. . . ." If dialogue would have been a major com-ponent of the film under Murnau's direction, then—in these days of the part-talkie at Fox—he would have had to work with a specialized dialogue writer and an intermediary director who would "stage scenes" from the per-spective of sound recording. Can it be a coincidence that Murnau's termi-nation agreement was settled at almost exactly the same time that Shee-han notified Wurtzel that he was hiring the East Coast playwright Elliott Lester to write the dialogue for the film?[91] Lester's source play, "The Mud Turtle," takes place entirely on the farm, and that is where the dialogue begins in the "part-talkie" version. In the play, Lester had given Kate such crass, pedestrian lines as: "I feel sorta like I'm buttin' in like a fly in a cup o' hot coffee" and "As soon as I saw Lem I knew he was on the square, an' I says to myself, gee, he can punch my meal ticket any time he wants to."[92] Murnau's conception of Kate was diametrically opposed to this clichéd type, and he had made her the center of his film.

Murnau's recommendations for completing the film are cited in their entirety by Eisner, who describes his statement as a letter to William Fox. A copy of the original document has not yet come to light, and we may wonder whether, at this late date, it really was a letter to William Fox, in the hope of bypassing the local studio heads, or whether this might have been the memo that Rose Kearin referred to in a letter she wrote to Mur-nau in Tahiti on July 4. "Buddy [A. F. Erickson] sent for your comment on 'Daily Bread,' but I did not give it to him. I reminded him that he was to come here and read it, for I believe that was what you suggested, so he did."

The silent version was completed before the part-talkie, but not immediately after Murnau's departure. Murnau's personal friends, the noted title writers and editors Katherine Hilliker and H. H. Caldwell, did not begin work on it until early July 1929. They are most likely the people responsible for saving Murnau's vision of his film to the greatest extent possible under the circumstances.[93] Hilliker and Caldwell had begun their association with Murnau at least as early as August 1926, when they wrote titles for the American version of *Faust*. They were familiar enough with the supposedly authoritarian German director to address him affectionately as "you poor dodo" after they saw the preview of *Tabu* in New York in February 1931, and sometimes they signed telegrams to him Dr. Jekyll and Mrs. Hyde.[94] Hilliker and Caldwell were no ordinary title writers. In August 1927 the studio confirmed that they were to receive "publicity credit as Production Editors on such pictures as you will edit and title" and that no one else at Fox was referred to in that capacity.[95] What exactly did Hilliker and Caldwell do? According to Katherine Hilliker, "Our duties ranged from consultation on story and cast, and the supervising of scripts before production, to the job of preparing the picture, after it was shot, for theater presentation. While we worked from time to time on program pictures, our chief concern was with the big specials like *Four Sons* (Ford), *Seventh Heaven* (Borzage), and *Carmen* (Raoul Walsh), and we were given practical control of the productions upon which we worked from the time the director made his first cut until we had it in shape to show an audience."[96] *Mother Machree*, *Sunrise* (titles only, they specified), *Seventh Heaven*, *Street Angel*, *The River*, and *Lucky Star* were among the many other films they handled.[97] (They were on a year-long vacation trip when *4 Devils* was loaded with 120 titles.) Hilliker wrote to Murnau that "*Sunrise* was the only picture we ever had handed us that didn't have to be re-constructed in the editing and titles; and in most cases we had to write in new sequences and have them shot in order to fill up the bad holes left by their pet writers. During our last contract on the lot, practically every big director they had asked to have us assigned on stories."[98] They reported to Sol Wurtzel, who must have had a great deal of authority in postproduction, considering how he was able to change *The River*. According to Hilliker's report: "I have been at the studio a good deal, doing quite a bit of work with the retakes. Sol had a brainstorm and added a sequence in the first reel, having the old woman come in and offer to help Rosalee after the arrest. It is terrible and I have been fighting Sol bitterly but amicably ever since I heard about it, but only succeeded in toning it down."[99]

The couple finished *City Girl* at the end of August 1929.[100] Their screen credit reads "edited and titled by." The second set of contracts, for shooting the dialogue section of the film, specified that work was to commence at the end of October and the beginning of November.[101] So perhaps no reshooting was done for the silent version but simply reediting and title rewrites, despite some additional shots requested in Hilliker and Caldwell's seven-page "Suggested new ending" submitted on August 2, which they deemed necessary "to make the picture releasable." (Their draft begins after Tustine shoots the lantern, barely missing Lem.) Hilliker and Caldwell concluded their memo, "As we have stated before, we believe the present ending to be highly detrimental to the success of the production." Their suggestions were not followed, but we don't know if the present ending is the one they recommended changing or still another one.

It was out of the question that Hilliker and Caldwell, or other experienced title writers, would be assigned to transform their titles to dialogue, which could have helped maintain a continuity of tone and restraint throughout the film. Soon they would find it difficult to find work in any capacity in Hollywood. The presumed dialogue specialist Elliott Lester wrote some nine drafts and revisions between about May and November 1929, and John Hunter Booth, the Broadway expert for *4 Devils*, contributed an early draft. Murnau's first recommendation for change ("which I would have made myself if I had worked longer on the picture") was to move the incident when Tustine slaps Kate just after she arrives at the farm. "I would take it out here," Murnau wrote, "because there is no sufficient reason for this girl, after she has received the slap, to stay on with the family instead of returning to the city." Instead, it should come near the end, when the father catches Kate with Mac. "In all scenes where he appears with the girl, build up the danger, so that in the climax the final night, it already has its dangerous background.... On this final evening, the scene between Mac and the girl should be by far more sensuous, so that we, as an audience, really fear that the girl might surrender." When Tustine sees them together and denounces Kate, "we should have the girl forget all her good feelings that might have grown through the love of the pure boy. She should become the hard-boiled waitress, who is only used to fighting men. She should yell at the old man all the truth this old tyrant could be told— of what he has done to her; what he has done to his son; what he has done to his whole family; and she should say it in the most bold, vigorous manner, so the audience would feel relieved that at last there is someone to tell him the truth. As an answer to this, which the old man considers an insult, outraged, he would slap her and call her a streetwalker."[102]

According to the scripts and continuity for the part-talking version, the slap was moved to the place that Murnau had suggested, but without building up a sense of menace between Mac and Kate prior to that point. And the tension between Kate and Lem has disappeared. Now they are blissful newlyweds who speak lines that would have been impossible in the story that the silent version tells, such as:

> LEM: Are you tired, darling?
>
> KATE: No I'm not. It's fun workin' for you.
>
> LEM: Don't you—don't you go workin' too hard now, and get yourself all tired out, will you?[103]

Kate isn't abruptly ordered out of her bedroom by Tustine to feed the reapers. Instead, she tells Lem's mother cheerfully, "Come on, ma, you're going to serve dinner and let me help. Feedin' gorillas is my racket." Kate becomes subservient in a much more radical and invisible manner in the new version of the film. She loses her place at the center of the dramatic conflict, which had been a test of will between the city woman and the country patriarch. The emphasis shifts to Lem, who plays a much more active, decisive role in keeping with the title of Lester's first draft, "Manhood." After Lem wins the fight with Mac, he confronts his father boldly and tells Kate to pack because they are going to leave together for the city. Kate becomes the mediator between Lem and his father, instead of Lem playing this role as he had in the silent version: she urges her husband to stay on the farm where they are needed. Lem forces Mac to apologize to Kate, but not his father, who never does apologize. Critic J. F. Lundy, who knew the play, criticized City Girl perceptively—except that he attributed its problems to the wrong person: "F. W. Murnau directed the production and has stuck closely to the legit version; too much, in fact, for the production's good. . . . Murnau has made a mistake in not developing more the character of the father. The climax comes with only a few sequences to show his stern nature. . . ."[104] Coincidentally, the review appeared the same day that the *Exhibitors Herald-World* broke the story that William Fox had sold off his shares in the companies that carried his name. Sheehan, who retained his position, announced: "War is over and we're back in the amusement business."[105]

When Murnau wrote to William Fox about this project at the end of 1927, he described it as "a tale about wheat, about the sacredness of bread, about the estrangement of the modern city dwellers and their ignorance about Nature's sources of sustenance." But that description doesn't fit Lester's play or any of the drafts of the script or the version of *City Girl*. Tustine thinks of his wheat only in terms of its cash value, setting a repressive tone from the beginning when he drives his young daughter to tears for playing with a few stalks of grain: "I raise wheat to sell, not to play with. Every grain counts." He takes them away from her and places them carefully inside his Bible, his face stony. When Tustine recites the Lord's Prayer before the midday meal ("Give us this day our daily bread"), his stern demeanor makes it evident that "the sacredness of bread" is no simple matter in this story. Tustine's moral authority has already been undermined because he puts monetary profit ahead of love for his family. The play, and to some extent the early drafts of the script, explains Tustine's harshness and his fixation on money as the result of emotional strain, because he will lose the farm if the wheat is not sold at a high enough price. His impulsive fits of anger give way to apologies and he shows affection sometimes. In the film, these softening touches have been eliminated, except for one brief moment with his wife when Tustine worries that if Lem "doesn't sell right, I'll never be able to make both ends meet." This single glimpse of Tustine's human side is quickly forgotten, for he rules his domain by unyielding laws he takes from the Bible. His family is reduced to silence in his presence. The moment he enters a scene, spontaneity and life die. In the film, he has become an abstract, negative force, prefiguring Hitu's role in *Tabu*.

Murnau takes care to show that in the country as well as in the city the physical presence of wheat is overcome by a dehumanizing abstraction that kills the pleasure that is so beautifully conveyed, for example, by the young couple running through the wheat fields before Kate is introduced to Lem's family. As in *Tabu*, abstraction goes hand in hand with a cash economy that is almost incomprehensible to the young lovers. Very early in the film, Lem's mother shapes bread dough to bake in the oven while Tustine sits at the table carefully writing out numbers that translate grain into dollars. His calculations (we see them in insert shots) show the price per bushel that will give him the money he needs. A dissolve takes us to the (Chicago) Board of Trade and a higher level of abstraction divorced from the physical presence of grain. The camera pans left over huge panels of numbers, stopping at "Wheat." A man quickly wipes away chalk figures, replacing them with lower fractions: the value of wheat has already fallen below Tustine's expectations even before Lem arrives in the city. We have seen him in the train on his way to Chicago, reading his father's note with his calculations and a reminder that if he doesn't get that price "it will be serious." After a brief look at the wheat futures board, we return to Tustine's figures back at the farm, but we have no way of knowing what, exactly, is at stake in the amount he has stipulated. The issue, strangely enough, does not arise later on, only the threat of the hailstorm. In the film, the need for money itself remains abstract (again prefiguring *Tabu*).

The story shifts from the farm to the city through the bread that people eat every day, not the abstraction of numbers corresponding to the arbitrariness of market value. As Tustine cuts bread for his family's meal, the image dissolves to slices of bread emerging from an automatic machine in a diner, where Kate puts them on lunch plates, and where she will soon become acquainted with Lem. Over thirty meals later (according to his meal ticket), Lem writes out his calculations in the diner as carefully as his father had done, figuring the price he got for the wheat compared to what he was supposed to get. The loss represented by these numbers will end up nearly killing him, first his spirit and then his life itself.

The silent version draws strong lines of tension between Kate and Tustine even before she arrives at the farm. It is from his point of view that the word "WAITRESS" emerges from Lem's telegram to dominate the screen, indicating the depth of Tustine's prejudice against her as an abstract figure representing danger to the world he has tightly controlled. Not merely an outsider, she is a sign of his son's independence, a true rival for his allegiance, and she will be blamed for the financial loss in the wheat transaction. The Oedipal dynamics are obvious enough. To show another level of conflict, Murnau stages three scenes almost identically, through point-of-view shots, to show how Kate is oppressed in the country exactly as she had been in the city because she is forced into the same dehumanizing category that had dominated Tustine's reading of the telegram: waitress. At the diner in Chicago, two men sitting on stools next to Lem had elbowed each other and made jokes when Kate stood on a stool and reached up to the top of a coffee machine, revealing her legs above her stockings. One of them tried to flirt with her and then grabbed her wrist. Lem defended her and won her heart because he was ready to fight that man. The same obvious crudeness greets Kate at the farmhouse after Tustine orders her out of her bedroom to serve lunch to the hired hands who have come to harvest the grain. Her door opens directly onto a long table filled with leering faces that fill the screen eager to see this woman from the city (the men have already heard that she and Lem are having marital problems). Mary Duncan's face and her entire body show how Kate has to struggle for dignity and to keep the men from touching her as she comes close to them to serve coffee from a heavy metal pot. This time, unlike in the city, Lem doesn't intervene. Bewildered by his father's hostility toward Kate and her reaction, he is immobilized.

Murnau then adds a second scene to emphasize Kate's subjection in the country and how it is killing her spirit. As the men line up for the lunch that she has brought to the field on a buckboard, they stare at her, grinning from ear to ear. Kate is visibly uncomfortable, yet she tries to do her job and ignore what they have on their minds. Murnau uses exactly the same shot/reverse shot structure in the wheat fields that he used in the diner (here, the camera pans down Kate's body from behind, resting on a close shot of her legs, and then shows us the men's faces as they make jokes to each other). Kate is as isolated in the sunshine outdoors as she had been in her lonely room in the city or in the dark farmhouse. Lem sits apart from the others, refusing to eat, demoralized. This is a much more complex portrait than Murnau had in mind when he originally wrote to William Fox about his idea for *Our Daily Bread*. The "city girl" in this film is nothing like the one-dimensional vamps in *Sunrise* and *4 Devils*. Kate yearns for nature as a kind of salvation, but her dream is blocked by Tustine's humiliation of his son and his violent rejection of her—not only his physical brutality but also the demeaning way he gives her orders and the sexual dimension of Kate's subordination as a waitress, which is intended to punish her rather than allow her to do her share of the work as a member of the family. To the extent to which Kate remains a "waitress," she cannot ignore the fact that she is excluded from the family, nor can the men who look at her.

Finally, nature itself becomes threatening, as if the violence of actions and their internalization leads to an overwhelming moral darkness. Like *Nosferatu* and *Tabu*, night dominates the last part of *City Girl*, when the purest characters are threatened with extinction by those who operate by inhuman, inexorable laws. The metaphor driving the narrative—an apparently idyllic environment hides a lethal force of negation—becomes literal in the black of night when a hailstorm endangers the entire crop (the loss that Lem incurred in Chicago would be trivial by comparison) and Tustine nearly kills his own son. How true to the logic of the film that Tustine cannot hear Lem's voice calling "FATHER," just as he has refused to listen to Lem or Kate since they arrived at the farm. How accurate a cinematic representation of Tustine's single-minded negativity that when he shoots at Lem, he shatters the lantern. Without any light, he has to wait as long as it takes for Lem to reach him to know that he has not hit him. In that interval, the father himself dies. When Lem stands before him, Tustine holds onto him tightly, only half-revived. His reaction is remarkably similar to Kate's when she found Lem again in the city after she thought she had lost him forever. She seemed to collapse from the inside out, expressing how her entire being was at stake. As in this scene with his father, Lem gently persuaded her to come back to life. Now Lem finds Kate walking alone in the dark, trying to get the train back to the city. She reacts to him with that same visceral mixture of hope and resignation, dropping her defenses in the presence of the man she loves. Lem brings her back through the gate that his father now holds open for them, and he introduces Kate to him as if for the first time. They are able to begin again. This second chance is the happy ending that closes the film, but it is followed by another literal descent into darkness as the father drives the buckboard with the couple away from us into the night.

If Murnau were not completely responsible for the silent version of *City Girl* as we know it, I believe that it was a question of his not having the time or resources to fill in certain gaps in the story (the night harvest and the threat of the hailstorm are barely present). The internal consistencies of the film as it stands, including the direction of the actors, are too strong and seem, in retrospect, too close to the logic of the more finely shaped *Tabu* not to have been created by Murnau, even if certain shots may have been made by an assistant director (which would not have been extraordinary in any event) and even if Murnau were absent during the final editing, which was supervised by his capable friends Hilliker and Caldwell.

FILMS OF THE FUTURE

Murnau's career was cut short by his death at the age of forty-two in an automobile accident the week before *Tabu* premiered in New York. It was released with a grand opening, like all of his films except *City Girl*. *Tabu* was one of the last great silent films (Chaplin's *City Lights* was the other famous example) at a point in time when nondialogue films were, for all practical purposes, a thing of the past. Fewer and fewer films were even being produced in dual versions. "It is not without significance," wrote David Flaherty, "that *Tabu* was made as a silent in the beginning of the era of talkies. This was a deliberate choice, dictated not by economic but by aesthetic considerations. If *Tabu* enjoys a certain universality and timeless-ness, credit this (for that time) bold decision."[106] Murnau believed, before leaving for Tahiti, that silent (nondialogue) film would continue indefi-nitely as an art form, a quality cinema with its own specialized theaters and audience. His death coincided with the end of the silent film era. But did that mean that, had he lived, he would have given up making films rather than adapt to the changes in the industry?

Murnau was too intelligent to be opposed to dialogue forever. More-over, he had always been fascinated by new technological possibilities. This is easiest to see in his preoccupation with the film image, for instance, his interest in Fox's 70mm Grandeur process, which he envisaged premiering with the epic beauty of expansive wheat fields in *Our Daily Bread*. In the same letter to William Fox (December 22, 1927, as mentioned earlier), he had inquired about a Danish color process ("for some time I have taken quite a personal interest in this invention and have great confidence in its possibilities, particularly on account of its simplicity of shooting and pro-jecting methods"), and he expected to shoot *Tabu* in Technicolor (the early two-color version) until Colorart, the production company backing the project that had promised the equipment and operators, proved unable to finance the film.[107] Although Murnau ran into problems because he had designed *4 Devils* and, much later and more seriously, *Our Daily Bread* as nondialogue films, his problem with sound stemmed more from studio practice in the days of dual-version films (silent and part-dialogue) where "talking sections" were often written and shot by different personnel with-out regard for the overall integrity of the film, and because of the absence of William Fox, from the withdrawal of financial support for his concep-tion of *Our Daily Bread*.

While Murnau was away from Hollywood (May 12, 1929, to November 8, 1930), sound fidelity and recording practices had made rapid progress. In May 1930, Edgar Ulmer sent a lengthy report to Murnau, through Rose Kearin, about sound recording and other technological advances that he believed Murnau would find appealing. (At the time, Ulmer was trying to persuade Murnau to allow him to arrange for the distribution of his new film and to act as his intermediary for several future productions.) According to Ulmer, sound recording and postproduction equipment had improved greatly so that directors could "shoot as they did in the silent days," because sound could be handled separately from the image; the studios were no longer using the "very annoying and disturbing" dialogue director; the camera had been silenced and had become "as flexible again as it was before"; color technology had improved and become cheaper; and "Fox has turned entirely away from the use of incandescent lights which handicapped photography and were responsible for the terrible photographic results in the early stage of sound pictures." [108] If Murnau decided, along with Flaherty, to make *Tabu* without synchronized dialogue even after his experience with *Our Daily Bread*, this was probably only partly to show how eloquently its story could be conveyed without spoken words. It must also have been a practical decision based on the fact that the nonprofessional cast would not have been able to speak their lines convincingly or in English.

We have every reason to believe that Murnau's ideas about the cinema would have continued to evolve as its possibilities expanded. The modernity and what we might call the mythological realism of his last two films (each representing its own European image of Paradise and Paradise Lost, despite *City Girl*'s happy ending) demonstrated that he could make a virtue of simplicity and adjust to modest budgets if he needed to. The extremes of Murnau's career at Fox—from complete control over *Sunrise* to his eradication from the part-talking sections of *4 Devils* and *City Girl*—readied him for *Tabu*, a film that should have been a sign of things to come rather than the end of his era.

NOTES

Thanks to the following individuals for generously providing access to documents or suggestions about where I might look: Kevin Brownlow, Yves de Peretti, Richard Koszarski, Ron Magliozzi, Richard Allen, Scott Eyman,

Brian Taves, Frieda Grafe, Enno Patalas, Michael Friend, Werner Sudendorf, Emmanuelle Toulet, Bruce Williams, Luciano Berriatúa, Joseph McBride, Joe Yranski, Dennis Doros, and Matthew Solomon.

1 This letter is dated December 28, 1927 in Lotte Eisner's *Murnau* (London: Secker and Warburg, 1973), 197, but this passage appears in Murnau's letter to Fox of December 22. Fox's response is dated December 27. The correspondence that Eisner cites is not included among her papers or in the Murnau Collection at the Bibliothèque du Film (BiFi), Paris (formerly in the collection of the Cinémathèque Française).

2 Eisner, *Murnau*, 198–99. Eisner does not provide a date; and I have not located a copy of the original. I believe Murnau wrote this memo at the time he left Fox.

3 In *Lost Films* (New York: Citadel Press, 1996), Frank Thompson quotes Fox's Pressbook regarding the presentation of the title: "Most newspapers, if not all of them, would spell out the word 'four,' but in the film, *4 Devils* flashes off and on from a huge electric sign, with the figure '4' prominent, and as the name of the picture was taken from that, it was decided to copy it exactly and use the numeral" (267).

4 Robert C. Allen and Douglas Gomery, *Film History: Theory and Practice* (New York: Knopf, 1985), 93. See *Moving Picture World*, July 17, 1926, 51.

5 *Fox Folks*, July 1926, 6.

6 F. W. Murnau, "The Ideal Picture Needs No Titles," *Theatre Magazine*, January 1928, 72.

7 Of prime importance are the Fox Story, Legal and Photo Files, which are housed in the Arts-Special Collections Library, at the University of California, Los Angeles. The Legal File is missing for *4 Devils*, but the Photo Files document nearly every scene in both versions of the film. The photos from this period have been withdrawn by Twentieth Century–Fox for preservation. Murnau's legal papers with Fox are located in the William K. Everson Collection, Department of Cinema Studies, New York University. The Production Code Administration Files (at the Margaret Herrick Library, Academy of Motion Picture Arts and Sciences) are missing for *Sunrise*, *4 Devils*, and *Our Daily Bread / City Girl*. Additional sources are indicated in subsequent notes.

8 See Richard Koszarski, "City Girl," *Film Comment* (summer 1971): 20–22. Alex Gordon was responsible for finding the print. Gordon described himself as the "one man head" of Film Restoration at Twentieth Century-Fox Studios from 1968 to 1978. He salvaged 375 "lost" films the studio made between 1914 and 1935. "I found a print marked *City Girl* with Ricardo Cortez and Phyllis Brooks," Gordon wrote, "shoved behind a radiator in a nitrate vault at Fox Studios in Hollywood. When I screened it, it turned out to be the silent version of the Murnau film. I had it transferred by Foto-Kem Laboratories in Los Angeles under my deal with the Museum of Modern Art in New York,

who funded the Fox restoration program I had set up, and a safety negative and print were struck" (letter to the author, September 4, 2001).

9 Eisner, *Murnau*, 200.

10 For the endings of *4 Devils*, see Eisner, *Murnau*, 194. She based her analysis on the final script and the "Dialogue as Taken from the Screen" (bound together as a book), in the Murnau Collection, BiFi.

11 Murnau's first contract covered directing one film (title unspecified), plus "his own manuscript, including the scenario and continuity manuscript," for which he would receive $40,000 total compensation. Beyond that, he would earn $1,000 per week "additional compensation, if production is delayed for period of one month by events entirely beyond the control of Mr. Murnau, payable each week subsequent to each such delay." I have not yet found a record of Murnau's final compensation for *Sunrise*. He was also entitled to 4 percent of the money received in New York from European distribution after 50 percent of the negative cost had been recovered from the European territories. Another clause took note of Murnau's request to employ Karl Freund, "who has been working with [Murnau] for an extended period of time and who has also photographed the recently produced picture 'THE LAST MAN' [*The Last Laugh*]," indicating that if Freund were engaged, his salary would be consistent with the rate usually paid in America to "high class cameramen." (Ultimately, Charles Rosher and Karl Struss photographed *Sunrise*.) The contract stipulated a release from UFA that would allow Murnau to enter into contract with Fox.

A note to Winfield Sheehan dated February 4, 1929, from the Fox Comptroller detailed the following disbursements to Murnau relative to his second, and much more lucrative, four-year contract, dated July 8, 1926 (effective date for starting: August 21, 1927). According to the terms of his contract, Murnau was expected to make one film per year. For each additional picture he made during the four-year period, he was entitled to $25,000.

	Yearly	Weekly
1st year	$125,000	$2403.05
2nd year	$150,000	$2884.62
3rd year	$175,000	$3365.38
4th year	$200,000	$3846.15

Status to date: (payments made)
"Four Devils" $125,000
"Our Daily Bread" $68,750.11 [handwritten:] "add 3 weeks"

In the figure of $68,750.11, the salary has been included up to and including February 2, 1929. The "added 3 weeks" cover February 2 (the date these figures were drawn up) through February 23, Murnau's last day at Fox. (I have not reproduced the entire note.) Another memo, dated February 9, 1929, lists, for tax purposes, Murnau's income from Fox for 1928 ($134,855.80) and 1929, up to February 23 ($23,076.96). Murnau's termination contract included a clause about Murnau providing advisory services through August 21, but Sheehan's cover memo to Jack Leo explained that these services would not be claimed or expected. The amount specified was to be paid to Murnau in Berlin and was meant to cover his income tax in Germany so that he would not have to pay tax in both countries (Everson Collection, NYU).

12 "New Talking Film Ready For Public," *Variety*, February 25, 1927, 25.

13 *Variety*, February 15, 1927, 14; "Fox Orders Vitaphone Equipment For Installation in His Houses," *Moving Picture World*, February 19, 1927, 1 [volume p. 541].

14 See the large ads for the Roxy Theater in the *New York Herald Tribune* and the *New York Times*, April 30, 1927, 12, 25.

15 "Talking News Reel as Part of Movietone" and "Movietone" (Roxy) by Sid, *Variety*, May 4, 1927; "Movietone Newspictures Give New Interest to Certain Forms and Styles of Subjects," *Moving Picture World*, May 7, 1927, 28. A seven-minute Movietone newsreel of the "West Point Cadets" was screened for the press at the Roxy on the morning of April 29; for the public it was trimmed to four minutes.

16 Allen and Gomery, *Film History*, 123.

17 "Lindbergh on Movietone," *Variety*, May 25, 1927, 9. "Charles A. Lindbergh's take-off on his trans-Atlantic flight Friday morning was Fox-Movietoned and presented at the Roxy the same evening. The Movietone showing followed other shots of Lindbergh arriving on the field. The audience response to the first shots were [*sic*] very strong and the Movietone addition lasting about three minutes, scored even better."

Mordaunt Hall's review of three films in the *New York Times* the same day (section VII, p. 5) ended with his appraisal of the Movietone sound system as demonstrated by the Lindbergh newsreel: "The most interesting film feature at the Roxy was William Fox's Movietone of Captain Lindbergh's departure from Long Island. Not only did one hear the whirring of the airplane's motor, but one also heard the cheers of the throng that saw the fearless young flyer take off on his dash to the French capital. This was Mr. Fox's second Movietone news reel and there is no doubt but that he has started a valuable contribution to the screen. It is probably one that can be made more readily through the registering of the sound by light than when it is accomplished on a wax disk."

18 "Fox News Presents Movietone Shots of Chamberlin's *Hopoff*," *Moving Picture World*, June 11, 1927, 433. The *New York Times* and *Variety* reported the event in the same way.

19 "Roxy," *Variety*, June 15, 1927, 28. "The Roxy crashed into the Lindbergh welcome week with a show that is nothing short of prodigal in outstanding features. [...] The Fox Movie Tone record of Col. Lindbergh's reception in Washington the day before, with reproduction of President Coolidge's address and the aviator's brief speech, would have been sufficient to pack the house. This item was the outstanding feature, of course, building up to a sensational burst

of enthusiasm from the audience. The reproduction of the speeches brought wild enthusiasm such as was reflected in the views about the grandstand in the screen shots. The record was flawless in tone and diction. Every word registered in precise synchronization. The reproduction of applause from the Washington crowd, the zoom of aeroplanes circling above the scene and festive noise effects contributed by the Roxy orchestra blended into a medley of sound truly inspiring. The Lindbergh record was used at the end of the news topical, running ten minutes. . . ."

20 E. I. Sponable, "Historical Development of Sound Films, Parts 3–7," *Journal of the Society of Motion Picture Engineers* (May 1947): 409. *What Price Glory*, Fox's first super-production and its big hit of 1926, had previously been re-released with a Movietone score. See Donald Crafton, "The Coming of Sound to the American Cinema," in *The Talkies: American Cinema's Transition to Sound, 1926–1931* (Berkeley: University of California Press, 1997), 94. See also Douglas Gomery, *The Hollywood Studio System* (New York: St. Martin's Press, 1986); and Gomery, *Shared Pleasures* (Madison: University of Wisconsin Press, 1992).

21 "Mussolini's Hope in Screen," *Variety*, September 21, 1927, 1.

22 "Mussolini" (Movietone) (Fox) by Sime, *Variety*, September 21, 1927, 20 (in the section for film reviews).

    Moving Picture World, on October 1, reviewed the opening of *Sunrise* in similar terms, as the victory of Movietone:

> What impressed the audience most at the opening of Fox's *Sunrise* at the Times Square Theatre last Friday, was not so much the fine picture made by Fred W. Murnau, nor the excellent work of George O'Brien and Janet Gaynor, who shared the stellar honors, as it was the Movietone accompaniment for the picture and the Movietone scenes, taken in Italy under the supervision of Winfield R. Sheehan, which preceded the main feature.
>
> The audience saw and heard, as if they were there upon the stage before them, the superb Vatican choir of sixty or seventy voices in the various views of the Vatican, the marching Fascisti, singing their patriotic songs, the Bersaglieri, those crack Italian troops who constitute Mussolini's personal guard, passing in review with their bands playing, and then the great Premier, himself, speaking in English and Italian, exactly as if he was actually in the theatre.
>
> The perfection of the synchronization of sound and picture has at last been attained and hereafter anyone who doubts the future of this form of entertainment must be classified with those who thought that the 'movie' was only a passing amusement for children and folks of inferior mental capacity.
>
> Similarly, the Movietone accompaniment to *Sunrise*, which included the entire orchestration and stage effects, was so perfect that it amazed

as well as delighted the audience. The exhibitor's musical problems will be simple, once this device is generally adopted and this doesn't mean— maybe (299).

A separate review devoted to *Sunrise* was published in the same issue.

23 J. Douglas Gomery, "The Coming of Sound to the American Cinema: A History of the Transformation of an Industry," Ph.D. dissertation, University of Wisconsin, Madison, 1975, 182–83.

24 *Film Daily*, November 30, 1927, 2; cited in Crafton, *The Talkies*, 98.

25 *Film Daily*, December 8, 1927, 2; cited in ibid.

26 Gomery, *Shared Pleasures*, 144–45; Gomery, *The Hollywood Studio System*, 81.

27 *Film Daily*, July 22, 1928, 3.

28 Gomery, *The Hollywood Studio System*, 82.

29 "The Case of William Fox," *Fortune*, May 1930, 49.

30 Paul Thompson, "Murnau's Trip to Hollywood Brings *Sunrise* to the Screen," *Motion Picture Classic*, July 1927, 36. "Coming and Going," *Motion Picture World*, March 26, 1927, 264; "Fox Re-Signs Murnau," *Film Daily*, March 6, 1927, 3–4.

31 My thanks to Joe Yranski for the photo which has the caption affixed to it.

32 Fox concluded that what was considered a demotion in Germany (going from doorman to washroom attendant) was the opposite in America, where the washroom attendant could earn more money. See William Fox, "Reminiscences and Observations," in *The Story of the Films*, ed. Joseph P. Kennedy (Chicago: A. W. Shaw, 1927), 307–8.

33 Koszarski, *An Evening's Entertainment: The Age of the Silent Feature Picture, 1915–1928* (Berkeley: University of California Press, 1990), 85–86.

34 "The Case of William Fox," 49.

35 Gomery, *The Hollywood Studio System*, 82–83.

36 "The Case of William Fox," 117; Gomery, *The Hollywood Studio System*, 82 and chapter 3.

37 Upton Sinclair, *Upton Sinclair Presents William Fox* (Los Angeles: self-published, 1933).

38 Fox Story Files, *4 Devils*.

39 A questionnaire dated July 3, 1928, following a preview in Fresno, California, was reproduced by Eisner along with some comments from an audience member (Eisner, 195, note 7). Copies of others are held in the Berlin Filmmuseum and the Fox Collection at the University of Southern California. Two of them, also dated July 3, refer to a preview the night before at the California theater in San Jose. The shot list may be found under copyright number L25737, copyright deposits (microfilm), Motion Picture/Broadcasting/Recorded Sound Reading Room, Library of Congress (date of deposit: October 18, 1928; the copyright date, according to the U.S. Copyright Office records, is October 1).

40 *Theatre Magazine*, January 1928, 41, 72.

41 F. W. Murnau, "Films of the Future," *McCall's*, September 1928, 90.

42 Murnau's letter is dated December 22, 1927. It is partly cited in Eisner, *Murnau*, and in Eyman, *The Speed of Sound* (New York: Simon and Schuster, 1997).

43 Fox's letter is dated December 27, 1927, and is partly cited by Eisner. The first page, which includes these quotations, and page 4 are reproduced in *Filmmuseum Berlin*, but Fox's remarks are identified in the caption as pertaining to the script for *Sunrise*. See *Filmmuseum Berlin*, ed. Wolfgang Jacobsen, Hans Helmut Prinzler, and Werner Sudendorf (Berlin: Filmmuseum Berlin–Deutsche Kinemathek and Nicolai, 2000), 124–25.

44 Pressbook for *4 Devils*, "Director, Play and Players Are the Thing in *4 Devils*."

45 Margaret Reid, "After *Sunrise* Comes What?" *Picture Play*, October 1928, 22–24, 116.

46 The first draft is dated November 7, 1927. It ends when Aimee appears at the Lady's villa in a cab. Viertel is credited for "Continuity" and Mayer for "Screen Treatment." The "Final Script" is dated December 3, 1927. The copyright document submitted to the Library of Congress lists the screen credits. The Pressbook states: "*4 Devils* is taken from an original story by Herman Bang and the scenario was prepared by Carl Mayer, Berthold Viertel and Marion Orth." The Fox Story Files for *4 Devils* also contain a German translation of Herman Bang's story (originally written in Danish); a play by Paul Knudsen, *The Four Devils*, adapted by Herman Bernstein (no date); English and German copies of *The Four Cingarellis* (no date) by Hans Mueller and Hans Wilhelm, adapted from Bang's *Four Devils*, which, the script indicates, had been produced by Italy Pictures, Milan, starring Sylvia Bellini as Marion; and Murnau's treatment of October 12, 1927 (in English, not divided into shots).

47 "Films of the Future," 90.

48 Cited in Eisner, *Murnau*, 188.

49 Pressbook for *4 Devils*, "Trapeze Stunts and Marvel 'Go-Devil' Amaze Film Extras." The "Go-Devil" is also described at length in "After *Sunrise* Comes What?" *Photoplay* published a picture of Murnau shooting with the "Go-Devil" in its September 1928 issue.

50 This is an incomplete copy of the December 3 script, annotated in German and sometimes English, interleaved with some production sketches. Apparently it was used as a shooting script.

51 See "Musical Suggestions for *4 Devils*" (David Robinson Collection), reproduced in Luciano Berriatúa, *Los proverbios chinos de F. W. Murnau: Etapa americana* (Madrid: Filmotecca Española, 1990), 530–31.

52 Eisner, *Murnau*, 190.

53 "Ernest Palmer on Frank Borzage and F. W. Murnau," interview by Richard Koszarski, *Griffithiana*, no. 46 (December 1992): 120.

54 Paul Ivano, American Film Institute Seminar, April 20, 1974 (published in

1977). In the English edition of Eisner's book, the lamp that allows the shadow of the net to be visible on screen is called "a newly developed arc-light switch" (195); the German edition refers to it as a new camera lens (Frankfurt/M: Kommunales Kino, 1979 [new, enlarged edition], 317).

55 "The Reminiscences of Janet Gaynor" (1958), Oral History Collection, Columbia University, New York, 17.

56 "Murnau 18 Days Behind," *Variety*, May 2, 1928, 12; "Devils Finished," *Variety*, May 16, 1928, 8. According to *Moving Picture World*, May 12, 1928, the production began on January 3.

57 Unpublished interview with Kevin Brownlow, March 26, 1971.

58 "The Reminiscences of Janet Gaynor," 7.

59 Not one horse, but two. *Variety*, October 10, 1928. See the photograph in Eisner, *Murnau*.

60 Murnau brought in one of the most famous trapeze acts of the day, the Flying Codonas, to train the actors to perform the less challenging parts of the routine themselves and to serve as uncredited stunt doubles for the difficult feats. The Leap of Death was reserved for Alfredo Codona, who executed the world-famous triple somersault that he had perfected in 1920. The Codonas had performed in Dupont's *Variety*, which had been a huge success in the United States and to which 4 *Devils* was almost always compared. *Variety* had been voted the best picture of 1926 by *Film Daily's* annual poll of critics (*Film Daily Yearbook*, 1927, 16–17).

61 "The Reminiscences of Janet Gaynor," 17–18.

62 The letter is dated April 13, 1929 (Fox Legal File, Ernest Palmer).

63 *Film Daily* reported, on May 19, 1929, that A. F. (Buddy) Erickson was currently directing the talking version of 4 *Devils*.

64 *Variety*, February 20, 1929, 7; "Janet Gaynor Honored," *New York Times*, May 22, 1929.

65 Robert Flaherty wrote to Erik Barnouw on May 14, 1929: "Murnau with his yacht the 'Bali,' my brother and a crew of six men left last Sunday [May 12] for the South Seas. I leave with the outfit on the 12th of June from Frisco" (Flaherty Collection, Columbia University).

66 This document is missing from the Fox Story Files at UCLA; the copy Eisner discusses is in the Murnau Collection, BiFi.

67 Letter from Kearin to Murnau, June 1, 1929, Deutsche Kinemathek, F. W. Murnau Collection, on permanent loan from the Murnau-Stiftung.

68 A program from the premiere is in the Murnau Collection at the Margaret Herrick Library. Eisner believed that the actress Dorothy Kitchen had been replaced by Nancy Drexel (to play the younger sister), but the actress's name had been changed. See Eisner, *Murnau*, 187, note 1, and Fox's Pressbook.

69 See *Variety's* second review "Four Devils (25% dialogue)," June 19, 1929, 24.

70 The synopsis in the Pressbook confirms the "Dialogue as Taken From the Screen," which includes several story events.

71 Hervé Dumont, *Frank Borzage: Sarastro à Hollywood* (Milan: Edizioni Gabriele Mazzotta/Cinémathèque Française Paris, 1993), 154.

72 *Variety*, October 10, 1928.

73 William Fox to Sol Wurtzel, in *William Fox, Sol M. Wurtzel and the Early Fox Film Corporation: Letters, 1917–1923*, ed. Lillian Wurtzel Semenov and Carla Winter (Jefferson, N.C.: McFarland, 2001), 25.

74 The first studio evaluation is dated August 12, 1926; Willis Goldbeck's script is dated August 27, 1926. Fox bought the rights to the play on September 9, 1926. The second synopsis is dated March 8, 1928; Bing's translation and Viertel's drafts of the script are not dated. *Variety* reported on May 2, 1928, that Viertel was then writing the adaption and continuity while Murnau finished shooting *4 Devils* ("Murnau 18 Days Behind," 12). Marion Orth's 278-page draft, dated July 7, 1928, is the first script with a shot breakdown. Berthold Viertel's 229-page shot breakdown for the whole film (called a "continuity") is undated. The script titled "Final Version" is undated. All script materials are in the Fox Story Files for *Our Daily Bread*, except the "Final Version," which is in the General Script Collection at UCLA. The contracts and legal records are in the Fox Legal File, *Our Daily Bread*.

75 Fox Legal File, *Our Daily Bread*.

76 The earliest report that Murnau bought a farm may have been published by Theodore Huff in "An Index to the Films of F. W. Murnau," supplement to *Sight and Sound*, no. 15 (August 1948): 13. The contracts for the Oregon shoot are in the Fox Legal File, *Our Daily Bread*. The Pressbook advertised the fact that a real farm had been used, and even that the cast and crew had to drive forty-five miles every day for six weeks to get from Pendleton to the ranch and back ("Fox Troupe Travels 200,000 Miles While Filming *City Girl*").

77 Unpublished interview with Kevin Brownlow, 1969. According to the Press-book, "Forty men worked two weeks" at a cost of $3,000 to accomplish this ("*City Girl* Picture Shows Wonders Done with Acres of Wheat").

78 "Murnau Operation Causes Postponement of Film," *Film Daily*, August 2, 1928, 5.

79 *Moving Picture World*, September 15, 1928. According to Hervé Dumont (140), Murnau had to wait until Borzage was finished shooting *The River* on September 5 before actors Charles Farrell, Mary Duncan, and Ivan Linow, cinematographer Ernest Palmer, and set designer Harry Oliver were free to travel to Oregon. The Legal File shows that a double was hired for Farrell, beginning August 29. *Film Daily*, after noting that Farrell had been cast on August 12 and stating that the production "will start in a few weeks upon the recovery of Murnau from an operation for removal of the appendix," announced only four days later (August 16): "Production has started on *Our Daily Bread*, with Jack Pennick and a company of players and technicians leaving for Portland, Ore, to film exteriors. Due to the illness of Director F. W. Murnau, William Tummell is in temporary charge, L. William O'Connell is in charge of the camera battery."

80 Fox Legal File, *Our Daily Bread.*

81 Charles Rosher told Kevin Brownlow: "I found it difficult to get Murnau to look through the camera. 'I'll tell you if I like it in the projection room,' he used to say." Brownlow took that as a sign of how much Murnau trusted him. At Murnau's request, Rosher had spent a year in Berlin before he shot *Sunrise*, while Murnau was making *Faust*, to discuss American versus German methods of cinematography and to watch Murnau and cinematographer Carl Hoffman at work. See Brownlow, *The Parade's Gone By* (Berkeley: University of California Press, 1968), 230–33. Palmer's statements come from his interview with Koszarski, 118–19.

82 Koszarski interview, 119–20.

83 "*Our Daily Bread*: First Version of Treatment" by Berthold Viertel [no date], Fox Story Files.

84 Salka Viertel, *The Kindness of Strangers* (New York: Holt, Rinehart and Winston), 135.

85 "Je pense que Mary Duncan est la femme la plus intelligente du cinéma, douée d'un discernement singulier et aidée par moments d'intuitions troubles" (Jean George Auriol, "Les Pêchés de Mary Duncan," *La Revue du Cinéma*, no. 13 [August 1930]: 24). He is referring to her performances in the silent versions of *The River, City Girl, 4 Devils*, and *Romance of the Rio Grande* (directed by Alfred Santell). The cover photo shows Kate in her room in the city, sitting alongside the cage with her mechanical bird. French promotional materials recount the plot in great detail, confirming that the silent version we know today corresponded to the French release print (*La Bru*, Fonds Rondel, Bibliothèque de l'Arsenal, Paris).

86 *Film Daily*, May 19, 1929: "A. E. Erickson is a Denver boy, who has made good in Hollywood. He is better known as 'Buddy' and has worked up from the ranks, starting as a 'prop' boy. After assisting F. W. Murnau, he was assigned to direct *The Woman from Hell* and his work was so well liked that he was immediately given direction of the talking version of *Four Devils*. Following *Four Devils*, he will make *The Family Upstairs*, which will be an all-talker."

87 J. F. Lundy, *The Billboard*, April 12, 1930.

88 Memo from Ben Jacksen to Wm. Crawford, May 6, 1930, regarding a report on the musical score for the dialogue version: "To make it clear to you, one picture was made part talking and part silent, and the foreign version was all silent. This is the portion that is half talking and half silent" (Fox Legal File, *Our Daily Bread*).

89 The second set of contracts (denoted as "Murnau #3—Erickson—*Our Daily Bread*") shows start dates of October 22 to November 4, 1929, for actors hired by the week, including the actors who played Tustine, his wife and daughter, Mac, and a quartet of musicians for an added party sequence. End dates are not indicated (Fox Legal File, *Our Daily Bread*). No one knows exactly where *City Girl* was shown. The New York reviews state it played at Loew's New York cinema for one day, April 3, 1930. A cursory look shows that *City Girl*

was listed in New York City at two Fox neighborhood theaters, the Audubon and the Crotona, from April 2 to 4, and at Loew's Sheridan from April 29 to 30 (*New York Times*), and in Los Angeles at the Fox Boulevard from April 17 to 23 (*Los Angeles Times*). The April screenings were preceded by a brief run in Chicago at Fox's Monroe cinema, February 9 to 13 (*Chicago Tribune*).

90 Waly, "*City Girl* (50% dialog)," *Variety*, April 9, 1930. *City Girl* had been scheduled to open at the huge, plush Roxy Theatre. It was listed in the Roxy "Weekly Review" and program for the opening of the dialogue version of *4 Devils* on June 15, 1929, among the "All Talking Fox Movietone Super Features" to come.

91 Memo from Sheehan to Wurtzel, February 18, 1929, regarding the contract with Elliott Lester (Fox Legal File, *Our Daily Bread*); Murnau's agreement is in the Everson Collection, NYU; Elliott's contract is dated February 25, 1929 (Fox Legal File, *Our Daily Bread*).

92 These are lines from Lester's uninspiringly titled *The Mud Turtle*. In the play, Kate tells Lem that his father "nagged at me like I was a mud turtle on my back in the mud an' he was pokin' at me with a stick—an' you let him do it" (Fox Story Files, *Our Daily Bread*). By an odd coincidence, Elliott Lester provided a link between Murnau and Robert Flaherty. Berthold Viertel's first contract with Fox (June 18, 1927) was for a script based on Ejnar Mikkelsen's novel *Frozen Justice*, to be directed by Murnau. That would have made *Frozen Justice* Murnau's second American film, rather than *4 Devils*. The Story File (dated June 21, 1926) contains a long series of drafts, including one by Viertel (October 17, 1927) and a later one (April 23, 1929) with "Dialogue by Elliott Lester." Among the extensive research materials on life in the sub-Arctic included in the file can be found Robert Flaherty's essay "How I Filmed *Nanook of the North*" (*World's Work*, September 1922). Fox Legal File, Berthold Viertel; Fox Story File, *Frozen Justice*, UCLA.

In December 1925 *Fox Folks* had announced that *Frozen Justice* would be directed by John Ford. In Joseph McBride's biography of Ford, he refers to a letter that Murnau wrote Sheehan on November 16, 1925, which Sheehan had copied to Ford on December 11 to show him how eager Murnau was to direct that film, in an effort to persuade Ford to do it instead. If Murnau had prevailed, *Frozen Justice* would have been his first American film instead of *Sunrise* (McBride, *Searching for John Ford* [New York: St. Martin's Press, 2001], 159, 734). These letters are in the John Ford Collection, Lilly Library, Indiana University. As Sheehan wrote Ford: "Mr. F. W. Murnau, of Berlin, is suffering mental anguish and untold tortures because FROZEN JUSTICE has been awarded to the 'Pride of Peak's Island, Maine.' I think the reading of Mr. Murnau's letter will convince you of the great value of this property and of the fine opportunity ahead."

Echoing Flaherty's *Nanook* and prefiguring *Tabu*, Murnau wanted to shoot for six months in Alaska "because the scenic atmosphere is one of the biggest attractions of this picture." Murnau explained: "What attracts me most of a film theme is always the absolute simplicity of the plot. From this point of view, this story is almost the ideal film subject, because it can be told in three words. It is the eternal, human theme of a man who seeks revenge for the unfaithfulness of his wife, however in the present story it is transplanted from the every-day atmosphere of the civilized life in the big cities to a people living in a primitive state of nature, with the action laid in the Far North, the land of the Eskimos, both—country and people—today more interesting to the entire civilized world than ever before. In addition to this there is the theme: what becomes of a happy, primitive race, if it comes in touch with civilized people...."

An undated legal memo summarizing Carl Mayer's payments from Fox listed *Frozen Justice* as the last of four scripts, following an "original story," *Sunrise* and *4 Devils* (Everson Collection, NYU). *Frozen Justice* was finally made for Fox by Alan Dwan in 1929.

93   Letter from Hilliker to Ella Bingham Morris, July 6, 1929. All correspondence related to Hilliker and Caldwell is in the Hilliker-Caldwell Collection, Museum of Modern Art, New York.

94   "You poor dodo! You would have an unhappy ending, wouldn't you? Not even the South Seas could cheer you up. I'm quite convinced if you ever strayed into Heaven by mistake, angels or no angels, you'd leap over the nearest cloud and straight down to Hell where you could be yourself again." Hilliker goes on to rave about how much she and her husband "the Captain" loved *Tabu*. Hilliker to Murnau, February 16, 1931. An exchange of telegrams about an editing suggestion following *Tabu*'s New York preview shows that they were still on excellent terms.

95   Memo from Vivian M. Moses (Jack Leo's office), August 6, 1927.

96   "A dossier from I, Katherine Hilliker, to Mrs. Pritchett, 10/1/36."

97   Hilliker to Vivian Moses, September 20, 1927.

98   Hilliker to Murnau, February 16, 1931.

99   Hilliker to Caldwell, March 23, 1929.

100 Letter from Hilliker to Ella Bingham Morris, July 6, 1929; "Dossier" from Hilliker to Mrs. Pritchett, October 1, 1936; "New Suggested Ending" by Hilliker and Caldwell, August 2, 1929.

101 The contracts for the dialogue shoot are identified as Murnau #3—Erickson "OUR DAILY BREAD" in the Fox Legal File for *Our Daily Bread*.

102 Quoted in Eisner, *Murnau*, 198–99.

103 "Dialogue as Taken from the Screen," Fox Story Files, *Our Daily Bread*.

104 Lundy, April 12, 1930. McBride describes a similar situation involving Ford. "Jack made *The Black Watch* [1929] as a part-talkie, but after he finished his work on it, Fox general manager Winfield Sheehan hired British cast member Lumsden Hare to direct some additional talking sequences.... Ford thought Hare's scenes were really horrible—long, talky things, had nothing to do with

the story—and completely screwed it up. I wanted to vomit when I saw them.' Hare received a 'staged by' credit for his interpolations. . . . Some reviewers didn't know where to lay the blame, thinking Ford was another silent-movie director who had trouble handling dialogue scenes" (McBride, *Searching for John Ford*, 170).

105 "Fox Settlement," *Exhibitors Herald-World*, April 12, 1930. The dateline for the lead article is "New York, April 8."

106 David Flaherty, "A Few Reminiscences," 16.

107 Robert Flaherty wrote to his wife from Tahiti on August 20, 1929: "[Murnau] has decided to finance the picture himself—to forget color—photograph it all with my Akeley—me photographing" (Flaherty Papers, Columbia University). Floyd Crosby ended up photographing the film. See Langer, "Tabu: The Making of a Film," who cites Flaherty, "Tabu Diary" (manuscript), June 13, 1929, and a telegram from Flaherty and Murnau to Colorart, July 25, 1929, Flaherty Papers, Columbia University.

108 Letter from Kearin to Murnau, May 13, 1930.

THE AMERICAN ORIGINS OF FILM NOIR
Realism in Urban Art and *The Naked City*
Sumiko Higashi

The force of documentary surely derives in part from the fact that the images might be more disturbing than the arguments enveloping them.

—Martha Rosler

Although the term "film noir," coined by the French critic Nino Frank in 1946, was once confined to academic discourse, it is now part of the lexicon of (post)modernist culture.[1] A Super Bowl commercial for Intel's pentium chip, for example, was filmed as a noir parody inviting viewers to solve a mystery. A *Vogue* article, titled "Out of the Past," publicized a Weegee exhibit at the International Center of Photography in New York by citing *The Naked City* (1948). The Queens Museum of Art labeled its exhibit of crime scene photos "New York Noir." The fashion designer Isaac Mizrahi transformed his runway into a documentary scene for "Rogue Chic," his 1997 fall collection. The *New York Times* headlined its review of the show, "Three Major Designers Clothe the Naked City."[2] Television commercials for Flonase assume that the audience is familiar with noir conventions. Filmmakers, reviewers, and video store clerks are all au courant. Academic discourse has expanded as well.

Since A. M. Karimi noted in his dissertation, published in 1976, "a lack of any work in English" (except for some articles) on film noir, studies have multiplied.[3] Yet such discourse remains highly Eurocentric and, apart from hard-boiled fiction, pays scarce attention to the American origins of noir, specifically nineteenth-century realism and its construct, the city as a social matrix.

Whether film noir constitutes a genre, style, movement, or cycle during a historical period has been rehearsed elsewhere, remains unresolved, and is not the focus of this essay. James Naremore's contention that "film noir has no essential characteristics" is the most expansive and, for my purposes, useful formulation.[4] Also discussed elsewhere is the evolution of film noir, a debate that should be further expanded. Paul Ottoson lists familiar antecedents including German expressionism, French poetic realism, American hard-boiled fiction, filmmaking influenced by wartime exigencies, postwar malaise (involving female employment, returning veterans, and McCarthyism), Freudian symbolism, Italian neorealism, and the style of *Citizen Kane* (1940).[5] Such a list, while useful, restricts a historical consideration of film noir to just a few decades and excludes nineteenth-century American realism. Both Foster Hirsch and Paul Kerr include Ashcan school paintings on their list but do not discuss them. Marc Vernet, also in a consideration of past practices, argues that chiaroscuro lighting dates back to Cecil B. DeMille's silent films.[6] The Ashcan painters and DeMille's early features are indeed intertexually related works that are expressions of American pictorial realism and a source of noir stylistics.

Despite the argument that low-key lighting is "not specific" to film noir, Vernet prompts a rethinking of American antecedents by focusing not on film as texts but on realism as a middle-class response to urbanization.[7] Granted, DeMille's lighting was not then standard, so that he had to instruct the cameraman Alvin Wyckoff: "'You musn't make this part so light . . . it should be dark.' So they all said, 'He likes it contrasty.' . . . It . . . meant make the whites whiter and the blacks blacker." But such lighting, attributable in part to the art director Wilfred Buckland, represented more than dramatic effect, advances in film language, or product differentation. Composition in light and shadow was, in fact, an expression of pictorial realism undergirded by evangelical Protestant values. Sessue Hayakawa is thus introduced as the racial other in *The Cheat* (1915) through the use of low-key lighting (in a shot to be tinted red, according to the script), and characters are morally compromised in scenes that are, in the director's words, "contrasty."[8] A significant dimension of American (as opposed to European) realism was the expression of the moral values of the genteel middle class, especially in relation to urban otherness.

Although American realism was a dominant cultural form expressed in urban iconography, most film critics have not investigated its relevance to noir stylistics. Rather, they have construed realism in theoretical terms as a transparency of images produced by the Hollywood studio system. J. P. Telotte argues, for example, that location-shot films "seem guided by a desire for a kind of transparent realism, one in which, as Colin Mac-Cabe puts it, 'the real is not articulated—it is.'" Paul Kerr asserts that low-key lighting represented B-studio attempts at product differentiation and was thus a form of "resistance to realistic aesthetic." Carl Richardson, dismissing trendy French (and, by implication, British) theorists, states in his study that "when it is invoked, reality will refer to empirical, experiential externality."[9] Actually, the nineteenth-century American realists who embraced science, democracy, and individualism exemplified such empiricism. David Shi defines realists as those who "affirmed the existence of a physical realm independent of the mind, a coherent and accessible world of objective facts capable of being known through observation, understood with the use of reason, and accurately represented in thought, literature, and the arts." Shi claims that realism "gains precision when studied in the fullness and complexity of its historical moment."[10]

Considering urban relations, Amy Kaplan and Nancy Glazener argue that realism was a response to social change, especially the late-nineteenth-century arrival of numerous immigrants forming an underclass. As a rebellion against the sentimentalism of genteel women, realist discourse was a masculine investigation about the hard facts of metropolitan life.[11] Yet realism and sentimentalism were both informed by strong moral, if not religious, values and often converged as the social and cultural practices of the middle class. At times, reform movements produced benefits for the less fortunate. What distinguished realism in an expanding consumer culture, however, was its "strategy of containment" in commodifying the poor. The middle class framed the lower orders within the parameters of a proscenium stage, a painting, a post-card, a photograph, a stereograph, and a movie screen. As Peter Conrad argues, "the frame, for the pictorial interpretation of the city, is a convenience for disengagement."[12] Such a vantage point enabled middle-class spectators to construct a social world in which alien peoples were the other. Fourteenth Street thus represented more than a geographical boundary line in Manhattan. Ghettos like the Lower East Side were labeled "colonies" and subject to tourism as vicarious experience.[13] Put another way, the middle-class gaze, rendered even more penetrating by moral rectitude, reinscribed social hierarchies. Scrutiny of the poor by journalists, reformers, and police could be interpreted, even without a Foucauldian panoptic model, as efforts to objectify, if not to manage them. As a discursive practice, then, realism overlaps with orientalism in that the masses are racialized and theatricalized as exotic spectacle.[14] Although the reformer Henry George protested against such voyeurism, absent for the most part was the postmodernist stance articulated by Giles Deleuze as the "indignity of speaking for others."[15]

As a realist construct that reverberates in countless noir films like *Murder, My Sweet* (1944), *The Big Sleep* (1946), *Kiss of Death* (1947), *The Lady from Shanghai* (1948), *The Naked City* (1948), *Night and the City* (1950), *Call Northside 777* (1948), *The Asphalt Jungle* (1950), *Macao* (1952), *Angel Face* (1953), and *The Crimson Kimono* (1959), the cityscape is a mysterious netherworld with ethnic and racialized peoples provoking curiosity and paranoia. (Wayne Wang inverts this scenario in *Chan Is Missing* [1980] by showing that Chinatown inhabitants, not whites, have cause to feel paranoid.)[16] Cities, as Alan Trachtenberg argues, "invite pursuit, require investigation, invasion of other spaces."[17] Among the institutions mystifying the urban scene in order to "dispel it as news" was the metropolitan newspaper. A product of technological innovation, penny presses became a daily vehicle for realist discourse based on sensational urban investigations.[18] George G. Foster defined the role of a news reporter and invented the "genre of nonfictional urban sensationalism" by dramatizing his nocturnal tours in the *New York Tribune*.[19] Fairly typical is the lurid opening of his book, *New York by Gas-Light: With Here and There a Streak of Sunshine* (1850): "What a task we have undertaken! To penetrate beneath the thick veil of night and lay bare the fearful mysteries of darkness in the metropolis—the festivities of prostitution, the orgies of pauperism, the haunts of theft and murder, and all the sad realities that go to make up the lower stratum—the under-ground story—of life in New York! . . . Go with us, and see. The duty of the present age is to discover the real facts of the actual

Matthew Hale Smith's frontispiece (1868) contrasts a mansion and a brewery representing extreme class difference in terms of darkness and light.

conditions of the wicked and wretched classes—so that Philanthropy and Justice may plant their blows aright."[20]

Actually, Foster was not entirely unsympathetic toward the working class, and he was appalled by the increasing polarization between the "upper ten thousand" and the destitute. Continuing in the same vein were Matthew Hale Smith's *Sunshine and Shadow in New York* (1868) and James Dabney McCabe Jr.'s *Lights and Shadows of New York Life* (1868), which denounced urban slums as a moral and economic abyss. Indeed, Charles Loring Brace titled his report on poverty *The Dangerous Classes of New York and Twenty Years among Them* (1872). Adding to such light and shadow depictions were engravings that appeared in news magazines like *Harper's Weekly*. Winslow Homer and William A. Rogers, for example, depicted Chinese opium smokers, ragged tenement dwellers, and down-and-out men.[21] During the 1890s, the publication of halftones and the popularity of lantern slide lectures enabled photographers inventing documentary practice, notably Jacob A. Riis, to publicize, as stated in the title of his book, *How the Other Half Lives: Studies among the Tenements of New York* (1890). Silent filmmakers like DeMille quoted Riis in early features like *Kindling* (1915), and in so doing they aestheticized urban scenes as picturesque but morally debased.[22] The representation of the city as a social matrix, in sum,

Scenes of tenements in Cecil B. DeMille's *Kindling* (1915) continued an
American pictorial tradition that dated back to engravings, paintings, and photos.
(Courtesy of George Eastman House)

has a complex history dating back to realism as middle-class discourse on
urbanization.

JACOB A. RIIS AND THE ASHCAN SCHOOL

Attention to urban iconography clarifies the intertextuality of realist art
with noir stylistics, as well as the social structure underlying such discourse.
And because that structure changes over time, so too does realist representation of the city. Several texts illustrate these issues, but particularly relevant are the works of Jacob A. Riis, the Ashcan paintings of the New York
realists or "the black school," and the photojournalism of Weegee (Arthur
Fellig).[23] A pioneer of social photography, Riis reported for the *New York
Tribune* before he capitalized on the invention of halftones and magnesium
flash powder, used to startling effect in the dark, to reveal lives of the poor.
Until his pathbreaking photos were published, the urban landscape was
represented according to grand-style conventions.[24] Such photographs
aestheticized the city in terms of panoramic vistas, broad avenues com-
posing geometric patterns, monumental buildings with Beaux Arts orna-
mentation, landscaped parks with scenic promenades, and technological
marvels like steel bridges. Photographed from high angles and in extreme

long shots, the metropolis exemplified the City Beautiful movement, with its emphasis on harmony, balance, and order. Absent was the diverse urban population reduced in scale or rendered invisible. As opposed to a bird's-eye view of the city, Riis offered a mole's-eye view with a realist perspective.[25] And he did so by producing a sensational and enthralling excursion for middle-class readers.

After publishing a *Scribner's* essay with nineteen line drawings based on his photos in 1889, Riis produced *How the Other Half Lives*, a work with forty-three illustrations, including fifteen halftones.[26] Accounting for its success was his mediation as expressed in captions and more than three hundred pages of text. As a narrator, Riis uses first-person pronouns, both singular and plural, and direct address. Put another way, he identifies with the middle-class reader whose subjectivity contrasts with the passive poor. An entertaining tour guide, he leads an excursion on the Lower East Side through ethnic neighborhoods like Chinatown, the scene of opium addiction and white slavery; stops at cheap lodging houses, stale-beer dives, Jew-town sweatshops, and almshouses and workhouses; focuses on portraits of women workers and children, including homeless boys labeled "street Arabs"; and discusses social issues, especially landlord despotism and foul tenements. Contributing to the schadenfreude of the reader, riveted by the misfortunes of the poor, were captioned illustrations. Several show slum dwellers entrapped by vertical and horizontal lines of buildings, dark shadowy areas, overcrowding, rubbish and filth, moods of despair, languor, and apathy.[27] A Danish immigrant and once a down-and-outer himself, Riis successfully encouraged tenement reform and lodging house abolition.[28] Yet his use of photos as evidence to document the condition of the social body subjected the poor not only to scrutiny and surveillance but to commodification. As John Tagg argues, characteristic of "the regime in which photographic evidence emerged ... was a ... social division between the power and privilege of *producing* and *possessing* and the burden of *being* meaning."[29]

Less than twenty years after the publication of *How the Other Half Lives*, the Ashcan painters, led by Robert Henri, held a well-publicized, well-attended, and well-received exhibit at the Macbeth Gallery on Fifth Avenue. As rebels against the conservative National Academy, William Glackens (despite being "the American Renoir"), George Luks, Everett Shinn, John Sloan, and later George Bellows painted ordinary people and created a distinctly American art. Characteristic of their work was a somber palette that contrasted with the atmospheric paintings of American impressionists like Childe Hassam. Indeed, Henri's *Street Scene with Snow* (1902) shows an inky carriage plowing through muddy snow, dark buildings lining the street, and a black spire puncturing a sky roiling with ominous clouds, whereas Hassam's *Late Afternoon, New York Winter* (1900) is saturated with light pastels. Attracted to the urban scene, Henri viewed the city as a virile expression of masculine forces and enjoyed its physicality. As a proponent of the strenuous life, he played golf with Sloan and accompanied his student Bellows to boxing matches. Luks adopted roguish ways, frequented bars, and bragged, "I can paint with a shoestring dipped in lard!" Descended from more diverse and less privileged families than were the American impressionists, these realists sympathized with the urban poor, and, at various times in their careers, contributed to the socialist publication *The Masses*.[30] Even so, their representation of life in lower Manhattan was informed by middle-class perceptions of ethnicity and race as immutable social difference.

As stressed by an exhibit of American impressionism and realism at the Metropolitan Museum of Art in New York in 1994, the Ashcan paintings are intertexually related to the work of Jacob A. Riis. Although Riis's work broke new ground, he worked in the tradition of urban iconography established by magazine engravers. Winslow Homer had preceded him into lodging houses and Chinatown clubhouses. Squatters in tenements, ragpickers, street vendors, opium smokers, and drunks were familiar characters in middle-class publications. Perhaps most iconic in the representation of tenements were engravings like William A. Rogers's *Ragpicker's Court, Mulberry Street* (1879) that showed laundry hanging from dilapidated tenements. Such scenes frequently reappear in documentary social photography, including Riis's work, as well as in Ashcan paintings like Bellows's *Cliff Dwellers* (1913), and Sloan's *Sunday, Women Drying Their Hair* (1912), *A Woman's Work* (1912), and *Backyards, Greenwich Village* (1914).[31] Indeed, Glackens, Luks, Shinn, and Sloan, formerly Philadelphians, had been employed as news illustrators in the 1890s and thus were part of the realist journalistic tradition before they became painters. Sloan, for example, worked for both the *Philadelphia Inquirer* and the *Philadelphia Press*.[32] Consequently, there is a marked degree of middle-class voyeurism and tourism in some of their works.

Consider, for example, Bellows's *Cliff Dwellers*, a painting in somber

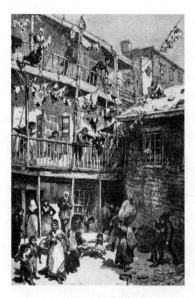

William A. Rogers's *Ragpicker's Court,
Mulberry Street* (1879), published in *Harper's*
magazine, presents an iconic view of the
slums that would be replicated by painters,
photographers, and filmmakers.

hues that shows slum dwellers crammed into a narrow street between
tenements with laundry lines and a tiny patch of sky. Granted, the work is
ambiguous in its representation of the poor as part of a lively street scene,
the title characterizes them as primitive. Significantly, the painting was
based on the frontispiece caption "Why Don't They Go to the Country
for a Vacation?" which speaks volumes as social commentary. Indeed, the
initial drawing for *The Masses* conveyed a more oppressive and claustro-
phobic feeling due to the crowd gathered on the street and the squalidness
of the atmosphere. Although the painting vitiates the darker mood of the
drawing, daylight "penetrates the tenement darkness from the side of the
viewer, as if a door had been thrown open," to reveal life on the Lower
East Side. Put another way, the spectator's gaze is still that of the middle-
class consumer on an excursion. Such a view is also inherent in Bellows's
visceral rendering of boxing matches that anticipated ringside photographers and filmmakers, namely *Both Members of the Club* (1912), originally
titled *A Nigger and a White Man*, and Ashcan paintings in general.[33] Sloan,
interestingly, described himself as an "incorrigible window watcher" with a
"little peeper instinct."[34] At least he expressed discomfort in scrutinizing
the poor and sympathized with their plight.

Although the importance of the Ashcan school was cut short by the
arrival of modernism at the Armory Show in 1913, it was influential in later

George Bellows's *Cliff Dwellers* (1913) typifies Ashcan school representations of urban life in the slums. (Courtesy of Los Angeles County Museum of Art)

decades.[35] Sloan's voyeurism, for example, was recycled in more prurient form during the Depression by Reginald Marsh, who, like other New York social realists, painted the inhabitants of lower Manhattan by reinscribing societal distinctions. As an artist whose work is linked with noir stylistics, Marsh was influenced by the Ashcan school. At sites like Coney Island, he focused on the sensual bodies of the masses as the corporeal essence of the city. But as Peter Conrad argues, his art became increasingly less realistic and verged on the mythological. Also departing from the realist tradition was Edward Hopper, another painter mentioned by film critics with respect to the noir style.[36] Although he was Henri's pupil, Hopper abstracted the urban scene so that, unlike Ashcan painters, he is not engaged in direct social observation. As a modernist, he is scarcely concerned with articulating middle-class values as a function of art, and thus he influenced more abstract renderings of the city in film noir.

WEEGEE'S NAKED CITY

Reginald Marsh's realist paintings of urban characters during the Depression are intertextually related, as Foster Hirsch argues, to the work of Weegee and Diane Arbus and to noir stylistics.[37] Weegee's photographs, in particular, continue the tradition of urban realism expressed in sensational news reporting. A Jewish immigrant reared on the Lower East Side, he once played the violin for a silent film theater because music was his first love. Weegee began his photographic career by working in a darkroom and excelled at printing photos, a skill that would stand him in good stead. Supplementing his income on Sundays, he photographed children in their best clothes, developed prints to emphasize contrasts, and sold them to parents. Years later, he recalled, "my customers, who were Italian, Polish, or Jewish liked their pictures dead-white." Graduating to freelance work, Weegee sold his images to Acme Newspictures, a firm used by three of New York's major papers, the *Daily News*, the *World Telegram*, and the *Herald Tribune*. Some of his best photos were published when he became a contributor to a sleek new paper, *P.M. Daily*. By installing a shortwave radio in his car to hear police and fire reports, Weegee was often first on the scene to capture mayhem. Although some thought his graphic pictures lacked social value, the Photo League mounted his first one-person exhibit, titled "Murder Is My Business," in 1941. The Museum of Modern Art then followed with exhibits like "Action Photography" in 1943 and "Art in Propaganda" in 1944. Dubbed "O. Henry with a camera" by the *Saturday Evening Post*, Weegee enjoyed his greatest success when a collection of his photos was published as *Naked City* (1945).[38] The title was a result of photographing murder scenes during the winter and nudist colonies in the summer.[39] Significantly, a follow-up that was less lurid, *Weegee's People* (1946), did not sell nearly as well.

By the time Weegee became famous in the 1940s, the demographics of the country had changed so that the genteel middle class was no longer the cultural arbiter. The salaried white-collar workers that now constituted the middle class, especially its lower rungs, were a more heterogeneous group and were likely to be consumers of popular, not highbrow, culture.[40] Within this changing social context, Weegee's work is modernist in the sense that he is unencumbered by middle-class moralism and reformist crusades. Yet his photographs show traces of realist origins by constructing spectatorship as vicarious experience. Clearly, Riis's documentary social photography precedes Weegee's work as urban journalism.[41] Just as Riis used magnesium flash powder to invade dark slums, Weegee used a flash to startle his subjects and infrared film to conceal his intrusion. Peter Conrad argues that, for Riis, flash illumination was both "a means and a symbol of indicment," whereas for Weegee it was a weapon. "The photographic act is the equivalent of a hold up." Yet Riis used a frying pan to ignite flash-lights, fired cartridges from a noisy revolver, and set fire to surroundings that included a room inhabited by the blind.[42] And both photographers resorted to manipulation, such as posing subjects and cropping pictures, that blurred the line between fiction and nonfiction. Although Weegee's photos, like those by Riis, are shot in chiaroscuro, his work is more mod-ernist than picturesque in constructing a narrative. Light and shadow are still dramatic but cease to convey the didactic Protestant values underlying much realist expression.

A scrutiny of *Naked City* in relation to *How the Other Half Lives* clarifies the intertexuality of the two works. Weegee, like Riis, mediates the darker aspects of urban life by taking the reader on a voyeuristic tour and by pro-viding captions but minimal text. Speaking colloquially in first person and at times engaging in direct address, he divides his chapters into events and sites such as fires, murders, sudden death, patrol wagons, the opera, the Bowery, Coney Island, and Harlem. According to Alain Bergala, Weegee's photos replicate the cinema in scale and fragmentation of shots, which are either too wide or too tight, and in slightly off-kilter angles that create im-balance and imply off-screen space.[43] Significantly, all the photos in each chapter are "edited" as if shots in a newsreel montage and thus comprise a narrative. "Murders . . . ," for example, shows an extreme long shot of several people leaning out their windows to see a corpse on the pavement below, then a closer shot of spectators, then a medium shot of the bleeding victim, gun in foreground, then a group of young boys staring at another crime scene. Also cinematic is the inclusion of point-of-view shots after medium close-ups of rapt spectators with whom the readers identify. Undoubtedly, the voyeurs captured both in and by the text were titillated by horrific, sor-did, and grim events. A number of prisoners in scenes of arrest or in patrol wagons, for example, are transvestites whose corporeality provokes curi-osity. Weegee, unlike Riis, makes few, if any, moral pronouncements about the urban other.[44] But if his tabloid photos do not reinscribe social hier-achies, they are still voyeuristic and implicitly set standards of normality, if not morality, for the reader. David Serlin and Jesse Lerner admit that objectification is the result, but they also argue that at issue for Weegee, as a Jewish immigrant, is an attempt at self-definition.[45] Acknowledged as such, his portrait of the other as himself in a specular relation represents, in my view, a form of self-loathing that is tragically part of the urban immigrant experience.

As an urban sociologist, Weegee, like the nineteeth-century journalists noted earlier, was outraged by the disparity between rich and poor. As he writes in his chapter on the opera, "the common people waited in the street in the rain . . . for standing room . . . while Society arrived wearing galoshes and pearls." Among his famous pictures is a rendering of such glaring contrasts. "The Critic," first published in *Life*, shows two wealthy society matrons in glittering jewels and white furs walking past a disheveled, angry, lower-class woman. (A row of onlookers to the left has been cropped in the *Naked City* print to heighten contrast.) What readers did not know was that the event had been staged. Weegee had picked up a woman at a Bowery bar, plied her with alcohol, and instructed an assistant to thrust her into the frame.[46] Such compositions recall the nineteenth-century engravings and photographs that provided social commentary by juxtaposing rich and poor. Also part of documentary practice was the blending of fact and fiction: staged events were nothing new in the history of either photojournalism or newsreels.[47] Yet Weegee was willing to demystify the photographic apparatus as a lens revealing urban mystery by encouraging readers to join him. Serving as bookends in *Naked City* are a portrait of himself with a camera (chapter 1), and, in a final section, detailed instructions to budding photographers. As a work that is to some extent self-reflexive, the book has claims to modernism as well as realism.[48] As such, it is intertextually related to many noir films, not the least of which is the semi-documentary that bears its title.

THE NAKED CITY

Whether or not *The Naked City* (1948) should be included in the noir canon depends on how critics define their terms. Raymond Borde and Etienne Chaumeton, Charles Higham and Joel Greenberg, A. M. Karimi, Jon Tuska, and Frank Krutnik label *The Naked City* a semi-documentary rather than noir. J. P. Telotte invents a hybridized term, "noir documentary," to categorize the film. Such films set trends since Louis de Rochemont, producer of *The March of Time*, successfully transformed *The House on 92nd Street* (1945) into a feature resembling a newsreel.[49] Robert G. Porfirio and Raymond Durgnat acknowledge that the postwar semi-documentary represented a stylistic innovation that influenced the look of film noir. Paul Schrader, who divides the evolution of noir into three phases, describes the films of the second period (1945–1949) as realistic works about crime and police investigation. Carl Richardson argues that film noir and semi-documentary are forms that intersected during the middle period of a cycle and then parted ways. Alain Silver argues that the dichotomy between realistic *policiers* and expressionistic detective films is false, and he states that "the visual conventions of film noir are, as often as not, actually more naturalistic."[50] Whatever its category, *The Naked City* is indebted to the conventions of American realism in its representation of the city as a social matrix.[51] But the film also illustrates how the Production Code and the blacklist era vitiated realist expression dating back to the nineteenth century. The film, in sum, unwittingly exposes tensions regarding realism during the McCarthy era.

Attention to the production of *The Naked City*, as revealed by the Mark Hellinger Papers at the University of Southern California, shows that its filmmakers were consciously crafting a realist film. As a former columnist for the New York *Daily Mirror*, Hellinger had produced *The Killers* (1946) and *Brute Force* (1947) since his move from Warner Bros. to Universal-International Pictures. In 1946 he teamed up with the scriptwriter Malvin Wald to make an authentic film of the city that was in his blood. Wald, who grew up in Brooklyn, had written documentary scripts while serving in the First Motion Picture Unit of the Army Air Force and convinced Hellinger to invest in location shooting.[52] As preparation, he spent a month in New York to do research for a story, titled *Homicide*, about a murdered blonde. That fall, he kept Hellinger informed about his progress:

> I have managed to read from cover to cover five complete case records—each one at least 200 pages of reports made by detectives. These reports, plus Inspector Donovan's personal interpretations . . . give me information no newspaperman ever had. . . .
>
> I'll do a quick couple of days of visiting the line-up, the Telegraph Bureau at Headquarters, the Photo Gallery, and the Manhattan homicide squad on West 30th Street. . . .
>
> At this point I am making no effort to figure out a story line. Every case

gives me more and more story material and characters. I think that when I get back to Hollywood it will be more of a job of editing what I have learned than creating something new.

The important thing is that I come back to Hollywood knowing more about New York homicide detectives than any writer in Hollywood—and I think I will by the time I'm finished here.[53]

When Wald returned, he wrote a story treatment and several drafts of a screenplay retitled *The Naked City*. A telegram in the Hellinger Papers reveals that the producer later agreed to pay Arthur Fellig (Weegee) $3,500 for the rights to the title.[54] After Albert Maltz became Wald's collaborator, a shooting script was submitted to the Production Code Administration. Apparently the story was too realistic, as Joseph Breen, representing urban Catholic interests, requested that the "suicide [of one of the characters] be changed" and urged caution about the "selection and photographing of the dresses and costumes for your women." Referring to a montage of scenes that, in part, recalls Weegee's photos, he added, "We presume that the husband and wife sleeping on the fire escape will be handled with delicacy and care." Among the other concerns he dictated were: "Murder will be handled in such way as not to be excessively brutal"; "Delete the specific reference to 'seconal'"; "It should be made clear that Qualen is not killed, inasmuch as he is a police officer"; and "The business of Garza being electrocuted by the third rail will not be handled in a gruesome manner."[55]

Despite the changes requested by Breen's office, Maltz, who understood documentary practice as well as Wald, continued to accentuate realism in his production notes prior to shooting:

1 That the CAMERA EYE, whenever possible, reflect the rich and infinite detail of the daily life of New York: the infinite variety of faces and natural types; the architectural beauty and squalor that exist side by side. . . .

2 That the musical score be blended with another music—the noises of the great city that are sometimes unpleasant but are always evocative and real. . . .

3 This film will depend for its effect upon a sense of absolute authenticity, upon its honest portrayal of people and life, upon the absence of forced effects, forced scenes, forced melodramatics.

Indeed the very introduction of New York City itself, as a factor in the

Mark Hellinger's *The Naked City*, titled after Weegee's book of the same name, reproduces the tradition of nineteenth-century social documentary photography in some of its location shooting. (Courtesy of the University of Southern California)

film and the very nature of the opening commentary, dictate the style necessary to the film. . . .

The director should have, as his working basis, real drama, real people
and real effects. It will then be his task to get drama from the real action and
sounds of a chase down an apartment house fire escape. . . . Absolute reality
is the slide rule.[56]

As Carl Richardson argues, contrary to the argument that noir was the
result of slashed budgets, realism in the form of location shooting was
expensive.[57] Given that *The Naked City* was not a proven box office formula, Hellinger personally financed the film by borrowing $878,000, or
65 percent of the negative cost, from the Bank of America.[58] The shooting
schedule of eighty-four days, producing nearly 225,000 feet of film shot
at 107 locations, was a logistical nightmare because Hellinger air mailed
dailies to Los Angeles and screened footage to determine if it should be
reshot.[59] A compulsive personality, Hellinger appeared on the set every day
even though he was suffering from a serious heart condition.[60] Adding to

the complications was the bureaucratic red tape in a city unaccustomed to location shooting. As Universal's New York office informed Hellinger: "An application is required for each location and must be filed at least twenty four hours in advance. Quite often we shoot three or four locations a day. . . . It is obvious that this form of application has been improvised for picture taking, because of a lack of any definite procedure for this type of work. This permit routine certainly creates a hardship for us."[61]

Further suggesting the importance of location shooting for a realist representation of the city was a set list that delineated thirty-four exteriors to include cast members.

Ext. East Side Pier

Ext. Hallorans Home in Queens

Ext. Dexter Apartment House

Ext. Police Headquarters "Centre Street"

Ext. Madison Avenue

Ext. 10th Precinct Station House

Ext. Homicide Building

Ext. at Billboard

Ext. Dead End Street

Ext. Madison Avenue Jewelry Store

Ext. East Side Street

Ext. East Side Pier

Int. and Ext. Lexington Avenue, Beauty Shop

Ext. Fashionable Jewelry Shop

Ext. Street in East Eighties (Niles Apt.)

Ext. Fire Escape to Alley—Niles Apt.

Int. Subway Platform

Int. Subway Station

Ext. Bridge above L.I.R.R. Yards

Ext. Times Square

Ext. Building under Construction

Ext. Street Corner

Ext. Cheap Movie Box Office

Ext. East Side Street

Ext. East Side Street and Soda Fountain

Ext. Rivington Street

Ext. Garza's Tenement House

Ext. Backyard and Alley of Tenement House

Ext. Alley at Rear of Store

Ext. Butcher Store and Street

Ext. Williamsburg Bridge[62]

Armed with realist tradition, the cameraman William Daniels (who had worked with the director Jules Dassin on *Brute Force*), along with his assistant Roy Tripp, shot street scenes from a camera concealed behind a two-way mirror on a moving van. Consequently, ordinary street people were unaware that, in the best realist tradition, they were being surreptitiously photographed.[63] The recruitment of New York stage and radio actors without previous film experience to play most of the featured roles was a further attempt to enhance realism.[64]

As the published script of *The Naked City* shows, the film replicates realist texts that construct urban spectatorship through a mediating narrator. As a showman with stage and radio experience, Hellinger decided to record the film's voice-over himself.[65] He speaks infrequently in first person, addresses characters and street people in second person, and describes in third person.[66] What he provides, in a conversational tone, is oversight of a murder investigation that results in an extended tour of the city and depicts its social structure. Walter Winchell, Hellinger's former colleague at the *Daily Mirror*, claimed that the film was "just like a trip to New York."[67] The film replicates urban class and ethnic relations in its characterization of Irish police detectives and white- and blue-collar criminals. Alluring women are stereotyped as a sexual threat. Jean Dexter (born Bartory), a working-class ethnic blonde, persuades Dr. Stoneman, a wealthy and respected dentist, and Frank Niles, a handsome ne'er-do-well, to become jewel thieves. The actual thefts are committed by two criminals from the Lower East Side, Garza and Backalis.[68] Indeed, Garza, a loathsome thug who personifies the film's ethnic other, murders his accomplice as well as Jean because he wants a bigger share of the profits. Contemplating these events at various city sites are veteran Lieutenant Mulvey (Muldoon in the film), who represents the moral center of the film, and his young assistant, Jimmy Halloran, who lives with his wife and child in a lower-middle-class, two-family house in suburban Queens.[69]

A scrutiny of Hellinger's memos as well as the script (in comparison with the film) reveals that the producer was slightly at odds with his scriptwriters. Wald and Maltz draw on realist iconography in the script by describing shots replicating Riis's social photography as well as Ashcan paintings. Concluding the film, for example, was a chase sequence on the Lower East Side with shots of tenements, "a mass of clotheslines, with wet wash hanging from every line," and "a long alleyway, with ash cans and piles of junk in evidence."[70] But at one moment during the chase, the script specifies a point-of-view shot that is Garza's, so that spectators momentarily identify with his being entrapped:

CAMERA IS GARZA'S EYES

A black police sedan is moving slowly along. A detective is questioning the two little girls who are playing jacks. One of them points toward Garza's tenement. CAMERA SWINGS to show cops and plainclothesmen leaping out of cars. CAMERA SWINGS other way to show Mulvey and others starting across street at a run.[71]

Alert to the meaning of these shots, Hellinger dictates changes in his notes on the chase sequence:

> We have been basing our Garza Chase finish on a misconception. We have lost our narrator, and our feeling of the city, and in so doing the picture has tailed off into the type of sequence that has been done a thousand and one times. We are personalizing the story of a man who was merely incidental to our entire yarn, and we can lose everything we have gained. . . . We should play most of this finish from either the narrator or the spectator angle. If, for example, we have a medium shot of Garza racing up the super-structure, and a voice says: "What has happened to you Garza?" . . . "Why are you running now?" . . . you stole—you murdered . . . and now look at you.[72]

By privileging the narrator, Hellinger reinforced realist practice that denied ethnic tenement dwellers their subjectivity and bolstered the moral position of the spectator.

Although Hellinger reworked *The Naked City* so that it conformed to documentary practice, the events of the blacklist era dictated that realism, scarcely a radical expression, be censored. When Hellinger died prematurely, Universal executives, mindful of the House Un-American Activities Committee, were skittish about a film written by Maltz, a former Communist Party member about to become one of the Hollywood Ten. A number of cuts were thus made in the release print that Hellinger had previewed before his death for his wife, Gladys Glad, and the actor Barry Fitzgerald.[73] Among the deletions were the shot of a couple sleeping on a tenement fire escape in the summer and Lieutenant Mulvey's explanation of crime: "It's a jungle, a city like this. Eight million people struggling for life, for food, for air, for a bit of happiness. Seems like there ain't enough of everything to go around . . . and so sometimes it breaks out in . . . violence."[74] Despite the accessibility of the script, it is difficult to specify the exact nature of cuts made because the extensive changes in voice-over (but not dialogue) reveal that Hellinger and Dassin improvised during filming and postproduction. Indeed, the spectacular Williamsburg Bridge as the site of Garza's death was specified in the set list but not in the script. What could not be attributed to squeamish Universal executives, however, was the casting of a white actor to play a "Negro patrolman" speaking a few lines in the plot.[75] At least Bellows, Riis, and Weegee had not refrained from including blacks as part of the mosaic of the city.

A police detective in *The Naked City* (1948) pursues a villain on the Lower East Side in a shot recalling earlier depictions of slum areas.

Maltz and Wald were apparently not the only source of realist social commentary in *The Naked City*. Jules Dassin, who would be blacklisted after Edward Dmytryk named him in his testimony, described the release as a butchered version of his final cut. Later, he claimed that he had enhanced the social exposition of the film while on location by using camera work to move beyond the script. Shots that were cut included a pan from a Bowery building named Hotel Progress to a man lying in the gutter, and a view of a jewelry store window that pulled back to reveal two derelicts.[76] Such representation of class inequity was ironic but still part of the realist iconography that reinscribed social hierarchies. Universal, however, was intimidated by a political climate in which stark expressions of class difference might be considered un-American. *The Naked City* thus showed that a realist representation of the city as a social matrix was subject to censorship not only directly by Breen, but indirectly by the House Un-American Activities Committee.

Despite politics, Universal executives realized that the brilliant location shooting (which would win an Academy Award) rendered *The Naked City* a distinctive realist film.[77] Undoubtedly, they were as concerned about the film's box office appeal as they were about alienating the House Un-American Activities Committee. A carefully orchestrated publicity and advertising campaign thus focused on Hellinger's lifelong love affair with New York: "Hellinger's own name is an impressive selling element. Hellinger was exploited for years by his newspaper syndicate as the modern O. Henry and the man who knew Manhattan history. This picture is Hellinger's inside story of the great city.... We will also make capital of the fact that this picture was filmed in its entirety on the sidewalks of New York."[78]

Ads for *The Naked City* trumpeted "THE MOST EXCITING STORY OF THE WORLD'S MOST EXCITING CITY!" A manual for exhibitors claimed that a selling point was the "realistic type of story which reveals police methods as they really are."[79] Critics were, for the most part, enthusiastic about the film's realism, and audiences crowded the box office.[80] Leo Mishkin wrote in the *New York Morning Telegraph* that the film was "the most accurate picture of New York City . . . captured on the screen" since Ralph Steiner and Willard Van Dyke's *The City* (1939), a documentary with disturbing realist images meant to provoke urban reform.[81] Bosley Crowther complained in the *New York Times*, however, that "the Hellinger interest in the seamier side of N.Y. life, expressed in a flood of soundtrack rhetoric, seems a shade immature in graphic view."[82] Crowther may have been unwittingly prescient. As a representation of the cityscape dating back to the nineteenth century, realism had been eclipsed in other art forms and would soon be displaced in film noir by a more modernist aesthetic. Still, realist conventions remain dominant in depictions of the other that reinforce racial, ethnic, and class stratification, especially on television. Indeed, *The Naked City* was recycled as a series on the small screen and anticipated detective shows like *Dragnet* (not to mention gritty contemporary dramas like *NYPD Blue* and *Homicide*, or even the evening news). As postscripts, such programs signify that a highbrow cultural form attesting to the ambivalence of the genteel classes toward urban life had, by midcentury, thoroughly saturated popular culture.

NOTES

An early version of this paper was presented at a symposium organized by Liana Vardi for the Department of History at the State University of New York, Buffalo, in March 1997. I am grateful to Ned Comstock at the University of Southern California for his thoughtfulness in assisting me with my research; to Robert Gilliam at the Interlibrary Loan office at the State University of New York, Brockport, for timely access to sources; to Archie Koontz at the Liftbridge Bookstore for tracking down out-of-print books; and to Robert J. Smith for reproducing photos. I am indebted to my late father, Setsuo Higashi, for sharing a sense of wonderment as we watched film noir together in postwar Los Angeles.

1 Charles O'Brien argues that, in fact, the term was used by French critics in the 1930s. See his "Film Noir in France: Before the Liberation," in *Iris* 21 (spring 1996): 7–20.

2 "Out of the Past," *Vogue*, November 1997, 218; "Three Major Designers Clothe the Naked City," *New York Times*, April 12, 1997, 27; Ken Bensinger, "Art and Money," *Wall Street Journal*, June 8, 2001, w4.

3 A. M. Karimi, *Toward a Definition of the American Film Noir* (New York: Arno Press, 1976), 5.

4 James Naremore, *More Than Night: Film Noir in Its Contexts* (Berkeley: University of California Press, 1998), 5. Naremore argues that film noir is modernist. See also Edward Dimendberg, "From Berlin to Bunker Hill: Urban Space, Late Modernity, and Film Noir in Fritz Lang's and Joseph Losey's *M*," *Wide Angle* 14 (October 1997): 62–92.

5 Paul Ottoson, *A Reference Guide to the American Film Noir, 1940–1958* (Metuchen, N.J.: Scarecrow Press, 1981), 2; Paul Kerr, "Out of What Past? Notes on the B Film Noir," in *The Hollywood Film Industry*, ed. Paul Kerr (London: Routledge and Kegan Paul, 1986), 221–22.

6 Marc Vernet, "Film Noir on the Edge of Doom," in *Shades of Noir: A Reader*, ed. Joan Copjec (London: Verso, 1983), 9–10; Kerr, "Out of What Past? 221; Foster Hirsch, *The Dark Side of the Screen: Film Noir* (New York: Da Capo, 1981), 82. Vernet credits Wyckoff for DeMille's chiaroscuro lighting, but more important was David Belasco's well-known set designer, Wilfred Buckland. Although there is low-key lighting in certain scenes in *The Squaw Man* (1913)—the first feature DeMille codirected with Oscar Apfel—the campfire scenes in *The Virginian* (1914) signal Buckland's arrival. Thomas Elsaesser, wondering what happened to low-key lighting in the 1920s and 1930s, quotes Vernet on its survival in B pictures. See his "A German Ancestry to Film Noir? Film History and Its Imaginary," *Iris* 21 (spring 1996): 134. Actually, DeMille, credited with spurring the postwar economy, ceased to represent consumption in moral terms and celebrated Jazz Age excess. As a result, his lighting technique changed. See my *Cecil B. DeMille and American Culture* (Berkeley: University of California Press, 1994). See also Peter Baxter, "On the History and Ideology of Film Lighting," *Screen* 16 (autumn 1975): 83–107; Lea Jacobs, "Lasky Lighting," in *The DeMille Legacy*, ed. Paolo Cherchi Usai and Lorenzo Codelli (Pordenone: Edizioni Biblioteca dell'Immagine, 1991), 250–61; Lea Jacobs, "Belasco, DeMille and the Development of Lasky Lighting," *Film History* 5 (December 1993): 405–18; and J. A. Place and L. S. Peterson, "Some Visual Motifs of Film Noir," in *Movies and Methods*, ed. Bill Nichols (Berkeley: University of California Press, 1976), 325–32.

7 Frank Krutnik, *In a Lonely Street: Film Noir, Genre, Masculinity* (London: Routledge, 1991), 19.

8 Interview with DeMille, June 28, 1957, in *The Squaw Man* folder, Personal:

Autobiography, DeMille Archives, Brigham Young University. Script of *The Cheat*, Special Collections, University of Southern California.

9 J. P. Telotte, "The Fantastic Realism of Film Noir: *Kiss Me Deadly*," *Wide Angle* 14 (January 1991): 6; Kerr, "Out of What Past?" 223–29; Carl Richardson, *Autopsy: An Element of Realism in Film Noir* (Metuchen, N.J.: Scarecrow, 1992), 3.

10 David Shi, *Facing Facts: Realism in American Thought and Culture, 1850–1920* (New York: Oxford University Press, 1995), 4–5. Although some critics do not differentiate between realism and naturalism, others point out that American realism validates individualism as opposed to environmental forces.

11 Amy Kaplan, *The Social Construction of American Realism* (Chicago: University of Chicago Press, 1988), introduction; Nancy Glazener, *Reading for Realism: The History of a U.S. Literary Institution, 1850–1910* (Durham, N.C.: Duke University Press, 1997), introduction; Alfred Habegger, *Gender, Fantasy, and Realism in American Literature* (New York: Columbia University Press, 1982), chapter 11. On sentimentalism, see especially Ann Douglas, *The Feminization of America* (New York: Knopf, 1977).

12 Peter Conrad, *The Art of the City: Views and Versions of New York* (New York: Oxford University Press, 1984), 69.

13 David Ward, *Poverty, Ethnicity and the American City: Changing Conceptions of the Slum and the Ghetto* (Cambridge: Cambridge University Press, 1989), 95.

14 See Michel Foucault, *Discipline and Punish: The Birth of the Prison*, trans. Alan Sheridan (New York: Pantheon, 1978); and Edward W. Said, *Orientalism* (New York: Random House, 1978). A truly panoptic moment occurs onscreen when James Stewart visits a prison in *Call Northside 777*. Shots of Stewart with his back to a guard surveying prisoners from the center of a circular floor plan approximate Jeremy Bentham's panopticon.

15 Ward, *Poverty, Ethnicity and the American City* 78; quoted in Craig Owens, "The Discourse of Others: Feminists and Postmodernism," in *The Anti-Aesthetic: Essays on Postmodern Culture*, ed. Hal Foster (Port Townsend, Wash.: Bay Press, 1983), 80.

16 On race in film noir, see Eric Lott, "The Whiteness of Film Noir," in *Whiteness: A Critical Reader*, ed. Mike Hill (New York: New York University Press, 1997), 81–101; E. Ann Kaplan, "'The Dark Continent of Film Noir': Race, Displacement and Metaphor in Tourneur's *Cat People* (1942) and Welles' *The Lady from Shanghai* (1948)," in *Women in Film Noir*, ed. E. Ann Kaplan (London: British Film Institute, 199), 183–201; and Julian Murphet, "Film Noir and the Rational Unconscious," *Screen* 39 (spring 1998): 23–35. See also Peter Feng, "Being Chinese American, Becoming Asian American: *Chan Is Missing*," *Cinema Journal* 35 (summer 1996): 88–118.

17 Alan Trachtenberg, "Experiments in Another Country: Stephen Crane's City Sketches," in *American Realism: New Essays*, ed. Eric Sundquist (Baltimore, Md.: Johns Hopkins University Press, 1972), 139–41.

18 On sensationalism and early film, see Ben Singer, *Melodrama and Modernity:*

Early Sensational Cinema and Its Contexts (New York: Columbia University Press, 2001), chapter 3.

19 Stuart M. Blumin, introduction to George G. Foster, *New York by Gas-Light and Other Urban Sketches* (Berkeley: University of California Press, 1990), 1. See also Stuart M. Blumin, "Explaining the New Metropolis: Perception, Depiction, and Analysis in Mid-Nineteenth Century New York," *Journal of Urban History* 11 (November 1984): 9–38.

20 Foster, *New York by Gas-Light*, 69.

21 John Grafton, *New York in the Nineteenth Century: 317 Engravings from Harper's Weekly and Other Contemporary Sources*, 2nd ed. (Mineola, N.Y.: Dover Publications, 1977), 68; Peter Beacon Hales, *Silver Cities: The Photography of American Urbanization, 1839–1915* (Philadelphia: Temple University Press, 1984), 188. See also John A. Kouwenhoven, *Adventures of America 1857–1900: A Pictorial Record from Harper's Weekly* (New York: Harper and Bros., 1938); Sally Lorenson Gross, *Toward an Urban View: The Nineteenth-Century American City in Prints* (New Haven, Conn.: Yale University Press, 1989).

22 What began as nickelodeon entertainment for the lower classes thus resulted not only in immigrants being seen through the eyes of their social "betters," but also seeing themselves as ethnic stereotypes.

23 Stories abound as to how Fellig was renamed. Some claim that he was named after the Ouija board.

24 Hales, *Silver Cities*, chapters 2, 3.

25 John F. Kasson, *Rudeness and Civility: Manners in Nineteenth-Century America* (New York: Hill and Wang, 1990), chapter 3.

26 Hales, *Silver Cities*, 178. Charles A. Madison argues that only thirty-eight pictures redrawn by artists were published in the first edition (Madison, preface to Jacob A. Riis, *How the Other Half Lives: Studies among the Tenements of New York* [New York: Dover Publications, 1971]).

27 Riis reviled the Chinese but was sympathetic toward blacks, as was Weegee.

28 See Mark Pittenger, "A World of Difference: Constructing the 'Underclass' in Progressive America," *American Quarterly* 49 (March 1997): 26–65.

29 John Tagg, *The Burden of Representation: Essays in Photographies and Histories* (Amherst: University of Massachusetts Press, 1988), 6. On Jacob A. Riis, see Alexander Alland Sr., *Jacob A. Riis: Photographer and Citizen* (Millerton, NY: Aperture, 1974); Hales, *Silver Cities*, chapter 4; Carol Schloss, *In Visible Light: Photography and the American Writer 1840–1940* (New York: Oxford University Press, 1987); and Maren Stange, *Symbols of Ideal Life: Social Documentary Photography in America 1890–1950* (Cambridge: Cambridge University Press, 1989), chapter 1.

30 Shi, *Facing Facts*, 253–58; Brendan Prendenville, *Realism in Twentieth-Century Painting* (London: Thames and Hudson, 2000), 24; Conrad, *The Art of the City* 93; H. Barbara Weinberg, Doreen Bolger, and David Park Curry, *American Impressionism and Realism: The Painting of Modern Life, 1885–1915* (New York: Metropolitan Museum of Art, 1994), 5, 38.

31 Grafton, *New York in the Nineteenth Century*, 62–63; Weinberg, Bolger, and Curry, *American Impressionism and Realism*, 194–96, 278, 287, 300.

32 Shi, *Facing Facts*, 254; Prendeville, *Realism in Twentieth-Century Painting*, 27–28. Prendeville argues that some Ashcan paintings were atmospheric in the sense that the photography of Alfred Stieglitz (whom Weegee admired) and Edward Steichen was pictorial. Some of this photography, as well as Riis's contrasting urban studies, influenced DeMille in *Kindling*.

33 Prendeville, *Realism in Twentieth-Century Painting*, 22–25; Weinberg, Bolger, and Curry, *American Impressionism and Realism*, 234–37.

34 Conrad, *The Art of the City*, 262. According to Conrad, Walker Evans was reticent about his surreptitious photographs of New York subway riders and did not publish them for twenty years.

35 See Martin Green, *New York 1913: The Armory Show and the Paterson Strike Pageant* (New York: Macmillan, 1988).

36 Hirsch, *The Dark Side of the Screen*, 80–83; Conrad, *The Art of the City*, 97–100.

37 Hirsch, *The Dark Side of the Screen*, 83.

38 Miles Barth, "Weegee's World," in *Weegee's World*, ed. Miles Barth (Boston: Little, Brown, 1997), 11–34.

39 Suzanne Burrey Johnston, "As I Remember Weegee," *Photo Review* 22 (winter 1999): 13.

40 On the middle classes, see Stuart M. Blumin, *The Emergence of the Middle Class: Social Experience in the American City, 1760–1900* (Cambridge: Cambridge University Press, 1989); and C. Wright Mills, *White Collar: The American Middle Classes* (New York: Oxford University Press, 1951).

41 According to Martha Rosler, "historical interests" have resulted in Jacob Riis and Weegee being placed in the pantheon alongside more "classical" photographers like Lewis Hine and Danny Lyon. See her essay "In, Around and Afterthoughts (on Documentary Photography)," in *The Context of Meaning: Critical Histories of Photography*, ed. Richard Bolton (Cambridge, Mass.: MIT Press, 1989), 318. See also *The Social Scene: The Ralph M. Parsons Foundation Photography Collection at the Museum of Contemporary Art, Los Angeles* (Los Angeles: Museum of Contemporary Art, 2000) for recent essays on documentary photography.

42 Conrad, *The Art of the City*, 155; Madison, preface, viii.

43 Alain Bergala, "Weegee and Film Noir," in *Weegee's World*, ed. Miles Barth (Boston: Little, Brown, 1997), 73. Weegee did make films that were shown in New York.

44 Weegee, *Naked City* (New York: Da Capo, 1973 [1945]), chapters 4 and 11. See also Miles Orvell, "Weegee's Voyeurism and the Mastery of Urban Disorder," in *After the Machine: Visual Arts and the Erasing of Cultural Boundaries* (Jackson: University of Mississippi Press, 1995), 71–96.

45 David Serlin and Jesse Lerner, "Weegee and the Jewish Question," *Wide Angle* 19 (October 1997): 94–107. The authors label Weegee's work "vulgar modernism," and they link him to Ashcan painters whom they also dub modernist.

But Robert Henri and John Sloan are realists, especially when their work is compared to the art unveiled at the Armory Show.

46 Weegee, *Naked City*, 128, 130–31; Barth, "Weegee's World," 26–27.

47 See Raymond Fielding, *The American Newsreel, 1911–1967* (Norman: University of Oklahoma Press, 1972).

48 Weegee, *Naked City*, chapters 1, 18. See note 65 below for parallels in the film version.

49 See Raymond Fielding, *The March of Time, 1935–1951* (New York: Oxford University Press, 1978).

50 Raymonde Borde and Etienne Chaumeton, "Toward a Definition of Film Noir," trans. Alain Silver, in *Film Noir Reader*, ed. Alain Silver and James Ursini (New York: Limelight, 1999), 19–21 (the excerpt is from *Panorama du film noir américain*); Charles Higham and Joel Greenberg, *Hollywood in the Forties* (New York: A. S. Barnes and Co., 1968), chapter 5; Karimi, *Toward a Definition of the American Film Noir*, 2; Jon Tuska, *Dark Cinema: American Film Noir in Cultural Perspective* (Westport, Conn.: Greenwood, 1984), 193; Krutnik, *In a Lonely Street*, 25; J. P. Telotte, *Voices in the Dark: The Narrative Pattern of Film Noir* (Urbana: University of Illinois Press, 1989), chapter 8; J. P. Telotte, "Outside the System: the Documentary Voice of Film Noir," *New Orleans Review* 14 (1987): 35–63; Robert G. Porfirio, "No Way Out: Existential Motifs in the Film Noir," *Sight and Sound* 45 (autumn 1976), 212; Raymond Durgnat, "Paint It Black: The Family Tree of the Film Noir," *Cinema*, no. 6/7 (August 1970): 49–56; Paul Schrader, "Notes on Film Noir," *Film Comment* (spring 1972): 12; Richardson, *Autopsy*, 5; Alain Silver, "Introduction," *Film Noir Reader*, ed. Silver and Ursini, 8. See also Alain Silver and Elizabeth Ward, eds., *Film Noir: An Encyclopedic Reference to the American Film Noir* (Woodstock, N.Y.: Overlook Press, 1979). Naremore argues that "there has never been a single noir style" (*More Than Night*, 7).

51 When I wrote this essay in 2001, I did not have the benefit of reading Edward Dimendberg's acclaimed *Film Noir and The Spaces of Modernity* (Cambridge, Mass.: Harvard University Press, 2004). Writing in chapter 1 about Weegee in relation to *The Naked City*, Dimendberg stresses conceptualizations of urban space, social organization, and subjectivity.

52 Malvin Wald, "Afterword: The Anatomy of a Hit," in Malvin Wald and Albert Maltz, *The Naked City* (Carbondale: Southern Illinois University Press, 1979), 135–48.

53 Malvin Wald to Mark Hellinger, undated, Mark Hellinger Papers, Special Collections, University of Southern California (hereafter, Hellinger Papers, USC).

54 Telegram from Mark Hellinger to Frank Henry, May 9, 1947, Hellinger Papers, USC.

55 Joseph Breen to Mark Hellinger, May 16, 1947, Hellinger Papers, USC.

56 Albert Maltz, Production Notes for Mark Hellinger, April 7, 1947, Hellinger Papers, USC.

57 Richardson, *Autopsy*, 98. See chapter 2 for an account of the production and significance of the film.

58 Loan Agreement, September 16, 1947, Hellinger Papers, USC.

59 Jim Bishop, *The Mark Hellinger Story: A Biography of Broadway and Hollywood* (New York: Appleton-Century Crofts, 1952), 337.

60 Ibid., 334.

61 Gilbert Kurland to Mark Hellinger, June 29, 1947, Hellinger Papers, USC.

62 Set List, Hellinger Papers, USC.

63 Bishop, *The Mark Hellinger Story*, 336–37; Conrad, *The Art of the City*, 158–59; Richardson, *Autopsy*, 88–95.

64 Production Notes, *The Naked City* clipping file, Margaret Herrick Library, Academy of Motion Picture Arts and Sciences, Los Angeles (hereafter, AMPAS). See also Herb A. Lightman, *American Cinematographer* 29 (May 1948): 152–79. Lightman based much of his article on the Production Notes.

65 See Sarah Kozloff, "Humanizing 'The Voice of God': Narration in *The Naked City*," *Cinema Journal* 23 (summer 1984): 41–53; Sarah Kozloff, *Invisible Storytellers: Voice-Over Narration in American Fiction Film* (Berkeley: University of California Press, 1988). Absent from the script is the beginning of the narration, in which Hellinger introduces himself and the film in a self-reflexive manner. Indeed, the film's credits, shown at the end, are stated in first-person plural and so continues the voice-over.

66 Wald and Maltz, *The Naked City*. Interestingly, all but one of the stills reproduced in the script are from some other takes than what appears in the film.

67 Telegram from Al Horwits to John Joseph-Maurice Bergman, January 26, 1948, in Hellinger Papers, USC.

68 The spelling of Garza's name is changed in the film to Garzah.

69 Wald and Maltz, *The Naked City*.

70 Ibid., 128.

71 Ibid., 127.

72 Notes on Chase Sequence—"The Naked City," undated, Hellinger Papers, USC.

73 Bishop, *The Mark Hellinger Story*, 357.

74 Wald and Maltz, *The Naked City*, 4, 70.

75 Ibid., 104.

76 John Francis Lane, "I See Dassin Make 'The Law,'" *Films and Filming* (September 1958): 28; Andrew Horton, "Jules Dassin: A Multi-National Filmmaker Considered," *Film Criticism* 8 (spring 1984): 24; "Jules Dassin: An Interview with Cynthia Grenier," *Sight and Sound* 27 (winter 1957/58): 142. Actually, the filmmakers could not legally clear the rights to photograph the Hotel Progress, but footage probably would have been deleted anyway.

77 Cameraman William Daniels and editor Paul Weatherwax received Academy Awards for their work on the film.

78 A Publicity and Advertising Campaign for "The Naked City," February 2, 1948, Hellinger Papers, USC.

79 Showman's Manual, *The Naked City* clipping file, AMPAS.

80 On the critical response to the film, see Richardson, *Autopsy*, chapter 3. Wald writes in the afterword to the script that according to a Consumer's Union report, 70 percent of the critics rated the film as excellent.

81 Produced by American Documentary Films, Inc., *The City*, outlined by Pare Lorentz and scripted by Henwar Rodakiewicz, was narrated by Lewis Mumford, who at the time was the architecture critic for the *New Yorker*. Some of its shots, such as children playing in the summer, are replicated in *The Naked City*. The documentary uses realist clichés to make a case for urban planning that assumes a homogeneous population and does not involve economic restructuring. Although realist, some of the film's images are indebted to Charles Sheeler and Paul Strand's *Manahatta* (1921), acknowledged as an early avant-garde film.

82 Reviews by Leo Mishkin and by Bosley Crowther, *The Naked City* clipping file, AMPAS.

BIBLIOGRAPHY

Abbott, Mary Allen. *Children's Responses to the Motion Picture "The Thief of Baghdad."* Rome: International Educational Cinematographic Institute, League of Nations, 1931.

Abel, Richard. *The Red Rooster Scare: Making Cinema American, 1900–1910.* Berkeley: University of California Press, 1999.

Addams, Jane. *The Spirit of Youth and City Streets.* New York: Macmillan Company, 1909.

Adorno, Theodor. "Freudian Theory and the Pattern of Fascist Propaganda." In *The Essential Frankfurt School Reader,* ed. Andrew Arato and Eike Gebhardt. New York: Continuum, 1982. 118–37.

Alland, Alexander Sr. *Jacob A. Riis: Photographer and Citizen.* Millerton, N.Y.: Aperture, 1974.

Allen, Holly Marie. "Fallen Women and Forgotten Men: Gendered Concepts of Community, Home and Nation, 1932–1945." Ph.D. dissertation, Yale University, 1996.

Allen, Robert C., and Douglas Gomery. *Film History: Theory and Practice.* New York: Knopf, 1985.

Anderson, Mark Lynn. "Shooting Star: Understanding Wallace Reid and His Public." In *Headline Hollywood: A Century of Film Scandal,* ed. Adrienne L. McLean and David A. Cook. New Brunswick, N.J.: Rutgers University Press, 2001. 83–106.

Ang, Ien. *Watching Dallas.* London: Methuen, 1985.

Arato, Andrew, and Eike Gebhardt, eds. *The Essential Frankfurt School Reader.* New York: Continuum, 1982.

Ariès, Philippe. *Centuries of Childhood: A Social History of Family Life.* Trans. Robert Baldick. New York: Vintage, 1962.

Arnold, Julean, ed. *China through the American Window.* Shanghai: American Chamber of Commerce, 1932.

Auty, Chris. "The Complete Spielberg." *Sight and Sound* (autumn 1982): 279.

Balio, Tino, ed. *The American Film Industry*. Madison: University of Wisconsin Press, 1985.

———. *Grand Design: Hollywood as a Modern Business Enterprise, 1930–1939*. Berkeley: University of California Press, 1995.

Barry, Iris. "Why Wait for Posterity?" *Hollywood Quarterly* 1, no. 2 (January 1946): 131–37.

Bart, Peter. *The Gross: The Hits, the Flops—The Summer That Ate Hollywood*. New York: St. Martin's Press, 1999.

Barth, Miles. *Weegee's World*. Boston: Little, Brown, 1997.

Baxter, Peter. "On the History and Ideology of Film Lighting." *Screen* 16, no. 3 (autumn 1975): 83–107.

Bean, Jennifer, and Diane Negra, eds. *A Feminist Reader in Early Cinema*. Durham, N.C.: Duke University Press, 2002.

Bellingham, Bruce. "Institution and Family: An Alternative View of Nineteenth Century Child Saving." *Social Problems* 33, no. 6 (1986): 533–57.

Bellour, Raymond, ed. *Le cinéma american: Analyses de films*. Vol. 1. Paris: Flammarion, 1980.

———. "On Fritz Lang." *Sub-Stance*, no. 9 (1974): 25–34.

Belton, John. *Widescreen Cinema*. Cambridge, Mass.: Harvard University Press, 1992.

Benjamin, Walter. "The Critique of Violence." In *Reflections*, ed. Peter Demetz; trans. Edmund Jephcott. New York: Harcourt Brace Jovanovich, 1978.

Bergala, Alain. "Weegee and Film Noir." In *Weegee's World*, ed. Miles Barth. Boston: Little, Brown, 1997.

Berriatúa, Luciano. *Los proverbios chinos de F. W. Murnau: Etapa amaericana*. Madrid: Filmotecca Española, 1990.

Black, Gregory D. *Hollywood Censored: Morality Codes, Catholics, and the Movies*. Cambridge: Cambridge University Press, 1994.

Blake, Roger. *The Porno Shops*. Cleveland, Ohio: Century Books, 1969.

Blaszczyk, Regina. *Imagining Consumers: Design and Innovation from Wedgwood to Corning*. Baltimore, Md.: Johns Hopkins University Press, 2000.

Blumer, Herbert, and Philip M. Hauser, *Movies, Delinquency and Crime* (New York: Macmillan, 1933.

Blumin, Stuart. *The Emergence of the Middle Class: Social Experience in the American City, 1760–1900*. Cambridge: Cambridge University Press, 1989.

———. "Explaining the New Metropolis: Perception, Depiction, and Analysis in Mid-Nineteenth Century New York." *Journal of Urban History* 11 (November 1984): 9–38.

Boddy, William. "Approaching *The Untouchables*: Social Science and Moral Panics in Early Sixties Television." *Cinema Journal* 35, no. 4 (summer 1996): 70–87.

Bolton, Richard, ed. *The Context of Meaning: Critical Histories of Photography*. Cambridge, Mass.: MIT Press, 1989.

Borde, Raymonde, and Etienne Chaumeton. "Toward a Definition of Film Noir." In *Film Noir Reader*, ed. Alain Silver and James Ursini. New York: Limelight, 1999. 19–21.

Bordwell, David. *On the History of Film Style*. Cambridge, Mass.: Harvard University Press, 1997.

Bowser, Eileen. *The Transformation of Cinema, 1907–1915*. Berkeley: University of California Press, 1994.

Boyarin, Daniel. *Unheroic Conduct: The Rise of Heterosexuality and the Invention of the Jewish Man*. Berkeley: University of California Press, 1997.

Britton, Andrew. "Blissing Out: The Politics of Reagnite Entertainment." *Movie*, no. 30/31 (1986): 1–42.

Brode, Douglas. *The Films of Steven Spielberg*. New York: Citadel, 1995.

Brodkin, Karen. *How Jews Became White Folks and What That Says About Race in America*. New Brunswick, N.J.: Rutgers University Press, 1999.

Browne, Nick. "The Spectator-in-the-Text: The Rhetoric of *Stagecoach*." *Film Quarterly* 29, no. 2 (winter 1975–76): 26–38.

Brownlow, Kevin. *Behind the Mask of Innocence: The Social Problem Films of the Silent Era*. New York: Knopf, 1990.

———. *The Parade's Gone By*. Berkeley: University of California Press, 1968.

Buscombe, Edward. "Notes on Columbia Pictures Corporation, 1926–1941." *Screen* 16, no. 3 (autumn 1975): 65–82.

Cahiers du Cinema Editorial Collective. "John Ford's *Young Mr. Lincoln*." In *Movies and Methods*, ed. Bill Nichols. Berkeley: University of California Press, 1976. 493–529.

Capra, Frank. *The Name above the Title: An Autobiography*. New York: Macmillan, 1971.

Carroll, Noël. "Film, Rhetoric, and Ideology." In *Explanation and Value in the Arts*, ed. Salim Kemal and Ivan Gaskell. Cambridge: Cambridge University Press, 1993.

Cartwright, Lisa. "U.S. Modernisms and the Emergence of 'The Right Wing of Film Art': The Films of James Sibley Watson, Jr. and Melville Webber." In *Lovers of Cinema: The First American Avant-Garde, 1919–1945*, ed. Jan-Christopher Horak. Madison: University of Wisconsin Press, 1995. 156–79.

Chauncey, George. *Gay New York: Gender, Urban Culture and the Making of the Gay Male World, 1890–1940*. New York: HarperCollins, 1994.

Clark, Clifford Edward Jr. *The American Family Home, 1800–1960*. Chapel Hill: University of North Carolina Press, 1986.

Clark, Danae. *Negotiating Hollywood: The Cultural Politics of Actors' Labor*. Minneapolis: University of Minnesota Press, 1995.

Clifford, James, and George E. Marcus, eds. *Writing Culture: The Poetics and Politics of Ethnography*. Berkeley: University of California Press, 1986.

Collins, Jim, Hilary Radner, and Ava Preacher Collins, eds. *Film Theory Goes to the Movies*. New York: Routledge, 1993.

Conrad, Peter. *The Art of the City: Views and Versions of New York*. New York: Oxford University Press, 1984.

Copjec, Joan, ed. *Film Noir: A Reader*. London: Verso, 1983.

Couvares, Francis G., ed. *Movie Censorship and American Culture*. Washington, D.C.: Smithsonian Institution Press, 1996.

Cowan, Ruth Schwartz. *More Work for Mother: The Ironies of Household Technology From the Open Hearth to the Microwave*. New York: Basic Books, 1983.

Crafton, Donald. *The Talkies: American Cinema's Transition to Sound, 1926–1931*. Berkeley: University of California Press, 1999.

Crapanzano, Vincent. "On the Writing of Ethnography." *Dialectical Anthropology* 2 (1977): 69–73.

Crow, Carl. *Four Hundred Million Customers: The Experiences—Some Happy, Some Sad of an American in China*. New York: Harper and Brothers, 1937.

Cunningham, Jo. *Collector's Encyclopedia of American Dinnerware*. Paducah, Ky.: Collector Books, 1982.

Curry, Ramona. *Too Much of a Good Thing: Mae West as Cultural Icon*. Minneapolis: University of Minnesota Press, 1996.

DeCordova, Richard. "Ethnography and Exhibition: The Child Audience, the Hays Office and Saturday Matinees." *Camera Obscura* 23 (May 1990): 91–106.

———. "The Mickey in Macy's Window: Childhood, Consumerism and Disney Animation." In *Disney Discourse: Producing the Magic Kingdom*, ed. Eric Smoodin. New York: Routledge, 1994. 203–13.

———. *Picture Personalities: The Emergence of the Star System in America*. Urbana: University of Illinois Press, 1990.

de Grazia, Edward, and Roger Newman. *Banned Films: Movies, Censors and the First Amendment*. New York: Bowker, 1982.

D'Emilio, John, and Estelle B. Freedman. *Intimate Matters: A History of Sexuality in America*. New York: Harper and Row, 1988.

Denning, Michael. *The Cultural Front: The Laboring of American Culture in the Twentieth Century*. London: Verso, 1996.

Di Lauro, Al, and Gerald Rabkin. *Dirty Movies: An Illustrated History of the Stag Film, 1915–1970*. New York: Chelsea House, 1976.

Dimendberg, Edward. *Film Noir and the Spaces of Modernity*. Cambridge, Mass.: Harvard University Press, 2004.

———. "From Berlin to Bunker Hill: Urban Space, Late Modernity, and Film Noir in Fritz Lang's and Joseph Losey's *M*." *Wide Angle* 14 (October 1997): 62–92.

Doherty, Thomas. *Pre-Code Hollywood: Sex, Immorality, and Insurrection in American Cinema, 1930–1934*. New York: Columbia University Press, 1999.

Doty, Alexander. *Making Things Perfectly Queer: Interpreting Mass Culture*. Minneapolis: University of Minnesota Press, 1993.

Douglas, Ann. *The Feminization of America*. New York: Knopf, 1977.

Dumont, Hervé. *Frank Borzage: Sarastro à Hollywood*. Milan: Edizioni Gabriele Mazzotta/Cinémathèque Française, 1993.

Durgnat, Raymond. "'Paint It Black': The Family Tree of the Film Noir." *Cinema*, nos. 6/7 (August 1970): 49–56.

Dyer, Richard. *Heavenly Bodies: Film Stars and Society*. New York: St. Martin's Press, 1986.

———. *Now You See It: Studies on Lesbian and Gay Film*. New York: Routledge, 1990.

———. *Stars*. London: British Film Institute, 1979.

Eckert, Charles. "The Carole Lombard in Macy's Window." In *Fabrications*, ed. Jane Gaines and Charlotte Herzog. New York: Routledge, 1990. 100–21.

Eisner, Lotte. *Murnau*. London: Secker and Warburg, 1973.

Elsaesser, Thomas. "A German Ancestry to Film Noir? Film History and Its Imaginary." *Iris* 21 (spring 1996): 129–44.

Enstad, Nan. *Ladies of Labor, Girls of Adventure: Working Women, Popular Culture, and Labor Politics at the Turn of the Twentieth Century*. New York: Columbia University Press, 1999.

Eyman, Scott. *The Speed of Sound*. New York: Simon and Schuster, 1997.

Feldman, Matthew. *The National Board of Censorship (Review) of Motion Pictures: 1909–1922*. New York: Arno, 1977.

Feng, Peter. "Being Chinese American, Becoming Asian American: *Chan Is Missing*." *Cinema Journal* 35, no. 4 (summer 1996): 88–118.

Ferguson, Otis. *The Film Criticism of Otis Ferguson*, Robert Wilson, ed. Philadelphia: Temple University Press, 1971.

Feuerwerker, Albert. *The Chinese Economy, 1912–1949*. Ann Arbor: University of Michigan Press, 1968.

Fielding, Raymond. *The American Newsreel, 1911–1967*. Norman: University of Oklahoma Press, 1972.

———. *The March of Time, 1935–1951*. New York: Oxford University Press, 1978.

Fiske, John. *Television Culture*. New York: Methuen, 1987.

Flaherty, David. "A Few Reminiscences." *Film Culture* 20 (1959): n.p.

Foster, George G. *New York by Gas-Light and other Urban Sketches*, ed. Stuart Blumin. Berkeley: University of California Press, 1990.

Foster, Hal, ed. *The Anti-Aesthetic: Essays on Postmodern Culture*. Port Townsend, Wash.: Bay Press, 1983.

Foucault, Michel. *Discipline and Punish: The Birth of the Prison*, trans. Alan Sheridan. New York: Pantheon, 1978.

———. *The History of Sexuality. Volume 1: An Introduction*, trans. Robert Hurley. New York: Vintage, 1980.

———, ed. *I, Pierre Rivière, Having Slaughtered My Mother, My Sister, and My Brother . . . A Case of Parracide in the Nineteenth Century*. Lincoln: University of Nebraska Press, 1982.

———. "What Is an Author?" In *Textual Strategies: Perspectives in Post-Structuralist Criticism*, ed. Josue V. Harari. Ithaca, N.Y.: Cornell University Press, 1979. 141–60.

Freeburg, Victor. *The Art of Photoplay Making*. New York: Macmillan, 1918.

Friedman, Andrea. "'The Habitats of Sex-Crazed Perverts': Campaigns Against Burlesque in Depression-Era New York City." *Journal of the History of Sexuality* 7, no. 2 (October 1996): 203–8.

Frugé, August. *A Skeptic among Scholars: August Frugé on University Publishing.* Berkeley: University of California Press, 1993.

Fuller, Kathryn. *At the Picture Show: Small Town Audiences and the Creation of Movie Fan Culture.* Charlottesville: University Press of Virginia, 2001 [1996].

———, ed. *Movie-Going History in Small Town America.* Berkeley: University of California Press, 2007.

Gaines, Jane, and Charlotte Herzog, eds. *Fabrications.* New York: Routledge, 1990.

Glazener, Nancy. *Reading for Realism: The History of a U.S. Literary Institution, 1850–1910.* Durham, N.C.: Duke University Press, 1997.

Gomery, Douglas. "The Coming of Sound to the American Cinema: A History of the Transformation of an Industry." Ph.D. dissertation, University of Wisconsin, Madison, 1975.

———. *The Hollywood Studio System.* New York: St. Martin's Press, 1986.

———. *Shared Pleasures: A History of Film Presentation in the United States.* Madison: University of Wisconsin Press, 1992.

Grafton, John. *New York in the Nineteenth Century: 317 Engravings from Harper's Weekly and Other Contemporary Sources.* Mineola, N.Y.: Dover Publications, 1977.

Green, Martin. *New York 1913: The Armory Show and the Paterson Strike Pageant.* New York: Macmillan, 1988.

Greimas, A. J. *Structural Semantics: An Attempt at a Method,* trans. Daniele McDowell, Ronald Schleifer, and Alan Velie. Lincoln: University of Nebraska Press, 1984.

Grenier, Cynthia. "Jules Dassin: An Interview with Cynthia Grenier." *Sight and Sound* 27, no. 3 (winter 1957–58): n.p.

Greven, Philip. *The Protestant Temperament: Patterns of Child-Rearing, Religious Experience and the Self in Early America.* New York: Knopf, 1977.

Grieveson, Lee. "The Thaw-White Scandal, *The Unwritten Law,* and the Scandal of Cinema." In *Headline Hollywood: A Century of Film Scandal,* ed. Adrienne L. McClean and David Cook. New Brunswick, N.J.: Rutgers University Press, 2001. 27–51.

Gross, Sally Lorenson. *Toward an Urban View: The Nineteenth-Century American City in Prints.* New Haven: Yale University Press, 1989.

Habegger, Alfred. *Gender, Fantasy, and Realism in American Literature.* New York: Columbia University Press, 1982.

Hales, Peter Beacon. *Silver Cities: The Photography of American Urbanization, 1839–1915.* Philadelphia: Temple University Press, 1984.

Halliday, Jon, ed. *Sirk on Sirk.* London: Secker and Warburg, 1971.

Hammond, Michael. "Laughter during Wartime: Comedy and the Language of

Trauma in British Cinema Regulation, 1917." *Screen* 44, no. 2 (summer 2003): 222–28.

Handel, Leo A. *Hollywood Looks at Its Audience*. Urbana: University of Illinois Press, 1950.

Haney, Robert W. *Comstockery in America: Patterns of Censorship and Control*. New York: Da Capo Press, 1974.

Hansen, Miriam. *Babel and Babylon: Spectatorship in American Silent Film*. Cambridge, Mass.: Harvard University Press, 1991.

Hastie, Amelie. "Circuits of Memory and History: *The Memoirs of Alice Guy-Blaché*." In *The Feminist Reader in Early Cinema*, ed. Jennifer Bean and Diane Negra. Durham, N.C.: Duke University Press, 2002. 29–59.

Heath, Stephen. "Narrative Space." *Screen* 17, no. 3 (autumn 1976): 68–112.

Herman, Ellen. *The Romance of American Psychology: Political Culture in the Age of Experts*. Berkeley: University of California Press, 1995.

Higashi, Sumiko. *Cecil B. DeMille and American Culture: The Silent* Era. Berkeley: University of California Press, 1994.

Higham, Charles, and Joel Greenberg. *Hollywood in the Forties*. New York: A. S. Barnes and Co., 1968.

Hill, Mike. *Whiteness: A Critical Reader*. New York: New York University Press, 1997.

Hirsch, Foster. *The Dark Side of the Screen: Film Noir*. New York: Da Capo, 1981.

Hollows, Joanne, and Mark Janovich, eds. *Approaches to Popular Film*. Manchester: Manchester University Press, 1995.

Hoover, J. Edgar. "Combating Merchants of Filth: The Role of the FBI." *University of Pittsburgh Law Review* 25 no. 3 (March 1964): 469–78.

Horak, Jan-Christopher. *Lovers of Cinema: The First American Avant-Garde, 1919–1945*. Madison: University of Wisconsin Press, 1995.

Horton, Andrew. "Jules Dassin: A Multi-National Filmmaker Considered." *Film Criticism* 8 (spring 1984): n.p.

Humphrey, Daniel. "Authorship, History and the Dialectic of Trauma: Derek Jarman's *The Last of England*." *Screen* 44, no. 2 (summer 2003): 208–15.

Iacovetta, Franca, and Wendy Mitchinson. *On the Case: Explorations in Social History*. Toronto: University of Toronto Press, 1998.

Ignatiev, Noel. *How the Irish Became White*. New York: Routledge, 1995.

Ivano, Paul. "American Film Institute Seminar, April 20, 1974." Los Angeles: American Film Institute, 1977.

Jacobs, Lea. "Belasco, DeMille and the Development of Lasky Lighting." *Film History* 5 (December 1993): 405–18.

———. "Lasky Lighting." In *The Demille Legacy*, ed. Paolo Cherchi Usai and Lorenzo Codelli. Pordenone, Italy: Edizioni Biblioteca dell'Immagine, 1991. 250–61.

———. *The Wages of Sin: Censorship and the Fallen Woman Film, 1928–1942*. Madison: University of Wisconsin Press, 1991.

Jacobson, Wolfgang, Hans Helmut Prinzler, and Werner Sudendorf, eds. *Film-museum Berlin*. Berlin: Filmmuseum Berlin–Deutsche Kinemathek and Nicolai, 2000.

Jameson, Fredric. *The Political Unconscious: Narrative as a Socially Symbolic Act*. Ithaca, N.Y.: Cornell University Press, 1981.

Jarvie, Ian. *Hollywood's Overseas Campaign: The North Atlantic Movie Trade, 1920–1950*. Cambridge: Cambridge University Press, 1992.

Jehlen, Myra, and Judith Walkowitz. "Patrolling the Borders: Feminist Historiography and the New Historicism." *Radical History Review* 43 (1989): 23–43.

Jenkins, Henry. "Historical Poetics." In *Approaches to Popular Film*, ed. Joanne Hollows and Mark Jancovich. Manchester: Manchester University Press, 1995. 99–122.

Johnston, Suzanne Burrey. "As I Remember Weegee." *Photo Review* 22 (winter 1999): n.p.

Jowett, Garth. *Film: The Democratic Art*. Boston: Little, Brown, 1976.

Kaplan, Amy. *The Social Construction of American Realism*. Chicago: University of Chicago Press, 1988.

Kaplan, E. Ann. "'The Dark Continent of Film Noir': Race, Displacement and Metaphor in Tourneur's *Cat People* (1942) and Welles' *The Lady from Shanghai* (1948)." In *Women in Film Noir*, ed. Ann Kaplan. London: British Film Institute, 1999. 183–201.

———. "Melodrama, Cinema and Trauma." *Screen* 42, no. 2 (summer 2001): 201–5.

Karimi, A. M. *Toward a Definition of the American Film Noir*. New York: Arno Press, 1976.

Kasson, John F. *Rudeness and Civility: Manners in Nineteenth-Century America*. New York: Hill and Wang, 1990.

Kattelle, Alan D. *Home Movies: A History of the American Industry, 1897–1979*. Hudson, Mass.: self-published, 2000.

Katz, Ephraim. *The Film Encyclopedia*. New York: Lippincott and Crowell, 1979.

Kennedy, Joseph P., ed. *The Story of the Film*. Chicago: A. S. Shaw, 1927.

Kerr, Paul, ed. *The Hollywood Film Industry*. London: Routledge and Kegan Paul, 1986.

Kett, Joseph F. *Rites of Passage: Adolescence in America, 1790 to the Present*. New York: Basic, 1977.

Kleinhans, Chuck. "Independent Features: Hopes and Dreams." In *The New American Cinema*, ed. Jon Lewis. Durham, N.C.: Duke University Press, 1998. 307–27.

Kolker, Robert. *A Cinema of Loneliness: Penn, Kubrick, Coppola, Scorsese, Altman*. New York: Oxford University Press, 1980.

Koszarski, Richard. "City Girl." *Film Comment* (summer 1971): 20–22.

———. *An Evening's Entertainment: The Age of the Silent Feature Picture, 1915–1928*. Berkeley: University of California Press, 1990.

————, interviewer. "Ernest Palmer on Frank Borzage and F. W. Murnau." *Griffithiana*, no. 46 (December 1992): 115–20.

Kouwenhoven, John A. *Adventures of America, 1857–1900: A Pictorial Record from Harper's Weekly*. New York: Harper and Bros., 1938.

Kozloff, Sarah. "Humanizing 'The Voice of God': Narration in *The Naked City*." *Cinema Journal* 23, no. 4 (summer 1984): 41–53.

————. *Invisible Storytellers: Voice-Over Narration in American Fiction Film*. Berkeley: University of California Press, 1988.

Kozol, Wendy. "Madonnas of the Fields: Photography, Gender and 1930s Farm Relief." *Genders* 2 (summer 1988): 1–23.

Kracauer, Siegfried. *From Caligari to Hitler: A Psychological History of the German Film*. Princeton, N.J.: Princeton University Press, 1947.

Krutnik, Frank. *In a Lonely Steet: Film Noir, Genre, Masculinity*. London: Routledge, 1991.

Kuhn, Annette. *Dreaming of Fred and Ginger: Cinema and Cultural Memory*. New York: New York University Press, 2002.

Kuntzell, Thierry. "Savoir, pouvoir, voir." In *Le cinèma american: Analyses de films*, vol. 1, ed. Raymond Bellour. Paris: Flammarion, 1980. 161–72.

Lane, Christina. "Hollywood Star Couples: Classical-Era Romance and Marriage." Ph.D. dissertation, University of Texas, Austin, 1999.

Lane, John Francis. "I See Dassin Make *The Law*." *Films and Filming* (September 1958): n.p.

Langer, Mark. "Flaherty's Hollywood Period: The Crosby Version." *Wide Angle* 20, no. 2 (April 1998): 38–57.

————. "*Tabu*: The Making of a Film." *Cinema Journal* 24, no. 3 (spring 1985): 43–64.

Lasker, Bruno, ed. *Problems of the Pacific 1931: Proceedings of the Fourth Conference of the Institute of Pacific Relations, Hangchow and Shanghai, China, October 21 to November 2*. Chicago: University of Chicago Press, 1932.

Lewis, Jon. *Hollywood v. Hard Core: How the Struggle over Censorship Saved the Modern Film Industry*. New York: New York University Press, 2000.

————, ed. *The New American Cinema*. Durham, N.C.: Duke University Press, 1998.

————. *Whom God Wishes to Destroy: Francis Coppola and the New Hollywood*. Durham, N.C.: Duke University Press, 1995.

Lipkin, Steven N. "*Sunrise*: A Film Meets Its Public." *Quarterly Review of Film Studies* (August 1977): 327–55.

Loos, Anita. *Gentlemen Prefer Blondes*. New York: Boni and Liveright, 1925.

Lott, Eric. "The Whiteness of Film Noir." In *Whiteness: A Critical Reader*, ed. Mike Hill. New York: New York University Press, 1997: 81–101.

Lowrey, Carolyn. *The First One Hundred Noted Men and Women of the Screen*. New York: Moffat, Yard and Co., 1920.

Lugowski, David. "Queering the (New) Deal: Lesbian and Gay Representation and the Depression-Era Cultural Politics of Hollywood's Production Code." *Cinema Journal* 38, no. 2 (winter 1999): 3–35.

———. "Queering the (New) Deal: Lesbian, Gay and Queer Representation in U.S. Cinema, 1929–1941." Ph.D. dissertation, New York University, 1999.

Lynd, Robert, and Helen Merrell Lynd. *Middletown: A Study in American Culture.* New York: Harcourt, 1929.

———. *Middletown in Transition: A Study in Cultural Conflicts.* New York: Harcourt Brace, 1937.

Maas, Frederica Sagor. *The Shocking Miss Pilgrim: A Writer in Early Hollywood.* Lexington: University Press of Kentucky, 1999.

MacGowan, Kenneth. *Behind the Screen: The History and Technique of the Motion Picture.* New York: Delacorte, 1965.

Maltby, Richard. "The Production Code and the Hays Office." In Tino Balio, *Grand Design: Hollywood as a Modern Business Industry, 1930–1939.* Berkeley: University of California Press, 1995. 37–72.

Marchand, Roland. *Advertising the American Dream: Making Way for Modernity, 1920–1940.* Berkeley: University of California Press, 1985.

Marchetti, Gina. *Romance and the "Yellow Peril."* Berkeley: University of California Press, 1993.

Marcus, George E. "Rhetoric and the Ethnographic Genre in Anthropological Research." *Current Anthropology* 21 (1980): 507–10.

Marcus, George E., and James Clifford, "The Making of Ethnographic Texts: A Preliminary Report." *Current Anthropology* 26 (1985): 267–71.

Marcus, George E., and Dick Cushman, "Ethnographies as Texts." *Annual Review of Anthropology* (1982): 25–69.

Martin, Olga J. *Hollywood's Movie Commandments.* New York: H. M. Wilson, 1937.

May, Ernest R., and John K. Fairbank, eds. *America's China Trade in Historical Perspective: The Chinese and American Performance.* Cambridge, Mass.: Harvard University Press, 1986.

Mayne, Judith. *Cinema and Spectatorship.* London: Routledge, 1993.

———. "Marlene Dietrich, *The Blue Angel,* and Female Performance." *Seduction and Theory: Readings of Gender, Representation, and Rhetoric,* ed. Dianne Hunter. Urbana: University of Illinois Press, 1989.

McBride, Joseph. *Frank Capra: The Catastrophe of Success.* New York: Simon and Schuster, 1992.

McElvaine, Robert, ed. *Down and Out in the Great Depression: Letters from the "Forgotten Man."* Chapel Hill: University of North Carolina Press, 1983.

———. *The Great Depression: America, 1929–1941.* New York: Times Books, 1984.

McFadden, Margaret. "'America's Boy Friend Who Couldn't Get a Date': Gender, Race and the Cultural Work of the Jack Benny Program 1932–1946." *Journal of American History* 80, no. 1 (June 1993): 113–34.

Merritt, "Nickelodeon Theatres, 1905–1914: Building an Audience for the Movies." In *The American Film Industry*, ed. Tino Balio. Madison: University of Wisconsin Press, 1985. 83–102.

Milne, Peter. *Motion Picture Directing*. New York: Falk Publishing, 1922.

Milner, Michael. *Sex on Celluloid*. New York: Macfadden, 1964.

Mills, C. Wright. *White Collar: The American Middle Class*. New York: Oxford University Press, 1951.

Mintz, Steven, and Susan Kellogg. *Domestic Revolutions: A Social History of American Family Life*. New York: Free Press, 1988.

Mitchell, Alice Miller. *Children and Movies* (Chicago: University of Chicago Press, 1929.

Moise, Edwin E. *Modern China: A History*. London: Longman, 1986.

Morley, David. *The Nationwide Audience: Structure and Decoding*. London: BFI, 1980.

Mosse, George. *The Image of Man: The Creation of Modern Masculinity*. New York: Oxford University Press, 1996.

Mulvey, Laura. "Visual Pleasure and Narrative Cinema." *Screen* 16, no. 3 (autumn 1975): 6–18.

Murphet, Julian. "Film Noir and the Rational Unconscious." *Screen* 39, no. 1 (spring 1998): 23–35.

Murray, Robert K. *Red Scare: A Study in National Hysteria, 1919–1920*. New York: McGraw-Hill, 1964.

Naison, Mark. *Communists in Harlem during the Depression*. New York: Grove Press, 1983.

Naremore, James. *More Than Night: Film Noir in Its Contexts*. Berkeley: University of California Press, 1998.

Nichols, Bill, ed. *Movies and Methods*, vol. 1. Berkeley: University of California Press, 1976.

Noriega, Chon. "'SOMETHING'S MISSING HERE!' Homosexuality and Film Reviews during the Production Code Era, 1934–1962." *Cinema Journal* 30, no. 1 (fall 1990): 20–41.

O'Brien, Charles. "Film Noir in France: Before the Liberation." *Iris* 21 (spring 1996): 7–20.

Orvell, Miles. *After the Machine: Visual Arts and the Erasing of Cultural Boundaries*. Jackson: University of Mississippi Press, 1995.

Ottoson, Paul. *A Reference Guide to the American Film Noir, 1940–1958*. Metuchen, N.J.: Scarecrow Press, 1981.

Owens, Craig. "The Discourse of Others: Feminists and Postmodernism." In *The Anti-Aesthetic: Essays on Postmodern Culture*. Port Townsend, Wash.: Bay Press, 1983. 57–82.

Palumbo-Liu, David. "The *Bitter Tea* of Frank Capra." *positions* 3, no. 3 (winter 1995): 759–89.

Paul, James C. N., and Murray L. Schwartz, *Federal Censorship: Obscenity in the Mail*. Westport, Conn.: Greenwood Press, 1977.

Pells, Richard. *Radical Visions and American Dreams: Cultural and Social Thought in the Depression Years.* Middletown, Conn.: Wesleyan University Press, 1973.

Pittenger, Mark. "A World of Difference: Constructing the 'Underclass' in Progressive America." *American Quarterly* 49, no. 1 (March 1997): 26–65.

Place, J. A., and L. S. Peterson. "Some Visual Motifs of Film Noir." In *Movies and Methods,* ed. Bill Nichols. Berkeley: University of California Press, 1976. 325–32.

Porfirio, Rogert G. "No Way Out: Existential Motifs in the Film Noir." *Sight and Sound* 45, no. 4 (autumn 1976): 212–17.

Potamianos, George. *Film Exhibition in Sacramento and Placerville.* Berkeley: University of California Press, forthcoming.

Prendeville, Brendan. *Realism in Twentieth-Century Painting.* London: Thames and Hudson, 2000.

Prince, Stephen. *Visions of Empire: Political Imagery in Contemporary American Film.* New York: Praeger, 1992.

Remer, C. F. *Foreign Investments in China.* New York: Macmillan, 1933.

Reynolds, Paige. "'Something for Nothing': Bank Night and the Refashioning of the American Dream." In *Movie-Going History in Small Town America,* ed. Kathryn Fuller-Seeley. Berkeley: University of California Press, 2007.

Richardson, Carl. *Autopsy: An Element of Realism in Film Noir.* Metuchen, N.J.: Scarecrow Press, 1992.

Riesman, David, and Evelyn T. Riesman. "Movies and Audiences." *American Quarterly* 4, no. 3 (fall 1952): 195–202.

Roberts, Edwin A. Jr. *The Smut Rakers: A Report in Depth on Obscenity and the Censors.* Silver Springs, Md.: National Observer, 1966.

Robinson. Gilbert L. "Transportation in Carter County, 1913–1917." *Chronicles of Oklahoma* 19, no. 4 (December 1941): 368–76.

Rose, Jacqueline. *The Case of Peter Pan: Or, The Impossibility of Children's Fiction.* London: Macmillan, 1984.

Rosenbloom, Nancy J. "Between Reform and Regulation: The Struggle over Film Censorship in Progressive America, 1909–1922." *Film History* 1 (1987): 307–25.

Rosler, Martha. "In, Around and Afterthoughts (on Documentary Photography)." In *The Context of Meaning: Critical Histories of Photography,* ed. Richard Bolton. Cambridge, Mass.: MIT Press, 1989: 303–40.

Russell, Hilary. "Training, Restraining and Sustaining: Infant and Child Care in the Late Nineteeth Century." *Material History Bulletin* 21 (1985): 35–49.

Ryan, Michael, and Douglas Kellner. *Camera Politica: The Politics and Ideology of Contemporary Hollywood Film.* Bloomington: Indiana University Press, 1990.

Sachar, Howard M. *A History of the Jews in America.* New York: Random House, 1992.

Said, Edward. *Orientalism.* New York: Random House, 1978.

Sarris, Andrew. *The American Cinema: Directors and Directions, 1929–1968.* New York: Dutton, 1968.

Saunders, Thomas. *Hollywood In Berlin: American Cinema and Weimar Germany*. Berkeley: University of California Press, 1994.

Schaefer, Eric. *"Bold! Daring! Shocking! True!" A History of Exploitation Films, 1919–1959*. Durham, N.C.: Duke University Press, 1999.

Schatz, Thomas. "The New Hollywood." In *Film Theory Goes to the Movies*, ed. Jim Collins, Hilary Radner, and Ava Preacher Collins. New York: Routledge, 1993.

Schrader, Paul. "Notes on Film Noir." *Film Comment* 8, no. 1 (1972): 8–13.

Scloss, Carol. *Visible Light: Photography and the American Writer 1840–1940*. New York: Oxford University Press, 1987.

Serlin, David, and Jesse Lerener. "Weegee and the Jewish Question." *Wide Angle* 19, no. 4 (1997): 94–107.

Servin, Manuel P., and Iris Higbie Wilson. *Southern California and Its University*. Los Angeles: Ward Ritchie Press, 1969.

Shepherd, Jean. *In God We Trust, All Others Pay Cash*. New York: Doubleday, 1966.

Shi, David. *Facing Facts: Realism in American Thought and Culture, 1850–1920*. New York: Oxford University Press, 1995.

Silver, Alain, and Elizabeth Ward, eds. *Film Noir: An Encyclopedic Reference to the American Film Noir*. Woodstock, N.Y.: Overlook Press, 1979.

Silver, Alain, and James Ursini, eds. *Film Noir Reader*. New York: Limelight, 1999.

Sinclair, Upton. *Upton Sinclair Presents William Fox*. Los Angeles: self-published, 1933.

Singer, Ben. *Melodrama and Modernity: Early Sensational Cinema and Its Contexts*. New York: Columbia University Press, 2001.

Sklar, Robert. *City Boys: Cagney, Bogart, Garfield*. Princeton, N.J.: Princeton University Press, 1992.

———. *Movie-Made America: A Cultural History of the Movies*. New York: Basic, 1975.

Slane, Andrea. *A Not So Foreign Affair: Fascism, Sexuality, and the Cultural Rhetoric of American Democracy*. Durham, N.C.: Duke University Press, 2001.

Smith, Greg M. "Blocking *Blockade*: Partisan Protest, Popular Debate, and Encapsulated Texts." *Cinema Journal* 36, no. 1 (fall 1996): 18–38.

Smoodin, Eric, ed. *Disney Discourse: Producing the Magic Kingdom*. New York: Routledge, 1994.

———. *Regarding Frank Capra: Audience, Celebrity, and American Film Studies, 1930–1960*. Durham, N.C.: Duke University Press, 2004.

Smoodin, Eric, and Ann Martin, eds. *Hollywood Quarterly: Film Culture in Postwar America, 1945–1957*. Berkeley: University of California Press, 2002.

The Social Scene: The Ralph M. Parsons Foundation Photography Collection at the Museum of Contemporary Art, Los Angeles. Los Angeles: Museum of Contemporary Art, 2000.

Stacey, Jackie. *Star Gazing: Hollywood Cinema and Female Spectatorship*. London: Routledge, 1994.

Staiger, Janet. *Bad Women: Regulating Sexuality in Early American Cinema*. Minneapolis: University of Minnesota Press, 1995.

———. *Interpreting Films: Studies in the Historical Reception of American Cinema*. Princeton, N.J.: Princeton University Press, 1992.

———, ed. *The Studio System*. New Brunswick, N.J.: Rutgers University Press, 1995.

Stamp, Shelley. "Lois Weber, Progressive Cinema and the Fate of 'The Work-A-Day Girl' in *Shoes*." *Camera Obscura* 56 (2004): 140–69.

———. *Movie-Struck Girls: Women and Motion Picture Culture after the Nickelodeon*. Princeton, N.J.: Princeton University Press, 2000.

Stange, Maren. *Symbols of Ideal Life: Social Documentary Photography in America 1890–1950*. Cambridge: Cambridge University Press, 1989.

Strasser, Susan. *Never Done: A History of American Housework*. New York: Pantheon Books, 1982.

Stratton, David H. *Tempest over Teapot Dome: The Story of Albert B. Fall*. Norman: University of Oklahoma Press, 1998.

Studlar, Gaylyn. "The Perils of Pleasure? Fan Magazine Discourse as Women's Commodified Culture in the 1920s." *Wide Angle* 13, no. 1 (1991): 6–33.

Sundquist, Eric, ed. *American Realism: New Essays*. Baltimore, Md.: Johns Hopkins University Press, 1972.

Tagg, John. *The Burden of Representation: Essays in Photographies and Histories*. Amherst: University of Massachusetts Press, 1988.

Telotte, J. P. "The Fantastic Realism of Film Noir: *Kiss Me Deadly*." *Wide Angle* 14, no. 1 (January 1991): 4–18.

———. "Outside the System: The Documentary Voice of Film Noir." *New Orleans Review* 14, no. 2 (summer 1987): 353–63.

Terkel, Studs. *Hard Times: An Oral History of the Great Depression*. New York: Avon, 1970.

Thomas, Peter. "Victimage and Violence: *Memento* and Trauma Theory." *Screen* 44, no. 2 (summer 2003): 200–7.

Thompson, Frank. *Lost Films*. New York: Citadel Press, 1996.

Thompson, Kristin. *Exporting Entertainment: America in the World Film Market, 1907–1934*. London: British Film Institute, 1985.

Thomson, David. *Overexposures*. New York: Morrow, 1981.

Thorp, Margaret Farrand. *America at the Movies*. New Haven, Conn.: Yale University Press, 1939.

Tibbets, John, ed. *Introduction to the Photoplay*. Shawnee Mission, Kan.: National Film Society, 1977.

Toplin, Robert Brent. "Film and History: The State of the Union." *Perspectives: American Historical Association Newsletter* 37, no. 4 (April 1999): 1, 8–9.

Trachtenberg, Alan. "Experiments in Another Country: Stephen Crane's City Sketches." In *American Realism: New Essays*, ed. Eric Sundquist. Baltimore, Md.: Johns Hopkins University Press, 1972. 138–54.

Tuchman, Mitch, and Anne Thompson. "I'm the Boss," *Film Comment* 17, no. 4 (1981): 50–51.

Turim, Maureen. "The Trauma of History: Flashbacks upon Flashbacks," *Screen* 42, no. 2 (summer 2001): 205–10.

Tuska, Jon. *Dark Cinema: American Film Noir in Cultural Perspective*. Westport, Conn.: Greenwood, 1984.

Tyler, Parker. *Screening the Sexes: Homosexuality in the Movies*. Garden City, N.Y.: Doubleday, 1973.

Usai, Paolo Cherchi, and Lorenzo Codelli, eds. *The DeMille Legacy*. Pordenone, Italy: Edizioni Biblioteca dell'Immagine, 1991.

Van Zile, Edward S. *That Marvel, the Movie*. New York: G. P. Putnam, 1923.

Vasey, Ruth. *The World According to Hollywood, 1918–1939*. Madison: University of Wisconsin Press, 1997.

Vernet, Marc. "Film Noir on the Edge of Doom." In *Shades of Noir: A Reader*, ed. Joan Copjec. London: Verso, 1983. 1–33.

Viertel, Salka. *The Kindness of Strangers*. New York: Holt, Rinehart and Winston, 1969.

Wakeman, Frederic Jr. *Policing Shanghai, 1927–1937*. Berkeley: University of California Press, 1996.

Wald, Marvin, and Albert Maltz. *The Naked City*. Carbondale: Southern Illinois University Press, 1979.

Walker, Janet. "Trauma Cinema: False Memories and True Experience." *Screen* 42, no. 2 (summer 2001): 211–16.

Waller, Gregory. *Main Street Amusements: Movies and Commercial Entertainment in a Southern City, 1896–1930*. Washington, D.C.: Smithsonian Institution Press, 1995.

Ward, David. *Poverty, Ethnicity and the American City: Changing Conceptions of the Slum and the Ghetto*. Cambridge: Cambridge University Press, 1989.

Wasser, Frederick. *Veni, Vidi, Video: The Hollywood Empire and the VCR*. Austin: University of Texas Press, 2001.

Wasson, Haidee. *Museum Movies: The Museum of Modern Art and the Birth of Art Cinema*. Berkeley: University of California Press, 2005.

Watkins, T. H. *The Great Depression: America in the 1930's*. Boston: Little, Brown, 1993.

Waugh, Thomas. *Hard to Imagine: Gay Male Eroticism in Photography and Film from Their Beginnings to Stonewall*. New York: Columbia University Press, 1996.

Weegee. *Naked City*. New York: E. P. Dutton, 1945.

Weinberg, H. Barbara, Doreen Bolger, and David Park Curry. *American Impressionism and Realism: The Painting of Modern Life, 1885–1915*. New York: Metropolitan Museum of Art, 1994.

Wells, Robert. "Family History and the Demographic Transition." In *The American Family in Social Historical Perspective*, ed. Michael Gordon. New York: St. Martin's Press, 1983. 372–92.

Wickets, Donald Furthman. "Why Sex Crimes Increase." *Physical Culture* 78, no. 1 (July 1937): 18–19, 73–74.

Wilkins, Mira. "The Impacts of American Multinational Enterprise on American-Chinese Economic Relations, 1786–1949." In *America's China Trade in Historical Perspective: The Chinese and American Performance*, ed. Ernest R. May and John K. Fairbank. Cambridge, Mass.: Harvard University Press, 1986. 259–88.

Williams, Linda. *Hard Core: Power, Pleasure and the "Frenzy of the Visible."* Berkeley: University of California Press, 1999.

Wishy, Bernard. *The Child and the Republic: The Dawn of Modern American Child Nurture*. Philadelphia: University of Pennsylvania Press, 1968.

Wood, Robin. *Hollywood from Vietnam to Reagan*. New York: Columbia University Press, 1986.

Worland, Rick. "OWI Meets the Monsters: Hollywood Horror Films and War Propaganda, 1942 to 1945." *Cinema Journal* 37, no. 1 (fall 1997): 47–65.

Wright, Gwendolyn. *Building the Dream: A Social History of Housing in America*. Cambridge, Mass.: MIT Press, 1981.

Wright, William Lord. *Photoplay Plot Encyclopedia*. Los Angeles: Palmer Photoplay Corporation, 1920.

———. *Photoplay Writing*. New York: Falk Publishing, 1922.

Wyatt, Justin. *High Concept: Movies and Marketing in Hollywood*. Austin: University of Texas Press, 1994.

Yallop, David Y. *The Day the Laughter Stopped: The True Story of Fatty Arbuckle*. New York: St. Martin's Press, 1976.

Zelizer, Viviana A. *Pricing the Priceless Child: The Changing Social Value of Children*. New York: Basic, 1985.

Zimmermann, Patricia R. *Reel Families: A Social History of Amateur Film*. Bloomington: Indiana University Press, 1995. 114–21.

CONTRIBUTORS

MARK LYNN ANDERSON is an assistant professor of film studies in the Department of English at the University of Pittsburgh. Interested in the roles of media institutions in American society between the two World Wars, he has written essays on celebrity scandal, film censorship, and early film education. His book, *Twilight of the Idols: Hollywood and the Human Sciences in the 1920s*, is forthcoming.

JANET BERGSTROM is a professor in the Department of Film, Television, and Digital Media at the University of California, Los Angeles. Her essays and DVD works on F. W. Murnau have been published in the United States, England, France, Germany, Japan, and Australia. She edited a special issue of *Film History* devoted to "The Year 1927," which includes her study "Murnau, Mussolini and Movietone." She has published many essays on emigré directors Fritz Lang and Jean Renoir. She is the editor of *Endless Night: Cinema and Psychoanalysis, Parallel Histories*, and she is completing a book on Murnau in America. She teaches seminars on the creation of DVD visual essays as an alternate venue for publishing original research.

RICHARD DECORDOVA taught film studies in the Department of Communication at DePaul University for many years. He is the author of *Picture Personalities: The Emergence of the Star System in America* as well as many articles.

KATHRYN FULLER-SEELEY teaches media history in the Communications Department at Georgia State University. She is the author of *At the Picture Show: Small Town Audiences and the Creation of Movie Fan Culture* (1996) and coauthor (with Garth Jowett and Ian Jarvie) of *Children and the Movies: Media Influence and the Payne Fund Controversy* (1996), and she has written essays on the cultural histories of film exhibition and media reception.

SUMIKO HIGASHI is a professor emerita in the Department of History at the State University of New York, Brockport, and a fellow in the Film Studies Program at Yale University. She is the author of *Cecil B. DeMille and American Culture: The Silent Era*, as well as numerous essays on film history as American cultural history, on women in film and television, and on film as historical representation.

JON LEWIS is a professor in the English Department at Oregon State University where he has taught film and cultural studies since 1983. He has published five books: *The Road to Romance and Ruin: Teen Films and Youth Culture* (which won a *Choice Magazine* Academic Book of the Year Award); *Whom God Wishes to Destroy . . . Francis Coppola and the New Hollywood*; *The New American Cinema*; *Hollywood v. Hard Core: How the Struggle over Censorship Saved the Modern Film Industry* (a *New York Times* New and Noteworthy paperback); and *The End of Cinema as We Know It: American Film in the Nineties*. In 2002, he was named editor of *Cinema Journal* and he presently sits on the Executive Council of the Society for Cinema and Media Studies.

DAVID M. LUGOWSKI is an associate professor of English and director of the Communication Studies Program at Manhattanville College in Purchase, N.Y. He has published in such journals as *Arizona Quarterly, Cineaste, Cinema Journal,* and *Senses of Cinema* and in reference works including *The International Encyclopedia of Queer Culture, The Motion Picture Annual,* and *The Encyclopedia of Documentary Film.* The essay "Queering Citizen Kane," in *Film and Sexual Politics: A Critical Reader* is forthcoming, as well as his entry for the year 1932 in U.S. film in the year-by-year anthology *American Cinema of the 1930s: Themes and Variations.*

DANA POLAN is a professor of cinema studies at New York University. He is the author of seven books on film and media including, most recently, *Scenes of Instruction: The Beginnings of the U.S. Study of Film* (2007). *The Sopranos* (forthcoming), and *The French Chef* (forthcoming).

ERIC SCHAEFER is an associate professor and director of media studies in the Department of Visual and Media Arts at Emerson College in Boston. He is the author of *Bold! Daring! Shocking! True! A History of Exploitation Films, 1919–1959* (Duke), and he has published articles on exploitation and sexploitation film in *Cinema Journal, Film History, Film Quarterly,* and other journals and anthologies. He is presently working on *Massacre of Pleasure: A History of Sexploitation Film, 1960–1979.*

ANDREA SLANE is an associate in the Intellectual Property Department of Osler, Hoskin & Harcourt LLP in Toronto. She is also affiliated with the Centre for Innovation Law and Policy at the University of Toronto, Faculty of Law. She is the author of articles in such journals as *Camera Obscura* and the *University of Ottawa Law & Technology Journal*. She is also the author of *A Not So Foreign Affair: Fascism, Sexuality and the Cultural Rhetoric of American Democracy* (Duke).

ERIC SMOODIN is a professor of American studies and director of film studies at the University of California, Davis. Most recently, he is author of *Regarding Frank Capra: Audience, Celebrity, and American Film Studies, 1930–1960* (Duke) and editor, with Ann Martin, of *Hollywood Quarterly: Film Culture in Postwar America, 1945–1957.*

SHELLEY STAMP is an associate professor of film and digital media at the University of California, Santa Cruz. She is the author of *Movie-Struck Girls: Women and Motion Picture Culture after the Nickelodeon* and coeditor (with Charlie Keil) of *American Cinema's Transitional Era: Audiences, Institutions, Practices*. Her current book project, *Lois Weber in Early Hollywood*, is supported by a Film Scholars Grant from the Academy of Motion Picture Arts and Sciences.

INDEX

JON LEWIS is a professor of English at Oregon State University.

ERIC SMOODIN is a professor of American studies and director of film studies at the University of California, Davis.

Library of Congress Cataloging-in-Publication Data

Looking past the screen : case studies in
American film history and method /
edited by Jon Lewis and Eric Smoodin.
p. cm.
Includes bibliographical references and index.
ISBN-13: 978-0-8223-3807-9 (cloth : alk. paper)
ISBN-13: 978-0-8223-3821-5 (pbk. : alk. paper)
1. Motion pictures—United States—History.
2. Film criticism—United States—History.
I. Lewis, Jon, 1955. II. Smoodin, Eric Loren.
PN1993.5.U6L58 2007
791.430973—dc22
2007008325